CLASSICS IN INSTITUTIONAL ECONOMICS

CLASSICS IN INSTITUTIONAL ECONOMICS

The Founders 1890–1945

Edited by
Malcolm Rutherford
& Warren J. Samuels

VOLUME I

~

THORSTEIN BUNDE VEBLEN

Routledge
Taylor & Francis Group
LONDON AND NEW YORK

First published 1997 by Pickering & Chatto (Publishers) Limited

Published 2016 by Routledge
2 Park Square, Milton Park, Abingdon, Oxon OX14 4RN
605 Third Avenue, New York, NY 10017

Routledge is an imprint of the Taylor & Francis Group, an informa business

BRITISH LIBRARY CATALOGUING IN PUBLICATION DATA
Classics in institutional economics : the founders,
1890–1945
1. Economists – United States – Biography 2. Institutional
economics 3. Economics – United States – History – 19th
century
I. Samuels, Warren J. (Warren Joseph) , 1933– II. Rutherford,
Malcolm, 1948–
330.1′55′0922

Set ISBN 1–85196–390–1
Volume I ISBN 1–85196–391–X

LIBRARY OF CONGRESS CATALOGING-IN-PUBLICATION DATA
Classics in institutional economics : the founders, 1890–1945 / edited
by Warren J. Samuels and Malcolm Rutherford.
p. cm.
Includes bibliographical references and index.
ISBN 1–85196–391–X (vol. 1 : alk. paper). — ISBN 1–85196–392–8
(vol. 2 : alk. paper). — ISBN 1–85196–393–6 (vol. 3 : alk. paper).
— ISBN 1–85196–394–4 (vol. 4 : alk. paper).— ISBN 1–85196–395–2
(Vol. 5 : alk. paper), — ISBN 1–85196–390–1 (set : alk. paper)
1. Institutional economics. I. Samuels, Warren J., 1933–
II. Rutherford, Malcolm, 1948–
HB99.5.C56 1997
330.1—dc21 96–21156
CIP

ISBN 13: 978-1-138-75178-1 (hbk)

New material typeset
by Wyvern 21 Ltd, Bristol

VOLUME I

CONTENTS

VOLUME II

CONTENTS

VOLUME III

CONTENTS

VOLUME IV

CONTENTS

Volume V

CONTENTS

COPY TEXTS

The following extracts are reproduced in facsimile except in the case of John Rogers Commons' *Political Economy and Law* which originally appeared in the religious journal *The Kingdom*.

In order to fit texts comfortably to the pages of this edition, certain liberties have been taken with the format of the original: occasionally right-hand pages have become left-hand pages (and vice versa) and text from consecutive pages has been fitted onto a single page. Endnotes in this edition refer to Pickering & Chatto page and line numbers. Readers wishing to consult the passages in the original are referred to the headnotes which appear immediately before each text.

Texts are reproduced by kind permission of the Library of Congress, the British Library Board and the British Library of Political and Economical Science.

ACKNOWLEDGEMENTS

We would like to thank the following for granting their kind permission to reproduce texts in this volume:

MIT Press Journals: 'Why is Economics Not an Evolutionary Science?', *Quarterly Journal of Economics* XII:4, July 1898, pp. 373–97

MIT Press: 'The Preconceptions of Economic Science', *Quarterly Journal of Economics* XIII:2, January 1899, pp. 121–50 and XIII:4, July 1899, pp. 396–426

American Economic Association: 'Industrial and Pecuniary Employments', *Publications of the American Economic Association* II, Third Series, 1901, pp. 190–235

University of Chicago Press: 'The Place of Science in Modern Civilization', *American Journal of Sociology* XI, 1906, pp. 585–609

INTRODUCTION

The authors featured in this collection are those whose work served to create and define the American institutionalist tradition in economics: Thorstein Veblen, Richard Theodore Ely, John Rogers Commons, Robert Franklin Hoxie, Wesley Clair Mitchell, and Walton Hale Hamilton. The material contained in this collection is of interest for a number of reasons. First, institutionalism is recognized as a peculiarly American development in economics. Nothing quite the same emerged in Britain or continental Europe, and a knowledge of the literature of institutionalism is a necessary part of understanding the history of American economics and of American social thought more broadly. This is true not just for the period of institutionalism's development and rise to prominence in American economics, but also for the subsequent period of relative decline in prestige and importance. Second, the literature on institutionalism is full of debate and disagreement concerning the unifying characteristics of the movement and its principal contributions. A collection of many of the most important items written by the founding figures provides a convenient vehicle for assessing these issues. Finally, many of the major concerns of institutionalists – with the role of institutions and with the development of an evolutionary approach – have been coming back into prominence as important issues in economics generally. There is the 'new' institutional economics of Douglas North and Oliver Williamson, the evolutionary economics of Nelson and Winter, and the attempt to develop a new evolutionary political economy by Geoff Hodgson and others. All of this has created a revival of interest in the work of Veblen, Commons, and the other founders of American institutionalism.

Institutionalism and the American Context

As pointed out by Ekelund and Hebert (1990: 454), eclecticism and pragmatism were hallmarks of American economics from the nineteenth until well into the twentieth century, and 'classical and neoclassical *theoretical* analysis consequently never had the hold upon American economists that it did on English economists.' In the nineteenth century there were American adherents to classical analysis, but also many who argued that the Ricardian and Malthusian theories of rent and population did not apply to American conditions, and some such as H. C. Carey who attempted to construct a distinctive national economics. In the last twenty years of the century, not only were marginalist and subjectivist ideas being imported and developed, but also German historicism, which along with its empirical and historical method and reformist ideology, had a profound influence through the many Americans who studied economics at German universities (Parrish 1967). At the same time the evolutionism of Darwin and Spencer impacted strongly on American philosophy and sociology and on intellectual life in general (Russett 1976). All of this created a considerable ferment within American economics, and, in the absence of any authoritative figure, such as Marshall in England, one that took a very long time to settle out. Basic concepts of value, cost, and distribution were much contested in the academic literature. Neoclassical, Austrian, historicist, and social-evolutionary ideas all contended, and were variously intermixed. The particular problems of public utilities, railroads, trusts, business depressions, immigration, and labor unrest were the stuff of agitated debate. Discussion of institutional issues, empirical and historical investigations, concern with the actual functioning of markets, and a desire to transcend the limits of static analysis were by no means limited to those later classified as institutionalists. The work of F. W. Taussig and A. T. Hadley are good examples of the eclecticism mentioned above, but out of these conditions institutional economics also emerged (Dorfman 1962). The unsettled state of economics and the fertile intellectual environment suggested to the founders of the institutionalist movement that a more substantial reworking of economics along evolutionary and institutional lines was both necessary and possible. However, in setting out on this task not all institutionalists adopted the same perspectives or guiding metaphors, or utilized the same techniques of investigation, giving rise to a significant amount of diversity within the institutionalist movement itself.

For the first few decades of the twentieth century American economics was highly variegated but not compartmentalized into well defined schools, and with little by the way of any dominant orthodoxy. Thus, despite the fact that the beginnings of American institutional economics can be dated quite precisely to the last few years of the nineteenth century, and the early writings of Thorstein Veblen and John R. Commons, it was not given its name until 1918, by Walton Hamilton at a meeting of the American Economics Association (Hamilton 1919), and the term did not come into common use as denoting a specific constellation of ideas or 'school' of economic thought until the late 1920s and early 1930s (Edie 1927; Roundtable 1931, 1932). Even then not all of those now normally classified as institutionalists used the term to describe themselves. This is not to say that lines of division were not visible, or that institutionalists never recognized their commonalities, but the processes of definition and self-identification were hindered both by the variety of views to be found among institutionalists themselves (a fact that has continued to complicate the discussion) and the diversity of American economics as a whole. Certainly, institutionalists did not think of themselves, or behave, as a group existing outside the mainstream of American economics. They published in the major journals, held positions at major schools or research institutes, belonged to the American Economics Association, and participated fully in the American discourse on economics and economic policy.

That institutional economics came to be regarded as a tradition (or school) of thought both separate from, and marginal to, a mainstream neoclassical orthodoxy had to do with later developments. First, the gradual stabilizing and development of a core of neoclassical microeconomic theory. As early as the 1930's this began to be contrasted favourably with the continued unstabilized state of institutional economics. Later, in the post Second World War period, the sweep of what appeared to be an analytically powerful and practically effective Keynesian macroeconomics, and the growth of mathematical and econometric techniques, techniques that became associated with notions of scientific rigour but which were not easily married to institutionalist predilections and concerns, completed the process.

Despite this marginalization within the discipline, institutional economics has remained alive and has, in more recent years, done reasonably well as a separate 'heterodox' group with its own association and journal and its own discourse. The fortunes of the movement have tended to vary directly with the prevailing degree of dissatisfaction with the neoclassical orthodoxy, but with recent developments in evolutionary and institutional approaches to economics it may possess a more viable future, in the United States and Europe, than is frequently appreciated (Samuels 1995).

The Coordinates of Institutional Economics

All schools of economic thought, including neoclassicism, display some degree of internal heterogeneity, but institutionalism as a whole has been characterized, probably more than any other school of economic thought, by the individualism of its members. There is an irony here: while all schools are comprised of individuals more or less going their own way, neoclassical economists have (1) preached methodological individualism while (2) more or less adhering to fairly common if not standardized doctrines (such as the rationality and competition assumptions), whereas institutionalists have (1) preached methodological collectivism while (2) more or less widely practicing a variety of individualized versions of institutionalism. The relative stabilization of neoclassical economics may account for its growing ascendency during the twentieth century. Be that as it may, one task of this collection is to indicate the common areas of agreement on fundamentals among the founding members of the institutionalist movement, while also eliciting the differences in approach, interest and emphasis.

Individual institutionalists have varied in their concepts of science, their methods of investigation, and in the groups of topics they have chosen to concentrate on. But beyond that, institutionalism has had two major strands, one following a path initiated by Thorstein Veblen, the other begun by John R. Commons (and before him by Richard T. Ely). It is important to recognize, however, that while differences between these two major strands exist, they are often matters more of emphasis than of fundamentals; that the differences became widened in the period following the 1970s, that is, beyond the period covered in this collection; that during the first half-century of institutionalism the emphasis was on what was held in common, albeit colored by more or less idiosyncratic individual interests and emphases; and that the writers featured in this collection pursued their own research agendas without much sense of intra-group conflict. While it is true that Commons and Mitchell did find things to criticize in Veblen's work, both were influenced by him and made much use of his ideas. They were also far from critical of each other despite their different approaches.

The analyses of any school of economic thought are sufficiently complex as to pose a problem of conceptually identifying the common elements. Many elements co-exist and the meaning of any one of them derives in part from inherent features and in part from their correlation and interaction with each other. And, of course, different scholars will present them differently. What follows is one approach.

(i) Institutions Matter

As the name itself indicates, institutional economics has a central concern with the role played by institutions in economic life. Institutions are defined broadly to include social norms, social conventions, laws and constitutions that together make up the set of general social rules, and the formal and informal organizations, such as families, firms, churches, charities, political parties, pressure groups, and so on, that operate within the broader social and legal environment. Organizations, of course, will have their own internal conventions and formal or informal rules of operation.

Veblen defined an institution as a habit of thought. Although he wrote in the language of instinct psychology, dominant in his day, his was fundamentally a behavioristic psychology. Individuals are inculcated in the ways of their society. These habits of thought and belief either reinforce or inhibit innate instincts or propensities. Commons defined an institution as collective action in both control and liberation of individual action. Much of his collective action can be interpreted as habits of thought; and Veblen's habits of thought can be interpreted as collective action controlling and liberating individual action. Thus, all institutional economists take as a central tenet that individuals are deeply affected by their institutional environment, not merely constrained by the rules, but socialized into them, molded by them, and also (differentially) enabled and empowered by them. This has a number of major implications.

First, institutionalists have always argued that individuals are not maximizers of psychologically given utility functions but are, to use Commons's term, 'institutionalized minds.' People are deeply affected by prevailing norms and conventions. In much of their behavior they are norm guided, but this does not mean that they are unintelligent or incapable of creativity, only that there is a context of social norms and other rules that provide the accepted goals of action and ways of thinking, the established means to those ends, and the areas open to individual discretion and initiative. For example, institutionalists see both the use of financial gain as a criterion of success, and the calculating rationality of the businessperson as institutional products: not eternal truths, but reflections of the prevailing pecuniary, business, culture. This, however, is not to deny that individual businesspeople can be creative in the ways that they devise to achieve their financial objectives.

Second, institutionalists believe that the economy is more than markets and that markets are themselves complexes of many institutions, including laws of property and contract, regulations of many kinds, and a whole array of conventional rules and practices. Some of these will vary from market to market. The economy is more than a price mechanism constituted by abstract forces of demand and supply. There is no such thing as 'the market' except in the abstracting and generalizing minds of economists. 'The market' does not exist, except as an abstraction; actual markets exist, and these are a function of many institutions. Neither economies writ large nor markets are given to humankind. In particular, economies, including markets, are what they are because of the forces – habitual, customary, legislative, and judicial – which have been used to make them.

Third, institutional economists pay close attention to the structure of power. Power can be in the form of legally enforceable rights and liberties or in the form of an economic power in the sense of a bargaining power or power to withhold. In so far as one is dealing with markets, the structure of power (both legal and economic) governs how markets will be formed and how, and to whose advantage, they will operate. Power governs the distributions of benefits and of sacrifice in society. In focussing on power, institutionalists do not deny the importance of the conventionally recognized 'basic economic problems' of resource allocation, level of income (and output, employment and prices), and distribution of income. They insist, however, that a fourth basic economic problem both transcends and interacts with those three, the problem of the organization and control of the economy. The problem of organization and control is a problem of the distribution of power in society.

Fourth, not only do institutionalists emphasize the importance of power and social control, many have focused attention on the central institution of social control, namely, government (the state). These institutionalists emphasize the role of government in providing the legal foundations of the economic system, including the laws of property, control, negotiable instruments, business organization (corporation, partnership, etc.), money, sales, agency, and so on. Every aspect of modern economic life, the dominant *laissez faire* and non-interventionist ideology notwithstanding, has a body of applicable law. Legal control is an integral part of the economy without which it would not be the economy as we know it; control is an integral part of business without which it would not be business at all. Legal control, the economy, and business are closely interrelated and have grown together.

In the institutionalist view, laws and regulations are not necessarily antagonistic to freedom. The question is neither whether to have government and law, nor how to minimize government or legal regulation. Law is an instrument for creating as well as restricting freedom, but for different people in different contexts. 'Intervention' in practice is not the intrusion of government into a situation in which it has been absent but a change in the interests to which government is giving its support. The critical question always tends to be whether government will be an instrument of the powerful and propertied, or a check on the powerful and propertied.

To all institutionalists, therefore, institutions matter. Accordingly, institutionalists, while not dismissing the pure theory of markets out of hand, insist on the importance of theorizing about actual institutions; the processes in which institutional adoption, adjustment and transformation take place; and the fundamentals of organization and control which transcend the consideration of pure markets. On the one hand institutionalists stress the problem of organization and control and the correlative importance of institutions including law. On the other hand, they are also interested in the standard neoclassical problem of the allocation of resources. In regard to it, they have a broader and deeper conception of what is involved in resource allocation and, what is more, a longer chain of explanatory variables. The institutionalist causal chain, which includes the exercise of individual choice based in part on socialized preferences, may be put thus: the allocation of resources is a function of the market, which is a function of demand and supply, which is a function of power structure (rights), which is a function in part of law, which is a function of government, which is a function of the control of government (and thereby whose interests will be given protection by government), which is a function of the contest over political ideology and the control of government, and so on.

(ii) Institutional Evolution and Change

Institutional economics was founded not only on the idea that institutions matter but also on the idea that institutions evolve and change over time. Institutionalists believe that institutions are artifacts, not only produced by humankind but also subject to change. This is obvious in the work of all of the founding figures of the institutionalist movement, but the exact formulations vary. For some institutionalists, such as Veblen, what is most important is the 'Darwinian' idea of causal process in which non-deliberative processes of institutional growth and evolution are stressed. For others, such as Commons, the emphasis is on the 'artificial selection' implied by deliberative processes of political and judicial dispute resolution and decision making. In both cases there is an awareness of the path dependence of evolutionary processes, that each change emerges out of the pre-existing situation. In Veblen's work this is stated explicitly in terms of his idea of 'cumulative causation'.

Veblen's notion of cumulative causation involves the idea that institutional evolution is to be explained primarily in terms of a causal sequence, one that relies not on intentionality but on a cumulative process of habituation. In Veblen, individuals take their basic habits of thought from the surrounding institutions. Fundamental changes to these institutions come about not as the result of any deliberate decision or choice to make such changes, but because of the economic and technological changes that go on and that gradually bring about new patterns of life and, through habituation, new ways of thinking that come to displace the old. This will give rise to an ideological conflict between the ways of thinking associated with the new material conditions and the habits of thought established in the prevailing institutions. Old ways of thinking die hard, and change may also be resisted by those with vested interests in the status quo. Veblen provides little analysis of the processes through which ideological and political conflicts are resolved, but suggests that the discipline of new patterns of life will tend to win out.

Veblen's ideas concerning habituation and the discipline of new patterns of life influenced the early work of both Mitchell and Hoxie, but others, most notably Commons, sought to give intentional processes in the form of judicial and political decision making a larger and more explicit role. Commons focused his attention on the pervasive nature of conflicts of interest and on the need to continually create and recreate a sufficient degree of mutuality between the major interests in society to maintain the workability of the system over time. These conflicts could have many sources, not just the impact of new material or technological conditions, and the resolving of the disputes takes place not only informally, through the evolution of habit and custom, but also through judicial and legislative decision making. Here a choice between conflicting rules must be made on the basis of some notion of the social good. In his discussions on institutional evolution Commons placed a special emphasis on the choices made by monarchs, legislatures, and judges, the resulting evolution of common and statute law, and of the slow adjustment of social values as new problems emerged and new practices and rules devised. In this, Commons was influenced by Ely and joined by others such as Walton Hamilton.

Of course, an emphasis on political and judicial processes of conflict resolution is not necessarily inconsistent with the argument that changes in economic and technical conditions can bring about far reaching changes in the way people organize their lives and think about the world. Some of Mitchell's sketches of institutional history, for example, combine insights from Veblen and Commons (Mitchell 1927: 66–74). In addition, the instrumentalist and reformist perspective adopted by virtually all institutionalists, provides a role for deliberative efforts at institutional change operating primarily through legislative action. In other words, for institutionalists the evolution of institutions implies their malleability, and their malleability implies the prospect of bringing about institutional reforms designed to solve economic and social problems; new forms of social control that could be designed and appraised with the aid of scientific investigation.

(iii) Institutional Reform and Instrumentalism

The institutionalists' emphasis on institutional evolution is related to their activist orientation toward socioeconomic institutions. They seek to understand the relation of particular institutions to perceived problems and to treat institutions not unlike any other variable, that is, as open to change and control. Instead of taking a static approach which reifies institutions as they are, institutionalists comprehend institutions in terms of their *becoming* rather than their *being*, and in terms of the conflicting interests, values, and ideologies that find institutional expression. Even without activist efforts at reform, institutions are the object of control, as individuals and groups within society attempt to change institutions for their own purposes. To ignore this is to both reify and ratify – give ontological status to – the activism of the already powerful.

Veblen's emphasis on unintentional processes of habituation resulted is his providing less of a clear role for activism within his theoretical framework than many other institutionalists, although he did become involved in the promotion of trade unions and, later, the engineering movement as possible vehicles of change. Veblen was highly critical of capitalism and looked to its eventual demise as a result of the growth of new habits of thought associated with modern science and technology – habits of thought at odds with inherited notions of property and natural rights. For Veblen and other more radical institutionalists, capitalism is another form of barbarism, a particular system of predatory power and behavior. The ills of capitalism – its concentrations of income, wealth and industrial power; its manipulative excesses; its instability; its industrial waste, and so on, all of which are interrelated – they trace to the preoccupation with pecuniary considerations and goals and its repression of industrial/technological capabilities. Neoclassical economics they see as capitalist apologetics.

The other institutionalists represented in this collection, are both less radical, seeking to reform capitalism rather than replace it, and also more active in their reformism, having been heavily influenced by the instrumentalism of American pragmatic philosophers such as John Dewey. Neither Commons nor Mitchell, for example, have any generic animus against capitalism. Their complaints about the existing system are not that different from Veblen's, but they also see the benefits of markets and of individual initiative, and believe the system can be reformed to operate both more smoothly and in the interests of a larger constituency. Mitchell was particularly concerned with the problem of business cycles, while Commons and his disciplines sought to give legal protection to the interests of consumers and workers. For those to whom capitalism meant the hegemony of business, this was anathema; for those who envisioned the extension of the pluralistic or democratic promise of capitalism, this was a continuation of past trends, now increasingly extended to the mass of the people. Commons was the great historian, interpreter and advocate of US non-revolutionary, 'bread and butter' labor unions. For him, the legal status of unions and welfare state legislation were compatible with capitalism. Government was being used to protect new interests; what hitherto had been protected as 'property' was now being protected as other kinds of rights.

The instrumentalist position that informs the work of most institutionalists views theories as instruments for human betterment. Theories are tools and should be judged as tools. The test of a theory is to be found in its application to the solution of social problems. This, of course, requires some set of goals or social values that can serve to define problems and successful solutions. For instrumentalists, however, there is no sharp dividing line between means and ends or between science and metaphysics. Ends are not ultimates, but 'ends in view' and these too can be appraised against the consequences of the attempt to achieve them. Valuation is also a process, and one that interrelates with scientific investigation and policy experimentation.

For those influenced by Dewey, the valuation process is conceived of as a discourse, consisting largely, in democratic countries, of the political discourse. For some institutionalists what is of key importance in this discourse is the representation of all interests and the reconciliation of conflicting interests, in the sense of determining what is reasonable under the circumstances. This is expressed in Commons's concept of reasonable value. For others, the key issue is that values be based on instrumentalities and not on ceremonialism: on what works to enhance human life and not on values or conventions inherited from the past. In both cases the social scientist has a role in the provision of knowledge, but there is some variation among institutionalists in the view taken of the proper relationship between the roles of scientist and policy advocate.

For Commons, the economist cannot pretend to know what is best or optimal for society. What is in the social interest is what emerges out of the debate over policies and values carried out by those with conflicting interests. In this, however, the social scientist can act legitimately in a variety of ways: as an investigator of actual social conditions and policy consequences, in order to provide information; as a facilitator, attempting to find creative solutions that could gain wide support; and also as a advocate of a particular position, in the knowledge that other positions will also have their advocates. In his own reform efforts Commons often sought to bring together progressive representatives of the interested parties to a problem and to elicit from them solutions which would protect and advance both interests of all. On the other hand, Mitchell was uncomfortable with advocacy, and felt that the scientist, as scientist, should be concerned with investigating the operation of the economic system and the consequences of policy. Social policy objectives and values should be a matter for democratic debate. Nevertheless, Mitchell was very much of the view that science should inform social policy and social policy debates, and that the appraisal of policy initiatives could ultimately contribute significantly to the debate over social values.

Whatever the details of their positions, institutionalists insist that there is a continuing and inexorable problem of determining the reasonableness of what Commons called the working rules of society, that some conception of public purpose must be worked out in order to reach decisions about the interests and policies to which government will give its support, and that informed and democratic political discourse is the social valuational process for working that out. In contrast, neoclassical economists typically seek to identify determinate unique optimal equilibrium solutions to allocative and other problems. The institutionalists argue that this is to ignore, trivialize, finesse, and render static the problem of structuring the processes through which such solutions or outcomes are in fact worked out. It is to ignore the problem of organization and control and the fact that unique solutions do not exist *ab initio*; the actually achieved outcome is a function of the existing structure of power, institutions, and set of social values.

(iv) Methodological Holism

A great deal of what has already been said leads to a form of holism. The term holism was not used by any of the founders of institutionalism, but it was introduced later to indicate the institutionalist stress on the importance of institutions; the need to analyse the behavior of individuals within their institutional context; the interconnectedness between different parts of the social system (economics, politics, law, etc.); and the evolution of the whole.

As has already been indicated, the institutionalists believe, first, that the economy encompasses more than either 'the market' or markets and, second, that a critical problem of analysis is that of the organization and control of the economic system and its evolution. Institutionalists therefore feel that instead of taking as given either capitalism (market economy) or its particular set of institutions prevalent in some time and place, they must develop a theory of capitalism itself. As for particular institutions, including both the market and the institutions which form and operate through markets, they study institutions both individually and as parts of the larger matrix of the economic order. In these respects, the broadly conceptualized economic system is understood to be a cultural and valuational process, not a static mechanism or equilibrium of stable relations.

Given these beliefs, it is hardly surprising that institutional economists envision their conception of the economy, and therefore their work as economists, to be holistic and evolutionary. It is holistic because, they believe, they must deal with the economy comprehended as a whole. It is evolutionary because, they believe, the meaning of any economic phenomenon resides not only in static and contemporary considerations but in light of the continuing transformation of the economic system.

The institutionalists accept that the ultimate agents of economic action are individuals. But they emphasize that society is more than just a group of independent individuals; that individuals act within institutional matrices; and that social institutions cannot themselves be explained in *purely* individualistic terms. It is sometimes claimed that institutionalists treat the social whole and other collective entities as actors with agential power of their own, but this is a mistaken interpretation. Commons's use of the term 'collective will', for example, actually implies nothing more than the outcome of collective, political and judicial, decision making. On the other hand, institutionalists do reject reductionist versions of individualism. Individuals always act within an institutional context, and to explain that context requires reference to a pre-existing context. Reductionist efforts to eliminate all references to social entities or to socially defined roles is likely to be impossible to achieve.

The holistic perspective of institutionalists is also related to their rejection of the highly abstract and formal methods of neoclassical economics. Their insistence on the institutional basis of behavior leads to a rejection of the maximizing and competitive assumptions that form the basis of neoclassical abstractions. In most neoclassical models the institutional context is either ignored altogether or treated as epiphenomenal, as a mere aggregate of independently arrived at individual decisions. Institutionalists want to include the institutional context, and seek to explain the behavior of any part by reference to the whole system and its place within that whole. Different institutionalists have, however, attempted to achieve these objectives in different ways.

(v) Methods of Investigation

The founding figures of institutionalism utilized a variety of techniques, but these differing techniques were usually seen as complementing each other, rather than indicating any deep methodological conflict. Veblen's technique was to develop a narrative account of some aspect of institutional history, or of the current economic situation, and running in terms of habituation, institutions, and technology. His work made use of available empirical studies, for example the *Report of the Industrial Commission*, but he conducted relatively few empirical or case studies himself.

Things were different with those who followed. Some, such as Hoxie, attempted to apply Veblenian categories to a more detailed study of specific cases. Hoxie's studies of unions actually led him to doubt Veblen's ideas concerning unions. Case studies were also a feature of Hamilton's work – notably his studies of the coal industry and of the price making practices of firms. Mitchell was of a much less speculative temper than Veblen and was also influenced by positivist ideas. He felt Veblen's conclusions needed careful empirical checking, and his own efforts focussed on the detailed statistical investigation of business cycles. Mitchell was one of the founders of the NBER and had much to do with the statistical nature of the work it conducted. Commons conducted vast investigations of the trade union movement; compiled a monumental documentary history of American industrial society; became closely involved in the drafting of legislation concerning such matters as public utility regulation, workman's compensation, and unemployment insurance; and pioneered the use of interview techniques. Although Commons did relatively little statistical work himself, he both supported it and was involved with the NBER.

This emphasis on empirical work in the form of case studies and statistical compilations has given rise to the impression that institutionalists engaged in purely descriptive work with no theoretical underpinnings or objectives. That this is not the case can be seen from a closer look at the work of Mitchell and Commons. Mitchell always placed his investigations of business cycles within an institutional context. Cycles, for Mitchell, were a result of the behavior patterns induced by the modern 'money economy' with its production for profit, its complex set of markets with various leads and lags in the adjustment of prices, its banking system, and so on. Statistical investigation he linked to institutional analysis through his view that statistics picked up the standardizing influence of institutions on the behavior of masses of individuals. Mitchell's work on cycles took place within a broad conceptual apparatus borrowed largely from Veblen. In terms of more specific theories of business cycles, of the exact set of causal relationships that produced cycles, Mitchell wanted to investigate the strengths and weaknesses of many alternative hypotheses and to define more closely the explanatory task remaining to the theorist. From this he developed his idea of 'analytic description' which was designed to keep theorizing and concrete empirical investigation in the closest possible contact.

Commons also worked within and sought to develop a theoretical framework. The early version of this framework is visible in Commons's work from the turn of the century. This framework was modified and much elaborated as a result of his wide reading in law and economics, and as a direct result of his case studies and experience in drafting legislation.

Commons deftly combined legal and economic historical materials with several bodies of interpretive theory, including theories of legal relations, transactions, human psychology, social change, and social control. Commons's concern was to develop 'formulas', to be understood as providing a formulation of the relation between different parts to each other and to the whole. These formulas were also designed to be tools for the resolution of specific problems. A nice example is Commons's formulas of rationing, bargaining and managerial transactions, that link the nature of transactions to the legal and customary rules of society, and that Commons uses to provide insight into many issues concerning the regulation of markets.

The methods used by institutionalists, then, are not descriptive or non-theoretical. They do seek to keep theorizing at a more concrete level, in touch with the institutional context within which economic activity takes place, and related to issues and problems of immediate concern. The techniques used by different institutionalists vary somewhat, but each can be seen as an attempt to find a method or methods consistent with the other key co-ordinates of institutionalism as outlined above.

The Founders of Institutional Economics

The early development of institutional economics is associated both with particular individuals and with particular universities and departments. Unquestionably the two leading figures in the establishment of what came to be called institutional economics were Thorstein Veblen (1857–1929) and John R. Commons (1862–1945). As the school became both self-conscious and observed by others, Veblen and Commons were unequivocally understood to be its founders. Still, other figures were both present and active in the early days of the school. Along with Veblen and Commons, Wesley Mitchell (1874–1948) has sometimes been seen as a co-founder of the movement. In addition, important roles were played by Richard T. Ely (1854–1943), Commons's teacher and mentor, by Robert F. Hoxie (1868–1916), and Walton H. Hamilton (1881–1958).

One of the centers for the early development of institutionalism was the University of Chicago. The first chair of the Department of Economics, Laurence Laughlin, brought Thorstein Veblen with him from Cornell in 1892. Veblen was first a Fellow and later an Assistant Professor at Chicago where he remained until 1906 when he moved to Stanford. While at Chicago Veblen had a substantial and direct influence on both Robert Hoxie and Wesley Mitchell. Hoxie had also followed Laughlin to Chicago from Cornell, first as a student and later as a Fellow. After some moving around he returned to Chicago in 1903 where he stayed on the faculty until his suicide in 1916. Mitchell was also at Chicago as a student of Laughlin's and Veblen's and became a junior member of the faculty there until moving to Berkeley in 1908, and later moving to Columbia. Walton Hamilton's training was at the University of Michigan where he came under the influence of H. C. Adams and C. H. Cooley. Hoxie persuaded Laughlin to bring him to Chicago in 1914, but despite forming a close friendship with Hoxie he moved on after a year, first to Amherst, then to Brookings, and finally to Yale Law School. Chicago did not remain a centre of institutionalism for long past this formative period, and in the inter-war years it was replaced by Columbia University (with Mitchell, Tugwell, and J. M. Clark) as one of the two main centres of institutional economics.

The other major center for the development was the University of Wisconsin. Richard T. Ely established the Department there and recruited his former student John R. Commons. Ely and Commons shared a particular interest in trade unions, labor problems, and the role of law in economic affairs. Wisconsin's position as a center of institutionalism remained intact through the inter-war period due to Commons's long tenure in the Department and the subsequent role played by his students.

(i) Thorstein Bunde Veblen

Thorstein Veblen was one of the most original observers and analysts of modern capitalist society. He investigated phenomena that others failed to perceive and he approached every subject in his own distinctive way. As noted above, Veblen was deeply influenced by the evolutionary method of Darwin – particularly his rejection of teleology – and sought to apply that method to social evolution. Veblen conceived of social evolution as a cumulative and never ending process of the adaptation – through habituation – of institutions to changing material circumstances. On this basis Veblen both criticised the mainstream economics of his time and sought to construct an alternative.

A number of Veblen's articles presented in this collection combine an articulation of his own evolutionary approach with criticisms of other types of economics. Perhaps the most outstanding example of this is Veblen's famous paper 'Why is Economics Not an Evolutionary Science?' (1898) that contains his devastating critique of the hedonistic conception of man as a 'lightning calculator' along with his own view of the necessary constituent parts of an modern, evolutionary, science. The same is true of Veblen's essays on Marx, on J. B. Clark, and on marginal utility theory. More purely critical is the lengthy essay on 'The Preconceptions of Economic Science' (1899–1900).

The excerpts from *The Theory of the Leisure Class* (1899) present the major elements of his analysis of consumption behavior. Veblen was one of the first – and perhaps still the foremost – analyst of the social foundations of consumption behavior: 'status emulation', 'conspicuous consumption' and 'invidious comparison' were terms either introduced or popularised by him. The major components of Veblen's theory of production are provided in the essays on 'Industrial and Pecuniary Employments' (1901) and 'On the Nature of Capital' (1908), and in the selections from *The Theory of Business Enterprise* (1904), *The Engineers and the Price System* (1921), and *Absentee Ownership* (1923). In these we read of his view of pecuniary and industrial modes of thought and practice; the nature of the modern, finance-driven business firm; the cultural incidence of the machine process; the nature of the modern credit economy; and so on. These excerpts display the fact that Veblen was one of the first analysts of capitalism as a corporate system. The material from *The Instinct of Workmanship* (1914) contains Veblen's theory of instincts and of institution formation that is crucial to an understanding of his theory of institutional change. Other excerpts reveal Veblen's powerful analyses of the predatory state and the nature and manipulation of patriotism and his critique of the nature, operation and role of the university in a business civilization.

In his analysis Veblen formulated a number of dichotomies. The most commonly expressed of these dichotomies is that between the industrial and the pecuniary aspects of culture, the conflict between making goods and making money that recurs in the work of many other institutionalists. This dichotomy is also expressed in more general terms as one between teleological or matter-of-fact habits of thought and ceremonial modes of thought, and is the basis of other dichotomies such as that between predatory and peaceable nations. In Veblen's work institutions tend to be seen as inhibitive of change, protecting the established system of status and distribution of income and wealth. Veblen was a critic of the institutionalized form which capitalism has taken, so much so that he was a critic of capitalism itself. This was related to his criticism of mainstream economic theory, which he felt perpetuated old but questionable philosophical views and represented an ideological rationalization of capitalism.

Veblen's negative focus on institutions as a matters of status emulation, power play, and retrogression is in contrast to Richard T. Ely's and John R. Commons's affirmation of institutions as determinative of economic organization and performance. Analytically, however, Veblen's view of institutions as widely held habits of thought is not inconsistent with that of Commons in which institutions represent collective action in both control and liberation of individual action. For both of these founders of institutional economics, institutions are socially constructed, and subject to reform. Admittedly, Veblen was more interested in clearing the ground for reform whereas Commons was interested in providing an analysis which could channel particular efforts at legal and institutional change.

(ii) John Rogers Commons

John R. Commons had several careers. He was the first and foremost labor historian of the United States and its foremost labor economist. He was an architect of pioneering social legislation – of labor legislation, labor relations legislation, public utility regulation, industrial safety, workers' compensation, unemployment compensation, and social security. He was active in numerous movements, including those centering on civil service reform and proportional representation as well as monetary reform and labor legislation. He was a major historian and interpreter of the complex legal and other foundations of capitalism, and he attempted to pull together a general theory of institutional economics in one magisterial work.

Commons's work in the field of labor is represented here by several contributions. To understand his approach, one has to appreciate that he recognized conflict between labor and capital and its relations to problems of class. But he saw such conflict not as systemically threatening but as generic to the modern industrial capitalist economy in which different groups pursued their interests given their position in the economy, i.e., a wholly constructive if not 'natural' phenomenon. This is reflected in his essay on class conflict and its growth and inevitability (1908); his famous essay on the American shoemakers (1909), which indicates his interpretation to what labor wants and how unions serve that objective; his interpretation of how law can protect the reasonable expectations and interests of both capital and labor, in the first chapter of his (and John B. Andrews') *Principles of Labor Legislation* (1920); and his introductory essay in volume 3 of *History of Labor in the United States, 1896-1932* (1935).

In a series of writings, represented here by 'Political Economy and Law'(1896), 'A Sociological View of Sovereignty' (1899–1900), 'Law and Economics'(1925), and by excerpts from *The Legal Foundations of Capitalism* (1924), *Institutional Economics* (1934) and *The Economics of Collective Action* (1950), Commons pursued a complex historical and theoretical project of enormous proportions. This project is related to his work on labor issues as it involves a theory of social evolution based on the prevalence of conflict of interest and on the need to overcome conflicts as they arise in order to maintain a workable degree of mutuality between different interest groups. Commons's discussion of the evolution of capitalism encompasses a theory of the transformation of the state, its distillation of the institution of private property out of the diminished position of the monarchy, the role of representative government in the formation of particular property rights, and the transformation of the legal concepts of property and freedom from a feudal to a capitalist to a joint capitalist-labor system. It is a theory of systemic power struggle and a theory of conflict resolution. The contrast with Veblen's theory is that Commons focuses on legal and political processes of conflict resolution as opposed to Veblen's stress on habituation. Commons used the analogy of 'artificial selection' as opposed to the unintentionalist or purely causal process of natural selection.

This also involved a theory of the economy as comprising more than market and price mechanism, especially a theory of transactions, including both bargaining transactions and transactions made through the decisions of some legal authority, and a theory of going concerns or organizations. A theory, too, of the legal-economic nexus, including a theory of the legal foundations of the economy and of the economic foundations of law. In all this he utilized English and US legal-economic history as both a source of his theories and as illustrating how they applied, working out a theory of governance ('sovereignty') whose central objective was a theory of the organization and control of the economic system. The issue for Commons was neither 'government or no government' nor 'minimization of government' but which, or whose, interests was government to be used to promote.

Commons's basic approach to legal-economic theory is represented here in part by the sections on working rules and public purpose from his *Legal Foundations of Capitalism*; the sections on transactions and concerns, sovereignty, and collective action from *Institutional Economics*; and the chapters on collective action, individual action, transactions and capitalism from his posthumous *Economics of Collective Action*. His treatment of broader methodological and disciplinary matters is represented by his essays, 'The Problem of Correlating Law, Economics and Ethics' (1932), 'The Place of Economics in Social Philosophy' (1939), and 'Twentieth Century Economics' (1939).

(iii) Robert Franklin Hoxie

Although his career was cut short, Robert Hoxie was an important figure in the early history of institutionalism. At the University of Chicago he came under Veblen's influence. Veblen's influence on Hoxie, particularly in terms of the adoption of the ideal of an evolutionary economics, can be clearly seen in Hoxie's methodological and pedagogical essays written between 1901 and 1907, and is particularly evident in 'The Empirical Method of Economic Instruction' (1901), which is full of Veblenian terminology. Nevertheless, Hoxie was no slave to Veblen and he did not think that the adoption of an evolutionary ideal did away with the need for careful analysis of static problems and classification on the basis of present form and function. This point of view is well displayed in his essay on 'The Demand and Supply Concepts' (1906). Hoxie's own method, and the one he claimed to use in his later work, is outlined in 'Historical Method versus Historical Narrative' (1906). Here he argues that the historical method, properly understood, is that of seeking the solution of a definite problem through attempting to explain how that (institutional) problem situation emerged out of the past.

Hoxie eventually settled on the issue of trade unionism and the labor problem, initially motivated by Veblen's analysis in *The Theory of Business Enterprise* concerning the impact of machine technology on the habits of thought of the industrial workman. The Veblenian preconceptions that lay behind his study of unions are explicitly laid out in his paper 'The Trade Union Point of View' (1907). Hoxie's findings, however, ultimately led him away from the Veblenian system and into his own analysis of the various types of American unionism. This analysis is found in 'Trade Unionism in the United States' (1914). Hoxie's findings that there were many types of unionism, and that the dominant type was what he called 'business unionism', not only led him away from Veblen's ideas of the machine discipline, but also may have played a part in Veblen's own change of heart concerning the nature of American unionism, as expressed later in *The Engineers and the Price System* (1921). Hoxie's work on trade unionism brought him into close contact with John R. Commons. Both were concerned with issues of the conflict between scientific management and unionism, but Hoxie's research on this topic was not fully completed and what was published created much controversy.

(iv) Walton Hale Hamilton

Walton Hamilton had a career which encompassed both economics and law. He contributed to both institutional economics and legal realism, the latter being the methodological analogue in jurisprudence that the former was in economics. Both schools of thought rejected the idea that formalistic manipulation of abstract concepts alone could adequately deal with their respective domains. Hamilton taught at Michigan, Chicago, Amherst and, though he lacked a law degree, for many years at the Yale Law School. In a series of writings, Hamilton reached many of the same conclusions as did Commons concerning the role of government in providing the legal foundations of the economy and of law as a mode of both conflict resolution and social change. He differed, however, in some of his specific policy advice.

Much of Hamilton's earlier work involved issues of the proper nature of economic theory. Hamilton's problem with the orthodox view of the market is displayed in 'The Price System and Social Policy' (1918). In this paper, Hamilton analyses how the dictates of money making leads to the subordination of social welfare. This is a function not of inherent selfishness but of the form of social organization. The 'Place of Value Theory in Economics' is both a critique of orthodox economics for its narrow concern with value theory and a call for the creation of a new economic theory along different lines and with a different focus. The nature of this new economics is outlined in his 'The Institutional Approach to Economic Theory' (1919), a paper that effectively gave the institutionalist movement its name. Equally important as a defining contribution is Hamilton's entry on the topic of 'Institution' in the *Encyclopedia of the Social Sciences* (1937).

As Hamilton's work developed he took an increasing interest in the processes of actual, real world, price formation and in various forms of price regulation. A key part of this work was Hamilton's notion of many private decisions being affected by a public interest and justifying some form of government interference or regulation. He believed that institutions should be treated as neither given nor natural but a matter of human construction; and if institutions often developed nondeliberatively they were also matters of conscious redesign and reform. Conflicts over claims of property and other rights were largely and increasingly worked out through government, and in the resolution of these conflicts some notion of the public interest was always given effect even if not explicitly articulated. The price system of the market thus both operated within and gave effect to legal and customary institutions, and reform of these institutions would likely have profound impact on the organization, operation and performance of markets. These themes are amply developed in the selection of Hamilton's writings from 'Affectation with the Public Interest' (1930) to the chapters from *The Politics of Industry* (1957).

(v) Richard Theodore Ely

Richard Theodore Ely was one of the most influential economists of his time. Trained initially in the belief system of a devout Presbyterian family in up-state New York and in Germany by the historicist Karl Knies, the young Ely combined inductivism, historicism and Social Gospel-Christian

Socialism. He was a leader of the young radical economists who were instrumental in the founding of the American Economic Association in 1885. In 1892 he became the first head of the School of Economics, Political Science and History at the University of Wisconsin; through its Department of Economics, and particularly the work of John R. Commons and his students, his program was instrumental in the adjustment and transformation of public policies in a variety of areas at the state and national levels. He was arguably the first major historian and analyst of socialism and of the labor movement in the United States. He promoted the study of land and public utility economics. His *Outlines of Economics* was, through numerous editions, one of the most in fluential economics texts of his period.

Ely can be seen as initiating the Wisconsin tradition of institutionalism, though his position as a founder of institutionalism generally is eclipsed by John R. Commons. Ely believed that markets, resource allocation and, most especially, distribution were profoundly influenced by legal and customary institutions. He believed that even in an individualist society, considerations of conflict resolution and of socioeconomic change necessarily meant that institutions of social control, such as the state, had to make decisions on the basis of some notion of social welfare, or what Commons later was to call 'public purpose'. Law, in particular, had to balance considerations of continuity – for example, protection to reasonably established and maintained expectations – with those of change – such as through the exercise of the policy power. This view of law and government was predicated not on notions of absolute or natural rights but on a view of law and of property as pragmatic socially constructed and revised institutions. He supported the legal protection of the interests of labor as reflective of the development of an increasingly pluralistic industrial economy and thought that government should protect labor interests much as it protected business interests. These ideas reverberate throughout his writings but especially in his *Property and Contract in Their Relations to the Distribution of Wealth* (1914). The selection from that study provides the core of his theory of property. The other selection from Ely's work evidences the economic history which served as the background, if not the foundation, of his analysis of institutions.

(vi) Wesley Clair Mitchell

Wesley Mitchell has been described as Veblen's most 'outstanding student' (Dorfman 1959: 360), but, like Hoxie, he was no slave to Veblen and developed his own approach to institutional economics. Under the direction of Laughlin, Mitchell initially worked on the history of the Greenbacks, but Veblen's influence was soon to make itself felt in the form of an ambitious project on the history and functioning of the 'money economy'. This project was to focus on the development and functioning of 'pecuniary institutions', including an examination of how such institutions affected the activities and habits of thought of the people subject to them. Sometime in 1910 Mitchell gave up work on this project as too large and too speculative, but a number of Mitchell's more obviously institutionalist essays came directly out of the work he had undertaken in connection with the money economy project. Most important of these are the two articles on 'The Rationality of Economic Activity' (1910), his well known paper on 'The Backward Art of Spending Money' (1912), and 'The Role of Money in Economic Theory' (1916). Mitchell's interest in the history of economic thought also grew out of this research. Mitchell was later to teach a famous course on Types of Economic Theory at Columbia University. His approach, like Veblen's, was to present economic ideas as expressions of the prevailing habits of thought. His well know essay on 'Bentham's Felicific Calculus' (1918) is included to represent this aspect of Mitchell's work.

When Mitchell gave up on the money economy project he turned his attention to what had been merely one part of it – the problem of business cycles. The immediate outcome of this reorientation was his book *Business Cycles* (1913), a book that established Mitchell as a major figure in the profession. Mitchell's quantitative approach set him a little apart from the other founders of institutionalism. He was influenced by positivist ideas of science and more concerned to imitate physics than biology – but it is important to understand that, for Mitchell, quantitative analysis was a path to an institutional economics. This is made clear in Mitchell's presidential address to the American Economic Association, 'Quantitative Analysis in Economic Theory' (1916). Furthermore, Mitchell always conceived of business cycles as a problem of the particular pecuniary institutions in force, and is presented in rather Veblenian terms. This is demonstrated in the selection from *Business Cycles: The Problem and its Setting* (1927). It is also worth noting both that Mitchell gave generous reviews to Commons's books, and that Commons actively supported statistical work such as Mitchell's.

Mitchell continued to work on the problem of business cycles but the project he envisioned was never completed. The selection from Mitchell and Burns, *Measuring Business Cycles* (1946) provides an outline of the work Mitchell planned to undertake. The book itself came under sharp attack from Koopmans for its methodological approach, caricatured as 'measurement without theory'.

Mitchell was a founder and, for many years, Director of Research of the

National Bureau of Economic Research. Under Mitchell's direction, the NBER conducted vast amounts of research on business cycles, price movements, income distribution and growth, and labor issues. The NBER was an expression of Mitchell's commitment to research and his desire to keep research separate from particular political agendas. Although Mitchell felt that there was a need for institutional reform to overcome problems such as business cycles, and that policy should be informed by scientific investigation, he was always highly cautious in offering policy advice himself, and was extremely concerned to maintain an objective and non-political stance for scientific investigation. Mitchell's views on the relationship between scientific research and policy issues are laid out in his 'Intelligence and the Guidance of Economic Evolution' (1936).

References

Dorfman, Joseph, *The Economic Mind in American Civilization*, vol. 4. (New York: Viking, 1959).

——, 'The Background of Institutional Economics', J. Dorfman et al (eds.), *Institutional Economics* (Berkeley: University of California Press, 1962).

Edie, Lionel D, 'The Institutional Concept', *Quarterly Journal of Economics*, 41: 405–40 (1927).

Ekelund, Robert B. and Hebert, Robert F, *A History of Economic Theory and Method* (New York: McGraw Hill), 3rd edn. (1990).

Hamilton, Walton H, 'The Institutional Approach to Economic Theory', *American Economic Review*, 9: 309–18, (1919).

Parrish, John B, 'The Rise of Economics as an Academic Discipline: The Formative Years to 1900' *Southern Economic Journal* 34: 1–16, (1967).

Roundtable, 1931. 'Institutionalism: What it is and What it Hopes to Become'. *American Economic Review*, Papers and Proceedings 21: 134–41, (1931).

——, 1932. 'Institutional Economics'. *American Economic Review*, Papers and Proceedings 22: 105–16 (1932).

Russett, Cynthia E, *Darwin in America: The Intellectual Response 1865-1912* (San Francisco: W. H. Freeman, 1976).

Samuels, Warren J, 'The Present State of Institutional Economics', *Cambridge Journal of Economics* 19: 569–90, (1995).

THORSTEIN BUNDE VEBLEN

Thorstein Bunde Veblen (1857–1929), the son of Norwegian immigrants residing in Minnesota, received a BA from Carleton College in 1880 and a PhD from Yale University in 1884. After seven years' unemployment, he enrolled at Cornell University in 1991, where he met and impressed James Laurence Laughlin. Laughlin took Veblen to the newly established University of Chicago in 1892 to help organize the economics department. While at Chicago Veblen became managing editor of the *Journal of Political Economy* and published a series of articles and books which became classic expressions of his point of view. Leaving Chicago in 1906 he subsequently taught at Stanford (1906–9), Missouri (1911–18) and the New School for Social Research (1918–26). Veblen was one of the most iconoclastic, critical, seminal and widely influential American economists, his work becoming a foundation for Institutional Economics.

[1]

Why is Economics not an Evolutionary Science?

Thorstein Bunde Veblen, 'Why is Economics Not an Evolutionary Science?', *Quarterly Journal of Economics*, vol. 12 (July 1898), pp. 373–97; reprinted in *The Place of Science in Modern Civilization* (New York: Viking Press, 1919); reprinted, New Brunswick: Transactions, 1990, pp. 32–55.

In this classic article, Veblen both criticizes the practices of most other economists and lays out his methodological program for the construction of an evolutionary economics. His criticism is that the orthodox equilibrium technique is static and runs in terms of 'normality and propensity to an end' and neglects both the problem of the organization and control of the economy and the dynamic forces which make for change. An evolutionary economics should instead be based on the idea of a non-teleological and cumulative sequence of cause and effect.

THE

QUARTERLY JOURNAL

OF

ECONOMICS

JULY, 1898

WHY IS ECONOMICS NOT AN EVOLUTIONARY SCIENCE?

M. G. de Lapouge recently said, "Anthropology is destined to revolutionize the political and the social sciences as radically as bacteriology has revolutionized the science of medicine." * In so far as he speaks of economics, the eminent anthropologist is not alone in his conviction that the science stands in need of rehabilitation. His words convey a rebuke and an admonition, and in both respects he speaks the sense of many scientists in his own and related lines of inquiry. It may be taken as the consensus of those men who are doing the serious work of modern anthropology, ethnology, and psychology, as well as of those in the biological sciences proper, that economics is helplessly behind the times, and unable to handle its subject-matter in a way to entitle it to standing as a modern science. The other political and social sci-

* "The Fundamental Laws of Anthropo-sociology," *Journal of Political Economy*. December, 1897, p. 54. The same paper, in substance, appears in the *Rivista Italiana di Sociologia* for November, 1897.

ences come in for their share of this obloquy, and perhaps on equally cogent grounds. Nor are the economists themselves buoyantly indifferent to the rebuke. Probably no economist to-day has either the hardihood or the inclination to say that the science has now reached a definitive formulation. either in the detail of results or as regards the fundamental features of theory. The nearest recent approach to such a position on the part of an economist of accredited standing is perhaps to be found in Professor Marshall's Cambridge address of a year and a half ago.* But these utterances are so far from the jaunty confidence shown by the classical economists of half a century ago that what most forcibly strikes the reader of Professor Marshall's address is the exceeding modesty and the uncalled-for humility of the spokesman for the "old generation." With the economists who are most attentively looked to for guidance, uncertainty as to the definitive value of what has been and is being done, and as to what we may, with effect, take to next, is so common as to suggest that indecision is a meritorious work. Even the Historical School, who made their innovation with so much of home-grown applause some time back, have been unable to settle down contentedly to the pace which they set themselves.

The men of the sciences that are proud to own themselves "modern" find fault with the economists for being still content to occupy themselves with repairing a structure and doctrines and maxims resting on natural rights, utilitarianism, and administrative expediency. This aspersion is not altogether merited, but is near enough to the mark to carry a sting. These modern sciences are evolutionary sciences, and their adepts contemplate that characteristic of their work with some complacency. Economics is not an evolutionary science — by the confession of its

* "The Old Generation of Economists and the New," in this Journal for January. 1897. p. 133.

spokesman; and the economists turn their eyes with something of envy and some sense of baffled emulation to these rivals that make broad their phylacteries with the legend, "Up to date."

Precisely wherein the social and political sciences, including economics, fall short of being evolutionary sciences, is not so plain. At least, it has not been satisfactorily pointed out by their critics. Their successful rivals in this matter — the sciences that deal with human nature among the rest — claim as their substantial distinction that they are realistic: they deal with facts. But economics, too, is realistic in this sense: it deals with facts, often in the most painstaking way, and latterly with an increasingly strenuous insistence on the sole efficacy of data. But this "realism" does not make economics an evolutionary science. The insistence on data could scarcely be carried to a higher pitch than it was carried by the first generation of the Historical School; and yet no economics is farther from being an evolutionary science than the received economics of the Historical School. The whole broad range of erudition and research that engaged the energies of that school commonly falls short of being science, in that, when consistent, they have contented themselves with an enumeration of data and a narrative account of industrial development, and have not presumed to offer a theory of anything or to elaborate their results into a consistent body of knowledge.

Any evolutionary science, on the other hand, is a close-knit body of theory. It is a theory of a process, of an unfolding sequence. But here, again, economics seems to meet the test in a fair measure, without satisfying its critics that its credentials are good. It must be admitted, *e.g.*, that J. S. Mill's doctrines of production, distribution, and exchange, are a theory of certain economic processes, and that he deals in a consistent and effective fashion with the sequences of fact that make up his subject-matter. So, also, Cairnes's discussion of normal value, of the rate of wages, and of international trade, are excellent instances of a theoretical handling of economic processes of sequence and the orderly unfolding development of fact. But an attempt to cite Mill and Cairnes as exponents of an evolutionary economics will produce no better effect than perplexity, and not a great deal of that. Very much of monetary theory might be cited to the same purpose and with the like effect. Something similar is true even of late writers who have avowed some penchant for the evolutionary point of view; as, *e.g.*, Professor Hadley,—to cite a work of unquestioned merit and unusual reach. Measurably, he keeps the word of promise to the ear; but any one who may cite his *Economics* as having brought political economy into line as an evolutionary science will convince neither himself nor his interlocutor. Something to the like effect may fairly be said of the published work of that later English strain of economists represented by Professors Cunningham and Ashley, and Mr. Cannan, to name but a few of the more eminent figures in the group.

Of the achievements of the classical economists, recent and living, the science may justly be proud; but they fall short of the evolutionist's standard of adequacy, not in failing to offer a theory of a process or of a developmental relation, but through conceiving their theory in terms alien to the evolutionist's habits of thought. The difference between the evolutionary and the pre-evolutionary sciences lies not in the insistence on facts. There was a great and fruitful activity in the natural sciences in collecting and collating facts before these sciences took on the character which marks them as evolutionary. Nor does the difference lie in the absence of efforts to formulate and explain schemes of process, sequence, growth, and development in the pre-evolutionary days. Efforts of this kind abounded, in number and diversity; and many schemes of development, of great subtlety and beauty, gained a vogue both as theories of organic and inorganic development and as schemes of the life history of nations and societies. It will not even hold true that our elders overlooked the presence of cause and effect in formulating their theories and reducing their data to a body of knowledge. But the terms which were accepted as the definitive terms of knowledge were in some degree different in the early days from what they are now. The terms of thought in which the investigators of some two or three generations back definitively formulated their knowledge of facts, in their last analyses. were different in kind from the terms in which the modern evolutionist is content to formulate his results. The analysis does not run back to the same ground, or appeal to the same standard of finality or adequacy, in the one case as in the other.

The difference is a difference of spiritual attitude or point of view in the two contrasted generations of scientists. To put the matter in other words, it is a difference in the basis of valuation of the facts for the scientific purpose, or in the interest from which the facts are appreciated. With the earlier as with the later generation the basis of valuation of the facts handled is, in matters of detail, the causal relation which is apprehended to subsist between them. This is true to the greatest extent for the natural sciences. But in their handling of the more comprehensive schemes of sequence and relation — in their definitive formulation of the results — the two generations differ. The modern scientist is unwilling to depart from the test of causal relation or quantitative sequence. When he asks the question, Why? he insists on an answer in terms of cause and effect. He wants to reduce his solution of all problems to terms of the conservation of energy or the persistence of quantity. This is his last recourse. And this last recourse has in our time been made available for the handling of schemes of development and theories of a comprehensive process by the notion of a cumulative causation. The great deserts of the evolutionist leaders — if they have great deserts as leaders — lie, on the one hand, in their refusal to go back of the colorless sequence of phenomena and seek higher ground for their ultimate syntheses, and, on the other hand, in their having shown how this colorless impersonal sequence of cause and effect can be made use of for theory proper, by virtue of its cumulative character.

For the earlier natural scientists, as for the classical economists, this ground of cause and effect is not definitive. Their sense of truth and substantiality is not satisfied with a formulation of mechanical sequence. The ultimate term in their systematization of knowledge is a "natural law." This natural law is felt to exercise some sort of a coercive surveillance over the sequence of events, and to give a spiritual stability and consistence to the causal relation at any given juncture. To meet the high classical requirement, a sequence — and a developmental process especially — must be apprehended in terms of a consistent propensity tending to some spiritually legitimate end. When facts and events have been reduced to these terms of fundamental truth and have been made to square with the requirements of definitive normality, the investigator rests content. Any causal sequence which is apprehended to traverse the imputed propensity in events is a "disturbing factor." Logical congruity with the apprehended propensity is, in this view, adequate ground of procedure in building up a scheme of knowledge or of development. The objective point of the efforts of the scientists working under the guidance of this classical tradition, is to formulate knowledge in terms of absolute truth; and this absolute truth is a spiritual fact. It means a coincidence of facts with the deliverances of an enlightened and deliberate common sense.

The development and the attenuation of this preconception of normality or of a propensity in events might be traced in detail from primitive animism down through the elaborate discipline of faith and metaphysics, overruling Providence, order of nature, natural rights, natural law, underlying principles. But all that may be necessary here is to point out that, by descent and by psychological content, this constraining normality is of a spiritual kind. It is for the scientific purpose an imputation of spiritual coherence to the facts dealt with. The question of interest is how this preconception of normality has fared at the hands of modern science, and how it has come to be superseded in the intellectual primacy by the latter-day preconception of a non-spiritual sequence. This question is of interest because its answer may throw light on the question as to what chance there is for the indefinite persistence of this archaic habit of thought in the methods of economic science.

Under primitive conditions, men stand in immediate personal contact with the material facts of the environment; and the force and discretion of the individual in shaping the facts of the environment count obviously, and to all appearance solely, in working out the conditions of life. There is little of impersonal or mechanical sequence visible to primitive men in their every-day life; and what there is of this kind in the processes of brute nature about them is in large part inexplicable and passes for inscrutable. It is accepted as malignant or beneficent, and is construed in the terms of personality that are familiar to all men at first hand,—the terms known to all men by first-hand knowledge of their own acts. The inscrutable movements of the seasons and of the natural forces are apprehended as actions guided by discretion, will power, or propensity looking to an end, much as human actions are. The processes of inanimate nature are agencies whose habits of life are to be learned, and who are to be coerced, outwitted, circumvented, and turned to account, much as the beasts are. At the same time the community is small, and the human contact of the individual is not wide. Neither the industrial life nor the non-industrial social life forces upon men's attention the ruthless impersonal sweep of events that no man can withstand or deflect, such as becomes visible in the more complex and comprehensive life process of the larger community of a later day. There is nothing decisive to hinder men's knowledge of facts and events being formulated in terms of personality — in terms of habit and propensity and will power.

As time goes on and as the situation departs from this archaic character,— where it does depart from it,— the circumstances which condition men's systematization of facts change in such a way as to throw the impersonal character of the sequence of events more and more into the foreground. The penalties for failure to apprehend facts in dispassionate terms fall surer and swifter. The sweep of events is forced home more consistently on men's minds. The guiding hand of a spiritual agency or a propensity in events becomes less readily traceable as men's knowledge of things grows ampler and more searching. In modern times, and particularly in the industrial countries, this coercive guidance of men's habits of thought in the realistic direction has been especially pronounced; and the effect shows itself in a somewhat reluctant but cumulative departure from the archaic point of view. The departure is most visible and has gone farthest in those homely branches of knowledge that have to do immediately with modern mechanical processes, such as engineering designs and technological contrivances generally. Of the sciences, those have wandered farthest on this way (of integration or disintegration, according as one may choose to view it) that have to do with mechanical sequence and process; and those have best and longest retained the archaic point of view intact which — like the moral, social, or spiritual sciences — have to do with process and sequence that is less tangible, less traceable by the use of the senses, and that therefore less immediately forces upon the attention the phenomenon of sequence as contrasted with that of propensity.

There is no abrupt transition from the pre-evolutionary to the post-evolutionary standpoint. Even in those natural sciences which deal with the processes of life and the evolutionary sequence of events the concept of dispassionate cumulative causation has often and effectively been helped out by the notion that there is in all this some sort of a meliorative trend that exercises a constraining guidance over the course of causes and effects. The faith in this meliorative trend as a concept useful to the science has gradually weakened, and it has repeatedly been disavowed; but it can scarcely be said to have yet disappeared from the field.

The process of change in the point of view, or in the terms of definitive formulation of knowledge, is a gradual one; and all the sciences have shared, though in an unequal degree, in the change that is going forward. Economics is not an exception to the rule, but it still shows too many reminiscences of the "natural" and the "normal," of "verities" and "tendencies," of "controlling principles" and "disturbing causes," to be classed as an evolutionary science. The history of the science shows a long and devious course of disintegrating animism,— from the days of the scholastic writers, who discussed usury from the point of view of its relation to the divine suzerainty, to the Physiocrats, who rested their case on an "*ordre naturel*" and a "*loi naturelle*" that decides what is substantially true and, in a general way, guides the course of events by the constraint of logical congruence. There has been something of a change from Adam Smith, whose recourse in perplexity was to the guidance of "an unseen hand," to Mill and Cairnes, who formulated the laws of "natural" wages and "normal" value, and the former of whom was so well content with his work as to say, "Happily, there is nothing in the laws of Value which remains for the present or any future writer to clear up: the theory of the subject is complete."* But the difference between the earlier and the later point of view is a difference of degree rather than of kind.

The standpoint of the classical economists, in their higher or definitive syntheses and generalizations, may not inaptly be called the standpoint of ceremonial adequacy. The ultimate laws and principles which they formulated were laws of the normal or the natural, according to a preconception regarding the ends to which, in the nature of things, all things tend. In effect, this preconception imputes to things a tendency to work out what the instructed common sense of the time accepts as the adequate or worthy end of human effort. It is a projection of the accepted ideal of conduct. This ideal of conduct is made to serve as a canon of truth, to the extent that the investigator contents himself with an appeal to its legitimation for premises that run back of the facts with which he is immediately dealing, for the "controlling principles" that are conceived intangibly to underlie the process discussed, and for the "tendencies" that run beyond the situation as it lies before him. As instances of the use of this ceremonial canon of knowledge may be cited the "conjectural history" that plays so large a part in the classical treatment of economic institutions, such as the normalized accounts of the beginnings of barter in the transactions of the putative hunter, fisherman, and boat-builder, or the man with the plane and the two planks, or the two men with the basket of apples and the basket of nuts.† Of a similar import is the characterization of money as "the great wheel of circulation"‡ or as "the medium of ex-

* *Political Economy*, Book III. chap. i.

† Marshall, *Principles of Economics* (2d ed.), Book V. chap. ii. p. 395, note.

‡ Adam Smith, *Wealth of Nations* (Bohn ed.), Book II. chap. ii. p. 289.

change." Money is here discussed in terms of the end which, "in the normal case," it should work out according to the given writer's ideal of economic life, rather than in terms of causal relation.

With later writers especially, this terminology is no doubt to be commonly taken as a convenient use of metaphor, in which the concept of normality and propensity to an end has reached an extreme attenuation. But it is precisely in this use of figurative terms for the formulation of theory that the classical normality still lives its attenuated life in modern economics; and it is this facile recourse to inscrutable figures of speech as the ultimate terms of theory that has saved the economists from being dragooned into the ranks of modern science. The metaphors are effective, both in their homiletical use and as a labor-saving device,— more effective than their user designs them to be. By their use the theorist is enabled serenely to enjoin himself from following out an elusive train of causal sequence. He is also enabled, without misgivings, to construct a theory of such an institution as money or wages or land-ownership without descending to a consideration of the living items concerned, except for convenient corroboration of his normalized scheme of symptoms. By this method the theory of an institution or a phase of life may be stated in conventionalized terms of the apparatus whereby life is carried on, the apparatus being invested with a tendency to an equilibrium at the normal, and the theory being a formulation of the conditions under which this putative equilibrium supervenes. In this way we have come into the usufruct of a cost-of-production theory of value which is pungently reminiscent of the time when Nature abhorred a vacuum. The ways and means and the mechanical structure of industry are formulated in a conventionalized nomenclature, and the observed motions of this mechanical apparatus are then reduced to a normalized scheme of relations. The scheme so arrived at is spiritually binding on the behavior of the phenomena contemplated. With this normalized scheme as a guide, the permutations of a given segment of the apparatus are worked out according to the values assigned the several items and features comprised in the calculation; and a ceremonially consistent formula is constructed to cover that much of the industrial field. This is the deductive method. The formula is then tested by comparison with observed permutations, by the polariscopic use of the "normal case"; and the results arrived at are thus authenticated by induction. Features of the process that do not lend themselves to interpretation in the terms of the formula are abnormal cases and are due to disturbing causes. In all this the agencies or forces causally at work in the economic life process are neatly avoided. The outcome of the method, at its best, is a body of logically consistent propositions concerning the normal relations of things — a system of economic taxonomy. At its worst, it is a body of maxims for the conduct of business and a polemical discussion of disputed points of policy.

In all this, economic science is living over again in its turn the experiences which the natural sciences passed through some time back. In the natural sciences the work of the taxonomist was and continues to be of great value, but the scientists grew restless under the régime of symmetry and system-making. They took to asking why, and so shifted their inquiries from the structure of the coral reefs to the structure and habits of life of the polyp that lives in and by them. In the science of plants, systematic botany has not ceased to be of service; but the stress of investigation and discussion among the botanists to-day falls on the biological value of any given feature of structure, function, or tissue rather than on its taxonomic bearing. All the talk about cytoplasm, centrosomes, and karyokinetic process, means that the inquiry now looks consistently to the life process, and aims to explain it in terms of cumulative causation.

What may be done in economic science of the taxonomic kind is shown at its best in Cairnes's work, where the method is well conceived and the results effectively formulated and applied. Cairnes handles the theory of the normal case in economic life with a master hand. In his discussion the metaphysics of propensity and tendencies no longer avowedly rules the formulation of theory, nor is the inscrutable meliorative trend of a harmony of interests confidently appealed to as an engine of definitive use in giving legitimacy to the economic situation at a given time. There is less of an exercise of faith in Cairnes's economic discussions than in those of the writers that went before him. The definitive terms of the formulation are still the terms of normality and natural law, but the metaphysics underlying this appeal to normality is so far removed from the ancient ground of the beneficent "order of nature" as to have become at least nominally impersonal and to proceed without a constant regard to the humanitarian bearing of the "tendencies" which it formulates. The metaphysics has been attenuated to something approaching in colorlessness the naturalist's conception of natural law. It is a natural law which, in the guise of "controlling principles," exercises a constraining surveillance over the trend of things; but it is no longer conceived to exercise its constraint in the interest of certain ulterior human purposes. The element of beneficence has been well-nigh eliminated, and the system is formulated in terms of the system itself. Economics as it left Cairnes's hand, so far as his theoretical work is concerned, comes near being taxonomy for taxonomy's sake.

No equally capable writer has come as near making economics the ideal "dismal" science as Cairnes in his discussion of pure theory. In the days of the early classical writers economics had a vital interest for the laymen of the time, because it formulated the common sense metaphysics of the time in its application to a department of human life. But in the hands of the later classical writers the science lost much of its charm in this regard. It was no longer a definition and authentication of the deliverances of current common sense as to what ought to come to pass; and it, therefore, in large measure lost the support of the people out of doors, who were unable to take an interest in what did not concern them; and it was also out of touch with that realistic or evolutionary habit of mind which got under way about the middle of the century in the natural sciences. It was neither vitally metaphysical nor matter-of-fact, and it found comfort with very few outside of its own ranks. Only for those who by the fortunate accident of birth or education have been able to conserve the taxonomic animus has the science during the last third of a century continued to be of absorbing interest. The result has been that from the time when the taxonomic structure stood forth as a completed whole in its symmetry and stability the economists themselves, beginning with Cairnes, have been growing restive under its discipline of stability, and have made many efforts, more or less sustained, to galvanize it into movement. At the hands of the writers of the classical line these excursions have chiefly aimed at a more complete and comprehensive taxonomic scheme of permutations; while the historical departure threw away the taxonomic ideal without getting rid of the preconceptions on which it is based; and the later Austrian group struck out on a theory of process, but presently came to a full stop because the process about which they busied themselves was not, in their apprehension of it, a cumulative or unfolding sequence.

But what does all this signify? If we are getting restless under the taxonomy of a monocotyledonous wage doctrine and a cryptogamic theory of interest, with involute, loculicidal, tomentous, and moniliform variants, what is the cytoplasm, centrosome, or karyokinetic process to which we may turn, and in which we may find surcease from the metaphysics of normality and controlling principles? What are we going to do about it? The question is rather, What are we doing about it? There is the economic life process still in great measure awaiting theoretical formulation. The active material in which the economic process goes on is the human material of the industrial community. For the purpose of economic science the process of cumulative change that is to be accounted for is the sequence of change in the methods of doing things,—the methods of dealing with the material means of life.

What has been done in the way of inquiry into this economic life process? The ways and means of turning material objects and circumstances to account lie before the investigator at any given point of time in the form of mechanical contrivances and arrangements for compassing certain mechanical ends. It has therefore been easy to accept these ways and means as items of inert matter having a given mechanical structure and thereby serving the material ends of man. As such, they have been scheduled and graded by the economists under the head of capital, this capital being conceived as a mass of material objects serviceable for human use. This is well enough for the purposes of taxonomy; but it is not an effective method of conceiving the matter for the purpose of a theory of the developmental process. For the latter purpose, when taken as items in a process of cumulative change or as items in the scheme of life, these productive goods are facts of human knowledge, skill, and predilection; that is to say, they are, substantially, prevalent habits of thought, and it is as such that they enter into the process of industrial development. The physical properties of the materials accessible to man are constants: it is the human agent that changes,—his insight and his appreciation of what these things can be used for is what develops. The accumulation of goods already on hand conditions his handling and utilization of the materials offered, but even on this side — the "limitation of industry by capital" — the limitation imposed is on what men can do and on the methods of doing it. The changes that take place in the mechanical contrivances are an expression of changes in the human factor. Changes in the material facts breed further change only through the human factor. It is in the human material that the continuity of development is to be looked for; and it is here, therefore, that the motor forces of the process of economic development must be studied if they are to be studied in action at all. Economic action must be the subject-matter of the science if the science is to fall into line as an evolutionary science.

Nothing new has been said in all this. But the fact is all the more significant for being a familiar fact. It is a fact recognized by common consent throughout much of the later economic discussion, and this current recognition of the fact is a long step towards centering discussion and inquiry upon it. If economics is to follow the lead or the analogy of the other sciences that have to do with a life process, the way is plain so far as regards the general direction in which the move will be made.

The economists of the classical trend have made no serious attempt to depart from the standpoint of taxonomy and make their science a genetic account of the economic life process. As has just been said, much the same is true for the Historical School. The latter have attempted an account of developmental sequence, but they have followed the lines of pre-Darwinian speculations on development rather than lines which modern science would recognize as evolutionary. They have given a narrative survey of phenomena, not a genetic account of an unfolding process. In this work they have, no doubt, achieved results of permanent value; but the results achieved are scarcely to be classed as economic theory. On the other hand, the Austrians and their precursors and their coadjutors in the value discussion have taken up a detached portion of economic theory, and have inquired with great nicety into the process by which the phenomena within their limited field are worked out. The entire discussion of marginal utility and subjective value as the outcome of a valuation process must be taken as a genetic study of this range of facts. But here, again, nothing further has come of the inquiry, so far as regards a rehabilitation of economic theory as a whole. Accepting Menger as their spokesman on this head, it must be said that the Austrians have on the whole showed themselves unable to break with the classical tradition that economics is a taxonomic science.

The reason for the Austrian failure seems to lie in a faulty conception of human nature,— faulty for the present purpose, however adequate it may be for any other. In all the received formulations of economic theory, whether at the hands of English economists or those of the Continent, the human material with which the inquiry is concerned is conceived in hedonistic terms; that is to say, in terms of a passive and substantially inert and immutably given human nature. The psychological and anthropological preconceptions of the economists have been those which were accepted by the psychological and social sciences some generations ago. The hedonistic conception of man is that of a lightning calculator of pleasures and pains, who oscillates like a homogeneous globule of desire of happiness under the impulse of stimuli that shift him about the area, but leave him intact. He has neither antecedent nor consequent. He is an isolated, definitive human datum, in stable equilibrium except for the buffets of the impinging forces that displace him in one direction or another. Self-poised in elemental space, he spins symmetrically about his own spiritual axis until the parallelogram of forces bears down upon him, whereupon he follows the line of the resultant. When the force of the impact is spent, he comes to rest, a self-contained globule of desire as before. Spiritually, the hedonistic man is not a prime mover. He is not the seat of a process of living, except in the sense that he is subject to a series of permutations enforced upon him by circumstances external and alien to him.

The later psychology, re-enforced by modern anthropological research, gives a different conception of human nature. According to this conception, it is the characteristic of man to do something, not simply to suffer pleasures and pains through the impact of suitable forces. He is not simply a bundle of desires that are to be saturated by being placed in the path of the forces of the environment, but rather a coherent structure of propensities and habits which seeks realization and expression in an unfolding activity. According to this view, human activity, and economic activity among the rest, is not apprehended as something incidental to the process of saturating given desires. The activity is itself the substantial fact of the process, and the desires under whose guidance the action takes place are circumstances of temperament which determine the specific direction in which the activity will unfold itself in the given case. These circumstances of temperament are ultimate and definitive for the individual who acts under them, so far as regards his attitude as agent in the particular action in which he is engaged. But, in the view of the science, they are elements of the existing frame of mind of the agent, and are the outcome of his antecedents and his life up to the point at which he stands. They are the products of his hereditary traits and his past experience, cumulatively wrought out under a given body of traditions, conventionalities, and material circumstances; and they afford the point of departure for the next step in the process. The economic life history of the individual is a cumulative process of adaptation of means to ends that cumulatively change as the process goes on, both the agent and his environment being at any point the outcome of the past process. His methods of life to-day are enforced upon him by his habits of life carried over from yesterday and by the circumstances left as the mechanical residue of the life of yesterday.

What is true of the individual in this respect is true of the group in which he lives. All economic change is a change in the economic community,— a change in the community's methods of turning material things to account. The change is always in the last resort a change in habits of thought. This is true even of changes in the mechanical processes of industry. A given contrivance for effecting certain material ends becomes a circumstance which affects the further growth of habits of thought — habitual methods of procedure — and so becomes a point of departure for further development of the methods of compassing the ends sought and for the further variation of ends that are sought to be compassed. In all this flux there is no definitively adequate method of life and no definitive or absolutely worthy end of action, so far as concerns the science which sets out to formulate a theory of the process of economic life. What remains as a hard and fast residue is the fact of activity directed to an objective end. Economic action is teleological, in the sense that men always and everywhere seek to do something. What, in specific detail, they seek, is not to be answered except by a scrutiny of the details of their activity; but, so long as we have to do with their life as members of the economic community, there remains the generic fact that their life is an unfolding activity of a teleological kind.

It may or may not be a teleological process in the sense that it tends or should tend to any end that is conceived to be worthy or adequate by the inquirer or by the consensus of inquirers. Whether it is or is not is a question with which the present inquiry is not concerned; and it is also a question of which an evolutionary economics need take no account. The question of a tendency in events can evidently not come up except on the ground of some preconception or prepossession on the part of the person looking for the tendency. In order to search for a tendency, we must be possessed of some notion of a definitive end to be sought, or some notion as to what is the legitimate trend of events. The notion of a legitimate trend in a course of events is an extra-evolutionary preconception, and lies outside the scope of an inquiry into the causal sequence in any process. The evolutionary point of view, therefore, leaves no place for a formulation of natural laws in terms of definitive normality, whether in economics or in any other branch of inquiry. Neither does it leave room for that other question of normality, What should be the end of the developmental process under discussion?

The economic life history of any community is its life history in so far as it is shaped by men's interest in the material means of life. This economic interest has counted for much in shaping the cultural growth of all communities. Primarily and most obviously, it has guided the formation, the cumulative growth, of that range of conventionalities and methods of life that are currently recognized as economic institutions; but the same interest has also pervaded the community's life and its cultural growth at points where the resulting structural features are not chiefly and most immediately of an economic bearing. The economic interest goes with men through life, and it goes with the race throughout its process of cultural development. It affects the cultural structure at all points, so that all institutions may be said to be in some measure economic institutions. This is necessarily the case, since the base of action — the point of departure — at any step in the process is the entire organic complex of habits of thought that have been shaped by the past process. The economic interest does not act in isolation, for it is but one of several vaguely isolable interests on which the complex of teleological activity carried out by the individual proceeds. The individual is but a single agent in each case; and he enters into each successive action as a whole, although the specific end sought in a given action may be sought avowedly on the basis of a particular interest; as *e.g.*, the economic, æsthetic, sexual, humanitarian, devotional interests. Since each of these passably isolable interests is a propensity of the organic agent man, with his complex of habits of thought, the expression of each is affected by habits of life formed under the guidance of all the rest. There is, therefore, no neatly isolable range of cultural phenomena that can be rigorously set apart under the head of economic institutions, although a category of "economic institutions" may be of service as a convenient caption, comprising those institutions in which the economic interest most immediately and consistently finds expression, and which most immediately and with the least limitation are of an economic bearing.

From what has been said it appears that an evolutionary economics must be the theory of a process of cultural growth as determined by the economic interest, a theory of a cumulative sequence of economic institutions stated in terms of the process itself. Except for the want of space to do here what should be done in some detail if it is done at all, many efforts by the later economists in this direction might be cited to show the trend of economic discussion in this direction. There is not a little evidence to this effect, and much of the work done must be rated as effective work for this purpose. Much of the work of the Historical School, for instance, and that of its later exponents especially, is too noteworthy to be passed over in silence, even with all due regard to the limitations of space.

We are now ready to return to the question why economics is not an evolutionary science. It is necessarily the aim of such an economics to trace the cumulative working out of the economic interest in the cultural sequence. It must be a theory of the economic life process of the race or the community. The economists have accepted the hedonistic preconceptions concerning human nature and human action, and the conception of the economic interest which a hedonistic psychology gives does not afford material for a theory of the development of human nature. Under hedonism the economic interest is not conceived in terms of action. It is therefore not readily apprehended or appreciated in terms of a cumulative growth of habits of thought, and does not provoke, even if it did lend itself to, treatment by the evolutionary method. At the same time the anthropological preconceptions current in that common-sense apprehension of human nature to which economists have habitually turned has not enforced the formulation of human nature in terms of a cumulative growth of habits of life. These received anthropological preconceptions are such as have made possible the normalized conjectural accounts of primitive barter with which all economic readers are familiar, and the no less normalized conventional derivation of landed property and its rent, or the sociologico-philosophical discussions of the "function" of this or that class in the life of society or of the nation.

The premises and the point of view required for an evolutionary economics have been wanting. The economists have not had the materials for such a science ready to their hand, and the provocation to strike out in such a direction has been absent. Even if it has been possible at any time to turn to the evolutionary line of speculation in economics, the possibility of a departure is not enough to bring it about. So long as the habitual view taken of a given range of facts is of the taxonomic kind and the material lends itself to treatment by that method, the taxonomic method is the easiest, gives the most gratifying immediate results, and best fits into the accepted body of knowledge of the range of facts in question. This has been the situation in economics. The other sciences of its group have likewise been a body of taxonomic discipline, and departures from the accredited method have lain under the odium of being meretricious innovations. The well-worn paths are easy to follow and lead into good company. Advance along them visibly furthers the accredited work which the science has in hand. Divergence from the paths means tentative work, which is necessarily slow and fragmentary and of uncertain value.

It is only when the methods of the science and the syntheses resulting from their use come to be out of line with habits of thought that prevail in other matters that the scientist grows restive under the guidance of the received methods and standpoints, and seeks a way out. Like other men, the economist is an individual with but one intelligence. He is a creature of habits and propensities given through the antecedents, hereditary and cultural, of which he is an outcome; and the habits of thought formed in any one line of experience affect his thinking in any other. Methods of observation and of handling facts that are familiar through habitual use in the general range of knowledge, gradually assert themselves in any given special range of knowledge. They may be accepted slowly and with reluctance where their acceptance involves innovation; but, if they have the continued backing of the general body of experience, it is only a question of time when they shall come into dominance in the special field. The intellectual attitude and the method of correlation enforced upon us in the apprehension and assimilation of facts in the more elementary ranges of knowledge that have to do with brute facts assert themselves also when the attention is directed to those phenomena of the life process with which economics has to do; and the range of facts which are habitually handled by other methods than that in traditional vogue in economics has now become so large and so insistently present at every turn that we are left restless, if the new body of facts cannot be handled according to the method of mental procedure which is in this way becoming habitual.

In the general body of knowledge in modern times the facts are apprehended in terms of causal sequence. This is especially true of that knowledge of brute facts which is shaped by the exigencies of the modern mechanical industry. To men thoroughly imbued with this matter-of-fact habit of mind the laws and theorems of economics, and of the other sciences that treat of the normal course of things, have a character of "unreality" and futility that bars out any serious interest in their discussion. The laws and theorems are "unreal" to them because they are not to be apprehended in the terms which these men make use of in handling the facts with which they are perforce habitually occupied. The same matter-of-fact spiritual attitude and mode of procedure have now made their way well up into the higher levels of scientific knowledge, even in the sciences which deal in a more elementary way with the same human material that makes the subject-matter of economics, and the economists themselves are beginning to feel the unreality of their theorems about "normal" cases. Provided the practical exigencies of modern industrial life continue of the same character as they now are, and so continue to enforce the impersonal method of knowledge, it is only a question of time when that (substantially animistic) habit of mind which proceeds on the notion of a definitive normality shall be displaced in the field of economic inquiry by that (substantially materialistic) habit of mind which seeks a comprehension of facts in terms of a cumulative sequence.

The later method of apprehending and assimilating

facts and handling them for the purposes of knowledge may be better or worse, more or less worthy or adequate, than the earlier; it may be of greater or less ceremonial or æsthetic effect; we may be moved to regret the incursion of underbred habits of thought into the scholar's domain. But all that is beside the present point. Under the stress of modern technological exigencies, men's every-day habits of thought are falling into the lines that in the sciences constitute the evolutionary method; and knowledge which proceeds on a higher, more archaic plane is becoming alien and meaningless to them. The social and political sciences must follow the drift, for they are already caught in it.

[2]

Excerpts from *The Theory of the Leisure Class*

Thorstein Bunde Veblen, 'Pecuniary Emulation', 'Conspicuous Leisure', 'Conspicuous Consumption' and 'The Pecuniary Standard of Living', *The Theory of the Leisure Class* (New York: Macmillan, 1899), pp. 33–118.

The famous book from which these excerpts are taken is noted for its anthropological approach to practices and institutions which most economists take for granted. Using his unique style of language, Veblen analyzes the social behavior norms of Americans in a manner that emphasizes the role of hierarchy and status emulation in the formation of consumption and other related habits. Once one has read and comprehended Veblen on this subject, one can no longer look at the conventional patterns of consumption, leisure, and family life in quite the same way as before. Among other things, Veblen's analysis suggests that many socially sanctioned patterns of behavior are survivals from earlier and more barbaric periods of history.

Pecuniary Emulation

In the sequence of cultural evolution the emergence of a leisure class coincides with the beginning of ownership. This is necessarily the case, for these two institutions result from the same set of economic forces. In the inchoate phase of their development they are but different aspects of the same general facts of social structure.

It is as elements of social structure — conventional facts — that leisure and ownership are matters of interest for the purpose in hand. An habitual neglect of work does not constitute a leisure class; neither does the mechanical fact of use and consumption constitute ownership. The present inquiry, therefore, is not concerned with the beginning of indolence, nor with the beginning of the appropriation of useful articles to individual consumption. The point in question is the origin and nature of a conventional leisure class on the one hand and the beginnings of individual ownership as a conventional right or equitable claim on the other hand.

The early differentiation out of which the distinction between a leisure and a working class arises is a division maintained between men's and women's work in the lower stages of barbarism. Likewise the earliest form of ownership is an ownership of the women by the able-bodied men of the community. The facts may be expressed in more general terms, and truer to the import of the barbarian theory of life, by saying that it is an ownership of the woman by the man.

There was undoubtedly some appropriation of useful articles before the custom of appropriating women arose. The usages of existing archaic communities in which there is no ownership of women is warrant for such a view. In all communities the members, both male and female, habitually appropriate to their individual use a variety of useful things; but these useful things are not thought of as owned by the person who appropriates and consumes them. The habitual appropriation and consumption of certain slight personal effects goes on without raising the question of ownership; that is to say, the question of a conventional, equitable claim to extraneous things.

The ownership of women begins in the lower barbarian stages of culture, apparently with the seizure of female captives. The original reason for the seizure and appropriation of women seems to have been their usefulness as trophies. The practice of seizing women from the enemy as trophies, gave rise to a form of ownership-marriage, resulting in a household with a male head. This was followed by an extension of slavery to other captives and inferiors, besides women, and by an extension of ownership-marriage to other women than those seized from the enemy. The outcome of emulation under the circumstances of a predatory life, therefore, has been on the one hand a form of marriage resting on coercion, and on the other hand the custom of ownership. The two institutions are not distinguishable in the initial phase of their development; both arise from the desire of the successful men to put their prowess in evidence by exhibiting some durable result of their exploits. Both also minister to that propensity for mastery which pervades all predatory communities. From the ownership of women the concept of ownership extends itself to include the products of their industry, and so there arises the ownership of things as well as of persons.

In this way a consistent system of property in goods is gradually installed. And although in the latest stages of the development, the serviceability of goods for consumption has come to be the most obtrusive element of their value, still, wealth has by no means yet lost its utility as a honorific evidence of the owner's prepotence.

Wherever the institution of private property is found, even in a slightly developed form, the economic process bears the character of a struggle between men for the possession of goods. It has been customary in economic theory, and especially among those economists who adhere with least faltering to the body of modernised classical doctrines, to construe this struggle for wealth as being substantially a struggle for subsistence. Such is, no doubt, its character in large part during the earlier and less efficient phases of industry. Such is also its character in all cases where the "niggardliness of nature" is so strict as to afford but a scanty livelihood to the community in return for strenuous and unremitting application to the business of getting the means of subsistence. But in all progressing communities an advance is presently made beyond this early stage of technological development. Industrial efficiency is presently carried to such a pitch as to afford something appreciably more than a bare livelihood to those engaged in the industrial process. It has not been unusual for economic theory to speak of the further struggle for wealth on this new industrial basis as a competition for an increase of the comforts of life, — primarily for an increase of the physical comforts which the consumption of goods affords.

The end of acquisition and accumulation is conventionally held to be the consumption of the goods accumulated — whether it is consumption directly by the owner of the goods or by the household attached to him and for this purpose identified with him in theory. This is at least felt to be the economically legitimate end of acquisition, which alone it is incumbent on the theory to take account of. Such consumption may of course be conceived to serve the consumer's physical wants — his physical comfort — or his so-called higher wants — spiritual, æsthetic, intellectual, or what not; the latter class of wants being served indirectly by an expenditure of goods, after the fashion familiar to all economic readers.

But it is only when taken in a sense far removed from its naïve meaning that consumption of goods can be said to afford the incentive from which accumulation invariably proceeds. The motive that lies at the root of ownership is emulation; and the same motive of emulation continues active in the further development of the institution to which it has given rise and in the development of all those features of the social structure which this institution of ownership touches. The possession of wealth confers honour; it is an invidious distinction. Nothing equally cogent can be said for the consumption of goods, nor for any other conceivable incentive to acquisition, and especially not for any incentive to the accumulation of wealth.

It is of course not to be overlooked that in a community where nearly all goods are private property the necessity of earning a livelihood is a powerful and ever-present incentive for the poorer members of the community. The need of subsistence and of an increase of physical comfort may for a time be the dominant motive of acquisition for those classes who are habitually employed at manual labour, whose subsistence is on a precarious footing, who possess little and ordinarily accumulate little; but it will appear in the course of the discussion that even in the case of these impecunious classes the predominance of the motive of physical want is not so decided as has sometimes been assumed. On the other hand, so far as regards those members and classes of the community who are chiefly concerned in the accumulation of wealth, the incentive of subsistence or of physical comfort never plays a considerable part. Ownership began and grew into a human institution on grounds unrelated to the subsistence minimum. The dominant incentive was from the outset the invidious distinction attaching to wealth, and, save temporarily and by exception, no other motive has usurped the primacy at any later stage of the development.

Property set out with being booty held as trophies of the successful raid. So long as the group had departed but little from the primitive communal organisation, and so long as it still stood in close contact with other hostile groups, the utility of things or persons owned lay chiefly in an invidious comparison between their possessor and the enemy from whom they were taken. The habit of distinguishing between the interests of the individual and those of the group to which he belongs is apparently a later growth. Invidious comparison between the possessor of the honorific booty and his less successful neighbours within the group was no doubt present early as an element of the utility of the things possessed, though this was not at the outset the chief element of their value. The man's prowess was still primarily the group's prowess, and the possessor of the booty felt himself to be primarily the keeper of the honour of his group. This appreciation of exploit from the communal point of view is met with also at later stages of social growth, especially as regards the laurels of war.

But so soon as the custom of individual ownership begins to gain consistency, the point of view taken in making the invidious comparison on which private property rests will begin to change. Indeed, the one change is but the reflex of the other. The initial phase of ownership, the phase of acquisition by naïve seizure and conversion, begins to pass into the subsequent stage of an incipient organisation of industry on the basis of private property (in slaves); the horde develops into a more or less self-sufficing industrial community;

possessions then come to be valued not so much as evidence of successful foray, but rather as evidence of the prepotence of the possessor of these goods over other individuals within the community. The invidious comparison now becomes primarily a comparison of the owner with the other members of the group. Property is still of the nature of trophy, but, with the cultural advance, it becomes more and more a trophy of successes scored in the game of ownership carried on between the members of the group under the quasi-peaceable methods of nomadic life.

Gradually, as industrial activity further displaces predatory activity in the community's everyday life and in men's habits of thought, accumulated property more and more replaces trophies of predatory exploit as the conventional exponent of prepotence and success. With the growth of settled industry, therefore, the possession of wealth gains in relative importance and effectiveness as a customary basis of repute and esteem. Not that esteem ceases to be awarded on the basis of other, more direct evidence of prowess; not that successful predatory aggression or warlike exploit ceases to call out the approval and admiration of the crowd, or to stir the envy of the less successful competitors; but the opportunities for gaining distinction by means of this direct manifestation of superior force grow less available both in scope and frequency. At the same time opportunities for industrial aggression, and for the accumulation of property by the quasi-peaceable methods of nomadic industry, increase in scope and availability. And it is even more to the point that property now becomes the most easily recognised evidence of a reputable degree of success as distinguished from heroic or signal achievement. It therefore becomes the conventional basis of esteem. Its possession in some amount becomes necessary in order to any reputable standing in the community. It becomes indispensable to accumulate, to acquire property, in order to retain one's good name. When accumulated goods have in this way once become the accepted badge of efficiency, the possession of wealth presently assumes the character of an independent and definitive basis of esteem. The possession of goods, whether acquired aggressively by one's own exertion or passively by transmission through inheritance from others, becomes a conventional basis of reputability. The possession of wealth, which was at the outset valued simply as an evidence of efficiency, becomes, in popular apprehension, itself a meritorious act. Wealth is now itself intrinsically honourable and confers honour on its possessor. By a further refinement, wealth acquired passively by transmission from ancestors or other antecedents presently becomes even more honorific than wealth acquired by the possessor's own effort; but this distinction belongs at a later stage in the evolution of the pecuniary culture and will be spoken of in its place.

Prowess and exploit may still remain the basis of award of the highest popular esteem, although the possession of wealth has become the basis of commonplace reputability and of a blameless social standing. The predatory instinct and the consequent approbation of predatory efficiency are deeply ingrained in the habits of thought of those peoples who have passed under the discipline of a protracted predatory culture. According to popular award, the highest honours within human reach may, even yet, be those gained by an unfolding of extraordinary predatory efficiency in war, or by a quasi-predatory efficiency in statecraft; but for the purposes of a commonplace decent standing in the community these means of repute have been replaced by the acquisition and accumulation of goods. In order to stand well in the eyes of the community, it is necessary to come up to a certain, somewhat indefinite, conventional standard of wealth; just as in the earlier predatory stage it is necessary for the barbarian man to come up to the tribe's standard of physical endurance, cunning, and skill at arms. A certain standard of wealth in the one case, and of prowess in the other, is a necessary condition of reputability, and anything in excess of this normal amount is meritorious.

Those members of the community who fall short of this, somewhat indefinite, normal degree of prowess or of property suffer in the esteem of their fellow-men; and consequently they suffer also in their own esteem, since the usual basis of self-respect is the respect accorded by one's neighbours. Only individuals with an aberrant temperament can in the long run retain their self-esteem in the face of the disesteem of their fellows. Apparent exceptions to the rule are met with, especially among people with strong religious convictions. But these apparent exceptions are scarcely real exceptions, since such persons commonly fall back on the putative approbation of some supernatural witness of their deeds.

So soon as the possession of property becomes the basis of popular esteem, therefore, it becomes also a requisite to that complacency which we call self-respect. In any community where goods are held in severalty it is necessary, in order to his own peace of mind, that an individual should possess as large a portion of goods as others with whom he is accustomed to class himself; and it is extremely gratifying to possess something more than others. But as fast as a person makes new acquisitions, and becomes accustomed to the resulting new standard of wealth, the new standard forthwith ceases to afford appreciably greater satisfaction than the earlier standard did. The tendency in any case is constantly to make the present pecuniary standard the point of departure for a fresh increase of wealth; and this in turn gives rise to a new standard of sufficiency and a new pecuniary classification of one's self as compared with one's neighbours. So far as concerns the present question, the end sought by accumulation is to rank high in comparison with the rest of the community in point of pecuniary strength. So long as the comparison is distinctly unfavourable to himself, the normal, average individual will live in chronic dissatisfaction with his present lot; and when he has reached what may be called the normal pecuniary standard of the community, or of his class in the community, this chronic dissatisfaction will give place to a restless straining to place a wider and ever-widening pecuniary interval between himself and this average standard. The invidious comparison can never become so favourable to the individual making it that he would not gladly rate himself still higher relatively to his competitors in the struggle for pecuniary reputability.

In the nature of the case, the desire for wealth can scarcely be satiated in any individual instance, and evidently a satiation of the average or general desire for wealth is out of the question. However widely, or equally, or "fairly," it may be distributed, no general increase of the community's wealth can make any approach to satiating this need, the ground of which is the desire of every one to excel every one else in the accumulation of goods. If, as is sometimes assumed, the incentive to accumulation were the want of subsistence or of physical comfort, then the aggregate economic wants of a community might conceivably be satisfied at some point in the advance of industrial efficiency; but since the struggle is substantially a race for reputability on the basis of an invidious comparison, no approach to a definitive attainment is possible.

What has just been said must not be taken to mean that there are no other incentives to acquisition and accumulation than this desire to excel in pecuniary standing and so gain the esteem and envy of one's fellow-men. The desire for added comfort and security from want is present as a motive at every stage of the process of accumulation in a modern industrial community; although the standard of sufficiency in tnese respects is in turn greatly affected by the habit of pecuniary emulation. To a great extent this emulation shapes the methods and selects the objects of expenditure for personal comfort and decent livelihood.

Besides this, the power conferred by wealth also

affords a motive to accumulation. That propensity for purposeful activity and that repugnance to all futility of effort which belong to man by virtue of his character as an agent do not desert him when he emerges from the naïve communal culture where the dominant note of life is the unanalysed and undifferentiated solidarity of the individual with the group with which his life is bound up. When he enters upon the predatory stage, where self-seeking in the narrower sense becomes the dominant note, this propensity goes with him still, as the pervasive trait that shapes his scheme of life. The propensity for achievement and the repugnance to futility remain the underlying economic motive. The propensity changes only in the form of its expression and in the proximate objects to which it directs the man's activity. Under the régime of individual ownership the most available means of visibly achieving a purpose is that afforded by the acquisition and accumulation of goods; and as the self-regarding antithesis between man and man reaches fuller consciousness, the propensity for achievement — the instinct of workmanship — tends more and more to shape itself into a straining to excel others in pecuniary achievement. Relative success, tested by an invidious pecuniary comparison with other men, becomes the conventional end of action. The currently accepted legitimate end of effort becomes the achievement of a favourable comparison with other men; and therefore the repugnance to futility to a good extent coalesces with the incentive of emulation. It acts to accentuate the struggle for pecuniary reputability by visiting with a sharper disapproval all shortcoming and all evidence of shortcoming in point of pecuniary success. Purposeful effort comes to mean, primarily, effort directed to or resulting in a more creditable showing of accumulated wealth. Among the motives which lead men to accumulate wealth, the primacy, both in scope and intensity, therefore, continues to belong to this motive of pecuniary emulation.

In making use of the term "invidious," it may perhaps be unnecessary to remark, there is no intention to extol or depreciate, or to commend or deplore any of the phenomena which the word is used to characterise. The term is used in a technical sense as describing a comparison of persons with a view to rating and grading them in respect of relative worth or value — in an æsthetic or moral sense — and so awarding and defining the relative degrees of complacency with which they may legitimately be contemplated by themselves and by others. An invidious comparison is a process of valuation of persons in respect of worth.

Conspicuous Leisure

If its working were not disturbed by other economic forces or other features of the emulative process, the immediate effect of such a pecuniary struggle as has just been described in outline would be to make men industrious and frugal. This result actually follows, in some measure, so far as regards the lower classes, whose ordinary means of acquiring goods is productive labour. This is more especially true of the labouring classes in a sedentary community which is at an agricultural stage of industry, in which there is a considerable subdivision of property, and whose laws and customs secure to these classes a more or less definite share of the product of their industry. These lower classes can in any case not avoid labour, and the imputation of labour is therefore not greatly derogatory to them, at least not within their class. Rather, since labour is their recognised and accepted mode of life, they take some emulative pride in a reputation for efficiency in their work, this being often the only line of emulation that is open to them. For those for whom acquisition and emulation is possible only within the field of productive efficiency and thrift, the struggle for pecuniary reputability will in some measure work out in an increase of diligence and parsimony. But certain secondary features of the emulative process, yet to be spoken of, come in to very materially circumscribe and modify emulation in these directions among the pecuniarily inferior classes as well as among the superior class.

But it is otherwise with the superior pecuniary class, with which we are here immediately concerned. For this class also the incentive to diligence and thrift is not absent; but its action is so greatly qualified by the secondary demands of pecuniary emulation, that any inclination in this direction is practically overborne and any incentive to diligence tends to be of no effect. The most imperative of these secondary demands of emulation, as well as the one of widest scope, is the requirement of abstention from productive work. This is true in an especial degree for the barbarian stage of culture. During the predatory culture labour comes to be associated in men's habits of thought with weakness and subjection to a master. It is therefore a mark of inferiority, and therefore comes to be accounted unworthy of man in his best estate. By virtue of this tradition labour is felt to be debasing, and this tradition has never died out. On the contrary, with the advance of social differentiation it has acquired the axiomatic force due to ancient and unquestioned prescription.

In order to gain and to hold the esteem of men it is not sufficient merely to possess wealth or power. The wealth or power must be put in evidence, for esteem is awarded only on evidence. And not only does the evidence of wealth serve to impress one's importance on others and to keep their sense of his importance alive and alert, but it is of scarcely less use in building up and preserving one's self-complacency. In all but the lowest stages of culture the normally constituted man is comforted and upheld in his self-respect by "decent surroundings" and by exemption from "menial offices." Enforced departure from his habitual standard of decency, either in the paraphernalia of life or in the kind and amount of his everyday activity, is felt to be a slight upon his human dignity, even apart from all conscious consideration of the approval or disapproval of his fellows.

The archaic theoretical distinction between the base and the honourable in the manner of a man's life retains very much of its ancient force even to-day. So much so that there are few of the better class who are not possessed of an instinctive repugnance for the vulgar forms of labour. We have a realising sense of ceremonial uncleanness attaching in an especial degree to the occupations which are associated in our habits of thought with menial service. It is felt by all persons of refined taste that a spiritual contamination is inseparable from certain offices that are conventionally required of servants. Vulgar surroundings, mean (that is to say, inexpensive) habitations, and vulgarly productive occupations are unhesitatingly condemned and avoided. They are incompatible with life on a satisfactory spiritual plane — with "high thinking." From the days of the Greek philosophers to the present, a degree of leisure and of exemption from contact with such industrial processes as serve the immediate everyday purposes of human life has ever been recognised by thoughtful men as a prerequisite to a worthy or beautiful, or even a blameless, human life. In itself and in its consequences the life of leisure is beautiful and ennobling in all civilised men's eyes.

This direct, subjective value of leisure and of other evidences of wealth is no doubt in great part secondary and derivative. It is in part a reflex of the utility of leisure as a means of gaining the respect of others, and in part it is the result of a mental substitution. The performance of labour has been accepted as a conventional evidence of inferior force; therefore it comes itself, by a mental short-cut, to be regarded as intrinsically base.

During the predatory stage proper, and especially during the earlier stages of the quasi-peaceable development of industry that follows the predatory stage, a life of leisure is the readiest and most conclusive evidence of pecuniary strength, and therefore of superior force; provided always that the gentleman of leisure can live in manifest ease and comfort. At this stage wealth consists chiefly of slaves, and the benefits accruing from the possession of riches and power take the form chiefly of personal service and the immediate products of personal service. Conspicuous abstention from labour therefore becomes the conventional mark of superior pecuniary achievement and the conventional index of reputability; and conversely, since application to productive labour is a mark of poverty and subjection, it becomes inconsistent with a reputable standing in the community. Habits of industry and thrift, therefore, are not uniformly furthered by a prevailing pecuniary emulation. On the contrary, this kind of emulation indirectly discountenances participation in productive labour. Labour would unavoidably become dishonourable, as being an evidence of poverty, even if it were not already accounted indecorous under the ancient tradition handed down from an earlier cultural stage. The ancient tradition of the predatory culture is that productive effort is to be shunned as being unworthy of able-bodied men, and this tradition is reinforced rather than set aside in the passage from the predatory to the quasi-peaceable manner of life.

Even if the institution of a leisure class had not come in with the first emergence of individual ownership, by force of the dishonour attaching to productive employment, it would in any case have come in as one of the early consequences of ownership. And it is to be remarked that while the leisure class existed in theory from the beginning of predatory culture, the institution takes on a new and fuller meaning with the transition from the predatory to the next succeeding pecuniary stage of culture. It is from this time forth a "leisure class" in fact as well as in theory. From this point dates the institution of the leisure class in its consummate form.

During the predatory stage proper the distinction between the leisure and the labouring class is in some degree a ceremonial distinction only. The able-bodied men jealously stand aloof from whatever is, in their apprehension, menial drudgery; but their activity in fact contributes appreciably to the sustenance of the group

The subsequent stage of quasi-peaceable industry is usually characterised by an established chattel slavery, herds of cattle, and a servile class of herdsmen and shepherds; industry has advanced so far that the community is no longer dependent for its livelihood on the chase or on any other form of activity that can fairly be classed as exploit. From this point on, the characteristic feature of leisure-class life is a conspicuous exemption from all useful employment.

The normal and characteristic occupations of the class in this mature phase of its life history are in form very much the same as in its earlier days. These occupations are government, war, sports, and devout observances. Persons unduly given to difficult theoretical niceties may hold that these occupations are still incidentally and indirectly "productive"; but it is to be noted as decisive of the question in hand that the ordinary and ostensible motive of the leisure class in engaging in these occupations is assuredly not an increase of wealth by productive effort. At this as at any other cultural stage, government and war are, at least in part, carried on for the pecuniary gain of those who engage in them; but it is gain obtained by the honourable method of seizure and conversion. These occupations are of the nature of predatory, not of productive, employment. Something similar may be said of the chase, but with a difference. As the community passes out of the hunting stage proper, hunting gradually becomes differentiated into two distinct employments. On the one hand it is a trade, carried on chiefly for gain; and from this the element of exploit is virtu ally absent, or it is at any rate not present in a sufficient degree to clear the pursuit of the imputation of gainful industry. On the other hand, the chase is also a sport — an exercise of the predatory impulse simply. As such it does not afford any appreciable pecuniary incentive, but it contains a more or less obvious element of exploit. It is this latter development of the chase — purged of all imputation of handicraft — that alone is meritorious and fairly belongs in the scheme of life of the developed leisure class.

Abstention from labour is not only a honorific or meritorious act, but it presently comes to be a requisite of decency. The insistence on property as the basis of reputability is very naïve and very imperious during the early stages of the accumulation of wealth. Abstention from labour is the conventional evidence of wealth and is therefore the conventional mark of social standing; and this insistence on the meritoriousness of wealth leads to a more strenuous insistence on leisure. *Nota notæ est nota rei ipsius.* According to well-established laws of human nature, prescription presently seizes upon this conventional evidence of wealth and fixes it in men's habits of thought as something that is in itself substantially meritorious and ennobling; while productive labour at the same time and by a like process becomes in a double sense intrinsically unworthy. Prescription ends by making labour not only disreputable in the eyes of the community, but morally impossible to the noble, freeborn man, and incompatible with a worthy life.

This tabu on labour has a further consequence in the industrial differentiation of classes. As the population increases in density and the predatory group grows into a settled industrial community, the constituted authorities and the customs governing ownership gain in scope and consistency. It then presently becomes impracticable to accumulate wealth by simple seizure, and, in logical consistency, acquisition by industry is equally impossible for high-minded and impecunious men. The alternative open to them is beggary or privation. Wherever the canon of conspicuous leisure has a chance undisturbed to work out its tendency, there will therefore emerge a secondary, and in a sense spurious, leisure class — abjectly poor and living a precarious life of want and discomfort, but morally unable to stoop to gainful pursuits. The decayed gentleman and the lady who has seen better days are by no means unfamiliar phenomena even now. This pervading sense of the indignity of the slightest manual labour is familiar to all civilised peoples, as well as to peoples of a less advanced pecuniary culture. In persons of delicate sensibility, who have long been habituated to gentle manners, the sense of the shamefulness of manual labour may become so strong that, at a critical juncture, it will even set aside the instinct of self-preservation. So, for instance, we are told of certain Polynesian chiefs, who, under the stress of good form, preferred to starve rather than carry their food to their mouths with their own hands. It is true, this conduct may have been due, at least in part, to an excessive sanctity or tabu attaching to the chief's person. The tabu would have been communicated by the contact of his hands, and so would have made anything touched by him unfit for human food. But the tabu is itself a derivative of the unworthiness or moral incompatibility of labour ; so that even when construed in this sense the conduct of the Polynesian chiefs is truer to the canon of honorific leisure than would at first appear. A better illustration, or at least a more unmistakable one, is afforded by a certain king of France, who is said to have lost his life through an excess of moral stamina in the observance of good form. In the absence of the functionary whose office it was to shift his master's seat, the king sat uncomplaining before the fire and suffered his royal person to be toasted beyond recovery. But in so doing he saved his Most Christian Majesty from menial contamination.

> Summum crede nefas animam præferre pudori,
> Et propter vitam vivendi perdere causas.

It has already been remarked that the term "leisure," as here used, does not connote indolence or quiescence. What it connotes is non-productive consumption of time. Time is consumed non-productively (1) from a sense of the unworthiness of productive work, and (2) as an evidence of pecuniary ability to afford a life of idleness. But the whole of the life of the gentleman of leisure is not spent before the eyes of the spectators who are to be impressed with that spectacle of honorific leisure which in the ideal scheme makes up his life. For some part of the time his life is perforce withdrawn from the public eye, and of this portion which is spent in private the gentleman of leisure should, for the sake of his good name, be able to give a convincing account. He should find some means of putting in evidence the leisure that is not spent in the sight of the spectators. This can be done only indirectly, through the exhibition of some tangible, lasting results of the leisure so spent — in a manner analogous to the familiar exhibition of tangible, lasting products of the labour performed for the gentleman of leisure by handicraftsmen and servants in his employ.

The lasting evidence of productive labour is its material product — commonly some article of consumption. In the case of exploit it is similarly possible and usual to procure some tangible result that may serve for exhibition in the way of trophy or booty. At a later phase of the development it is customary to assume some badge or insignia of honour that will serve as a conventionally accepted mark of exploit, and which at the same time indicates the quantity or degree of exploit of which it is the symbol. As the population increases in density, and as human relations grow more complex and numerous, all the details of life undergo a process of elaboration and selection; and in this process of elaboration the use of trophies develops into a system of rank, titles, degrees and insignia, typical examples of which are heraldic devices, medals, and honorary decorations.

As seen from the economic point of view, leisure, considered as an employment, is closely allied in kind with the life of exploit; and the achievements which characterise a life of leisure, and which remain as its decorous criteria, have much in common with the trophies of exploit. But leisure in the narrower sense, as distinct from exploit and from any ostensibly productive employment of effort on objects which are of no intrinsic use, does not commonly leave a material product. The criteria of a past performance of leisure therefore commonly take the form of "immaterial" goods. Such immaterial evidences of past leisure are quasi-scholarly or quasi-artistic accomplishments and a knowledge of processes and incidents which do not conduce directly to the furtherance of human life. So, for instance, in our time there is the knowledge of the dead languages and the occult sciences; of correct spelling; of syntax and prosody; of the various forms of domestic music and other household art; of the latest proprieties of dress, furniture, and equipage; of games, sports, and fancy-bred animals, such as dogs and race-horses. In all these branches of knowledge the initial motive from which their acquisition proceeded at the outset, and through which they first came into vogue, may have been something quite different from the wish to show that one's time had not been spent in industrial employment; but unless these accomplishments had approved themselves as serviceable evidence of an unproductive expenditure of time, they would not have survived and held their place as conventional accomplishments of the leisure class.

These accomplishments may, in some sense, be classed as branches of learning. Beside and beyond these there is a further range of social facts which shade off from the region of learning into that of physical habit and dexterity. Such are what is known as manners and breeding, polite usage, decorum, and formal and ceremonial observances generally. This class of facts are even more immediately and obtrusively presented to the observation, and they are therefore more widely and more imperatively insisted on as required evidences of a reputable degree of leisure. It is worth while to remark that all that class of ceremonial observances which are classed under the general head of manners hold a more important place in the esteem of men during the stage of culture at which conspicuous leisure has the greatest vogue as a mark of reputability, than at later stages of the cultural development. The barbarian of the quasi-peaceable stage of industry is notoriously a more high-bred gentleman, in all that concerns decorum, than any but the very exquisite among the men of a later age. Indeed, it is well known, or at least it is currently believed, that manners have progressively deteriorated as society has receded from the patriarchal stage. Many a gentleman of the old school has been provoked to remark regretfully upon the under-bred manners and bearing of even the better classes in the modern industrial communities; and the decay of the ceremonial code — or as it is otherwise called, the vulgarisation of life — among the industrial classes proper has become one of the chief enormities of latter-day civilisation in the eyes of all persons of delicate sensibilities. The decay which the code has suffered at the hands of a busy people testifies — all deprecation apart — to the fact that decorum is a product and an exponent of leisure-class life and thrives in full measure only under a régime of status.

The origin, or better the derivation, of manners is,

no doubt, to be sought elsewhere than in a conscious effort on the part of the well-mannered to show that much time has been spent in acquiring them. The proximate end of innovation and elaboration has been the higher effectiveness of the new departure in point of beauty or of expressiveness. In great part the ceremonial code of decorous usages owes its beginning and its growth to the desire to conciliate or to show good-will, as anthropologists and sociologists are in the habit of assuming, and this initial motive is rarely if ever absent from the conduct of well-mannered persons at any stage of the later development. Manners, we are told, are in part an elaboration of gesture, and in part they are symbolical and conventionalised survivals representing former acts of dominance or of personal service or of personal contact. In large part they are an expression of the relation of status, — a symbolic pantomime of mastery on the one hand and of subservience on the other. Wherever at the present time the predatory habit of mind, and the consequent attitude of mastery and of subservience, gives its character to the accredited scheme of life, there the importance of all punctilios of conduct is extreme, and the assiduity with which the ceremonial observance of rank and titles is attended to approaches closely to the ideal set by the barbarian of the quasi-peaceable nomadic culture. Some of the Continental countries afford good illustrations of this spiritual survival. In these communities the archaic ideal is similarly approached as regards the esteem accorded to manners as a fact of intrinsic worth.

Decorum set out with being symbol and pantomime and with having utility only as an exponent of the facts and qualities symbolised; but it presently suffered the transmutation which commonly passes over symbolical facts in human intercourse. Manners presently came, in popular apprehension, to be possessed of a substantial utility in themselves; they acquired a sacramental character, in great measure independent of the facts which they originally prefigured. Deviations from the code of decorum have become intrinsically odious to all men, and good breeding is, in everyday apprehension, not simply an adventitious mark of human excellence, but an integral feature of the worthy human soul. There are few things that so touch us with instinctive revulsion as a breach of decorum; and so far have we progressed in the direction of imputing intrinsic utility to the ceremonial observances of etiquette that few of us, if any, can dissociate an offence against etiquette from a sense of the substantial unworthiness of the offender. A breach of faith may be condoned, but a breach of decorum can not. "Manners maketh man."

None the less, while manners have this intrinsic utility, in the apprehension of the performer and the beholder alike, this sense of the intrinsic rightness of decorum is only the proximate ground of the vogue of manners and breeding. Their ulterior, economic ground is to be sought in the honorific character of that leisure or non-productive employment of time and effort without which good manners are not acquired. The knowledge and habit of good form come only by long-continued use. Kefined tastes, manners, and habits of life are a useful evidence of gentility, because good breeding requires time, application, and expense, and can therefore not be compassed by those whose time and energy are taken up with work. A knowledge of good form is *prima facie* evidence that that portion of the well-bred person's life which is not spent under the observation of the spectator has been worthily spent in acquiring accomplishments that are of no lucrative effect. In the last analysis the value of manners lies in the fact that they are the voucher of a life of leisure. Therefore, conversely, since leisure is the conventional means of pecuniary repute, the acquisition of some proficiency in decorum is incumbent on all who aspire to a modicum of pecuniary decency.

So much of the honourable life of leisure as is not spent in the sight of spectators can serve the purposes of reputability only in so far as it leaves a tangible, visible result that can be put in evidence and can be measured and compared with products of the same class exhibited by competing aspirants for repute. Some such effect, in the way of leisurely manners and carriage, etc., follows from simple persistent abstention from work, even where the subject does not take thought of the matter and studiously acquire an air of leisurely opulence and mastery. Especially does it seem to be true that a life of leisure in this way persisted in through several generations will leave a persistent, ascertainable effect in the conformation of the person, and still more in his habitual bearing and demeanour. But all the suggestions of a cumulative life of leisure, and all the proficiency in decorum that comes by the way of passive habituation, may be further improved upon by taking thought and assiduously acquiring the marks of honourable leisure, and then carrying the exhibition of these adventitious marks of exemption from employment out in a strenuous and systematic discipline. Plainly, this is a point at which a diligent application of effort and expenditure may materially further the attainment of a decent proficiency in the leisure-class proprieties. Conversely, the greater the degree of proficiency and the more patent the evidence of a high degree of habituation to observances which serve no lucrative or other directly useful purpose, the greater the consumption of time and substance impliedly involved in their acquisition, and the greater the resultant good repute. Hence, under the competitive struggle for proficiency in good manners, it comes about that much pains is taken with the cultivation of habits of decorum; and hence the details of decorum develop into a comprehensive discipline, conformity to which is required of all who would be held blameless in point of repute. And hence, on the other hand, this conspicuous leisure of which decorum is a ramification grows gradually into a laborious drill in deportment and an education in taste and discrimination as to what articles of consumption are decorous and what are the decorous methods of consuming them.

In this connection it is worthy of notice that the possibility of producing pathological and other idiosyncrasies of person and manner by shrewd mimicry and a systematic drill have been turned to account in the deliberate production of a cultured class — often with a very happy effect. In this way, by the process vulgarly known as snobbery, a syncopated evolution of gentle birth and breeding is achieved in the case of a goodly number of families and lines of descent. This syncopated gentle birth gives results which, in point of serviceability as a leisure-class factor in the population, are in no wise substantially inferior to others who may have had a longer but less arduous training in the pecuniary proprieties.

There are, moreover, measureable degrees of conformity to the latest accredited code of the punctilios as regards decorous means and methods of consumption. Differences between one person and another in the degree of conformity to the ideal in these respects can be compared, and persons may be graded and scheduled with some accuracy and effect according to a progressive scale of manners and breeding. The award of reputability in this regard is commonly made in good faith, on the ground of conformity to accepted canons of taste in the matters concerned, and without conscious regard to the pecuniary standing or the degree of leisure practised by any given candidate for reputability; but the canons of taste according to which the award is made are constantly under the surveillance of the law of conspicuous leisure, and are indeed constantly undergoing change and revision to bring them into closer conformity with its requirements. So that while the proximate ground of discrimination may be of another kind, still the pervading principle and abiding test of good breeding is the requirement of a substantial and patent waste of time. There may be some considerable range of variation in detail within the scope of this principle, but they are variations of form and expression, not of substance.

Much of the courtesy of everyday intercourse is of course a direct expression of consideration and kindly good-will, and this element of conduct has for the most part no need of being traced back to any underlying ground of reputability to explain either its presence or the approval with which it is regarded; but the same is not true of the code of proprieties. These latter are expressions of status. It is of course sufficiently plain, to any one who cares to see, that our bearing towards menials and other pecuniarily dependent inferiors is the bearing of the superior member in a relation of status, though its manifestation is often greatly modified and softened from the original expression of crude dominance. Similarly, our bearing towards superiors, and in great measure towards equals, expresses a more or less conventionalised attitude of subservience. Witness the masterful presence of the high-minded gentleman or lady, which testifies to so much of dominance and independence of economic circumstances, and which at the same time appeals with such convincing force to our sense of what is right and gracious. It is among this highest leisure class, who have no superiors and few peers, that decorum finds its fullest and maturest expression; and it is this highest class also that gives decorum that definitive formulation which serves as a canon of conduct for the classes beneath. And here also the code is most obviously a code of status and shows most plainly its incompatibility with all vulgarly productive work. A divine assurance and an imperious complaisance, as of one habituated to require subservience and to take no thought for the morrow, is the birthright and the criterion of the gentleman at his best; and it is in popular apprehension even more than that, for this demeanour is accepted as an intrinsic attribute of superior worth, before which the base-born commoner delights to stoop and yield.

As has been indicated in an earlier chapter, there is reason to believe that the institution of ownership has begun with the ownership of persons, primarily women. The incentives to acquiring such property have apparently been: (1) a propensity for dominance and coercion; (2) the utility of these persons as evidence of the prowess of their owner; (3) the utility of their services.

Personal service holds a peculiar place in the economic development. During the stage of quasi-peaceable industry, and especially during the earlier development of industry within the limits of this general stage, the utility of their services seems commonly to be the dominant motive to the acquisition of property in persons. Servants are valued for their services. But the dominance of this motive is not due to a decline in the absolute importance of the other two utilities possessed by servants. It is rather that the altered circumstances of life accentuate the utility of servants for this last-named purpose. Women and other slaves are highly valued, both as an evidence of wealth and as a means of accumulating wealth. Together with cattle, if the tribe is a pastoral one, they are the usual form of investment for a profit. To such an extent may female slavery give its character to the economic life under the quasi-peaceable culture that the woman even comes to serve as a unit of value among peoples occupying this cultural stage — as for instance in Homeric times. Where this is the case there need be little question but that the basis of the industrial system is chattel slavery and that the women are commonly slaves. The great, pervading human relation in such a system is that of master and servant. The accepted evidence of wealth is the possession of many women, and presently also of other slaves engaged in attendance on their master's person and in producing goods for him.

A division of labour presently sets in, whereby personal service and attendance on the master becomes the special office of a portion of the servants, while those who are wholly employed in industrial occupations proper are removed more and more from all immediate relation to the person of their owner. At the same time those servants whose office is personal service, including domestic duties, come gradually to be exempted from productive industry carried on for gain.

This process of progressive exemption from the common run of industrial employment will commonly begin with the exemption of the wife, or the chief wife. After the community has advanced to settled habits of life, wife-capture from hostile tribes becomes impracticable as a customary source of supply. Where this cultural advance has been achieved, the chief wife is ordinarily of gentle blood, and the fact of her being so will hasten her exemption from vulgar employment. The manner in which the concept of gentle blood originates, as well as the place which it occupies in the development of marriage, cannot be discussed in this place. For the purpose in hand it will be sufficient to say that gentle blood is blood which has been ennobled by protracted contact with accumulated wealth or unbroken prerogative. The woman with these antecedents is preferred in marriage, both for the sake of a resulting alliance with her powerful relatives and because a superior worth is felt to inhere in blood which has been associated with many goods and great power. She will still be her husband's chattel, as she was her father's chattel before her purchase, but she is at the same time of her father's gentle blood; and hence there is a moral incongruity in her occupying herself with the debasing employments of her fellow-servants. However completely she may be subject to her master, and however inferior to the male members of the social stratum in which her birth has placed her, the principle that gentility is transmissible will act to place her above the common slave; and so soon as this principle has acquired a prescriptive authority it will act to invest her in some measure with that prerogative of leisure which is the chief mark of gentility. Furthered by this principle of transmissible gentility the wife's exemption gains in scope, if the wealth of her owner permits it, until it includes exemption from debasing menial service as well as from handicraft. As the industrial development goes on and property becomes massed in relatively fewer hands, the conventional standard of wealth of the upper class rises. The same tendency to exemption from handicraft, and in the course of time from menial domestic employments, will then assert itself as regards the other wives, if such there are, and also as regards other servants in immediate attendance upon the person of their master. The exemption comes more tardily the remoter the relation in which the servant stands to the person of the master.

If the pecuniary situation of the master permits it, the development of a special class of personal or body servants is also furthered by the very grave importance which comes to attach to this personal service. The master's person, being the embodiment of worth and honour, is of the most serious consequence. Both for his reputable standing in the community and for his self-respect, it is a matter of moment that he should have at his call efficient specialised servants, whose attendance upon his person is not diverted from this their chief office by any by-occupation. These specialised servants are useful more for show than for service actually performed. In so far as they are not kept for exhibition simply, they afford gratification to their master chiefly in allowing scope to his propensity for dominance. It is true, the care of the continually increasing household apparatus may require added labour; but since the apparatus is commonly increased in order to serve as a means of good repute rather than as a means of comfort, this qualification is not of great weight. All these lines of utility are better served by a larger number of more highly specialised servants. There results, therefore, a constantly increasing differentiation and multiplication of domestic and body servants, along with a concomitant progressive exemption of such servants from productive labour. By virtue of their serving as evidence of ability to pay, the office of such domestics regularly tends to include continually fewer duties, and their service tends in the end to become nominal only. This is especially true of those servants who are in most immediate and obvious attendance upon their master. So that the utility of these comes to consist, in great part, in their conspicuous exemption from productive labour and in the evidence which this exemption affords of their master's wealth and power.

After some considerable advance has been made in the practice of employing a special corps of servants for the performance of a conspicuous leisure in this manner, men begin to be preferred above women for services that bring them obtrusively into view. Men, especially lusty, personable fellows, such as footmen and other menials should be, are obviously more powerful and more expensive than women. They are better fitted for this work, as showing a larger waste of time and of human energy Hence it comes about that in the economy of the leisure class the busy housewife of the early patriarchal days, with her retinue of hard-working handmaidens, presently gives place to the lady and the lackey.

In all grades and walks of life, and at any stage of the economic development, the leisure of the lady and of the lackey differs from the leisure of the gentleman in his own right in that it is an occupation of an ostensibly laborious kind. It takes the form, in large measure, of a painstaking attention to the service of the master, or to the maintenance and elaboration of the household paraphernalia; so that it is leisure only in the sense that little or no productive work is performed by this class, not in the sense that all appearance of labour is avoided by them. The duties performed by the lady, or by the household or domestic servants, are frequently arduous enough, and they are also frequently directed to ends which are considered extremely necessary to the comfort of the entire household. So far as these services conduce to the physical efficiency or comfort of the master or the rest of the household, they are to be accounted productive work. Only the residue of employment left after deduction of this effective work is to be classed as a performance of leisure.

But much of the services classed as household cares in modern everyday life, and many of the "utilities" required for a comfortable existence by civilised man, are of a ceremonial character. They are, therefore, properly to be classed as a performance of leisure in the sense in which the term is here used. They may be none the less imperatively necessary from the point of view of decent existence; they may be none the less requisite for personal comfort even, although they may be chiefly or wholly of a ceremonial character. But in so far as they partake of this character they are imperative and requisite because we have been taught to require them under pain of ceremonial uncleanness or unworthiness. We feel discomfort in their absence, but not because their absence results directly in physical discomfort, nor would a taste not trained to discriminate between the conventionally good and the conventionally bad take offence at their omission In so far as this is true the labour spent in these services is to be classed as leisure; and when performed by others than the economically free and self-directing head of the establishment, they are to be classed as vicarious leisure.

The vicarious leisure performed by housewives and menials, under the head of household cares, may frequently develop into drudgery, especially where the competition for reputability is close and strenuous. This is frequently the case in modern life. Where this happens, the domestic service which comprises the duties of this servant class might aptly be designated as wasted effort, rather than as vicarious leisure. But the latter term has the advantage of indicating the line of derivation of these domestic offices, as well as of neatly suggesting the substantial economic ground of their utility; for these occupations are chiefly useful as a method of imputing pecuniary reputability to the master or to the household on the ground that a given amount of time and effort is conspicuously wasted in that behalf.

In this way, then, there arises a subsidiary or derivative leisure class, whose office is the performance of a vicarious leisure for the behoof of the reputability of the primary or legitimate leisure class. This vicarious leisure class is distinguished from the leisure class proper by a characteristic feature of its habitual mode of life. The leisure of the master class is, at least ostensibly, an indulgence of a proclivity for the avoidance of labour and is presumed to enhance the master's own well-being and fulness of life; but the leisure of the servant class exempt from productive labour is in some sort a performance exacted from them, and is not normally or primarily directed to their own comfort. The leisure of the servant is not his own leisure. So far as he is a servant in the full sense, and not at the same time a member of a lower order of the leisure class proper, his leisure normally passes under the guise of specialised service directed to the furtherance of his master's fulness of life. Evidence of this relation of subservience is obviously present in the servant's carriage and manner of life. The like is often true of the wife throughout the protracted economic stage during which she is still primarily a servant — that is to say, so long as the household with a male head remains in force. In order to satisfy the requirements of the leisure-class scheme of life, the servant should show not only an attitude of subservience, but also the effects of special training and practice in subservience. The servant or wife should not only perform certain offices and show a servile disposition, but it is quite as imperative that they should show an acquired facility in the tactics of subservience — a trained conformity to the canons of effectual and conspicuous subservience. Even to-day it is this aptitude and acquired skill in the formal manifestation of the servile relation that constitutes the chief element of utility in our highly paid servants, as well as one of the chief ornaments of the well-bred housewife.

The first requisite of a good servant is that he should conspicuously know his place. It is not enough that he knows how to effect certain desired mechanical results; he must, above all, know how to effect these results in due form. Domestic service might be said to be a spiritual rather than a mechanical function. Gradually there grows up an elaborate system of good form, specifically regulating the manner in which this vicarious leisure of the servant class is to be performed. Any departure from these canons of form is to be deprecated, not so much because it evinces a shortcoming in mechanical efficiency, or even that it shows an absence of the servile attitude and temperament, but because, in the last analysis, it shows the absence of special training. Special training in personal service costs time and effort, and where it is obviously present in a high degree, it argues that the servant who possesses it, neither is nor has been habitually engaged in any productive occupation. It is *prima facie* evidence of a vicarious leisure extending far back in the past. So that trained service has utility, not only as gratifying the master's instinctive liking for good and skilful workmanship and his propensity for conspicuous dominance over those whose lives are subservient to his own, but it has utility also as putting in evidence a much larger consumption of human service than would be shown by the mere present conspicuous leisure performed by an untrained person. It is a serious grievance if a gentleman's butler or footman performs his duties about his master's table or carriage in such unformed style as to suggest that his habitual occupation may be ploughing or sheepherding. Such bungling work would imply inability on the master's part to procure the service of specially trained servants; that is to say, it would imply inability to pay for the consumption of time, effort, and instruction required to fit a trained servant for special service under an exacting code of forms. If the performance of the servant argues lack of means on the part of his master, it defeats its chief substantial end; for the chief use of servants is the evidence they afford of the master's ability to pay.

What has just been said might be taken to imply that the offence of an under-trained servant lies in a direct suggestion of inexpensiveness or of usefulness. Such, of course, is not the case. The connection is much less immediate. What happens here is what happens generally. Whatever approves itself to us on any ground at the outset, presently comes to appeal to us as a gratifying thing in itself; it comes to rest in our habits of thought as substantially right. But in order that any specific canon of deportment shall maintain itself in favour, it must continue to have the support of, or at least not be incompatible with, the habit or aptitude which constitutes the norm of its development. The need of vicarious leisure, or conspicuous consumption of service, is a dominant incentive to the keeping of servants. So long as this remains true it may be set down without much discussion that any such departure from accepted usage as would suggest an abridged apprenticeship in service would presently be found insufferable. The requirement of an expensive vicarious leisure acts indirectly, selectively, by guiding the formation of our taste,—of our sense of what is right in these matters,—and so weeds out unconformable departures by withholding approval of them.

As the standard of wealth recognized by common

consent advances, the possession and exploitation of servants as a means of showing superfluity undergoes a refinement. The possession and maintenance of slaves employed in the production of goods argues wealth and prowess, but the maintenance of servants who produce nothing argues still higher wealth and position. Under this principle there arises a class of servants, the more numerous the better, whose sole office is fatuously to wait upon the person of their owner, and so to put in evidence his ability unproductively to consume a large amount of service. There supervenes a division of labour among the servants or dependents whose life is spent in maintaining the honour of the gentleman of leisure. So that, while one group produces goods for him, another group, usually headed by the wife, or chief wife, consumes for him in conspicuous leisure; thereby putting in evidence his ability to sustain large pecuniary damage without impairing his superior opulence.

This somewhat idealized and diagrammatic outline of the development and nature of domestic service comes nearest being true for that cultural stage which has here been named the "quasi-peaceable" stage of industry. At this stage personal service first rises to the position of an economic institution, and it is at this stage that it occupies the largest place in the community's scheme of life. In the cultural sequence, the quasi-peaceable stage follows the predatory stage proper, the two being successive phases of barbarian life. Its characteristic feature is a formal observance of peace and order, at the same time that life at this stage still has too much of coercion and class antagonism to be called peaceable in the full sense of the word. For many purposes, and from another point of view than the economic one, it might as well be named the stage of status. The method of human relation during this stage, and the spiritual attitude of men at this level of culture, is well summed up under that term. But as a descriptive term to characterise the prevailing methods of industry, as well as to indicate the trend of industrial development at this point in economic evolution, the term "quasi-peaceable" seems preferable. So far as concerns the communities of the Western culture, this phase of economic development probably lies in the past; except for a numerically small though very conspicuous fraction of the community in whom the habits of thought peculiar to the barbarian culture have suffered but a relatively slight disintegration.

Personal service is still an element of great economic importance, especially as regards the distribution and consumption of goods; but its relative importance even in this direction is no doubt less than it once was. The best development of this vicarious leisure lies in the past rather than in the present; and its best expression in the present is to be found in the scheme of life of the upper leisure class. To this class the modern culture owes much in the way of the conservation of traditions, usages, and habits of thought which belong on a more archaic cultural plane, so far as regards their widest acceptance and their most effective development.

In the modern industrial communities the mechanical contrivances available for the comfort and convenience of everyday life are highly developed. So much so that body servants, or, indeed, domestic servants of any kind, would now scarcely be employed by anybody except on the ground of a canon of reputability carried over by tradition from earlier usage. The only exception would be servants employed to attend on the persons of the infirm and the feeble-minded. But such servants properly come under the head of trained nurses rather than under that of domestic servants, and they are, therefore, an apparent rather than a real exception to the rule.

The proximate reason for keeping domestic servants, for instance, in the moderately well-to-do household of to-day, is (ostensibly) that the members of the household are unable without discomfort to compass the work required by such a modern establishment. And the reason for their being unable to accomplish it is (1) that they have too many "social duties," and (2) that the work to be done is too severe and that there is too much of it. These two reasons may be restated as follows: (1) Under a mandatory code of decency, the time and effort of the members of such a household are required to be ostensibly all spent in a performance of conspicuous leisure, in the way of calls, drives, clubs, sewing-circles, sports, charity organisations, and other like social functions. Those persons whose time and energy are employed in these matters privately avow that all these observances, as well as the incidental attention to dress and other conspicuous consumption, are very irksome but altogether unavoidable. (2) Under the requirement of conspicuous consumption of goods, the apparatus of living has grown so elaborate and cumbrous, in the way of dwellings, furniture, bric-a-brac, wardrobe and meals, that the consumers of these things cannot make way with them in the required manner without help. Personal contact with the hired persons whose aid is called in to fulfil the routine of decency is commonly distasteful to the occupants of the house, but their presence is endured and paid for, in order to delegate to them a share in this onerous consumption of household goods. The presence of domestic servants, and of the special class of body servants in an eminent degree, is a concession of physical comfort to the moral need of pecuniary decency.

The largest manifestation of vicarious leisure in modern life is made up of what are called domestic duties. These duties are fast becoming a species of services performed, not so much for the individual behoof of the head of the household as for the reputability of the household taken as a corporate unit — a group of which the housewife is a member on a footing of ostensible equality As fast as the household for which they are performed departs from its archaic basis of ownership-marriage, these household duties of course tend to fall out of the category of vicarious leisure in the original sense; except so far as they are performed by hired servants. That is to say, since vicarious leisure is possible only on a basis of status or of hired service, the disappearance of the relation of status from human intercourse at any point carries with it the disappearance of vicarious leisure so far as regards that much of life. But it is to be added, in qualification of this qualification, that so long as the household subsists, even with a divided head, this class of non-productive labour performed for the sake of household reputability must still be classed as vicarious leisure, although in a slightly altered sense. It is now leisure performed for the quasi-personal corporate household, instead of, as formerly, for the proprietary head of the household.

Conspicuous Consumption

In what has been said of the evolution of the vicarious leisure class and its differentiation from the general body of the working classes, reference has been made to a further division of labour,—that between different servant classes. One portion of the servant class, chiefly those persons whose occupation is vicarious leisure, come to undertake a new, subsidiary range of duties—the vicarious consumption of goods. The most obvious form in which this consumption occurs is seen in the wearing of liveries and the occupation of spacious servants' quarters. Another, scarcely less obtrusive or less effective form of vicarious consumption, and a much more widely prevalent one, is the consumption of food, clothing, dwelling, and furniture by the lady and the rest of the domestic establishment.

But already at a point in economic evolution far antedating the emergence of the lady, specialised consumption of goods as an evidence of pecuniary strength had begun to work out in a more or less elaborate system. The beginning of a differentiation in consumption even antedates the appearance of anything that can fairly be called pecuniary strength. It is traceable back to the initial phase of predatory culture, and there is even a suggestion that an incipient differentiation in this respect lies back of the beginnings of the predatory life. This most primitive differentiation in the consumption of goods is like the later differentiation with which we are all so intimately familiar, in that it is largely of a ceremonial character, but unlike the latter it does not rest on a difference in accumulated wealth. The utility of consumption as an evidence of wealth is to be classed as a derivative growth. It is an adaptation to a new end, by a selective process, of a distinction previously existing and well established in men's habits of thought.

In the earlier phases of the predatory culture the only economic differentiation is a broad distinction between an honourable superior class made up of the able-bodied men on the one side, and a base inferior class of labouring women on the other. According to the ideal scheme of life in force at that time it is the office of the men to consume what the women produce. Such consumption as falls to the women is merely incidental to their work; it is a means to their continued labour, and not a consumption directed to their own comfort and fulness of life. Unproductive consumption of goods is honourable, primarily as a mark of prowess and a perquisite of human dignity; secondarily it becomes substantially honourable in itself, especially the consumption of the more desirable things. The consumption of choice articles of food, and frequently also of rare articles of adornment, becomes tabu to the women and children; and if there is a base (servile) class of men, the tabu holds also for them. With a further advance in culture this tabu may change into simple custom of a more or less rigorous character; but whatever be the theoretical basis of the distinction which is maintained, whether it be a tabu or a larger conventionality, the features of the conventional scheme of consumption do not change easily. When the quasi-peaceable stage of industry is reached, with its fundamental institution of chattel slavery, the general principle, more or less rigorously applied, is that the base, industrious class should consume only what may be necessary to their subsistence. In the nature of things, luxuries and the comforts of life belong to the leisure class. Under the tabu, certain victuals, and more particularly certain beverages, are strictly reserved for the use of the superior class.

The ceremonial differentiation of the dietary is best seen in the use of intoxicating beverages and narcotics. If these articles of consumption are costly, they are felt to be noble and honorific. Therefore the base classes, primarily the women, practise an enforced continence with respect to these stimulants, except in countries where they are obtainable at a very low cost. From archaic times down through all the length of the patriarchal régime it has been the office of the women to prepare and administer these luxuries, and it has been the perquisite of the men of gentle birth and breeding to consume them. Drunkenness and the other pathological consequences of the free use of stimulants therefore tend in their turn to become honorific, as being a mark, at the second remove, of the superior status of those who are able to afford the indulgence. Infirmities induced by over-indulgence are among some peoples freely recognised as manly attributes. It has even happened that the name for certain diseased conditions of the body arising from such an origin has passed into everyday speech as a synonym for "noble" or "gentle." It is only at a relatively early stage of culture that the symptoms of expensive vice are conventionally accepted as marks of a superior status, and so tend to become virtues and command the deference of the community; but the reputability that attaches to certain expensive vices long retains so much of its force as to appreciably lessen the disapprobation visited upon the men of the wealthy or noble class for any excessive indulgence. The same invidious distinction adds force to the current disapproval of any indulgence of this kind on the part of women, minors, and inferiors. This invidious traditional distinction has not lost its force even among the more advanced peoples of to-day. Where the example set by the leisure class retains its imperative force in the regulation of the conventionalities, it is observable that the women still in great measure practise the same traditional continence with regard to stimulants.

This characterisation of the greater continence in the use of stimulants practised by the women of the reputable classes may seem an excessive refinement of logic at the expense of common sense. But facts within easy reach of any one who cares to know them go to say that the greater abstinence of women is in some part due to an imperative conventionality; and this conventionality is, in a general way, strongest where the patriarchal tradition — the tradition that the woman is a chattel — has retained its hold in greatest vigour. In a sense which has been greatly qualified in scope and rigour, but which has by no means lost its meaning even yet, this tradition says that the woman, being a chattel, should consume only what is necessary to her sustenance, — except so far as her further consumption contributes to the comfort or the good repute of her master. The consumption of luxuries, in the true sense, is a consumption directed to the comfort of the consumer himself, and is, therefore, a mark of the master. Any such consumption by others can take place only on a basis of sufferance. In communities where the popular habits of thought have been profoundly shaped by the patriarchal tradition we may accordingly look for survivals of the tabu on luxuries at least to the extent of a conventional deprecation of their use by the unfree and dependent class. This is more particularly true as regards certain luxuries, the use of which by the dependent class would detract sensibly from the comfort or pleasure of their masters, or which are held to be of doubtful legitimacy on other grounds. In the apprehension of the great conservative middle class of Western civilisation the use of these various stimulants is obnoxious to at least one, if not both, of these objections; and it is a fact too significant to be passed over that it is precisely among these middle classes of the Germanic culture, with their strong surviving sense of the patriarchal proprieties, that the women are to the greatest extent subject to a qualified tabu on narcotics and alcoholic beverages. With many qualifications — with more qualifications as the patriarchal tradition has gradually weakened — the general rule is felt to be right and binding that women should consume only for the benefit of their masters. The objection of course presents itself that expenditure on women's dress and household paraphernalia is an obvious exception to this rule; but it will appear in the sequel that this exception is much more obvious than substantial.

During the earlier stages of economic development, consumption of goods without stint, especially consumption of the better grades of goods, — ideally all consumption in excess of the subsistence minimum, — pertains normally to the leisure class. This restriction tends to disappear, at least formally, after the later peaceable stage has been reached, with private ownership of goods and an industrial system based on wage labour or on the petty household economy. But during the earlier quasi-peaceable stage, when so many of the traditions through which the institution of a leisure class has affected the economic life of later times were taking form and consistency, this principle has had the force of a conventional law. It has served as the norm to which consumption has tended to conform, and any appreciable departure from it is to be regarded as an aberrant form, sure to be eliminated sooner or later in the further course of development.

The quasi-peaceable gentleman of leisure, then, not only consumes of the staff of life beyond the minimum required for subsistence and physical efficiency, but his consumption also undergoes a specialisation as regards the quality of the goods consumed. He consumes freely and of the best, in food, drink, narcotics, shelter, services, ornaments, apparel, weapons and accoutrements, amusements, amulets, and idols or divinities. In the process of gradual amelioration which takes place in the articles of his consumption, the motive principle and the proximate aim of innovation is no doubt the higher efficiency of the improved and more elaborate products for personal comfort and well-being. But that does not remain the sole purpose of their consumption. The canon of reputability is at hand and seizes upon such innovations as are, according to its standard, fit to survive. Since the consumption of these more excellent goods is an evidence of wealth, it becomes honorific; and conversely, the failure to consume in due quantity and quality becomes a mark of inferiority and demerit.

This growth of punctilious discrimination as to qualitative excellence in eating, drinking, etc., presently affects not only the manner of life, but also the training and intellectual activity of the gentleman of leisure. He is no longer simply the successful, aggressive male, the man of strength, resource, and intrepidity. In order to avoid stultification he must also cultivate his tastes, for it now becomes incumbent on him to discriminate with some nicety between the noble and the ignoble in consumable goods. He becomes a connoisseur in creditable viands of various degrees of merit, in manly beverages and trinkets, in seemly apparel and architecture, in weapons, games, dancers, and the narcotics. This cultivation of the æsthetic faculty requires time and application, and the demands made upon the gentleman in this direction therefore tend to change his life of leisure into a more or less arduous application to the business of learning how to live a life of ostensible leisure in a becoming way. Closely related to the requirement that the gentleman must consume freely and of the right kind of goods, there is the requirement that he must know how to consume them in a seemly manner. His life of leisure must be conducted in due form. Hence arise good manners in the way pointed out in an earlier chapter. High-bred manners and ways of living are items of conformity to the norm of conspicuous leisure and conspicuous consumption.

Conspicuous consumption of valuable goods is a means of reputability to the gentleman of leisure. As wealth accumulates on his hands, his own unaided effort will not avail to sufficiently put his opulence in evidence by this method. The aid of friends and competitors is therefore brought in by resorting to the giving of valuable presents and expensive feasts and entertainments. Presents and feasts had probably another origin than that of naïve ostentation, but they acquired their utility for this purpose very early, and they have retained that character to the present; so that their utility in this respect has now long been the substantial ground on which these usages rest. Costly entertainments, such as the potlatch or the ball, are peculiarly adapted to serve this end. The competitor with whom the entertainer wishes to institute a comparison is, by this method, made to serve as a means to the end. He consumes vicariously for his host at the same time that he is a witness to the consumption of that excess of good things which his host is unable to dispose of single-handed, and he is also made to witness his host's facility in etiquette.

In the giving of costly entertainments other motives, of a more genial kind, are of course also present. The custom of festive gatherings probably originated in motives of conviviality and religion; these motives are also present in the later development, but they do not continue to be the sole motives. The latter-day leisure-class festivities and entertainments may continue in some slight degree to serve the religious need and in a higher degree the needs of recreation and conviviality, but they also serve an invidious purpose; and they serve it none the less effectually for having a colourable non-invidious ground in these more avowable motives. But the economic effect of these social amenities is not therefore lessened, either in the vicarious consumption of goods or in the exhibition of difficult and costly achievements in etiquette.

As wealth accumulates, the leisure class develops further in function and structure, and there arises a differentiation within the class. There is a more or less elaborate system of rank and grades. This differentiation is furthered by the inheritance of wealth and the consequent inheritance of gentility. With the inheritance of gentility goes the inheritance of obligatory leisure; and gentility of a sufficient potency to entail a life of leisure may be inherited without the complement of wealth required to maintain a dignified leisure. Gentle blood may be transmitted without goods enough to afford a reputably free consumption at one's ease. Hence results a class of impecunious gentlemen of leisure, incidentally referred to already. These half-caste gentlemen of leisure fall into a system of hierarchical gradations. Those who stand near the higher and the highest grades of the wealthy leisure class, in point of birth, or in point of wealth, or both, outrank the remoter-born and the pecuniarily weaker. These lower grades, especially the impecunious, or marginal, gentlemen of leisure, affiliate themselves by a system of dependence or fealty to the great ones; by so doing they gain an increment of repute, or of the means with which to lead a life of leisure, from their patron. They become his courtiers or retainers, servants; and being fed and countenanced by their patron they are indices of his rank and vicarious consumers of his superfluous wealth. Many of these affiliated gentlemen of leisure are at the same time lesser men of substance in their own right; so that some of them are scarcely at all, others only partially, to be rated as vicarious consumers. So many of them, however, as make up the retainers and hangers-on of the patron may be classed as vicarious consumers without qualification. Many of these again, and also many of the other aristocracy of less degree, have in turn attached to their persons a more or less comprehensive group of vicarious consumers in the persons of their wives and children, their servants, retainers, etc.

Throughout this graduated scheme of vicarious leisure and vicarious consumption the rule holds that these offices must be performed in some such manner, or under some such circumstance or insignia, as shall point plainly to the master to whom this leisure or consumption pertains, and to whom therefore the resulting increment of good repute of right inures. The consumption and leisure executed by these persons for their master or patron represents an investment on his part with a view to an increase of good fame. As regards feasts and largesses this is obvious enough, and the imputation of repute to the host or patron here takes place immediately, on the ground of common notoriety. Where leisure and consumption is performed vicariously by henchmen and retainers, imputation of the resulting repute to the patron is effected by their residing near his person so that it may be plain to all men from what source they draw. As the group whose good esteem is to be secured in this way grows larger, more patent means are required to indicate the imputation of merit for the leisure performed, and to this end uniforms, badges, and liveries come into vogue. The wearing of uniforms or liveries implies a considerable degree of dependence, and may even be said to be a mark of servitude, real or ostensible. The wearers of uniforms and liveries may be roughly divided into two classes—the free and the servile, or the noble and the ignoble. The services performed by them are likewise divisible into noble and ignoble. Of course the distinction is not observed with strict consistency in practice; the less debasing of the base services and the less honorific of the noble functions are not infrequently merged in the same person. But the general distinction is not on that account to be overlooked. What may add some perplexity is the fact that this fundamental distinction between noble and ignoble, which rests on the nature of the ostensible service performed, is traversed by a secondary distinction into honorific and humiliating, resting on the rank of the person for whom the service is performed or whose livery is worn. So, those offices which are by right the proper employment of the leisure class are noble; such are government, fighting, hunting, the care of arms and accoutrements, and the like, — in short, those which may be classed as ostensibly predatory employments. On the other hand, those employments which properly fall to the industrious class are ignoble; such as handicraft or other productive labour, menial services, and the like. But a base service performed for a person of very high degree may become a very honorific office; as for instance the office of a Maid of Honour or of a Lady in Waiting to the Queen, or the King's Master of the Horse or his Keeper of the Hounds. The two offices last named suggest a principle of some general bearing. Whenever, as in these cases, the menial service in question has to do directly with the primary leisure employments of fighting and hunting, it easily acquires a reflected honorific character. In this way great honour may come to attach to an employment which in its own nature belongs to the baser sort.

In the later development of peaceable industry, the usage of employing an idle corps of uniformed men-at-arms gradually lapses. Vicarious consumption by dependents bearing the insignia of their patron or master narrows down to a corps of liveried menials. In a heightened degree, therefore, the livery comes to be a badge of servitude, or rather of servility. Something of a honorific character always attached to the livery of the armed retainer, but this honorific character disappears when the livery becomes the exclusive badge of the menial. The livery becomes obnoxious to nearly all who are required to wear it. We are yet so little removed from a state of effective slavery as still to be fully sensitive to the sting of any imputation of servility. This antipathy asserts itself even in the case of the liveries or uniforms which some corporations prescribe as the distinctive dress of their employees. In this country the aversion even goes the length of discrediting — in a mild and uncertain way — those government employments, military and civil, which require the wearing of a livery or uniform.

With the disappearance of servitude, the number of vicarious consumers attached to any one gentleman tends, on the whole, to decrease. The like is of course true, and perhaps in a still higher degree, of the number of dependents who perform vicarious leisure for him. In a general way, though not wholly nor consistently, these two groups coincide. The dependent who was first delegated for these duties was the wife, or the chief wife; and, as would be expected, in the later development of the institution, when the number of persons by whom these duties are customarily performed gradually narrows, the wife remains the last. In the higher grades of society a large volume of both these kinds of service is required; and here the wife is of course still assisted in the work by a more or less numerous corps of menials. But as we descend the social scale, the point is presently reached where the duties of vicarious leisure and consumption devolve upon the wife alone. In the communities of the Western culture, this point is at present found among the lower middle class.

And here occurs a curious inversion. It is a fact of common observation that in this lower middle class there is no pretence of leisure on the part of the head of the household. Through force of circumstances it has fallen into disuse. But the middle-class wife still carries on the business of vicarious leisure, for the good name of the household and its master. In descending the social scale in any modern industrial community, the primary fact — the conspicuous leisure of the master of the household — disappears at a relatively high point. The head of the middle-class household has been reduced by economic circumstances to turn his hand to gaining a livelihood by occupations which often partake largely of the character of industry, as in the case of the ordinary business man of to-day. But the derivative fact — the vicarious leisure and consumption rendered by the wife, and the auxiliary vicarious performance of leisure by menials — remains in vogue as a conventionality which the demands of reputability will not suffer to be slighted. It is by no means an uncommon spectacle to find a man applying himself to work with the utmost assiduity, in order that his wife may in due form render for him that degree of vicarious leisure which the common sense of the time demands.

The leisure rendered by the wife in such cases is, of

course, not a simple manifestation of idleness or indolence. It almost invariably occurs disguised under some form of work or household duties or social amenities, which prove on analysis to serve little or no ulterior end beyond showing that she does not and need not occupy herself with anything that is gainful or that is of substantial use. As has already been noticed under the head of manners, the greater part of the customary round of domestic cares to which the middle-class housewife gives her time and effort is of this character. Not that the results of her attention to household matters, of a decorative and mundificatory character, are not pleasing to the sense of men trained in middle-class proprieties; but the taste to which these effects of household adornment and tidiness appeal is a taste which has been formed under the selective guidance of a canon of propriety that demands just these evidences of wasted effort. The effects are pleasing to us chiefly because we have been taught to find them pleasing. There goes into these domestic duties much solicitude for a proper combination of form and colour, and for other ends that are to be classed as æsthetic in the proper sense of the term; and it is not denied that effects having some substantial æsthetic value are sometimes attained. Pretty much all that is here insisted on is that, as regards these amenities of life, the housewife's efforts are under the guidance of traditions that have been shaped by the law of conspicuously wasteful expenditure of time and substance. If beauty or comfort is achieved, — and it is a more or less fortuitous circumstance if they are, — they must be achieved by means and methods that commend themselves to the great economic law of wasted effort. The more reputable, "presentable" portion of middle-class household paraphernalia are, on the one hand, items of conspicuous consumption, and on the other hand, apparatus for putting in evidence the vicarious leisure rendered by the housewife.

The requirement of vicarious consumption at the hands of the wife continues in force even at a lower point in the pecuniary scale than the requirement of vicarious leisure. At a point below which little if any pretence of wasted effort, in ceremonial cleanness and the like, is observable, and where there is assuredly no conscious attempt at ostensible leisure, decency still requires the wife to consume some goods conspicuously for the reputability of the household and its head. So that, as the latter-day outcome of this evolution of an archaic institution, the wife, who was at the outset the drudge and chattel of the man, both in fact and in theory, — the producer of goods for him to consume, — has become the ceremonial consumer of goods which he produces. But she still quite unmistakably remains his chattel in theory; for the habitual rendering of vicarious leisure and consumption is the abiding mark of the unfree servant.

This vicarious consumption practised by the household of the middle and lower classes can not be counted as a direct expression of the leisure-class scheme of life, since the household of this pecuniary grade does not belong within the leisure class. It is rather that the leisure class scheme of life here comes to an expression at the second remove. The leisure class stands at the head of the social structure in point of reputability; and its manner of life and its standards of worth therefore afford the norm of reputability for the community. The observance of these standards, in some degree of approximation, becomes incumbent upon all classes lower in the scale. In modern civilized communities the lines of demarcation between social classes have grown vague and transient, and wherever this happens the norm of reputability imposed by the upper class extends its coercive influence with but slight hindrance down through the social structure to the lowest strata. The result is that the members of each stratum accept as their ideal of decency the scheme of life in vogue in the next higher stratum, and bend their energies to live up to that ideal. On pain of forfeiting their good name and their self-respect in case of failure, they must conform to the accepted code, at least in appearance.

The basis on which good repute in any highly organised industrial community ultimately rests is pecuniary strength; and the means of showing pecuniary strength, and so of gaining or retaining a good name, are leisure and a conspicuous consumption of goods. Accordingly, both of these methods are in vogue as far down the scale as it remains possible; and in the lower strata in which the two methods are employed, both offices are in great part delegated to the wife and children of the household. Lower still, where any degree of leisure, even ostensible, has become impracticable for the wife, the conspicuous consumption of goods remains and is carried on by the wife and children. The man of the household also can do something in this direction, and, indeed, he commonly does; but with a still lower descent into the levels of indigence — along the margin of the slums — the man, and presently also the children, virtually cease to consume valuable goods for appearances, and the woman remains virtually the sole exponent of the household's pecuniary decency. No class of society, not even the most abjectly poor, foregoes all customary conspicuous consumption. The last items of this category of consumption are not given up except under stress of the direst necessity. Very much of squalor and discomfort will be endured before the last trinket or the last pretence of pecuniary decency is put away. There is no class and no country that has yielded so abjectly before the pressure of physical want as to deny themselves all gratification of this higher or spiritual need.

From the foregoing survey of the growth of conspicuous leisure and consumption, it appears that the utility of both alike for the purposes of reputability lies in the element of waste that is common to both. In the one case it is a waste of time and effort, in the other it is a waste of goods. Both are methods of demonstrating the possession of wealth, and the two are conventionally accepted as equivalents. The choice between them is a question of advertising expediency simply, except so far as it may be affected by other standards of propriety, springing from a different source. On grounds of expediency the preference may be given to the one or the other at different stages of the economic development. The question is, which of the two methods will most effectively reach the persons whose convictions it is desired to affect. Usage has answered this question in different ways under different circumstances.

So long as the community or social group is small enough and compact enough to be effectually reached by common notoriety alone, — that is to say, so long as the human environment to which the individual is required to adapt himself in respect of reputability is comprised within his sphere of personal acquaintance and neighbourhood gossip, — so long the one method is about as effective as the other. Each will therefore serve about equally well during the earlier stages of social growth. But when the differentiation has gone farther and it becomes necessary to reach a wider human environment, consumption begins to hold over leisure as an ordinary means of decency. This is especially true during the later, peaceable economic stage. The means of communication and the mobility of the population now expose the individual to the observation of many persons who have no other means of judging of his reputability than the display of goods (and perhaps of breeding) which he is able to make while he is under their direct observation.

The modern organisation of industry works in the same direction also by another line. The exigencies of the modern industrial system frequently place individuals and households in juxtaposition between whom there is little contact in any other sense than that of juxtaposition. One's neighbours, mechanically speaking, often are socially not one's neighbours, or even acquaintances ; and still their transient good opinion has a high degree of utility. The only practicable means of impressing one's pecuniary ability on these unsympathetic observers of one's everyday life is an unremitting demonstration of ability to pay. In the modern community there is also a more frequent attendance at large gatherings of people to whom one's everyday life is unknown ; in such places as churches, theatres, ballrooms, hotels, parks, shops, and the like. In order to impress these transient observers, and to retain one's self-complacency under their observation, the signature of one's pecuniary strength should be written in characters which he who runs may read. It is evident, therefore, that the present trend of the development is in the direction of heightening the utility of conspicuous consumption as compared with leisure.

It is also noticeable that the serviceability of consumption as a means of repute, as well as the insistence on it as an element of decency, is at its best in those portions of the community where the human contact of the individual is widest and the mobility of the population is greatest. Conspicuous consumption claims a relatively larger portion of the income of the urban than of the rural population, and the claim is also more imperative. The result is that, in order to keep up a decent appearance, the former habitually live hand-to-mouth to a greater extent than the latter. So it comes, for instance, that the American farmer and his wife and daughters are notoriously less modish in their dress, as well as less urbane in their manners, than the city artisan's family with an equal income. It is not that the city population is by nature much more eager for the peculiar complacency that comes of a conspicuous consumption, nor has the rural population less regard for pecuniary decency. But the provocation to this line of evidence, as well as its transient effectiveness, are more decided in the city. This method is therefore more readily resorted to, and in the struggle to outdo one another the city population push their normal standard of conspicuous consumption to a higher point, with the result that a relatively greater expenditure in this direction is required to indicate a given degree of pecuniary decency in the city. The requirement of conformity to this higher conventional standard becomes mandatory. The standard of decency is higher, class for class, and this requirement of decent appearance must be lived up to on pain of losing caste.

Consumption becomes a larger element in the standard of living in the city than in the country. Among the country population its place is to some extent taken by savings and home comforts known through the medium of neighbourhood gossip sufficiently to serve the like general purpose of pecuniary repute. These home comforts and the leisure indulged in — where the indulgence is found — are of course also in great part to be classed as items of conspicuous consumption; and much the same is to be said of the savings. The smaller amount of the savings laid by by the artisan class is no doubt due, in some measure, to the fact that in the case of the artisan the savings are a less effective means of advertisement, relative to the environment in which he is placed, than are the savings of the people living on farms and in the small villages. Among the latter, everybody's affairs, especially everybody's pecuniary status, are known to everybody else. Considered by itself simply — taken in the first degree — this added provocation to which the artisan and the urban labouring classes are exposed may not very seriously decrease the amount of savings; but in its cumulative action, through raising the standard of decent expenditure, its deterrent effect on the tendency to save cannot but be very great.

A felicitous illustration of the manner in which this canon of reputability works out its results is seen in the practice of dram-drinking, "treating," and smoking in public places, which is customary among the labourers and handicraftsmen of the towns, and among the lower middle class of the urban population generally. Journeymen printers may be named as a class among whom this form of conspicuous consumption has a great vogue, and among whom it carries with it certain well-marked consequences that are often deprecated. The peculiar habits of the class in this respect are commonly set down to some kind of an ill-defined moral deficiency with which this class is credited, or to a morally deleterious influence which their occupation is supposed to exert, in some unascertainable way, upon the men employed in it. The state of the case for the men who work in the composition and press rooms of the common run of printing-houses may be summed up as follows. Skill acquired in any printing-house or any city is easily turned to account in almost any other house or city; that is to say, the inertia due to special training is slight. Also, this occupation requires more than the average of intelligence and general information, and the men employed in it are therefore ordinarily more ready than many others to take advantage of any slight variation in the demand for their labour from one place to another. The inertia due to the home feeling is consequently also slight. At the same time the wages in the trade are high enough to make movement from place to place relatively easy. The result is a great mobility of the labour employed in printing; perhaps greater than in any other equally well-defined and considerable body of workmen. These men are constantly thrown in contact with new groups of acquaintances, with whom the relations established are transient or ephemeral, but whose good opinion is valued none the less for the time being. The human proclivity to ostentation, reënforced by sentiments of goodfellowship, leads them to spend freely in those directions which will best serve these needs. Here as elsewhere prescription seizes upon the custom as soon as it gains a vogue, and incorporates it in the accredited standard of decency. The next step is to make this standard of decency the point of departure for a new move in advance in the same direction, — for there is no merit in simple spiritless conformity to a standard of dissipation that is lived up to as a matter of course by every one in the trade.

The greater prevalence of dissipation among printers than among the average of workmen is accordingly attributable, at least in some measure, to the greater ease of movement and the more transient character of acquaintance and human contact in this trade. But the substantial ground of this high requirement in dissipation is in the last analysis no other than that same propensity for a manifestation of dominance and pecuniary decency which makes the French peasant-proprietor parsimonious and frugal, and induces the American millionaire to found colleges, hospitals and museums. If the canon of conspicuous consumption were not offset to a considerable extent by other features of human nature, alien to it, any saving should logically be impossible for a population situated as the artisan and labouring classes of the cities are at present, however high their wages or their income might be.

But there are other standards of repute and other, more or less imperative, canons of conduct, besides wealth and its manifestation, and some of these come in to accentuate or to qualify the broad, fundamental canon of conspicuous waste. Under the simple test of effectiveness for advertising, we should expect to find leisure and the conspicuous consumption of goods dividing the field of pecuniary emulation pretty evenly between them at the outset. Leisure might then be expected gradually to yield ground and tend to obsolescence as the economic development goes forward, and the community increases in size; while the conspicuous consumption of goods should gradually gain in importance, both absolutely and relatively, until it had absorbed all the available product, leaving nothing over beyond a bare livelihood. But the actual course of development has been somewhat different from this ideal scheme. Leisure held the first place at the start, and came to hold a rank very much above wasteful consumption of goods, both as a direct exponent of wealth and as an element in the standard of decency, during the quasi-peaceable culture. From that point onward, consumption has gained ground, until, at present, it unquestionably holds the primacy, though it is still far from absorbing the entire margin of production above the subsistence minimum.

The early ascendency of leisure as a means of reputability is traceable to the archaic distinction between noble and ignoble employments. Leisure is honourable and becomes imperative partly because it shows exemption from ignoble labour. The archaic differentiation into noble and ignoble classes is based on an invidious distinction between employments as honorific or debasing; and this traditional distinction grows into an imperative canon of decency during the early quasi-peaceable stage. Its ascendency is furthered by the fact that leisure is still fully as effective an evidence of wealth as consumption. Indeed, so effective is it in the relatively small and stable human environment to which the individual is exposed at that cultural stage, that, with the aid of the archaic tradition which deprecates all productive labour, it gives rise to a large impecunious leisure class, and it even tends to limit the production of the community's industry to the subsistence minimum. This extreme inhibition of industry is avoided because slave labour, working under a compulsion more rigorous than that of reputability, is forced to turn out a product in excess of the subsistence minimum of the working class. The subsequent relative decline in the use of conspicuous leisure as a basis of repute is due partly to an increasing relative effectiveness of consumption as an evidence of wealth ; but in part it is traceable to another force, alien, and in some degree antagonistic, to the usage of conspicuous waste.

This alien factor is the instinct of workmanship. Other circumstances permitting, that instinct disposes men to look with favour upon productive efficiency and on whatever is of human use. It disposes them to deprecate waste of substance or effort. The instinct of workmanship is present in all men, and asserts itself even under very adverse circumstances. So that however wasteful a given expenditure may be in reality, it must at least have some colourable excuse in the way of an ostensible purpose. The manner in which, under special circumstances, the instinct eventuates in a taste for exploit and an invidious discrimination between noble and ignoble classes has been indicated in an earlier chapter. In so far as it comes into conflict with the law of conspicuous waste, the instinct of workmanship expresses itself not so much in insistence on substantial usefulness as in an abiding sense of the odiousness and æsthetic impossibility of what is obviously futile. Being of the nature of an instinctive affection, its guidance touches chiefly and immediately the obvious and apparent violations of its requirements. It is only less promptly and with less constraining force that it reaches such substantial violations of its requirements as are appreciated only upon reflection.

So long as all labour continues to be performed exclusively or usually by slaves, the baseness of all productive effort is too constantly and deterrently present in the mind of men to allow the instinct of workmanship seriously to take effect in the direction of industrial usefulness; but when the quasi-peaceable stage (with slavery and status) passes into the peaceable stage of industry (with wage labour and cash payment), the instinct comes more effectively into play. It then begins aggressively to shape men's views of what is meritorious, and asserts itself at least as an auxiliary canon of self-complacency. All extraneous considerations apart, those persons (adults) are but a vanishing minority to-day who harbour no inclination to the accomplishment of some end, or who are not impelled of their own motion to shape some object or fact or relation for human use. The propensity may in large measure be overborne by the more immediately constraining incentive to a reputable leisure and an avoidance of indecorous usefulness, and it may therefore work itself out in make-believe only; as for instance in "social duties," and in quasi-artistic or quasi-scholarly accomplishments, in the care and decoration of the house, in sewing-circle activity or dress reform, in proficiency at dress, cards, yachting, golf, and various sports. But the fact that it may under stress of circumstances eventuate in inanities no more disproves the presence of the instinct than the reality of the brooding instinct is disproved by inducing a hen to sit on a nestful of china eggs.

This latter-day uneasy reaching-out for some form of purposeful activity that shall at the same time not be indecorously productive of either individual or collective gain marks a difference of attitude between the modern leisure class and that of the quasi-peaceable stage. At the earlier stage, as was said above, the all-dominating institution of slavery and status acted resistlessly to discountenance exertion directed to other than naïvely predatory ends. It was still possible to find some habitual employment for the inclination to action in the way of forcible aggression or repression directed against hostile groups or against the subject classes within the group; and this served to relieve the pressure and draw off the energy of the leisure class without a resort to actually useful, or even ostensibly useful employments. The practice of hunting also served the same purpose in some degree. When the community developed into a peaceful industrial organisation, and when fuller occupation of the land had reduced the opportunities for the hunt to an inconsiderable residue, the pressure of energy seeking purposeful employment was left to find an outlet in some other direction. The ignominy which attaches to useful effort also entered upon a less acute phase with the disappearance of compulsory labour; and the instinct of workmanship then came to assert itself with more persistence and consistency.

The line of least resistance has changed in some measure, and the energy which formerly found a vent in predatory activity, now in part takes the direction of some ostensibly useful end. Ostensibly purposeless leisure has come to be deprecated, especially among that large portion of the leisure class whose plebeian origin acts to set them at variance with the tradition of the *otium cum dignitate*. But that canon of reputability which discountenances all employment that is of the nature of productive effort is still at hand, and will permit nothing beyond the most transient vogue to any employment that is substantially useful or productive. The consequence is that a change has been wrought in the conspicuous leisure practised by the leisure class; not so much in substance as in form. A reconciliation between the two conflicting requirements is effected by a resort to make-believe. Many and intricate polite observances and social duties of a ceremonial nature are developed; many organisations are founded, with some specious object of amelioration embodied in their official style and title; there is much coming and going, and a deal of talk, to the end that the talkers may not have occasion to reflect on what is the effectual economic value of their traffic. And along with the make-believe of purposeful employment, and woven inextricably into its texture, there is commonly, if not invariably, a more or less appreciable element of purposeful effort directed to some serious end.

In the narrower sphere of vicarious leisure a similar change has gone forward. Instead of simply passing her time in visible idleness, as in the best days of the patriarchal régime, the housewife of the advanced peaceable stage applies herself assiduously to household cares. The salient features of this development of domestic service have already been indicated.

Throughout the entire evolution of conspicuous expenditure, whether of goods or of services or human life, runs the obvious implication that in order to effectually mend the consumer's good fame it must be an expenditure of superfluities. In order to be reputable it must be wasteful. No merit would accrue from the consumption of the bare necessaries of life, except by comparison with the abjectly poor who fall short even of the subsistence minimum; and no standard of expenditure could result from such a comparison, except the most prosaic and unattractive level of decency. A standard of life would still be possible which should admit of invidious comparison in other respects than that of opulence; as, for instance, a comparison in various directions in the manifestation of moral, physical, intellectual, or æsthetic force. Comparison in all these directions is in vogue to-day; and the comparison made in these respects is commonly so inextricably bound up with the pecuniary comparison as to be scarcely distinguishable from the latter. This is especially true as regards the current rating of expressions of intellectual and æsthetic force or proficiency; so that we frequently interpret as æsthetic or intellectual a difference which in substance is pecuniary only.

The use of the term "waste" is in one respect an unfortunate one. As used in the speech of everyday life the word carries an undertone of deprecation. It is here used for want of a better term that will adequately describe the same range of motives and of phenomena, and it is not to be taken in an odious sense, as implying an illegitimate expenditure of human products or of human life. In the view of economic theory the expenditure in question is no more and no less legitimate than any other expenditure. It is here called "waste" because this expenditure does not serve human life or human well-being on the whole, not because it is waste or misdirection of effort or expenditure as viewed from the standpoint of the individual consumer who chooses it. If he chooses it, that disposes of the question of its relative utility to him, as compared with other forms of consumption that would not be deprecated on account of their wastefulness. Whatever form of expenditure the consumer chooses, or whatever end he seeks in making his choice, has utility to him by virtue of his preference. As seen from the point of view of the individual consumer, the question of wastefulness does not arise within the scope of economic theory proper. The use of the word "waste" as a technical term, therefore, implies no deprecation of the motives or of the ends sought by the consumer under this canon of conspicuous waste.

But it is, on other grounds, worth noting that the term "waste" in the language of everyday life implies deprecation of what is characterised as wasteful. This common-sense implication is itself an outcropping of the instinct of workmanship. The popular reprobation of waste goes to say that in order to be at peace with himself the common man must be able to see in any and all human effort and human enjoyment an enhancement of life and well-being on the whole. In order to meet with unqualified approval, any economic fact must approve itself under the test of impersonal usefulness — usefulness as seen from the point of view of the generically human. Relative or competitive advantage of one individual in comparison with another does not satisfy the economic conscience, and therefore competitive expenditure has not the approval of this conscience.

In strict accuracy nothing should be included under the head of conspicuous waste but such expenditure as is incurred on the ground of an invidious pecuniary comparison. But in order to bring any given item or element in under this head it is not necessary that it should be recognised as waste in this sense by the person incurring the expenditure. It frequently happens that an element of the standard of living which set out with being primarily wasteful, ends with becoming, in the apprehension of the consumer, a necessary of life; and it may in this way become as indispensable as any other item of the consumer's habitual expenditure. As items which sometimes fall under this head, and are therefore available as illustrations of the manner in which this principle applies, may be cited carpets and tapestries, silver table service, waiter's services, silk hats, starched linen, many articles of jewellery and of dress. The indispensability of these things after the habit and the convention have been formed, however, has little to say in the classification of expenditures as waste or not waste in the technical meaning of the word. The test to which all expenditure must be brought in an attempt to decide that point is the question whether it serves directly to enhance human life on the whole — whether it furthers the life process taken impersonally. For this is the basis of award of the instinct of workmanship, and that instinct is the court of final appeal in any question of economic truth or adequacy. It is a question as to the award rendered by a dispassionate common sense. The question is, therefore, not whether, under the existing circumstances of individual habit and social custom, a given expenditure conduces to the particular consumer's gratification or peace of mind; but whether, aside from acquired tastes and from the canons of usage and conventional decency, its result is a net gain in comfort or in the fulness of life. Customary expenditure must be classed under the head of waste in so far as the custom on which it rests is traceable to the habit of making an invidious pecuniary comparison — in so far as it is conceived that it could not have become customary and prescriptive without the backing of this principle of pecuniary reputability or relative economic success.

It is obviously not necessary that a given object of expenditure should be exclusively wasteful in order to come in under the category of conspicuous waste. An article may be useful and wasteful both, and its utility to the consumer may be made up of use and waste in the most varying proportions. Consumable goods, and even productive goods, generally show the two elements in combination, as constituents of their utility; although, in a general way, the element of waste tends to predominate in articles of consumption, while the contrary is true of articles designed for productive use. Even in articles which appear at first glance to serve for pure ostentation only, it is always possible to detect the presence of some, at least ostensible, useful purpose; and on the other hand, even in special machinery and tools contrived for some particular industrial process, as well as in the rudest appliances of human industry, the traces of conspicuous waste, or at least of the habit of ostentation, usually become evident on a close scrutiny. It would be hazardous to assert that a useful purpose is ever absent from the utility of any article or of any service, however obviously its prime purpose and chief element is conspicuous waste; and it would be only less hazardous to assert of any primarily useful product that the element of waste is in no way concerned in its value, immediately or remotely.

CHAPTER V

The Pecuniary Standard of Living

For the great body of the people in any modern community, the proximate ground of expenditure in excess of what is required for physical comfort is not a conscious effort to excel in the expensiveness of their visible consumption, so much as it is a desire to live up to the conventional standard of decency in the amount and grade of goods consumed. This desire is not guided by a rigidly invariable standard, which must be lived up to, and beyond which there is no incentive to go. The standard is flexible; and especially it is indefinitely extensible, if only time is allowed for habituation to any increase in pecuniary ability and for acquiring facility in the new and larger scale of expenditure that follows such an increase. It is much more difficult to recede from a scale of expenditure once adopted than it is to extend the accustomed scale in response to an accession of wealth. Many items of customary expenditure prove on analysis to be almost purely wasteful, and they are therefore honorific only, but after they have once been incorporated into the scale of decent consumption, and so have become an integral part of one's scheme of life, it is quite as hard to give up these as it is to give up many items that conduce directly to one's physical comfort, or even that may be necessary to life and health. That is to say, the conspicuously wasteful honorific expenditure that confers spiritual well-being may become more indispensable than much of that expenditure which ministers to the "lower" wants of physical well-being or sustenance only. It is notoriously just as difficult to recede from a "high" standard of living as it is to lower a standard which is already relatively low; although in the former case the difficulty is a moral one, while in the latter it may involve a material deduction from the physical comforts of life.

But while retrogression is difficult, a fresh advance in conspicuous expenditure is relatively easy; indeed, it takes place almost as a matter of course. In the rare cases where it occurs, a failure to increase one's visible consumption when the means for an increase are at hand is felt in popular apprehension to call for explanation, and unworthy motives of miserliness are imputed to those who fall short in this respect. A prompt response to the stimulus, on the other hand, is accepted as the normal effect. This suggests that the standard of expenditure which commonly guides our efforts is not the average, ordinary expenditure already achieved; it is an ideal of consumption that lies just beyond our reach, or to reach which requires some strain. The motive is emulation — the stimulus of an invidious comparison which prompts us to outdo those with whom we are in the habit of classing ourselves. Substantially the same proposition is expressed in the commonplace remark that each class envies and emulates the class next above it in the social scale, while it rarely compares itself with those below or with those who are considerably in advance. That is to say, in other words, our standard of decency in expenditure, as in other ends of emulation, is set by the usage of those next above us in reputability; until, in this way, especially in any community where class distinctions are somewhat vague, all canons of reputability and decency, and all standards of consumption, are traced back by insensible gradations to the usages and habits of thought of the highest social and pecuniary class — the wealthy leisure class.

It is for this class to determine, in general outline, what scheme of life the community shall accept as decent or honorific; and it is their office by precept and example to set forth this scheme of social salvation in its highest, ideal form. But the higher leisure class can exercise this quasi-sacerdotal office only under certain material limitations. The class cannot at discretion effect a sudden revolution or reversal of the popular habits of thought with respect to any of these ceremonial requirements. It takes time for any change to permeate the mass and change the habitual attitude of the people; and especially it takes time to change the habits of those classes that are socially more remote from the radiant body. The process is slower where the mobility of the population is less or where the intervals between the several classes are wider and more abrupt. But if time be allowed, the scope of the discretion of the leisure class as regards questions of form and detail in the community's scheme of life is large; while as regards the substantial principles of reputability, the changes which it can effect lie within a narrow margin of tolerance. Its example and precept carries the force of prescription for all classes below it; but in working out the precepts which are handed down as governing the form and method of reputability — in shaping the usages and the spiritual attitude of the lower classes — this authoritative prescription constantly works under the selective guidance of the canon of conspicuous waste, tempered in varying degree by the instinct of workmanship. To these norms is to be added another broad principle of human nature — the predatory animus — which in point of generality and of psychological content lies between the two just named. The effect of the latter in shaping the accepted scheme of life is yet to be discussed.

The canon of reputability, then, must adapt itself to the economic circumstances, the traditions, and the degree of spiritual maturity of the particular class whose scheme of life it is to regulate. It is especially to be noted that however high its authority and however true to the fundamental requirements of reputability it may have been at its inception, a specific formal observance can under no circumstances maintain itself in force if with the lapse of time or on its transmission to a lower pecuniary class it is found to run counter to the ultimate ground of decency among civilised peoples, namely, serviceability for the purpose of an invidious comparison in pecuniary success.

It is evident that these canons of expenditure have much to say in determining the standard of living for any community and for any class. It is no less evident that the standard of living which prevails at any time or at any given social altitude will in its turn have much to say as to the forms which honorific expenditure will take, and as to the degree to which this "higher" need will dominate a people's consumption. In this respect the control exerted by the accepted standard of living is chiefly of a negative character; it acts almost solely to prevent recession from a scale of conspicuous expenditure that has once become habitual.

A standard of living is of the nature of habit. It is an habitual scale and method of responding to given stimuli. The difficulty in the way of receding from an accustomed standard is the difficulty of breaking a habit that has once been formed. The relative facility with which an advance in the standard is made means that the life process is a process of unfolding activity and that it will readily unfold in a new direction whenever and wherever the resistance to self-expression decreases. But when the habit of expression along such a given line of low resistance has once been formed, the discharge will seek the accustomed outlet even after a change has taken place in the environment whereby the external resistance has appreciably risen. That heightened facility of expression in a given direction which is called habit may offset a considerable increase in the resistance offered by external circumstances to the unfolding of life in the given direction. As between the various habits, or habitual modes and directions of expression, which go to make up an individual's standard of living, there is an appreciable difference in point of persistence under counteracting circumstances and in point of the degree of imperativeness with which the discharge seeks a given direction.

That is to say, in the language of current economic theory, while men are reluctant to retrench their expenditures in any direction, they are more reluctant to retrench in some directions than in others; so that while any accustomed consumption is reluctantly given up, there are certain lines of consumption which are given up with relatively extreme reluctance. The articles or forms of consumption to which the consumer clings with the greatest tenacity are commonly the so-called necessaries of life, or the subsistence minimum. The subsistence minimum is of course not a rigidly determined allowance of goods, definite and invariable in kind and quantity; but for the purpose in hand it may be taken to comprise a certain, more or less definite, aggregate of consumption required for the maintenance of life. This minimum, it may be assumed, is ordinarily given up last in case of a progressive retrenchment of expenditure That is to say, in a general way, the most ancient and ingrained of the habits which govern the individual's life — those habits that touch his existence as an organism — are the most persistent and imperative. Beyond these come the higher wants — later-formed habits of the individual or the race — in a somewhat irregular and by no means invariable gradation. Some of these higher wants, as for instance the habitual use of certain stimulants, or the need of salvation (in the eschatological sense), or of good repute, may in some cases take precedence of the lower or more elementary wants. In general, the longer the habituation, the more unbroken the habit and the more nearly it coincides with previous habitual forms of the life process, the more persistently will the given habit assert itself. The habit will be stronger if the particular traits of human nature which its action involves, or the particular aptitudes that find exercise in it, are traits or aptitudes that are already largely and profoundly concerned in the life process or that are intimately bound up with the life history of the particular racial stock.

The varying degrees of ease with which different habits are formed by different persons, as well as the varying degrees of reluctance with which different habits are given up, goes to say that the formation of specific habits is not a matter of length of habituation simply. Inherited aptitudes and traits of temperament count for quite as much as length of habituation in deciding what range of habits will come to dominate any individual's scheme of life. And the prevalent type of transmitted aptitudes, or in other words the type of temperament belonging to the dominant ethnic element in any community, will go far to decide what will be the scope and form of expression of the community's habitual life process. How greatly the transmitted idiosyncracies of aptitude may count in the way of a rapid and definitive formation of habit in individuals is illustrated by the extreme facility with which an all-dominating habit of alcoholism is sometimes formed; or in the similar facility and the similarly inevitable formation of a habit of devout observances in the case of persons gifted with a special aptitude in that direc tion. Much the same meaning attaches to that peculiar facility of habituation to a specific human environment that is called romantic love.

Men differ in respect of transmitted aptitudes, or in respect of the relative facility with which they unfold their life activity in particular directions; and the habits which coincide with or proceed upon a relatively strong specific aptitude or a relatively great specific facility of expression become of great consequence to the man's well-being. The part played by this element of aptitude in determining the relative tenacity of the several habits which constitute the standard of living goes to explain the extreme reluctance with which men give up any habitual expenditure in the way of conspicuous consumption. The aptitudes or propensities to which a habit of this kind is to be referred as its ground are those aptitudes whose exercise is comprised in emulation; and the propensity for emulation — for invidious comparison — is of ancient growth and is a pervading trait of human nature. It is easily called into vigorous activity in any new form, and it asserts itself with great insistence under any form under which it has once found habitual expression. When the individual has once formed the habit of seeking expression in a given line of honorific expenditure, — when a given set of stimuli have come to be habitually responded to in activity of a given kind and direction under the guidance of these alert and deep-reaching propensities of emulation, — it is with extreme reluctance that such an habitual expenditure is given up. And on the other hand, whenever an accession of pecuniary strength puts the individual in a position to unfold his life process in larger scope and with additional reach, the ancient propensities of the race will assert themselves in determining the direction which the new unfolding of life is to take. And those propensities which are already actively in the field under some related form of expression, which are aided by the pointed suggestions afforded by a current accredited scheme of life, and for the exercise of which the material means and opportunities are readily available, — these will especially have much to say in shaping the form and direction in which the new accession to the individual's aggregate force will assert itself. That is to say, in concrete terms, in any community where conspicuous consumption is an element of the scheme of life, an increase in an individual's ability to pay is likely to take the form of an expenditure for some accredited line of conspicuous consumption.

With the exception of the instinct of self-preservation, the propensity for emulation is probably the strongest and most alert and persistent of the economic motives proper. In an industrial community this propensity for emulation expresses itself in pecuniary emulation; and this, so far as regards the Western civilised communities of the present, is virtually equivalent to saying that it expresses itself in some form of conspicuous waste. The need of conspicuous waste, therefore, stands ready to absorb any increase in the community's industrial efficiency or output of goods, after the most elementary physical wants have been provided for. Where this esult does not follow, under modern conditions, the eason for the discrepancy is commonly to be sought in a rate of increase in the individual's wealth too rapid for the habit of expenditure to keep abreast of it ; or it may be that the individual in question defers the conspicuous consumption of the increment to a later date — ordinarily with a view to heightening the spectacular effect of the aggregate expenditure contemplated. As increased industrial efficiency makes it possible to procure the means of livelihood with less labour, the energies of the industrious members of the community are bent to the compassing of a higher result in conspicuous expenditure, rather than slackened to a more comfortable pace. The strain is not lightened as industrial efficiency increases and makes a lighter strain possible, but the increment of output is turned to use to meet this want, which is indefinitely expansible, after the manner commonly imputed in economic theory to higher or spiritual wants. It is owing chiefly to the presence of this element in the standard of living that J. S. Mill was able to say that "hitherto it is questionable if all the mechanical inventions yet made have lightened the day's toil of any human being."

The accepted standard of expenditure in the community or in the class to which a person belongs largely determines what his standard of living will be. It does this directly by commending itself to his common sense as right and good, through his habitually contemplating it and assimilating the scheme of life in which it belongs ; but it does so also indirectly through popular insistence on conformity to the accepted scale of expenditure as a matter of propriety, under pain of disesteem and ostracism. To accept and practise the standard of living which is in vogue is both agreeable and expedient, commonly to the point of being indispensable to personal comfort and to success in life. The standard of living of any class, so far as concerns the element of conspicuous waste, is commonly as high as the earning capacity of the class will permit — with a constant tendency to go higher. The effect upon the serious activities of men is therefore to direct them with great singleness of purpose to the largest possible acquisition of wealth, and to discountenance work that brings no pecuniary gain. At the same time the effect on consumption is to concentrate it upon the lines which are most patent to the observers whose good opinion is sought; while the inclinations and aptitudes whose exercise does not involve a honorific expenditure of time or substance tend to fall into abeyance through disuse.

Through this discrimination in favour of visible consumption it has come about that the domestic life of most classes is relatively shabby, as compared with the éclat of that overt portion of their life that is carried on before the eyes of observers. As a secondary consequence of the same discrimination, people habitually screen their private life from observation. So far as concerns that portion of their consumption that may without blame be carried on in secret, they withdraw from all contact with their neighbours. Hence the exclusiveness of people, as regards their domestic life, in most of the industrially developed communities; and hence, by remoter derivation, the habit of privacy and reserve that is so large a feature in the code of proprieties of the better classes in all commu nities. The low birthrate of the classes upon whom the requirements of reputable expenditure fall with great urgency is likewise traceable to the exigencies of a standard of living based on conspicuous waste. The conspicuous consumption, and the consequent increased expense, required in the reputable maintenance of a child is very considerable and acts as a powerful deterrent. It is probably the most effectual of the Malthusian prudential checks.

The effect of this factor of the standard of living, both in the way of retrenchment in the obscurer elements of consumption that go to physical comfort and maintenance, and also in the paucity or absence of children, is perhaps seen at its best among the classes given to scholarly pursuits. Because of a presumed superiority and scarcity of the gifts and attainments that characterise their life, these classes are by convention subsumed under a higher social grade than their pecuniary grade should warrant. The scale of decent expenditure in their case is pitched correspondingly high, and it consequently leaves an exceptionally narrow margin disposable for the other ends of life. By force of circumstances, their own habitual sense of what is good and right in these matters, as well as the expectations of the community in the way of pecuniary decency among the learned, are excessively high — as measured by the prevalent degree of opulence and earning capacity of the class, relatively to the non-scholarly classes whose social equals they nominally are. In any modern community where there is no priestly monopoly of these occupations, the people of scholarly pursuits are un avoidably thrown into contact with classes that are pecuniarily their superiors. The high standard of pecuniary decency in force among these superior classes is transfused among the scholarly classes with but little mitigation of its rigour; and as a consequence there is no class of the community that spends a larger proportion of its substance in conspicuous waste than these.

[3]

The Preconceptions of Economic Science, I-III

Thorstein Bunde Veblen, 'The Preconceptions of Economic Science, I-III', *Quarterly Journal of Economics*, vol. 13 (January and July 1899), pp. 121–50, 396–426; vol. 14 (February 1900), pp. 240–69; reprinted in *The Place of Science in Modern Civilization* (New York: Viking Press, 1919) ; reprinted, New Brunswick: Transactions, 1990, pp. 82–179

Veblen believed that all economic theory, and the uses to which it is put, reflect and give effect to certain underlying preconceptions. These essays focus on classical and neoclassical economics, Veblen's argument being that their preconceptions are vestiges of past social forms and structures and related metaphors and modes of thought. Their identification involves Veblen in both the demystification of long-held beliefs and the analysis of the role of these beliefs in the organization and control of the economy. The established preconceptions Veblen finds to be incongruent with existential reality and dysfunctional when put into use. Their general acceptance, however, is a barrier to new ways of thinking. The critical analysis of these preconceptions, he thought, would, or at least should, suffice to call them into question.

THE PRECONCEPTIONS OF ECONOMIC SCIENCE.

I.

In an earlier paper * the view has been expressed that the economics handed down by the great writers of a past generation is substantially a taxonomic science. A view of much the same purport, so far as concerns the point here immediately in question, is presented in an admirably lucid and cogent way by Professor Clark in a recent number of this journal.† There is no wish hereby to burden Professor Clark with a putative sponsorship of any ungraceful or questionable generalizations reached in working outward from this main position, but expression may not be denied the comfort which his unintended authentication of the main position affords. It is true, Professor Clark does not speak of taxonomy, but employs the term

* "Why is Economics not an Evolutionary Science?" *Quarterly Journal of Economics*, July, 1898.

† "The Future of Economic Theory," *Ibid.*, October, 1898.

"statics," which is perhaps better suited to his immediate purpose. Nevertheless, in spite of the high authority given the term "statics," in this connection, through its use by Professor Clark and by other writers eminent in the science, it is fairly to be questioned whether the term can legitimately be used to characterize the received economic theories. The word is borrowed from the jargon of physics, where it is used to designate the theory of bodies at rest or of forces in equilibrium. But there is much in the received economic theories to which the analogy of bodies at rest or of forces in equilibrium will not apply. It is perhaps not too much to say that those articles of economic theory that do not lend themselves to this analogy make up the major portion of the received doctrines. So, for instance, it seems scarcely to the point to speak of the statics of production, exchange, consumption, circulation. There are, no doubt, appreciable elements in the theory of these several processes that may fairly be characterized as statical features of the theory; but the doctrines handed down are after all, in the main, theories of the process discussed under each head, and the theory of a process does not belong in statics. The epithet "statical" would, for instance, have to be wrenched somewhat ungently to make it apply to Quesnay's classic *Tableau Économique* or to the great body of Physiocratic speculations that take their rise from it. The like is true for Books II. and III. of Adam Smith's *Wealth of Nations*, as also for considerable portions of Ricardo's work, or, to come down to the present generation, for much of Marshall's *Principles*, and for such a modern discussion as Smart's *Studies in Economics*, as well as for the fruitful activity of the Austrians and of the later representatives of the Historical School.

But to return from this terminological digression. While economic science in the remoter past of its history has been mainly of a taxonomic character, later writers of all schools show something of a divergence from the taxonomic line and an inclination to make the science a genetic account of the economic life process, sometimes even without an ulterior view to the taxonomic value of the results obtained. This divergence from the ancient canons of theoretical formulation is to be taken as an episode of the movement that is going forward in latter-day science generally; and the progressive change which thus affects the ideals and the objective point of the modern sciences seems in its turn to be an expression of that matter-of-fact habit of mind which the prosy but exacting exigencies of life in a modern industrial community breed in men exposed to their unmitigated impact.

In speaking of this matter-of-fact character of the modern sciences it has been broadly characterized as "evolutionary"; and the evolutionary method and the evolutionary ideals have been placed in antithesis to the taxonomic methods and ideals of pre-evolutionary days. But the characteristic attitude, aims, and ideals which are so designated here are by no means peculiar to the group of sciences that are professedly occupied with a process of development, taking that term in its most widely accepted meaning. The latter-day inorganic sciences are in this respect like the organic. They occupy themselves with "dynamic" relations and sequences. The question which they ask is always, What takes place next, and why? Given a situation wrought out by the forces under inquiry, what follows as the consequence of the situation so wrought out? or what follows upon the accession of a further element of force? Even in so non-evolutionary a science as inorganic chemistry the inquiry consistently runs on a process, an active sequence, and the value of the resulting situation as a point of departure for the next step in an interminable cumulative sequence. The last step in the chemist's experimental inquiry into any substance is, What comes of the substance determined? What will it do? What will it lead to, when it is made the point of departure in further chemical action? There is no ultimate term, and no definitive solution except in terms of further action. The theory worked out is always a theory of a genetic succession of phenomena, and the relations determined and elaborated into a body of doctrine are always genetic relations. In modern chemistry no cognizance is taken of the honorific bearing of reactions or molecular formulæ. The modern chemist, as contrasted with his ancient congener, knows nothing of the worth, elegance, or cogency of the relations that may subsist between the particles of matter with which he busies himself, for any other than the genetic purpose. The spiritual element and the elements of worth and propensity no longer count. Alchemic symbolism and the hierarchical glamour and virtue that once hedged about the nobler and more potent elements and reagents are almost altogether a departed glory of the science. Even the modest imputation of propensity involved in the construction of a scheme of coercive normality, for the putative guidance of reactions, finds little countenance with the later adepts of chemical science. The science has outlived that phase of its development at which the taxonomic feature was the dominant one.

In the modern sciences, of which chemistry is one, there has been a gradual shifting of the point of view from which the phenomena that the science treats of are apprehended and passed upon; and to the historian of chemical science this shifting of the point of view must be a factor of great weight in the development of chemical knowledge. Something of a like nature is true for economic science; and it is the aim here to present, in outline, some of the successive phases that have passed over the spiritual attitude of the adepts of the science, and to point out the manner in which the transition from one point of view to the next has been made.

As has been suggested in the paper already referred to, the characteristic spiritual attitude or point of view of a given generation or group of economists is shown not so much in their detail work as in their higher syntheses — the terms of their definitive formulations — the grounds of their final valuation of the facts handled for purpose of theory. This line of recondite inquiry into the spiritual past and antecedents of the science has not often been pursued seriously or with singleness of purpose, perhaps because it is, after all, of but slight consequence to the practical efficiency of the present-day science. Still, not a little substantial work has been done towards this end by such writers as Hasbach, Oncken, Bonar, Cannan, and Marshall. And much that is to the purpose is also due to writers outside of economics, for the aims of economic speculation have never been insulated from the work going forward in other lines of inquiry. As would necessarily be the case, the point of view of economists has always been in large part the point of view of the enlightened common sense of their time. The spiritual attitude of a given generation of economists is therefore in good part a special outgrowth of the ideals and preconceptions current in the world about them.

So, for instance, it is quite the conventional thing to say that the speculations of the Physiocrats were dominated and shaped by the preconception of Natural Rights. Account has been taken of the effect of natural-rights preconceptions upon the Physiocratic schemes of policy and economic reform, as well as upon the details of their doctrines.* But little has been said of the significance of these preconceptions for the lower courses of the Physiocrats' theoretical structure. And yet that habit of mind to which the natural-rights view is wholesome and adequate is answerable both for the point of departure and

* See, for instance, Hasbach, *Allgemeine philosophische Grundlagen der von François Quesnay und Adam Smith begründeten politischen Oekonomie.*

for the objective point of the Physiocratic theories, both for the range of facts to which they turned and for the terms in which they were content to formulate their knowledge of the facts which they handled. The failure of their critics to place themselves at the Physiocratic point of view has led to much destructive criticism of their work; whereas, when seen through Physiocratic eyes, such doctrines as those of the net product and of the barrenness of the artisan class appear to be substantially true.

The speculations of the Physiocrats are commonly accounted the first articulate and comprehensive presentation of economic theory that is in line with later theoretical work. The Physiocratic point of view may, therefore, well be taken as the point of departure in an attempt to trace that shifting of aims and norms of procedure that comes into view in the work of later economists when compared with earlier writers.

Physiocratic economics is a theory of the working-out of the Law of Nature (*loi naturelle*) in its economic bearing, and this Law of Nature is a very simple matter.

> Les lois naturelles sont où physiques ou morales.
>
> On entend ici, par loi physique, *le cours réglé de tout événement physique de l'ordre naturel, évidemment le plus avantageux au genre humain.*
>
> On entend ici, par loi morale, *la règle de toute action humaine de l'ordre morale, conforme à l'ordre physique évidemment le plus avantageux au genre humain.*
>
> Ces lois forment ensemble ce qu'on appelle la *loi naturelle.* Tous les hommes et toutes les puissances humaines doivent être soumis à ces lois souveraines, instituées par l'Être-Suprême: elles sont immuables et irréfragables, et les meilleures lois possible.*

The settled course of material facts tending beneficently to the highest welfare of the human race,—this is the final term in the Physiocratic speculations. This is the touchstone of substantiality. Conformity to these "immutable

* Quesnay. *Droit Naturel*, ch. v. (Ed. Daire, *Physiocrates*, pp. 52-53).

and unerring" laws of nature is the test of economic truth. The laws are immutable and unerring, but that does not mean that they rule the course of events with a blind fatality that admits of no exception and no divergence from the direct line. Human nature may, through infirmity or perversity, wilfully break over the beneficent trend of the laws of nature; but to the Physiocrat's sense of the matter the laws are none the less immutable and irrefragable on that account. They are not empirical generalizations on the course of phenomena, like the law of falling bodies or of the angle of reflection; although many of the details of their action are to be determined only by observation and experience, helped out, of course, by interpretation of the facts of observation under the light of reason. So, for instance, Turgot, in his *Réflections*, empirically works out a doctrine of the reasonable course of development through which wealth is accumulated and reaches the existing state of unequal distribution; so also his doctrines of interest and of money. The immutable natural laws are rather of the nature of canons of conduct governing nature than generalizations of mechanical sequence, although in a general way the phenomena of mechanical sequence are details of the conduct of nature working according to these canons of conduct. The great law of the order of nature is of the character of a propensity working to an end, to the accomplishment of a purpose. The processes of nature working under the quasi-spiritual stress of this immanent propensity may be characterized as nature's habits of life. Not that nature is conscious of its travail, and knows and desires the worthy end of its endeavors; but for all that there is a quasi-spiritual nexus between antecedent and consequent in the scheme of operation in which nature is engaged. Nature is not uneasy about interruptions of its course or occasional deflections from the direct line through an untoward conjunction of mechanical causes, nor does the validity of the great overruling law suffer through such an episode. The introduction of a mere mechanically effective causal factor cannot thwart the course of nature from reaching the goal to which she animistically tends. Nothing can thwart this teleological propensity of nature except counter-activity or divergent activity of a similarly teleological kind. Men can break over the law, and have short-sightedly and wilfully done so; for men are also agents who guide their actions by an end to be achieved. Human conduct is activity of the same kind — on the same plane of spiritual reality or competency — as the course of nature, and it may therefore traverse the latter. The remedy for this short-sighted traffic of misguided human nature is enlightenment,—"instruction publique et privée des lois de l'ordre naturel." *

The nature in terms of which all knowledge of phenomena — for the present purpose economic phenomena — is to be finally synthesized is, therefore, substantially of a quasi-spiritual or animistic character. The laws of nature are in the last resort teleological: they are of the nature of a propensity. The substantial fact in all the sequences of nature is the end to which the sequence naturally tends, not the brute fact of mechanical compulsion or causally effective force. Economic theory is accordingly the theory (1) of how the efficient causes of the *ordre naturel* work in an orderly unfolding sequence, guided by the underlying natural laws — the propensity immanent in nature to establish the highest well-being of mankind, and (2) of the conditions imposed upon human conduct by these natural laws in order to reach the ordained goal of supreme human welfare. The conditions so imposed on human conduct are as definitive as the laws and the order by force of which they are imposed; and the theoretical conclusions reached, when these laws and this order are known, are therefore expressions

* Quesnay, *Droit Naturel*, ch. v. (Ed. Daire, *Physiocrates*, p. 53).

of absolute economic truth. Such conclusions are an expression of reality, but not necessarily of fact.

Now, the objective end of this propensity that determines the course of nature is human well-being. But economic speculation has to do with the workings of nature only so far as regards the *ordre physique*. And the laws of nature in the *ordre physique*, working through mechanical sequence, can only work out the physical well-being of man, not necessarily the spiritual. This propensity to the physical well-being of man is therefore the law of nature to which economic science must bring its generalizations, and this law of physical beneficence is the substantial ground of economic truth. Wanting this, all our speculations are vain; but having its authentication they are definitive. The great, typical function, to which all the other functioning of nature is incidental if not subsidiary, is accordingly that of the alimentation, nutrition of mankind. In so far, and only in so far as the physical processes contribute to human sustenance and fulness of life, can they, therefore, further the great work of nature. Whatever processes contribute to human sustenance by adding to the material available for human assimilation and nutrition, by increasing the substance disposable for human comfort, therefore count towards the substantial end. All other processes, however serviceable in other than this physiological respect, lack the substance of economic reality. Accordingly, human industry is productive, economically speaking, if it heightens the effectiveness of the natural processes out of which the material of human sustenance emerges; otherwise not. The test of productivity, of economic reality in material facts, is the increase of nutritive material. Whatever employment of time or effort does not afford an increase of such material is unproductive, however profitable it may be to the person employed, and however useful or indispensable it may be to the community. The type of such productive industry is the husbandman's employment, which yields a substantial (nutritive) gain. The artisan's work may be useful to the community and profitable to himself, but its economic effect does not extend beyond an alteration of the form in which the material afforded by nature already lies at hand. It is formally productive only, not really productive. It bears no part in the creative or generative work of nature; and therefore it lacks the character of economic substantiality. It does not enhance nature's output of vital force. The artisan's labors, therefore, yield no net product, whereas the husbandman's labors do.

Whatever constitutes a material increment of this output of vital force is wealth, and nothing else is. The theory of value contained in this position has not to do with value according to men's appraisement of the valuable article. Given items of wealth may have assigned to them certain relative values at which they exchange, and these conventional values may differ more or less widely from the natural or intrinsic value of the goods in question; but all that is beside the substantial point. The point in question is not the degree of predilection shown by certain individuals or bodies of men for certain goods. That is a matter of caprice and convention, and it does not directly touch the substantial ground of the economic life. The question of value is a question of the extent to which the given item of wealth forwards the end of nature's unfolding process. It is valuable, intrinsically and really, in so far as it avails the great work which nature has in hand.

Nature, then, is the final term in the Physiocratic speculations. Nature works by impulse and in an unfolding process, under the stress of a propensity to the accomplishment of a given end. This propensity, taken as the final cause that is operative in any situation, furnishes the basis on which to co-ordinate all our knowledge of those efficient causes through which Nature works to her ends. For the purpose of economic theory proper, this is the ultimate ground of reality to which our quest of economic truth must penetrate. But back of Nature and her works there is, in the Physiocratic scheme of the universe, the Creator, by whose all-wise and benevolent power the order of nature has been established in all the strength and beauty of its inviolate and immutable perfection. But the Physiocratic conception of the Creator is essentially a deistic one: he stands apart from the course of nature which he has established, and keeps his hands off. In the last resort, of course, "Dieu seul est producteur. Les hommes travaillent, recueillent, économisent, conservent; mais *économiser* n'est pas *produire*." * But this last resort does not bring the Creator into economic theory as a fact to be counted with in formulating economic laws. He serves a homiletical purpose in the Physiocratic speculations rather than fills an office essential to the theory. He comes within the purview of the theory by way of authentication rather than as a subject of inquiry or a term in the formulation of economic knowledge. The Physiocratic God can scarcely be said to be an economic fact, but it is otherwise with that nature whose ways and means constitute the subject-matter of the Physiocratic inquiry.

When this natural system of the Physiocratic speculations is looked at from the side of the psychology of the investigators, or from that of the logical premises employed, it is immediately recognized as essentially animistic. It runs consistently on animistic ground; but it is animism of a high grade,— highly integrated and enlightened, but, after all, retaining very much of that primitive force and naïveté which characterize the animistic explanations of phenomena in vogue among the untroubled bar-

* Dupont de Nemours, *Correspondance avec J.-B. Say* (Ed. Daire, *Physiocrates*, première partie, p. 399).

barians. It is not the disjected animism of the vulgar, who see a wilful propensity — often a wilful perversity — in given objects or situations to work towards a given outcome, good or bad. It is not the gambler's haphazard sense of fortuitous necessity or the housewife's belief in lucky days, numbers or phases of the moon. The Physiocrat's animism rests on a broader outlook, and does not proceed by such an immediately impulsive imputation of propensity. The teleological element — the element of propensity — is conceived in a large way, unified and harmonized, as a comprehensive order of nature as a whole. But it vindicates its standing as a true animism by never becoming fatalistic and never being confused or confounded with the sequence of cause and effect. It has reached the last stage of integration and definition, beyond which the way lies downward from the high, quasi-spiritual ground of animism to the tamer levels of normality and causal uniformities.

There is already discernible a tone of dispassionate and colorless "tendency" about the Physiocratic animism, such as to suggest a wavering towards the side of normality. This is especially visible in such writers as the half-protestant Turgot. In his discussion of the development of farming, for instance, Turgot speaks almost entirely of human motives and the material conditions under which the growth takes place. There is little metaphysics in it, and that little does not express the law of nature in an adequate form. But, after all has been said, it remains true that the Physiocrat's sense of substantiality is not satisfied until he reaches the animistic ground; and it remains true also that the arguments of their opponents made little impression on the Physiocrats so long as they were directed to other than this animistic ground of their doctrine. This is true in great measure even of Turgot, as witness his controversy with Hume. Whatever criticism is directed against them on other grounds is met with impatience, as being inconsequential, if not disingenuous.*

To an historian of economic theory the source and the line of derivation whereby this precise form of the order-of-nature preconception reached the Physiocrats are of first-rate importance; but it is scarcely a question to be taken up here,—in part because it is too large a question to be handled here, in part because it has met with adequate treatment at more competent hands,† and in part because it is somewhat beside the immediate point under discussion. This point is the logical, or perhaps better the psychological, value of the Physiocrats' preconception, as a factor in shaping their point of view and the terms of their definitive formulation of economic knowledge. For this purpose it may be sufficient to point out that the preconception in question belongs to the generation in which the Physiocrats lived, and that it is the guiding norm of all serious thought that found ready assimilation into the common-sense views of that time. It is the characteristic and controlling feature of what may be called the common-sense metaphysics of the eighteenth century, especially so far as concerns the enlightened French community.

It is to be noted as a point bearing more immediately on the question in hand that this imputation of final causes to the course of phenomena expresses a spiritual attitude which has prevailed, one might almost say, always and everywhere, but which reached its finest, most effective development, and found its most finished expression, in the eighteenth-century metaphysics. It is nothing recondite; for it meets us at every turn, as a matter of course, in the vulgar thinking of to-day,—in the pulpit and in the market place,—although it is not so ingenuous,

* So, for instance, the concluding chapters of La Rivière's *Ordre Naturel des Sociétés Politiques*.

† *E.g.*, Hasbach, *loc. cit.*; Bonar, *Philosophy and Political Economy*, Book II.; Ritchie, *Natural Rights*.

nor does it so unquestionedly hold the primacy in the thinking of any class to-day as it once did. It meets us likewise, with but little change of features, at all past stages of culture, late or early. Indeed, it is the most generic feature of human thinking, so far as regards a theoretical or speculative formulation of knowledge. Accordingly, it seems scarcely necessary to trace the lineage of this characteristic preconception of the era of enlightenment, through specific channels, back to the ancient philosophers or the jurists of the empire. Some of the specific forms of its expression — as, for instance, the doctrine of Natural Rights — are no doubt traceable through mediæval channels to the teachings of the ancients; but there is no need of going over the brook for water, and tracing back to specific teachings the main features of that habit of mind or spiritual attitude of which the doctrines of Natural Rights and the Order of Nature are specific elaborations only. This dominant habit of mind came to the generation of the Physiocrats on the broad ground of group inheritance, not by lineal devolution from any one of the great thinkers of past ages who had thrown its deliverances into a similarly competent form for the use of his own generation.

In leaving the Physiocratic discipline and the immediate sphere of Physiocratic influence for British ground, we are met by the figure of Hume. Here, also, it will be impracticable to go into details as to the remoter line of derivation of the specific point of view that we come upon on making the transition, for reasons similar to those already given as excuse for passing over the similar question with regard to the Physiocratic point of view. Hume is, of course, not primarily an economist; but that placid unbeliever is none the less a large item in any inventory of eighteenth-century economic thought. Hume was not gifted with a facile acceptance of the group inheritance that made the habit of mind of his generation. Indeed, he was gifted with an alert, though somewhat histrionic, scepticism touching everything that was well received. It is his office to prove all things, though not necessarily to hold fast that which is good.

Aside from the strain of affectation discernible in Hume's scepticism, he may be taken as an accentuated expression of that characteristic bent which distinguishes British thinking in his time from the thinking of the Continent, and more particularly of the French. There is in Hume, and in the British community, an insistence on the prosy, not to say the seamy, side of human affairs. He is not content with formulating his knowledge of things in terms of what ought to be or in terms of the objective point of the course of things. He is not even content with adding to the teleological account of phenomena a chain of empirical, narrative generalizations as to the usual course of things. He insists, in season and out of season, on an exhibition of the efficient causes engaged in any sequence of phenomena; and he is sceptical — irreverently sceptical — as to the need or the use of any formulation of knowledge that outruns the reach of his own matter-of-fact, step-by-step argument from cause to effect.

In short, he is too modern to be wholly intelligible to those of his contemporaries who are most neatly abreast of their time. He out-Britishes the British; and, in his footsore quest for a perfectly tame explanation of things, he finds little comfort, and indeed scant courtesy, at the hands of his own generation. He is not in sufficiently naïve accord with the range of preconceptions then in vogue.

But, while Hume may be an accentuated expression of a national characteristic, he is not therefore an untrue expression of this phase of British eighteenth-century thinking. The peculiarity of point of view and of method for which he stands has sometimes been called the critical attitude, sometimes the inductive method, sometimes the materialistic or mechanical, and again, though less aptly, the historical method. Its characteristic is an insistence on matter of fact.

This matter-of-fact animus that meets any historian of economic doctrine on his introduction to British economics is a large, but not the largest, feature of the British scheme of early economic thought. It strikes the attention because it stands in contrast with the relative absence of this feature in the contemporary speculations of the Continent. The most potent, most formative habit of thought concerned in the early development of economic teaching on British ground is best seen in the broader generalizations of Adam Smith, and this more potent factor in Smith is a bent that is substantially identical with that which gives consistency to the speculations of the Physiocrats. In Adam Smith the two are happily combined, not to say blended; but the animistic habit still holds the primacy, with the matter-of-fact as a subsidiary though powerful factor. He is said to have combined deduction with induction. The relatively great prominence given the latter marks the line of divergence of British from French economics, not the line of coincidence; and on this account it may not be out of place to look more narrowly into the circumstances to which the emergence of this relatively greater penchant for a matter-of-fact explanation of things in the British community is due.

To explain the characteristic animus for which Hume stands on grounds that might appeal to Hume, we should have to inquire into the peculiar circumstances — ultimately material circumstances — that have gone to shape the habitual view of things within the British community, and that so have acted to differentiate the British preconceptions from the French, or from the general range of preconceptions prevalent on the Continent. These peculiar formative circumstances are no doubt to some extent racial peculiarities; but the racial complexion of the British community is not widely different from the French, and especially not widely different from certain other Continental communities which are for the present purpose roughly classed with the French. Race difference can therefore not wholly, nor indeed for the greater part, account for the cultural difference of which this difference in preconceptions is an outcome. Through its cumulative effect on institutions the race difference must be held to have had a considerable effect on the habit of mind of the community; but, if the race difference is in this way taken as the remoter ground of an institutional peculiarity, which in its turn has shaped prevalent habits of thought, then the attention may be directed to the proximate causes, the concrete circumstances, through which this race difference has acted, in conjunction with other ulterior circumstances, to work out the psychological phenomena observed. Race differences, it may be remarked, do not so nearly coincide with national lines of demarcation as differences in the point of view from which things are habitually apprehended or differences in the standards according to which facts are rated.

If the element of race difference be not allowed definitive weight in discussing national peculiarities that underlie the deliverances of common sense, neither can these national peculiarities be confidently traced to a national difference in the transmitted learning that enters into the common-sense view of things. So far as concerns the concrete facts embodied in the learning of the various nations within the European culture, these nations make up but a single community. What divergence is visible does not touch the character of the positive information with which the learning of the various nations is occupied. Divergence is visible in the higher syntheses, the methods of handling the material of knowledge, the basis of valuation of the facts taken up, rather than in the material of knowledge. But this divergence must be set down to a cultural difference, a difference of point of view, not to a difference in inherited information. When a given body of information passes the national frontiers it acquires a new complexion, a new national, cultural physiognomy. It is this cultural physiognomy of learning that is here under inquiry, and a comparison of early French economics (the Physiocrats) with early British economics (Adam Smith) is here entered upon merely with a view to making out what significance this cultural physiognomy of the science has for the past progress of economic speculation.

The broad features of economic speculation, as it stood at the period under consideration, may be briefly summed up, disregarding the element of policy, or expediency, which is common to both groups of economists, and attending to their theoretical work alone. With the Physiocrats, as with Adam Smith, there are two main points of view from which economic phenomena are treated: (*a*) the matter-of-fact point of view or preconception, which yields a discussion of causal sequences and correlations; and (*b*) what, for want of a more expressive word, is here called the animistic point of view or preconception, which yields a discussion of teleological sequences and correlations,—a discussion of the function of this and that "organ," of the legitimacy of this or the other range of facts. The former preconception is allowed a larger scope in the British than in the French economics: there is more of "induction" in the British. The latter preconception is present in both, and is the definitive element in both; but the animistic element is more colorless in the British, it is less constantly in evidence, and less able to stand alone without the support of arguments from cause to effect. Still, the animistic element is the controlling factor in the higher syntheses of both; and for both alike it affords the definitive ground on which the argument finally comes to rest. In neither group of thinkers is the sense of substantiality appeased until this quasi-spiritual ground, given by the natural propensity of the course of events, is reached. But the propensity in events, the natural or normal course of things, as appealed to by the British speculators, suggests less of an imputation of will-power, or personal force, to the propensity in question. It may be added, as has already been said in another place, that the tacit imputation of will-power or spiritual consistency to the natural or normal course of events has progressively weakened in the later course of economic speculation, so that in this respect, the British economists of the eighteenth century may be said to represent a later phase of economic inquiry than the Physiocrats.

Unfortunately, but unavoidably, if this question as to the cultural shifting of the point of view in economic science is taken up from the side of the causes to which the shifting is traceable, it will take the discussion back to ground on which an economist must at best feel himself to be but a raw layman, with all a layman's limitations and ineptitude, and with the certainty of doing badly what might be done well by more competent hands. But, with a reliance on charity where charity is most needed, it is necessary to recite summarily what seems to be the psychological bearing of certain cultural facts.

A cursory acquaintance with any of the more archaic phases of human culture enforces the recognition of this fact,—that the habit of construing the phenomena of the inanimate world in animistic terms prevails pretty much universally on these lower levels. Inanimate phenomena are apprehended to work out a propensity to an end: the movements of the elements are construed in terms of quasi-personal force. So much is well authenticated by the observations on which anthropologists and ethnologists draw for their materials. This animistic habit, it may be said, seems to be more effectual and far-reaching among those primitive communities that lead a predatory life.

But along with this feature of archaic methods of thought or of knowledge, the picturesqueness of which has drawn the attention of all observers, there goes a second feature, no less important for the purpose in hand, though less obtrusive. The latter is of less interest to the men who have to do with the theory of cultural development, because it is a matter of course. This second feature of archaic thought is the habit of also apprehending facts in non-animistic, or impersonal, terms. The imputation of propensity in no case extends to all the mechanical facts in the case. There is always a substratum of matter of fact, which is the outcome of an habitual imputation of causal sequence, or, perhaps better, an imputation of mechanical continuity, if a new term be permitted. The agent, thing, fact, event, or phenomenon, to which propensity, will-power, or purpose, is imputed, is always apprehended to act in an environment which is accepted as spiritually inert. There are always opaque facts as well as self-directing agents. Any agent acts through means which lend themselves to his use on other grounds than that of spiritual compulsion, although spiritual compulsion may be a large feature in any given case.

The same features of human thinking, the same two complementary methods of correlating facts and handling them for the purposes of knowledge, are similarly in constant evidence in the daily life of men in our own community. The question is, in great part, which of the two bears the greater part in shaping human knowledge at any given time and within any given range of knowledge or of facts.

Other features of the growth of knowledge, which are remoter from the point under inquiry, may be of no less consequence to a comprehensive theory of the development of culture and of thought; but it is of course out of the question here to go farther afield. The present inquiry will have enough to do with these two. No other features are correlative with these, and these merit discussion on account of their intimate bearing on the point of view of economics. The point of interest with respect to these two correlative and complementary habits of thought is the question of how they have fared under the changing exigencies of human culture; in what manner they come, under given cultural circumstances, to share the field of knowledge between them; what is the relative part of each in the composite point of view in which the two habits of thought express themselves at any given cultural stage.

The animistic preconception enforces the apprehension of phenomena in terms generically identical with the terms of personality or individuality. As a certain modern group of psychologists would say, it imputes to objects and sequences an element of habit and attention similar in kind, though not necessarily in degree, to the like spiritual attitude present in the activities of a personal agent. The matter-of-fact preconception, on the other hand, enforces a handling of facts without imputation of personal force or attention, but with an imputation of mechanical continuity, substantially the preconception which has reached a formulation at the hands of scientists under the name of conservation of energy or persistence of quantity. Some appreciable resort to the latter method of knowledge is unavoidable at any cultural stage, for it is indispensable to all industrial efficiency. All technological processes and all mechanical contrivances rest, psychologically speaking, on this ground. This habit of thought is a selectively necessary consequence of industrial life, and, indeed, of all human experience in making use of the material means of life. It should therefore follow that, in a general way, the higher the culture, the greater the share of the mechanical preconception in shaping human thought and knowledge, since, in a general way, the stage of culture attained depends on the efficiency of industry. The rule, while it does not hold with anything like extreme generality, must be admitted to hold to a good extent; and to that extent it should hold also that, by a selective adaptation of men's habits of thought to the exigencies of those cultural phases that have actually supervened, the mechanical method of knowledge should have gained in scope and range. Something of the sort is borne out by observation.

A further consideration enforces the like view. As the community increases in size, the range of observation of the individuals in the community also increases; and continually wider and more far-reaching sequences of a mechanical kind have to be taken account of. Men have to adapt their own motives to industrial processes that are not safely to be construed in terms of propensity, predilection, or passion. Life in an advanced industrial community does not tolerate a neglect of mechanical fact; for the mechanical sequences through which men, at an appreciable degree of culture, work out their livelihood, are no respecters of persons or of will-power. Still, on all but the higher industrial stages, the coercive discipline of industrial life, and of the scheme of life that inculcates regard for the mechanical facts of industry, is greatly mitigated by the largely haphazard character of industry, and by the great extent to which man continues to be the prime mover in industry. So long as industrial efficiency is chiefly a matter of the handicraftsman's skill, dexterity, and diligence, the attention of men in looking to the industrial process is met by the figure of the workman, as the chief and characteristic factor; and thereby it comes to run on the personal element in industry.

But, with or without mitigation, the scheme of life

which men perforce adopt under the exigencies of an advanced industrial situation shapes their habits of thought on the side of their behavior, and thereby shapes their habits of thought to some extent for all purposes. Each individual is but a single complex of habits of thought, and the same psychical mechanism that expresses itself in one direction as conduct expresses itself in another direction as knowledge. The habits of thought formed in the one connection, in response to stimuli that call for a response in terms of conduct, must, therefore, have their effect when the same individual comes to respond to stimuli that call for a response in terms of knowledge. The scheme of thought or of knowledge is in good part a reverberation of the scheme of life. So that, after all has been said, it remains true that with the growth of industrial organization and efficiency there must, by selection and by adaptation, supervene a greater resort to the mechanical or dispassionate method of apprehending facts.

But the industrial side of life is not the whole of it, nor does the scheme of life in vogue in any community or at any cultural stage comprise industrial conduct alone. The social, civic, military, and religious interests come in for their share of attention, and between them they commonly take up by far the larger share of it. Especially is this true so far as concerns those classes among whom we commonly look for a cultivation of knowledge for knowledge's sake. The discipline which these several interests exert does not commonly coincide with the training given by industry. So the religious interest, with its canons of truth and of right living, runs exclusively on personal relations and the adaptation of conduct to the predilections of a superior personal agent. The weight of its discipline, therefore, falls wholly on the animistic side. It acts to heighten our appreciation of the spiritual bearing of phenomena and to discountenance a matter-of-fact apprehension of things. The sceptic of the type of Hume has never been in good repute with those who stand closest to the accepted religious truths. The bearing of this side of our culture upon the development of economics is shown by what the mediæval scholars had to say on economic topics.

The disciplinary effects of other phases of life, outside of the industrial and the religious, is not so simple a matter; but the discussion here approaches nearer to the point of immediate inquiry,— namely, the cultural situation in the eighteenth century, and its relation to economic speculation,— and this ground of interest in the question may help to relieve the topic of the tedium that of right belongs to it.

In the remoter past of which we have records, and even in the more recent past, Occidental man, as well as man elsewhere, has eminently been a respecter of persons. Wherever the warlike activity has been a large feature of the community's life, much of human conduct in society has proceeded on a regard for personal force. The scheme of life has been a scheme of personal aggression and subservience, partly in the naïve form, partly conventionalized in a system of status. The discipline of social life for the present purpose, in so far as its canons of conduct rest on this element of personal force in the unconventionalized form, plainly tends to the formation of a habit of apprehending and co-ordinating facts from the animistic point of view. So far as we have to do with life under a system of status, the like remains true, but with a difference. The régime of status inculcates an unremitting and very nice discrimination and observance of distinctions of personal superiority and inferiority. To the criterion of personal force, or will-power, taken in its immediate bearing on conduct, is added the criterion of personal excellence-in-general, regardless of the first-hand potency of the given person as an agent. This criterion of conduct requires a constant and painstaking imputation of personal value, regardless of fact. The discrimination enjoined by the canons of status proceeds on an invidious comparison of persons in respect of worth, value, potency, virtue, which must, for the present purpose, be taken as putative. The greater or less personal value assigned a given individual or a given class under the canons of status is not assigned on the ground of visible efficiency, but on the ground of a dogmatic allegation accepted on the strength of an uncontradicted categorical affirmation simply. The canons of status hold their ground by force of pre-emption. Where distinctions of status are based on a putative worth transmitted by descent from honorable antecedents, the sequence of transmission to which appeal is taken as the arbiter of honor is of a putative and animistic character rather than a visible mechanical continuity. The habit of accepting as final what is prescriptively right in the affairs of life has as its reflex in the affairs of knowledge the formula, *Quid ab omnibus, quid ubique creditur credendum est.*

Even this meagre account of the scheme of life that characterizes a régime of status should serve to indicate what is its disciplinary effect in shaping habits of thought, and therefore in shaping the habitual criteria of knowledge and of reality. A culture whose institutions are a framework of invidious comparisons implies, or rather involves and comprises, a scheme of knowledge whose definitive standards of truth and substantiality are of an animistic character; and, the more undividedly the canons of status and ceremonial honor govern the conduct of the community, the greater the facility with which the sequence of cause and effect is made to yield before the higher claims of a spiritual sequence or guidance in the course of events. Men consistently trained to an unremitting discrimination of honor, worth, and personal force in their daily conduct, and to whom these criteria afford the definitive ground of sufficiency in co-ordinating facts for the purposes of life, will not be satisfied to fall short of the like definitive ground of sufficiency when they come to co-ordinate facts for the purposes of knowledge simply. The habits formed in unfolding his activity in one direction, under the impulse of a given interest, assert themselves when the individual comes to unfold his activity in any other direction, under the impulse of any other interest. If his last resort and highest criterion of truth in conduct is afforded by the element of personal force and invidious comparison, his sense of substantiality or truth in the quest of knowledge will be satisfied only when a like definitive ground of animistic force and invidious comparison is reached. But when such ground is reached he rests content and pushes the inquiry no farther. In his practical life he has acquired the habit of resting his case on an authentic deliverance as to what is absolutely right. This absolutely right and good final term in conduct has the character of finality only when conduct is construed in a ceremonial sense; that is to say, only when life is conceived as a scheme of conformity to a purpose outside and beyond the process of living. Under the régime of status this ceremonial finality is found in the concept of worth or honor. In the religious domain it is the concept of virtue, sanctity, or tabu. Merit lies in what one is, not in what one does. The habit of appeal to ceremonial finality, formed in the school of status, goes with the individual in his quest of knowledge, as a dependence upon a similarly authentic norm of absolute truth,—a similar seeking of a final term outside and beyond the range of knowledge.

The discipline of social and civic life under a régime of status, then, re-enforces the discipline of the religious life; and the outcome of the resulting habituation is that the canons of knowledge are cast in the animistic mould and converge to a ground of absolute truth, and this absolute truth is of a ceremonial nature. Its subject-matter is a reality regardless of fact.

The outcome, for science, of the religious and social life of the civilization of status, in Occidental culture, was a structure of quasi-spiritual appreciations and explanations, of which astrology, alchemy, and mediæval theology and metaphysics are competent, though somewhat one-sided, exponents. Throughout the range of this early learning the ground of correlation of phenomena is in part the supposed relative potency of the facts correlated; but it is also in part a scheme of status, in which facts are scheduled according to a hierarchical gradation of worth or merit, having only a ceremonial relation to the observed phenomena. Some elements (some metals, for instance) are noble, others base; some planets, on grounds of ceremonial efficacy, have a sinister influence, others a beneficent one; and it is a matter of serious consequence whether they are in the ascendant, and so on.

The body of learning through which the discipline of animism and invidious comparison transmitted its effects to the science of economics was what is known as natural theology, natural rights, moral philosophy, and natural law. These several disciplines or bodies of knowledge had wandered far from the naïve animistic standpoint at the time when economic science emerged, and much the same is true as regards the time of the emergence of other modern sciences. But the discipline which makes for an animistic formulation of knowledge continued to hold the primacy in modern culture, although its dominion was never altogether undivided or unmitigated. Occidental culture has long been largely an industrial culture; and, as already pointed out, the discipline of industry, and of life in an industrial community, does not favor the animistic preconception. This is especially true as regards industry which makes large use of mechanical contrivances. The difference in these respects between Occidental industry and science, on the one hand, and the industry and science of other cultural regions, on the other hand, is worth noting in this connection. The result has been that the sciences, as that word is understood in later usage, have come forward gradually, and in a certain rough parallelism with the development of industrial processes and industrial organization. It is possible to hold that both modern industry (of the mechanical sort) and modern science centre about the region of the North Sea. It is still more palpably true that within this general area the sciences, in the recent past, show a family likeness to the civil and social institutions of the communities in which they have been cultivated, this being true to the greatest extent of the higher or speculative sciences; that is, in that range of knowledge in which the animistic preconception can chiefly and most effectively find application. There is, for instance, in the eighteenth century a perceptible parallelism between the divergent character of British and Continental culture and institutions, on the one hand, and the dissimilar aims of British and Continental speculation, on the other hand.

Something has already been said of the difference in preconceptions between the French and the British economists of the eighteenth century. It remains to point out the correlative cultural difference between the two communities, to which it is conceived that the difference in scientific animus is in great measure due. It is, of course, only the general features, the general attitude of the speculators, that can be credited to the difference in culture. Differences of detail in the specific doctrines held could be explained only on a much more detailed analysis than can be entered on here, and after taking account of facts which cannot here be even allowed for in detail.

Aside from the greater resort to mechanical contrivances and the larger scale of organization in British industry, the further cultural peculiarities of the British community run in the same general direction. British religious life and beliefs had less of the element of fealty — personal or discretionary mastery and subservience — and more of a tone of fatalism. The civil institutions of the British had not the same rich personal content as those of the French. The British subject owned allegiance to an impersonal law rather than to the person of a superior. Relatively, it may be said that the sense of status, as a coercive factor, was in abeyance in the British community. Even in the warlike enterprise of the British community a similar characteristic is traceable. Warfare is, of course, a matter of personal assertion. Warlike communities and classes are necessarily given to construing facts in terms of personal force and personal ends. They are always superstitious. They are great sticklers for rank and precedent, and zealously cultivate those distinctions and ceremonial observances in which a system of status expresses itself. But, while warlike enterprise has by no means been absent from the British scheme of life, the geographical and strategic isolation of the British community has given a characteristic turn to their military relations. In recent times British warlike operations have been conducted abroad. The military class has consequently in great measure been segregated out from the body of the community, and the ideals and prejudices of the class have not been transfused through the general body with the same facility and effect that they might otherwise have had. The British community at home has seen the campaign in great part from the standpoint of the "sinews of war."

The outcome of all these national peculiarities of circumstance and culture has been that a different scheme of life has been current in the British community from what has prevailed on the Continent. There has resulted the formation of a different body of habits of thought and a different animus in their handling of facts. The preconception of causal sequence has been allowed larger scope in the correlation of facts for purposes of knowledge; and, where the animistic preconception has been resorted to, as it always has in the profounder reaches of learning, it has commonly been an animism of a tamer kind.

Taking Adam Smith as an exponent of this British attitude in theoretical knowledge, it is to be noted that, while he formulates his knowledge in terms of a propensity (natural laws) working teleologically to an end, the end or objective point which controls the formulation has not the same rich content of vital human interest or advantage as is met with in the Physiocratic speculations. There is perceptibly less of an imperious tone in Adam Smith's natural laws than in those of the contemporary French economists. It is true, he sums up the institutions with which he deals in terms of the ends which they should subserve, rather than in terms of the exigencies and habits of life out of which they have arisen; but he does not with the same tone of finality appeal to the end subserved as a final cause through whose coercive guidance the complex of phenomena is kept to its appointed task. Under his hands the restraining, compelling agency retires farther into the background, and appeal is taken to it neither so directly nor on so slight provocation.

But Adam Smith is too large a figure to be disposed of in a couple of concluding paragraphs. At the same time his work and the bent which he gave to economic speculation are so intimately bound up with the aims and bias that characterize economics in its next stage of development that he is best dealt with as the point of departure for the Classical School rather than merely as a British counterpart of Physiocracy. Adam Smith will accordingly be considered in immediate connection with the bias of the classical school and the incursion of utilitarianism into economics.

THORSTEIN VEBLEN.

THE UNIVERSITY OF CHICAGO.

THE PRECONCEPTIONS OF ECONOMIC SCIENCE.

II.

ADAM SMITH'S animistic bent asserts itself more plainly and more effectually in the general trend and aim of his discussion than in the details of theory. "Adam Smith's *Wealth of Nations* is, in fact, so far as it has one single purpose, a vindication of the unconscious law present in the separate actions of men when these actions are directed by a certain strong personal motive." * Both in the *Theory of the Moral Sentiments* and in the *Wealth of Nations* there are many passages that testify to his abiding conviction that there is a wholesome trend in the natural course of things, and the characteristically optimistic tone in which he speaks for natural liberty is but an expression of this conviction. An extreme resort to this animistic ground occurs in his plea for freedom of investment.†

In the proposition that men are "led by an invisible hand," Smith does not fall back on a meddling Providence who is to set human affairs straight when they are in danger of going askew. He conceives the Creator to be very continent in the matter of interference with the natural course of things. The Creator has established

* Bonar, *Philosophy and Political Economy*, pp. 177, 178.

† "Every individual is continually exerting himself to find out the most advantageous employment for whatever capital he can command. It is his own advantage, and not that of the society, which he has in view. But the study of his own advantage naturally, or rather necessarily, leads him to prefer that employment which is most advantageous to the society. . . . By directing that industry in such a manner as its produce may be of the greatest value, he intends only his own gain; and he is in this, as in many other cases, led by an invisible hand to promote an end which was no part of his intention. Nor is it always the worse for society that it was no part of it. By pursuing his own interest he frequently promotes that of the society more effectually than when he really intends to promote it." *Wealth of Nations*, Book IV. chap. ii.

the natural order to serve the ends of human welfare; and he has very nicely adjusted the efficient causes comprised in the natural order, including human aims and motives, to this work that they are to accomplish. The guidance of the invisible hand takes place not by way of interposition, but through a comprehensive scheme of contrivances established from the beginning. For the purpose of economic theory, man is conceived to be consistently self-seeking; but this economic man is a part of the mechanism of nature, and his self-seeking traffic is but a means whereby, in the natural course of things, the general welfare is worked out. The scheme as a whole is guided by the end to be reached, but the sequence of events through which the end is reached is a causal sequence which is not broken into episodically. The benevolent work of guidance was performed in first establishing an ingenious mechanism of forces and motives capable of accomplishing an ordained result, and nothing beyond the enduring constraint of an established trend remains to enforce the divine purpose in the resulting natural course of things.

The sequence of events, including human motives and human conduct, is a causal sequence; but it is also something more, or, rather, there is also another element of continuity besides that of brute cause and effect, present even in the step-by-step process whereby the natural course of things reaches its final term. The presence of such a quasi-spiritual or non-causal element is evident from two (alleged) facts. (1) The course of things may be deflected from the direct line of approach to that consummate human welfare which is its legitimate end. The natural trend of things may be overborne by an untoward conjuncture of causes. There is a distinction, often distressingly actual and persistent, between the legitimate and the observed course of things. If "natural," in Adam Smith's use, meant necessary, in the sense of causally determined, no divergence of events from the natural or legitimate course of things would be possible. If the mechanism of nature, including man, were a mechanically competent contrivance for achieving the great artificer's design, there could be no such episodes of blundering and perverse departure from the direct path as Adam Smith finds in nearly all existing arrangements. Institutional facts would then be "natural." * (2) When things have gone wrong, they will right themselves if interference with the natural course ceases; whereas, in the case of a causal sequence simply, the mere cessation of interference will not leave the outcome the same as if no interference had taken place. This recuperative power of nature is of an extra-mechanical character. The continuity of sequence by force of which the natural course of things prevails is, therefore, not of the nature of cause and effect, since it bridges intervals and interruptions in the causal sequence.† Adam Smith's use of the term "real" in statements of theory — as, for example, "real value," "real price" ‡ — is evidence to this effect. "Natural" commonly has the same meaning as "real" in this connection.§ Both "natural" and "real" are placed in contrast with the actual; and, in Adam Smith's apprehension, both have a substantiality

* The discrepancy between the actual, causally determined situation and the divinely intended consummation is the metaphysical ground of all that inculcation of morality and enlightened policy that makes up so large a part of Adam Smith's work. The like, of course, holds true for all moralists and reformers who proceed on the assumption of a providential order.

† "In the political body, however, the wisdom of nature has fortunately made ample provision for remedying many of the bad effects of the folly and injustice of man; in the same manner as it has done in the natural body, for remedying those of his sloth and intemperance." *Wealth of Nations*, Book IV. chap. ix.

‡ *E.g.*, "the real measure of the exchangeable value of all commodities." *Wealth of Nations*, Book I. chap. v., and repeatedly in the like connection.

§ *E.g.*, Book I. chap. vii.: "When the price of any commodity is neither more nor less than what is sufficient to pay the rent of the land, the wages of the labor, and the profits of the stock employed in raising, preparing, and different from and superior to facts. The view involves a distinction between reality and fact, which survives in a weakened form in the theories of "normal" prices, wages, profits, costs, in Adam Smith's successors.

This animistic prepossession seems to pervade the earlier of his two monumental works in a greater degree than the latter. In the *Moral Sentiments* recourse is had to the teleological ground of the natural order more freely and with perceptibly greater insistence. There seems to be reason for holding that the animistic preconception weakened or, at any rate, fell more into the background as his later work of speculation and investigation proceeded. The change shows itself also in some details of his economic theory, as first set forth in the *Lectures*, and afterwards more fully developed in the *Wealth of Nations*. So, for instance, in the earlier presentation of the matter, "the division of labor is the immediate cause of opulence"; and this division of labor, which is the chief condition of economic well-being, "flows from a direct propensity in human nature for one man to barter with another." * The "propensity" in question is here appealed to as a natural endowment immediately given to man with a view to the welfare of human society, and without any attempt at further explanation of how man has come by it. No causal explanation of its presence or character is offered. But the corresponding passage of the *Wealth of Nations* handles the question more cautiously.† Other parallel passages might be compared with much the same effect. The

bringing it to market, according to their *natural* rates, the commodity is then sold for what may be called its *natural* price." "The actual price at which any commodity is commonly sold is called its market price. It may be either above or below or exactly the same with its natural price."

† *Lectures of Adam Smith* (Ed. Cannan, 1896), p. 169.

† "This division of labor, from which so many advantages are derived, is not originally the effect of any human wisdom, which foresees and intends that general opulence to which it gives occasion. It is the necessary though

guiding hand has withdrawn farther from the range of human vision.

However, these and other like filial expressions of a devout optimism need, perhaps, not be taken as integral features of Adam Smith's economic theory, or as seriously affecting the character of his work as an economist. They are the expression of his general philosophical and theological views, and are significant for the present purpose chiefly as evidences of an animistic and optimistic bent. They go to show what is Adam Smith's accepted ground of finality,— the ground to which all his speculations on human affairs converge; but they do not in any great degree show the teleological bias guiding the formulation of economic theory in detail.

The effective working of the teleological bias is best seen in Smith's more detailed handling of economic phenomena — in his discussion of what may loosely be called economic institutions — and in the criteria and principles of procedure by which he is guided in incorporating these features of economic life into the general structure of his theory. A fair instance, though perhaps not the most telling one, is the discussion of the "real and nominal price," and of the "natural and market price" of commodities, already referred to above.* The "real" price of commodities is their value in terms of human life. At this point Smith differs from the Physiocrats, with whom the ultimate terms of value are afforded by human sustenance taken as a product of the functioning of brute nature; the cause of the difference being that the Physiocrats conceived the natural order which works towards

very slow and gradual consequence of a certain propensity in human nature which has in view no such extensive utility,— the propensity to truck, barter, and exchange one thing for another. Whether this propensity be one of those original principles in human nature of which no further account can be given, or whether, as seems more probable, it be the necessary consequence of the faculties of reason and speech, it belongs not to our present subject to inquire." *Wealth of Nations*, Book I. chap. ii.

* *Wealth of Nations*, Book I. chaps. v.–vii.

the material well-being of man to comprise the non-human environment only, whereas Adam Smith includes man in this concept of the natural order, and, indeed, makes him the central figure in the process of production. With the Physiocrats, production is the work of nature: with Adam Smith, it is the work of man and nature, with man in the foreground. In Adam Smith, therefore, labor is the final term in valuation. This "real" value of commodities is the value imputed to them by the economist under the stress of his teleological preconception. It has little, if any, place in the course of economic events, and no bearing on human affairs, apart from the sentimental influence which such a preconception in favor of a "real value" in things may exert upon men's notions of what is the good and equitable course to pursue in their transactions. It is impossible to gauge this real value of goods; it cannot be measured or expressed in concrete terms. Still, if labor exchanges for a varying quantity of goods, "it is their value which varies, not that of the labor which purchases them." * The values which practically attach to goods in men's handling of them are conceived to be determined without regard to the real value which Adam Smith imputes to the goods; but, for all that, the substantial fact with respect to these market values is their presumed approximation to the real values teleologically imputed to the goods under the guidance of inviolate natural laws. The real, or natural, value of articles has no causal relation to the value at which they exchange. The discussion of how values are determined in practice runs on the motives of the buyers and sellers, and the relative advantage enjoyed by the parties to the transaction.† It is a discussion of a process of valuation, quite unrelated to the "real," or "natural," price of things, and

* *Wealth of Nations*, Book I. chap. v.

† As, *e.g.*, the entire discussion of the determination of Wages, Profits, and Rent, in Book I. chaps. viii.-xi.

quite unrelated to the grounds on which things are held to come by their real, or natural, price; and yet, when the complex process of valuation has been traced out in terms of human motives and the exigencies of the market, Adam Smith feels that he has only cleared the ground. He then turns to the serious business of accounting for value and price theoretically, and making the ascertained facts articulate with his teleological theory of economic life.*

The occurrence of the words "ordinary" and "average" in this connection need not be taken too seriously. The context makes it plain that the equality which commonly subsists between the ordinary or average rates, and the natural rates, is a matter of coincidence, not of identity. Not only are there temporary deviations, but there may be a permanent divergence between the ordinary and the natural price of a commodity; as in case of a monopoly or of produce grown under peculiar circumstances of soil or climate.†

The natural price coincides with the price fixed by competition, because competition means the unimpeded play of those efficient forces through which the nicely adjusted mechanism of nature works out the design to accomplish which it was contrived. The natural price is reached through the free interplay of the factors of

* "There is in every society or neighborhood an ordinary or average rate both of wages and profit in every different employment of labor and stock. This rate is naturally regulated, . . . partly by the general circumstances of the society. . . . There is, likewise, in every society or neighborhood an ordinary or average rate of rent, which is regulated, too. . . . These ordinary or average rates may be called the natural rates of wages, profit, and rent, at the time and place in which they commonly prevail. When the price of any commodity is neither more nor less than what is sufficient to pay the rent of the land, the wages of the labor, and the profits of the stock employed in raising, preparing, and bringing it to market, according to their natural rates, the commodity is then sold for what may be called its natural price." *Wealth of Nations*, Book I. chap. vii.

† "Such commodities may continue for whole centuries together to be sold at this high price; and that part of it which resolves itself into the rent of land is, in this case, the part which is generally paid above its natural rate." Book I. chap. vii.

production, and it is itself an outcome of production. Nature, including the human factor, works to turn out the goods; and the natural value of the goods is their appraisement from the standpoint of this productive process of nature. Natural value is a category of production: whereas, notoriously, exchange value or market price is a category of distribution. And Adam Smith's theoretical handling of market price aims to show how the factors of human predilection and human wants at work in the higgling of the market bring about a result in passable consonance with the natural laws that are conceived to govern production.

The natural price is a composite result of the blending of the three "component parts of the price of commodities,"—the natural wages of laborer, the natural profits of stock, and the natural rent of land; and each of these three components is in its turn the measure of the productive effect of the factor to which it pertains. The further discussion of these shares in distribution aims to account for the facts of distribution on the ground of the productivity of the factors which are held to share the product between them. That is to say, Adam Smith's preconception of a productive natural process as the basis of his economic theory dominates his aims and procedure, when he comes to deal with phenomena that cannot be stated in terms of production. The causal sequence in the process of distribution is, by Adam Smith's own showing, unrelated to the causal sequence in the process of production; but, since the latter is the substantial fact, as viewed from the standpoint of a teleological natural order, the former must be stated in terms of the latter before Adam Smith's sense of substantiality, or "reality," is satisfied. Something of the same kind is, of course, visible in the Physiocrats and in Cantillon. It amounts to an extension of the natural-rights preconception to economic theory. Adam Smith's discussion of distribution as a function of productivity might be traced in detail through his handling of Wages, Profits, and Rent; but, since the aim here is a brief characterization only, and not an exposition, no farther pursuit of this point seems feasible.

It may, however, be worth while to point out another line of influence along which the dominance of the teleological preconception shows itself in Adam Smith. This is the normalization of data, in order to bring them into consonance with an orderly course of approach to the putative natural end of economic life and development. The result of this normalization of data is, on the one hand, the use of what James Steuart calls "conjectural history" in dealing with past phases of economic life, and, on the other hand, a statement of present-day phenomena in terms of what legitimately ought to be according to the God-given end of life rather than in terms of unconstrued observation. Account is taken of the facts (supposed or observed) ostensibly in terms of causal sequence, but the imputed causal sequence is construed to run on lines of teleological legitimacy.

A familiar instance of this "conjectural history," in a highly and effectively normalized form, is the account of "that early and rude state of society which precedes both the accumulation of stock and the appropriation of land." * It is needless at this day to point out that this "early and rude state," in which "the whole produce of labor belongs to the laborer," is altogether a figment. The whole narrative, from the putative origin down, is not only supposititious, but it is merely a schematic presentation of what should have been the course of past development, in order to lead up to that ideal economic situation which would satisfy Adam Smith's preconception.† As the narrative comes nearer the region of

* *Wealth of Nations*, Book I. chap. vi.; also chap. viii.

† For an instance of how these early phases of industrial development appear, when not seen in the light of Adam Smith's preconception, see, among others, Bücher, *Entstehung der Volkswirtschaft*.

known latter-day facts, the normalization of the data becomes more difficult and receives more detailed attention; but the change in method is a change of degree rather than of kind. In the "early and rude state" the coincidence of the "natural" and the actual course of events is immediate and undisturbed, there being no refractory data at hand; but in the later stages and in the present situation, where refractory facts abound, the co-ordination is difficult, and the coincidence can be shown only by a free abstraction from phenomena that are irrelevant to the teleological trend and by a laborious interpretation of the rest. The facts of modern life are intricate, and lend themselves to statement in the terms of the theory only after they have been subjected to a "higher criticism."

The chapter "Of the Origin and Use of Money" * is an elegantly normalized account of the origin and nature of an economic institution, and Adam Smith's further discussion of money runs on the same lines. The origin of money is stated in terms of the purpose which money should legitimately serve in such a community as Adam Smith considered right and good, not in terms of the motives and exigencies which have resulted in the use of money and in the gradual rise of the existing method of payment and accounts. Money is "the great wheel of circulation," which effects the transfer of goods in process of production and the distribution of the finished goods to the consumers. It is an organ of the economic commonwealth rather than an expedient of accounting and a conventional repository of wealth.

It is perhaps superfluous to remark that to the "plain man," who is not concerned with the "natural course of things" in a consummate *Geldwirtschaft*, the money that passes his hand is not a "great wheel of circulation." To the Samoyed, for instance, the reindeer which serves him

* Book I. chap. iv.

as unit of value is wealth in the most concrete and tangible form. Much the same is true of coin, or even of bank-notes, in the apprehension of unsophisticated people among ourselves to-day. And yet it is in terms of the habits and conditions of life of these "plain people" that the development of money will have to be accounted for if it is to be stated in terms of cause and effect.

The few scattered passages already cited may serve to illustrate how Adam Smith's animistic or teleological bent shapes the general structure of his theory and gives it consistency. The principle of definitive formulation in Adam Smith's economic knowledge is afforded by a putative purpose that does not at any point enter causally into the economic life process which he seeks to know. This formative or normative purpose or end is not freely conceived to enter as an efficient agent in the events discussed, or to be in any way consciously present in the process. It can scarcely be taken as an animistic agency engaged in the process. It sanctions the course of things, and gives legitimacy and substance to the sequence of events, so far as this sequence may be made to square with the requirements of the imputed end. It has therefore a ceremonial or symbolical force only, and lends the discussion a ceremonial competency; although with economists who have been in passable agreement with Adam Smith as regards the legitimate end of economic life this ceremonial consistency, or consistency *de jure*, has for many purposes been accepted as the formulation of a causal continuity in the phenomena that have been interpreted in its terms. Elucidations of what normally ought to happen, as a matter of ceremonial necessity, have in this way come to pass for an account of matters of fact.

But, as has already been pointed out, there is much more to Adam Smith's exposition of theory than a formulation of what ought to be. Much of the advance he achieved over his predecessors consists in a larger and more painstaking scrutiny of facts, and a more consistent tracing out of causal continuity in the facts handled. No doubt, his superiority over the Physiocrats, that characteristic of his work by virtue of which it superseded theirs in the farther growth of economic science, lies to some extent in his recourse to a different, more modern ground of normality,— a ground more in consonance with the body of preconceptions that have had the vogue in later generations. It is a shifting of the point of view from which the facts are handled; but it comes in great part to a substitution of a new body of preconceptions for the old, or a new adaptation of the old ground of finality, rather than an elimination of all metaphysical or animistic norms of valuation. With Adam Smith, as with the Physiocrats, the fundamental question, the answer to which affords the point of departure and the norm of procedure, is a question of substantiality or economic "reality." With both, the answer to this question is given naively, as a deliverance of common sense. Neither is disturbed by doubts as to this deliverance of common sense or by any need of scrutinizing it. To the Physiocrats this substantial ground of economic reality is the nutritive process of Nature. To Adam Smith it is Labor. His reality has the advantage of being the deliverance of the common sense of a more modern community, and one that has maintained itself in force more widely and in better consonance with the facts of latter-day industry. The Physiocrats owe their preconception of the productiveness of nature to the habits of thought of a community in whose economic life the dominant phenomenon was the owner of agricultural land. Adam Smith owes his preconception in favor of labor to a community in which the obtrusive economic feature of the immediate past was handicraft and agriculture, with commerce as a scarcely secondary phenomenon.

So far as Adam Smith's economic theories are a tracing out of the causal sequence in economic phenomena, they are worked out in terms given by these two main directions of activity,— human effort directed to the shaping of the material means of life, and human effort and discretion directed to a pecuniary gain. The former is the great, substantial productive force: the latter is not immediately, or proximately, productive.* Adam Smith still has too lively a sense of the nutritive purpose of the order of nature freely to extend the concept of productiveness to any activity that does not yield a material increase of the creature comforts. His instinctive appreciation of the substantial virtue of whatever effectually furthers nutrition, even leads him into the concession that "in agriculture nature labors along with man," although the general tenor of his argument is that the productive force with which the economist always has to count is human labor. This recognized substantiality of labor as productive is, as has already been remarked, accountable for his effort to reduce to terms of productive labor such a category of distribution as exchange value.

With but slight qualification, it will hold that, in the causal sequence which Adam Smith traces out in his economic theories proper (contained in the first three books of the *Wealth of Nations*), the causally efficient factor is conceived to be human nature in these two relations,— of productive efficiency and pecuniary gain through exchange. Pecuniary gain — gain in the material means of life through barter — furnishes the motive force to the economic activity of the individual; although productive efficiency is the legitimate, normal end of the community's economic life. To such an extent does this concept of man's seeking his ends through "truck, barter, and exchange" pervade Adam Smith's treatment of eco-

* See *Wealth of Nations*, Book II. chap. v., "Of the Different Employment of Capitals."

nomic processes that he even states production in its terms, and says that "labor was the first price, the original purchase-money, that was paid for all things." * The human nature engaged in this pecuniary traffic is conceived in somewhat hedonistic terms, and the motives and movements of men are normalized to fit the requirements of a hedonistically conceived order of nature. Men are very much alike in their native aptitudes and propensities; † and, so far as economic theory need take account of these aptitudes and propensities, they are aptitudes for the production of the "necessaries and conveniences of life," and propensities to secure as great a share of these creature comforts as may be.

Adam Smith's conception of normal human nature — that is to say, the human factor which enters causally in the process which economic theory discusses — comes, on the whole, to this: Men exert their force and skill in a mechanical process of production, and their pecuniary sagacity in a competitive process of distribution, with a view to individual gain in the material means of life. These material means are sought in order to the satisfaction of men's natural wants through their consumption. It is true, much else enters into men's endeavors in the struggle for wealth, as Adam Smith points out; but this consumption comprises the legitimate range of incentives, and a theory which concerns itself with the natural course of things need take but incidental account of what does not come legitimately in the natural course. In point of fact, there are appreciable "actual," though scarcely "real," departures from this rule. They are spurious and insubstantial departures, and do not properly come

* *Wealth of Nations*, Book I. chap. v. See also the plea for free trade, Book IV. chap. ii.: "But the annual revenue of every society is always precisely equal to the exchangeable value of the whole annual produce of its industry, or, rather, is precisely the same thing with that exchangeable value."

† "The difference of natural talents in different men is in reality much les than we are aware of." *Wealth of Nations*, Book I. chap. ii.

within the purview of the stricter theory. And, since human nature is strikingly uniform, in Adam Smith's apprehension, both the efforts put forth and the consumptive effect accomplished may be put in quantitative terms and treated algebraically, with the result that the entire range of phenomena comprised under the head of consumption need be but incidentally considered; and the theory of production and distribution is complete when the goods or the values have been traced to their disappearance in the hands of their ultimate owners. The reflex effect of consumption upon production and distribution is, on the whole, quantitative only.

Adam Smith's preconception of a normal teleological order of procedure in the natural course, therefore, affects not only those features of theory where he is avowedly concerned with building up a normal scheme of the economic process. Through his normalizing the chief causal factor engaged in the process, it affects also his arguments from cause to effect.* What makes this latter feature worth particular attention is the fact that his successors carried this normalization farther, and employed it with less frequent reference to the mitigating exceptions which Adam Smith notices by the way.

The reason for that farther and more consistent normalization of human nature which gives us the "economic man" at the hands of Adam Smith's successors lies, in great part, in the utilitarian philosophy that entered in force and in consummate form at about the turning of the century. Some credit in the work of normalization is due

* "Mit diesen philosophischen Ueberzeugungen tritt nun Adam Smith an die Welt der Enfahrung heran, und es ergiebt sich ihm die Richtigkeit der Principien. Der Reiz der Smith'schen Schriften beruht zum grossen Teile darauf, dass Smith die Principien in so innige Verbindung mit dem Thatsächlichen gebracht. Hie und da werden dann auch die Principien, was durch diese Verbindung veranlasst wird, an ihren Spitzen etwas abgeschliffen, ihre allzuscharfe Ausprägung dadurch vermieden. Nichtsdestoweniger aber bleiben sie stets die leitenden Grundgedanken." Richard Zeyss, *Adam Smith und der Eigennutz* (Tübingen, 1889), p. 110.

also to the farther supersession of handicraft by the "capitalistic" industry that came in at the same time and in pretty close relation with the utilitarian views.

After Adam Smith's day, economics fell into profane hands. Apart from Malthus, who, of all the greater economists, stands nearest to Adam Smith on such metaphysical heads as have an immediate bearing upon the premises of economic science, the next generation do not approach their subject from the point of view of a divinely instituted order; nor do they discuss human interests with that gently optimistic spirit of submission that belongs to the economist who goes to his work with the fear of God before his eyes. Even with Malthus the recourse to the divinely sanctioned order of nature is somewhat sparing and temperate. But it is significant for the later course of economic theory that, while Malthus may well be accounted the truest continuer of Adam Smith, it was the undevout utilitarians that became the spokesmen of the science after Adam Smith's time.

There is no wide breach between Adam Smith and the utilitarians, either in details of doctrine or in the concrete conclusions arrived at as regards questions of policy. On these heads Adam Smith might well be classed as a moderate utilitarian, particularly so far as regards his economic work. Malthus has still more of a utilitarian air,—so much so, indeed, that he is not infrequently spoken of as a utilitarian. This view, convincingly set forth by Mr. Bonar,* is no doubt well borne out by a detailed scrutiny of Malthus's economic doctrines. His humanitarian bias is evident throughout, and his weakness for considerations of expediency is the great blemish of his scientific work. But, for all that, in order to an appreciation of the change that came over classical economics with the

* See, *e.g.*, *Malthus and his Work*, especially Book III., as also the chapter on Malthus in *Philosophy and Political Economy*, Book III., Modern Philosophy: Utilitarian Economics, chap. i., "Malthus."

rise of Benthamism, it is necessary to note that the agreement in this matter between Adam Smith and the disciples of Bentham, and less decidedly that between Malthus and the latter, is a coincidence of conclusions rather than an identity of preconceptions.*

With Adam Smith the ultimate ground of economic reality is the design of God, the teleological order; and his utilitarian generalizations, as well as the hedonistic character of his economic man, are but methods of the working out of this natural order, not the substantial and self-legitimating ground. Shifty as Malthus's metaphysics are, much the same is to be said for him.† Of the utilitarians proper the converse is true, although here, again, there is by no means utter consistency. The substantial economic ground is pleasure and pain: the teleological order (even the design of God, where that is admitted) is the method of its working out.

It may be unnecessary here to go into the farther implications, psychological and ethical, which this preconception of the utilitarians involves. And even this much may seem a taking of excessive pains with a distinction that marks no tangible difference. But a reading of the classical doctrines, with something of this metaphysics of political economy in mind, will show how, and in great part why, the later economists of the classical line diverged from Adam Smith's tenets in the early years of the century, until it has been necessary to interpret Adam Smith somewhat shrewdly in order to save him from heresy.

The post-Bentham economics is substantially a theory of value. This is altogether the dominant feature of the

* Ricardo is here taken as a utilitarian of the Benthamite color, although he cannot be classed as a disciple of Bentham. His hedonism is but the uncritically accepted metaphysics comprised in the common sense of his time, and his substantial coincidence with Bentham goes to show how well diffused the hedonist preconception was at the time.

† *Cf.* Bonar, *Malthus and his Work*, pp. 323–336.

body of doctrines; the rest follows from, or is adapted to, this central discipline. The doctrine of value is of very great importance also in Adam Smith; but Adam Smith's economics is a theory of the production and apportionment of the material means of life.* With Adam Smith, value is discussed from the point of view of production. With the utilitarians, production is discussed from the point of view of value. The former makes value an outcome of the process of production: the latter makes production the outcome of a valuation process.

The point of departure with Adam Smith is the "productive power of labor." † With Ricardo it is a pecuniary problem concerned in the distribution of ownership; ‡ but the classical writers are followers of Adam Smith, and improve upon and correct the results arrived at by him, and the difference of point of view, therefore, becomes evident in their divergence from him, and the different distribution of emphasis, rather than in a new and antagonistic departure.

The reason for this shifting of the centre of gravity from production to valuation lies, proximately, in Bentham's revision of the "principles" of morals. Bentham's philosophical position is, of course, not a self-explanatory phenomenon, nor does the effect of Benthamism extend only to those who are avowed followers of Bentham; for Bentham is the exponent of a cultural change that affects the habits of thought of the entire community.

* His work is an inquiry into "the Nature and Causes of the Wealth of Nations."

† "The annual labor of every nation is the fund which originally supplies it with all the necessaries and conveniences of life which it annually consumes, and which consist always either in the immediate produce of that labor or in what is purchased with that produce from other nations." *Wealth of Nations*, "Introduction and Plan," opening paragraph.

‡ "The produce of the earth — all that is derived from its surface by the united application of labor, machinery, and capital — is divided among three classes of the community. . . . To determine the laws which regulate this distribution, is the principal problem of political economy." *Political Economy*, Preface.

The immediate point of Bentham's work, as affecting the habits of thought of the educated community, is the substitution of hedonism (utility) in place of achievement of purpose, as a ground of legitimacy and a guide in the normalization of knowledge. Its effect is most patent in speculations on morals, where it inculcates determinism. Its close connection with determinism in ethics points the way to what may be expected of its working in economics. In both cases the result is that human action is construed in terms of the causal forces of the environment, the human agent being, at the best, taken as a mechanism of commutation, through the workings of which the sensuous effects wrought by the impinging forces of the environment are, by an enforced process of valuation, transmuted without quantitative discrepancy into moral or economic conduct, as the case may be. In ethics and economics alike the subject-matter of the theory is this valuation process that expresses itself in conduct, resulting, in the case of economic conduct, in the pursuit of the greatest gain or least sacrifice.

Metaphysically or cosmologically considered, the human nature into the motions of which hedonistic ethics and economics inquire is an intermediate term in a causal sequence, of which the initial and the terminal members are sensuous impressions and the details of conduct. This intermediate term conveys the sensuous impulse without loss of force to its eventuation in conduct. For the purpose of the valuation process through which the impulse is so conveyed, human nature may, therefore, be accepted as uniform; and the theory of the valuation process may be formulated quantitatively, in terms of the material forces affecting the human sensory and of their equivalents in the resulting activity. In the language of economics, the theory of value may be stated in terms of the consumable goods that afford the incentive to effort and the expenditure undergone in order to procure them.

Between these two there subsists a necessary equality; but the magnitudes between which the equality subsists are hedonistic magnitudes, not magnitudes of kinetic energy nor of vital force, for the terms handled are sensuous terms. It is true, since human nature is substantially uniform, passive, and unalterable in respect of men's capacity for sensuous affection, there may also be presumed to subsist a substantial equality between the psychological effect to be wrought by the consumption of goods, on the one side, and the resulting expenditure of kinetic or vital force, on the other side; but such an equality is, after all, of the nature of a coincidence, although there should be a strong presumption in favor of its prevailing on an average and in the common run of cases. Hedonism, however, does not postulate uniformity between men except in the respect of sensuous cause and effect.

The theory of value which hedonism gives is, therefore, a theory of cost in terms of discomfort. By virtue of the hedonistic equilibrium reached through the valuation process, the sacrifice or expenditure of sensuous reality involved in acquisition is the equivalent of the sensuous gain secured. An alternative statement might perhaps be made, to the effect that the measure of the value of goods is not the sacrifice or discomfort undergone, but the sensuous gain that accrues from the acquisition of the goods; but this is plainly only an alternative statement, and there are special reasons in the economic life of the time why the statement in terms of cost, rather than in terms of "utility," should commend itself to the earlier classical economists.

On comparing the utilitarian doctrine of value with earlier theories, then, the case stands somewhat as follows. The Physiocrats and Adam Smith contemplate value as a measure of the productive force that realizes itself in the valuable article. With the Physiocrats this productive force is the "anabolism" of Nature (to resort to a physiological term): with Adam Smith it is chiefly human labor directed to heightening the serviceability of the materials with which it is occupied. Production causes value in either case. The post-Bentham economics contemplates value as a measure of, or as measured by, the irksomeness of the effort involved in procuring the valuable goods. As Mr. E. C. K. Gonner has admirably pointed out,* Ricardo — and the like holds true of classical economics generally — makes cost the foundation of value, not its cause. This resting of value on cost takes place through a valuation. Any one who will read Adam Smith's theoretical exposition to as good purpose as Mr. Gonner has read Ricardo will scarcely fail to find that the converse is true in Adam Smith's case. But the causal relation of cost to value holds only as regards "natural" or "real" value in Adam Smith's doctrine. As regards market price, Adam Smith's theory does not differ greatly from that of Ricardo on this head. He does not overlook the valuation process by which market price is adjusted and the course of investment is guided, and his discussion of this process runs in terms that should be acceptable to any hedonist.

The shifting of the point of view that comes into economics with the acceptance of utilitarian ethics and its correlate, the associationist psychology, is in great part a shifting to the ground of causal sequence as contrasted with that of serviceability to a preconceived end. This is indicated even by the main fact already cited,— that the utilitarian economists make exchange value the central feature of their theories, rather than the conduciveness of industry to the community's material welfare. Hedonistic exchange value is the outcome of a valuation process enforced by the apprehended pleasure-giving capacities of the items valued. And in the utilitarian

* In the introductory essay to his edition of Ricardo's *Political Economy*. See, *e.g.*, paragraphs 9 and 24.

theories of production, arrived at from the standpoint so given by exchange value, the conduciveness to welfare is not the objective point of the argument. This objective point is rather the bearing of productive enterprise upon the individual fortunes of the agents engaged, or upon the fortunes of the several distinguishable classes of beneficiaries comprised in the industrial community; for the great immediate bearing of exchange values upon the life of the collectivity is their bearing upon the distribution of wealth. Value is a category of distribution. The result is that, as is well shown by Mr. Cannan's discussion,* the theories of production offered by the classical economists have been sensibly scant, and have been carried out with a constant view to the doctrines on distribution. An incidental but telling demonstration of the same facts is given by Professor Bücher;† and in illustration may be cited Torrens's *Essay on the Production of Wealth*, which is to a good extent occupied with discussions of value and distribution. The classical theories of production have been theories of the production of "wealth"; and "wealth," in classical usage, consists of material things having exchange value. During the vogue of the classical economics the accepted characteristic by which "wealth" has been defined has been its amenability to ownership. Neither in Adam Smith nor in the Physiocrats is this amenability to ownership made so much of, nor is it in a similar degree accepted as a definite mark of the subject-matter of the science.

As their hedonistic preconception would require, then, it is to the pecuniary side of life that the classical economists give their most serious attention, and it is the pecuniary bearing of any given phenomenon or of any institution that commonly shapes the issue of the argu-

* *Theories of Production and Distribution*, 1776–1848.

† *Entstehung der Volkswirtschaft* (second edition). *Cf.* especially chaps. ii., iii., vi., and vii.

ment. The causal sequence about which the discussion centres is a process of pecuniary valuation. It runs on distribution, ownership, acquisition, gain, investment, exchange.* In this way the doctrines on production come to take a pecuniary coloring; as is seen in a less degree also in Adam Smith, and even in the Physiocrats, although these earlier economists very rarely, if ever, lose touch with the concept of generic serviceability as the characteristic feature of production. The tradition derived from Adam Smith, which made productivity and serviceability the substantial features of economic life, was not abruptly put aside by his successors, though the emphasis was differently distributed by them in following out the line of investigation to which the tradition pointed the way. In the classical economics the ideas of production and of acquisition are not commonly held apart, and very much of what passes for a theory of production is occupied with phenomena of investment and acquisition. Torrens's *Essay* is a case in point, though by no means an extreme case.

This is as it should be; for to the consistent hedonist the sole motive force concerned in the industrial process is the self-regarding motive of pecuniary gain, and industrial activity is but an intermediate term between the expenditure or discomfort undergone and the pecuniary gain sought. Whether the end and outcome is an invidious gain for the individual (in contrast with or at the cost of his neighbors), or an enhancement of the facility of human life on the whole, is altogether a by-question in any discussion of the range of incentives by which men are prompted to their work or the direction which their efforts take. The serviceability of the given line of activ-

* "Even if we put aside all questions which involve a consideration of the effects of industrial institutions in modifying the habits and character of the classes of the community, . . . that enough still remains to constitute a separate science, the mere enumeration of the chief terms of economics — wealth, value, exchange, credit money, capital, and commodity — will suffice to show." Shirres, *Analysis of the Ideas of Economics* (London, 1893), pp. 8 and 9.

ity, for the life purposes of the community or for one's neighbors, "is not of the essence of this contract." These features of serviceability come into the account chiefly as affecting the vendibility of what the given individual has to offer in seeking gain through a bargain.*

In hedonistic theory the substantial end of economic life is individual gain; and for this purpose production and acquisition may be taken as fairly coincident, if not identical. Moreover, society, in the utilitarian philosophy, is the algebraic sum of the individuals; and the interest of the society is the sum of the interests of the individuals. It follows by easy consequence, whether strictly true or not, that the sum of individual gains is the gain of the society, and that, in serving his own interest in the way of acquisition, the individual serves the collective interest of the community. Productivity or serviceability is, therefore, to be presumed of any occupation or enterprise that looks to a pecuniary gain; and so, by a roundabout path, we get back to the ancient conclusion of Adam Smith, that the remuneration of classes or persons engaged in industry coincides with their productive contribution to the output of services and consumable goods.

A felicitous illustration of the working of this hedonistic norm in classical economic doctrine is afforded by the theory of the wages of superintendence,—an element in distribution which is not much more than suggested in Adam Smith, but which receives ampler and more painstaking attention as the classical body of doctrines reaches a fuller development. The "wages of superintendence" are the gains due to pecuniary management. They are the gains that come to the director of the "business,"—not those that go to the director of the mechanical proc-

* "If a commodity were in no way useful, . . . it would be destitute of exchangeable value; . . . (but), possessing utility, commodities derive their exchangeable value from two sources," etc. Ricardo, *Political Economy*, chap. i. sect. 1.

ess or to the foreman of the shop. The latter are wages simply. This distinction is not altogether clear in the earlier writers, but it is clearly enough contained in the fuller development of the theory.

The undertaker's work is the management of investment. It is altogether of a pecuniary character, and its proximate aim is "the main chance." If it leads, indirectly, to an enhancement of serviceability or a heightened aggregate output of consumable goods, that is a fortuitous circumstance incident to that heightened vendibility on which the investor's gain depends. Yet the classical doctrine says frankly that the wages of superintendence are the remuneration of superior productivity,* and the classical theory of production is in good part a doctrine of investment in which the identity of production and pecuniary gain is taken for granted.

The substitution of investment in the place of industry as the central and substantial fact in the process of production is due not to the acceptance of hedonism simply, but rather to the conjunction of hedonism with an economic situation of which the investment of capital and its management for gain was the most obvious feature. The situation which shaped the common-sense apprehension of economic facts at the time was what has since been called a capitalistic system, in which pecuniary enterprise and the phenomena of the market were the dominant and tone-giving facts. But this economic situation was also the chief ground for the vogue of hedonism in economics; so that hedonistic economics may be taken as an interpretation of human nature in terms of the market-place. The market and the "business world," to which the busi-

* *Cf.*, for instance, Senior, *Political Economy* (London, 1872), particularly pp. 88, 89, and 130–135, where the wages of superintendence are, somewhat reluctantly, classed under profits; and the work of superintendence is thereupon conceived as being, immediately or remotely, an exercise of "abstinence" and a productive work. The illustration of the bill-broker is particularly apt. The like view of the wages of superintendence is an article of theory with more than one of the later descendants of the classical line.

ness man in his pursuit of gain was required to adapt his motives, had by this time grown so large that the course of business events was beyond the control of any one person; and at the same time those far-reaching organizations of invested wealth which have latterly come to prevail and to coerce the market were not then in the foreground. The course of market events took its passionless way without traceable relation or deference to any man's convenience and without traceable guidance towards an ulterior end. Man's part in this pecuniary world was to respond with alacrity to the situation, and so adapt his vendible effects to the shifting demand as to realize something in the outcome. What he gained in his traffic was gained without loss to those with whom he dealt, for they paid no more than the goods were worth to them. One man's gain need not be another's loss; and, if it is not, then it is net gain to the community.

Among the striking remoter effects of the hedonistic preconception, and its working out in terms of pecuniary gain, is the classical failure to discriminate between capital as investment and capital as industrial appliances. This is, of course, closely related to the point already spoken of. The appliances of industry further the production of goods, therefore capital (invested wealth) is productive; and the rate of its average remuneration marks the degree of its productiveness.* The most obvious fact limiting the pecuniary gain secured by means of invested wealth is the sum invested. Therefore, capital limits the productiveness of industry; and the chief and indispensable condition to an advance in material well-being is the accumulation of invested wealth. In discussing the conditions of industrial improvement, it is usual to assume that "the state of the arts remains unchanged," which is,

* *Cf.* Böhm-Bawerk, *Capital and Interest*, Books II. and IV., as well as the Introduction and chaps. iv. and v. of Book I. Böhm-Bawerk's discussion bears less immediately on the present point than the similarity of the terms employed would suggest.

for all purposes but that of a doctrine of profits per cent., an exclusion of the main fact. Investments may, further, be transferred from one enterprise to another. Therefore, and in that degree, the means of production are "mobile."

Under the hands of the great utilitarian writers, therefore, political economy is developed into a science of wealth, taking that term in the pecuniary sense, as things amenable to ownership. The course of things in economic life is treated as a sequence of pecuniary events, and economic theory becomes a theory of what should happen in that consummate situation where the permutation of pecuniary magnitudes takes place without disturbance and without retardation. In this consummate situation the pecuniary motive has its perfect work, and guides all the acts of economic man in a guileless, colorless, unswerving quest of the greatest gain at the least sacrifice. Of course, this perfect competitive system, with its untainted "economic man," is a feat of the scientific imagination, and is not intended as a competent expression of fact. It is an expedient of abstract reasoning; and its avowed competency extends only to the abstract principles, the fundamental laws of the science, which hold only so far as the abstraction holds. But, as happens in such cases, having once been accepted and assimilated as real, though perhaps not as actual, it becomes an effective constituent in the inquirer's habits of thought, and goes to shape his knowledge of facts. It comes to serve as a norm of substantiality or legitimacy; and facts in some degree fall under its constraint, as is exemplified by many allegations regarding the "tendency" of things.

To this consummation, which Senior speaks of as "the natural state of man,"* human development tends by force of the hedonistic character of human nature; and in terms of its approximation to this natural state, therefore, the immature actual situation had best be stated. The

* *Political Economy*, p. 87.

pure theory, the "hypothetical science" of Cairnes, "traces the phenomena of the production and distribution of wealth up to their causes, in the principles of human nature and the laws and events — physical, political, and social — of the external world." * But since the principles of human nature that give the outcome in men's economic conduct, so far as it touches the production and distribution of wealth, are but the simple and constant sequence of hedonistic cause and effect, the element of human nature may fairly be eliminated from the problem, with great gain in simplicity and expedition. Human nature being eliminated, as being a constant intermediate term, and all institutional features of the situation being also eliminated (as being similar constants under that natural or consummate pecuniary *régime* with which the pure theory is concerned), the laws of the phenomena of wealth may be formulated in terms of the remaining factors. These factors are the vendible items that men handle in these processes of production and distribution; and economic laws come, therefore, to be expressions of the algebraic relations subsisting between the various elements of wealth and investment,— capital, labor, land, supply and demand of one and the other, profits, interest, wages. Even such items as credit and population become dissociated from the personal factor, and figure in the computation as elemental factors acting and reacting through a permutation of values over the heads of the good people whose welfare they are working out.

To sum up: the classical economics, having primarily to do with the pecuniary side of life, is a theory of a process of valuation. But since the human nature at whose hands and for whose behoof the valuation takes place is simple and constant in its reaction to pecuniary stimulus,

* *Character and Logical Method of Political Economy* (New York, 1875), p. 71. Cairnes may not be altogether representative of the high tide of classicism, but his characterization of the science is none the less to the point.

and since no other feature of human nature is legitimately present in economic phenomena than this reaction to pecuniary stimulus, the valuer concerned in the matter is to be overlooked or eliminated; and the theory of the valuation process then becomes a theory of the pecuniary interaction of the facts valued. It is a theory of valuation with the element of valuation left out,—a theory of life stated in terms of the normal paraphernalia of life.

In the preconceptions with which classical economics set out were comprised the remnants of natural rights and of the order of nature, infused with that peculiarly mechanical natural theology that made its way into popular vogue on British ground during the eighteenth century and was reduced to a neutral tone by the British penchant for the commonplace — stronger at this time than at any earlier period. The reason for this growing penchant for the commonplace, for the explanation of things in causal terms, lies partly in the growing resort to mechanical processes and mechanical prime movers in industry, partly in the (consequent) continued decline of the aristocracy and the priesthood, and partly in the growing density of population and the consequent greater specialization and wider organization of trade and business. The spread of the discipline of the natural sciences, largely incident to the mechanical industry, counts in the same direction; and obscurer factors in modern culture may have had their share.

The animistic preconception was not lost, but it lost tone; and it partly fell into abeyance, particularly so far as regards its avowal. It is visible chiefly in the unavowed readiness of the classical writers to accept as imminent and definitive any possible outcome which the writer's habit or temperament inclined him to accept as right and good. Hence the visible inclination of classical economists to a doctrine of the harmony of interests, and their somewhat uncircumspect readiness to state their generalizations in terms of what ought to happen according to the ideal requirements of that consummate *Geldwirtschaft* to which men "are impelled by the provisions of nature." * By virtue of their hedonistic preconceptions, their habituation to the ways of a pecuniary culture, and their unavowed animistic faith that nature is in the right, the classical economists knew that the consummation to which, in the nature of things, all things tend, is the frictionless and beneficent competitive system. This competitive ideal, therefore, affords the normal, and conformity to its requirements affords the test of absolute economic truth. The standpoint so gained selectively guides the attention of the classical writers in their observation and apprehension of facts, and they come to see evidence of conformity or approach to the normal in the most unlikely places. Their observation is, in great part, interpretative, as observation commonly is. What is peculiar to the classical economists in this respect is their particular norm of procedure in the work of interpretation. And, by virtue of having achieved a standpoint of absolute economic normality, they became a "deductive" school, so called, in spite of the patent fact that they were pretty consistently employed with an inquiry into the causal sequence of economic phenomena.

The generalization of observed facts becomes a normalization of them, a statement of the phenomena in terms of their coincidence with, or divergence from, that normal tendency that makes for the actualization of the absolute economic reality. This absolute or definitive ground of economic legitimacy lies beyond the causal sequence in which the observed phenomena are conceived to be interlinked. It is related to the concrete facts neither as cause nor as effect in any such way that the causal relation may be traced in a concrete instance. It has little causally to do either with the "mental" or with the "physical"

* Senior, *Political Economy*, p. 87.

data with which the classical economist is avowedly employed. Its relation to the process under discussion is that of an extraneous — that is to say, a ceremonial — legitimation. The body of knowledge gained by its help and under its guidance is, therefore, a taxonomic science.

So, by way of a concluding illustration, it may be pointed out that money, for instance, is normalized in terms of the legitimate economic tendency. It becomes a measure of value and a medium of exchange. It has become primarily an instrument of pecuniary commutation, instead of being, as under the earlier normalization of Adam Smith, primarily a great wheel of circulation for the diffusion of consumable goods. The terms in which the laws of money, as of the other phenomena of pecuniary life, are formulated, are terms which connote its normal function in the life history of objective values as they live and move and have their being in the consummate pecuniary situation of the "natural" state. To a similar work of normalization we owe those creatures of the mythmaker, the quantity theory and the wages-fund.

THORSTEIN VEBLEN.

THE UNIVERSITY OF CHICAGO.

THE PRECONCEPTIONS OF ECONOMIC SCIENCE.

III.

In what has already been said, it has appeared that the changes which have supervened in the preconceptions of the earlier economists constitute a somewhat orderly succession. The feature of chief interest in this development has been a gradual change in the received grounds of finality to which the successive generations of economists have brought their theoretical output, on which they have been content to rest their conclusions, and beyond which they have not been moved to push their analysis of events or their scrutiny of phenomena. There has been a fairly unbroken sequence of development in what may be called the canons of economic reality, or, to put it in other words, there has been a precession of the point of view from which facts have been handled and valued for the purpose of economic science.

The notion which has in its time prevailed so widely, that there is in the sequence of events a consistent trend which it is the office of the science to ascertain and turn to account,—this notion may be well founded or not. But that there is something of such a consistent trend in the sequence of the canons of knowledge under whose guidance the scientist works is not only a generalization from the past course of things, but lies in the nature of the case; for the canons of knowledge are of the nature of habits of thought, and habit does not break with the past, nor do the hereditary aptitudes that find expression in habit vary gratuitously with the mere lapse of time. What is true in this respect, for instance, in the domain of law and institutions is true, likewise, in the domain of science. What men have learned to accept as good and definitive for the guidance of conduct and of human relations remains true and definitive and unimpeachable until the exigencies of a later, altered situation enforce a variation from the norms and canons of the past, and so give rise to a modification of the habits of thought that decide what is, for the time, right in human conduct. So in science the ancient ground of finality remains a good and valid test of scientific truth until the altered exigencies of later life enforce habits of thought that are not wholly in consonance with the received notions as to what constitutes the ultimate, self-legitimating term — the substantial reality — to which knowledge in any given case must penetrate.

This ultimate term or ground of knowledge is always of a metaphysical character. It is something in the way of a preconception, accepted uncritically, but applied in criticism and demonstration of all else with which the science is concerned. So soon as it comes to be criticised, it is in a way to be superseded by a new, more or less altered formulation; for criticism of it means that it is no longer fit to survive unaltered in the altered complex of habits of thought to which it is called upon to serve as fundamental principle. It is subject to natural selection and selective adaptation, as are other conventions. The underlying metaphysics of scientific research and purpose, therefore, changes gradually and, of course, incompletely, much as is the case with the metaphysics underlying the common law and the schedule of civil rights. As in the legal framework the now avowedly useless and meaningless preconceptions of status and caste and precedent are even yet at the most metamorphosed and obsolescent rather than overpassed,— witness the facts of inheritance, vested interests, the outlawry of debts through lapse of time, the competence of the State to coerce individuals into support of a given policy,— so in the science the living generation has not seen an abrupt and traceless disappearance of the metaphysics that fixed the point of view of the early classical political economy. This is true even for those groups of economists who have most incontinently protested against the absurdity of the classical doctrines and methods. In Professor Marshall's words, "There has been no real breach of continuity in the development of the science."

But, while there has been no breach, there has none the less been change,— more far-reaching change than some of us are glad to recognize; for who would not be glad to read his own modern views into the convincing words of the great masters?

Seen through modern eyes and without effort to turn past gains to modern account, the metaphysical or preconceptional furniture of political economy as it stood about the middle of this century may come to look quite curious. The two main canons of truth on which the science proceeded, and with which the inquiry is here concerned, were: (*a*) a hedonistic-associational psychology, and (*b*) an uncritical conviction that there is a meliorative trend in the course of events, apart from the conscious ends of the individual members of the community. This axiom of a meliorative developmental trend fell into shape as a belief in an organic or quasi-organic (physiological)* life process on the part of the economic community or of the nation; and this belief carried with it something of a constraining sense of self-realizing cycles of growth, maturity and decay in the life history of nations or communities.

Neglecting what may for the immediate purpose be negligible in this outline of fundamental tenets, it will bear the following construction. (*a*) On the ground of the hedonistic or associational psychology, all spiritual continuity and any consequent teleological trend is tacitly denied so far as regards individual conduct, where the

* So, *e.g.*, Roscher, Comte, the early socialists, J. S. Mill, and later Spencer. Schaeffle, Wagner.

later psychology, and the sciences which build on this later psychology, insist upon and find such a teleological trend at every turn. (*b*) Such a spiritual or quasi-spiritual continuity and teleological trend is uncritically affirmed as regards the non-human sequence or the sequence of events in the affairs of collective life, where the modern sciences diligently assert that nothing of the kind is discernible, or that, if it is discernible, its recognition is beside the point, so far as concerns the purposes of the science.

This position, here outlined with as little qualification as may be admissible, embodies the general metaphysical ground of that classical political economy that affords the point of departure for Mill and Cairnes, and also for Jevons. And what is to be said of Mill and Cairnes in this connection will apply to the later course of the science, though with a gradually lessening force.

By the middle of the century the psychological premises of the science are no longer so neat and succinct as they were in the days of Bentham and James Mill. At J. S. Mill's hands, for instance, the naïvely quantitative hedonism of Bentham is being supplanted by a sophisticated hedonism, which makes much of an assumed qualitative divergence between the different kinds of pleasures that afford the motives of conduct. This revision of hedonistic dogma, of course, means a departure from the strict hedonistic ground. Correlated with this advance more closely in the substance of the change than in the assignable dates, is a concomitant improvement — at least, set forth as an improvement — upon the received associational psychology, whereby "similarity" is brought in to supplement "contiguity" as a ground of connection between ideas. This change is well shown in the work of J. S. Mill and Bain. In spite of all the ingenuity spent in maintaining the associational legitimacy of this new article of theory, it remains a patent innovation and a departure from the ancient standpoint. As is true of the improved hedonism, so it is true of the new theory of association that it is no longer able to construe the process which it discusses as a purely mechanical process, a concatenation of items simply. Similarity of impressions implies a comparison of impressions by the mind in which the association takes place, and thereby it implies some degree of constructive work on the part of the perceiving subject. The perceiver is thereby construed to be an agent engaged in the work of perception; therefore, he must be possessed of a point of view and an end dominating the perceptive process. To perceive the similarity, he must be guided by an interest in the outcome, and must "attend." The like applies to the introduction of qualitative distinctions into the hedonistic theory of conduct. Apperception in the one case and discretion in the other cease to be the mere registration of a simple and personally uncolored sequence of permutations enforced by the factors of the external world. There is implied a spiritual — that is to say, active — "teleological" continuity of process on the part of the perceiving or of the discretionary agent, as the case may be.

It is on the ground of their departure from the stricter hedonistic premises that Mill and, after him, Cairnes are able, for instance, to offer their improvement upon the earlier doctrine of cost of production as determining value. Since it is conceived that the motives which guide men in their choice of employments and of domicile differ from man to man and from class to class, not only in degree, but in kind, and since varying antecedents, of heredity and of habit, variously influence men in their choice of a manner of life, therefore the mere quantitative pecuniary stimulus cannot be depended on to decide the outcome without recourse. There are determinable variations in the alacrity with which different classes or communities respond to the pecuniary stimulus; and in so far as this condition prevails, the classes or communities in question are non-competing. Between such non-competing groups the norm that determines values is not the unmitigated norm of cost of production taken absolutely, but only taken relatively. The formula of cost of production is therefore modified into a formula of reciprocal demand. This revision of the cost-of-production doctrine is extended only sparingly, and the emphasis is thrown on the pecuniary circumstances on which depend the formation and maintenance of non-competing groups. Consistency with the earlier teaching is carefully maintained, so far as may be; but extra-pecuniary factors are, after all, even if reluctantly, admitted into the body of the theory. So also, since there are higher and lower motives, higher and lower pleasures,—as well as motives differing in degree,—it follows that an unguided response even to the mere quantitative pecuniary stimuli may take different directions, and so may result in activities of widely differing outcome. Since activities set up in this way through appeal to higher and lower motives are no longer conceived to represent simply a mechanically adequate effect of the stimuli, working under the control of natural laws that tend to one beneficent consummation, therefore the outcome of activity set up even by the normal pecuniary stimuli may take a form that may or may not be serviceable to the community. Hence *laissez-faire* ceases to be a sure remedy for the ills of society. Human interests are still conceived normally to be at one; but the detail of individual conduct need not, therefore, necessarily serve these generic human interests.* Therefore, other inducements than the unmitigated impact of pecuniary

* "Let us not confound the statement that *human* interests are at one with the statement that *class* interests are at one. The latter I believe to be as false as the former is true. . . . But accepting the major premises of the syllogism, that the interests of human beings are fundamentally the same, how as to the minor?—how as to the assumption that people know their interests in the sense in which they are identical with the interests of others, and that they spontaneously follow them *in this sense?*" Cairnes, *Essays in Political Economy* (London, 1873), p. 245. This question cannot consistently be asked by an adherent of the stricter hedonism.

exigencies may be necessary to bring about a coincidence of class or individual endeavor with the interests of the community. It becomes incumbent on the advocate of *laissez-faire* to "prove his minor premise." It is no longer self-evident that: "Interests left to themselves tend to harmonious combinations, and to the progressive preponderance of the general good." *

The natural-rights preconception begins to fall away as soon as the hedonistic mechanics have been seriously tampered with. Fact and right cease to coincide, because the individual in whom the rights are conceived to inhere has come to be something more than the field of intersection of natural forces that work out in human conduct. The mechanics of natural liberty — that assumed constitution of things by force of which the free hedonistic play of the laws of nature across the open field of individual choice is sure to reach the right outcome — is the hedonistic psychology; and the passing of the doctrine of natural rights and natural liberty, whether as a premise or as a dogma, therefore coincides with the passing of that mechanics of conduct on the validity of which the theoretical acceptance of the dogma depends. It is, therefore, something more than a coincidence that the half-century which has seen the disintegration of the hedonistic faith and of the associational psychology has also seen the dissipation, in scientific speculations, of the concomitant faith in natural rights and in that benign order of nature of which the natural-rights dogma is a corollary.

It is, of course, not hereby intended to say that the later psychological views and premises imply a less close dependence of conduct on environment than do the earlier ones. Indeed, the reverse may well be held to be true. The pervading characteristic of later thinking is the constant recourse to a detailed analysis of phenomena in causal terms. The modern catchword, in the present con-

* Bastiat, quoted by Cairnes. *Essays*, p. 319.

nection, is "response to stimulus"; but the manner in which this response is conceived has changed. The fact, and ultimately the amplitude, at least in great part, of the reaction to stimulus, is conditioned by the forces in impact; but the constitution of the organism, as well as its attitude at the moment of impact, in great part decides what will serve as a stimulus, as well as what the manner and direction of the response will be.

The later psychology is biological, as contrasted with the metaphysical psychology of hedonism. It does not conceive the organism as a causal hiatus. The causal sequence in the "reflex arc" is, no doubt, continuous; but the continuity is not, as formerly, conceived in terms of spiritual substance transmitting a shock: it is conceived in terms of the life activity of the organism. Human conduct, taken as the reaction of such an organism under stimulus, may be stated in terms of tropism, involving, of course, a very close-knit causal sequence between the impact and the response, but at the same time imputing to the organism a habit of life and a self-directing and selective attention in meeting the complex of forces that make up its environment. The selective play of this tropismatic complex that constitutes the organism's habit of life under the impact of the forces of the environment counts as discretion.

So far, therefore, as it is to be placed in contrast with the hedonistic phase of the older psychological doctrines, the characteristic feature of the newer conception is the recognition of a selectively self-directing life process in the agent. While hedonism seeks the causal determinant of conduct in the (probable) outcome of action, the later conception seeks this determinant in the complex of propensities that constitutes man a functioning agent, that is to say, a personality. Instead of pleasure ultimately determining what human conduct shall be, the tropismatic propensities that eventuate in conduct ultimately determine what shall be pleasurable. For the purpose in hand, the consequence of the transition to the altered conception of human nature and its relation to the environment is that the newer view formulates conduct in terms of personality, whereas the earlier view was content to formulate it in terms of its provocation and its by-product. Therefore, for the sake of brevity, the older preconceptions of the science are here spoken of as construing human nature in inert terms, as contrasted with the newer, which construes it in terms of functioning.

It has already appeared above that the second great article of the metaphysics of classical political economy — the belief in a meliorative trend or a benign order of nature — is closely connected with the hedonistic conception of human nature; but this connection is more intimate and organic than appears from what has been said above. The two are so related as to stand or fall together, for the latter is but the obverse of the former. The doctrine of a trend in events imputes purpose to the sequence of events; that is, it invests this sequence with a discretionary, teleological character, which asserts itself in a constraint over all the steps in the sequence by which the supposed objective point is reached. But discretion touching a given end must be single, and must alone cover all the acts by which the end is to be reached. Therefore, no discretion resides in the intermediate terms through which the end is worked out. Therefore, man being such an intermediate term, discretion cannot be imputed to him without violating the supposition. Therefore, given an indefeasible meliorative trend in events, man is but a mechanical intermediary in the sequence. It is as such a mechanical intermediate term that the stricter hedonism construes human nature.* Accordingly, when more of

* It may be remarked, by the way, that the use of the differential calculus and similar mathematical expedients in the discussion of marginal utility and the like, proceeds on this psychological ground, and that the theoretical results so arrived at are valid to the full extent only if this hedonistic psychology is accepted.

teleological activity came to be imputed to man, less was thereby allowed to the complex of events. Or it may be put in the converse form: when less of a teleological continuity came to be imputed to the course of events, more was thereby imputed to man's life process. The latter form of statement probably suggests the direction in which the causal relation runs, more nearly than the former. The change whereby the two metaphysical premises in question have lost their earlier force and symmetry, therefore, amounts to a (partial) shifting of the seat of putative personality from inanimate phenomena to man.

It may be mentioned in passing, as a detail lying perhaps afield, yet not devoid of significance for latter-day economic speculation, that this elimination of personality, and so of teleological content, from the sequence of events, and its increasing imputation to the conduct of the human agent, is incident to a growing resort to an apprehension of phenomena in terms of process rather than in terms of outcome, as was the habit in earlier schemes of knowledge. On this account the categories employed are, in a gradually increasing degree, categories of process,—"dynamic" categories. But categories of process applied to conduct, to discretionary action, are teleological categories: whereas categories of process applied in the case of a sequence where the members of the sequence are not conceived to be charged with discretion, are, by the force of this conception itself, non-teleological, quantitative categories. The continuity comprised in the concept of process as applied to conduct is consequently a spiritual, teleological continuity: whereas the concept of process under the second head, the non-teleological sequence, comprises a continuity of a quantitative, causal kind, substantially the conservation of energy. In its turn the growing resort to categories of process in the formulation of knowledge is probably due to the epistemological discipline of modern mechanical industry, the technological exigencies of which enforce a constant recourse to the apprehension of phenomena in terms of process, differing therein from the earlier forms of industry, which neither obtruded visible mechanical process so constantly upon the apprehension nor so imperatively demanded an articulate recognition of continuity in the processes actually involved. The contrast in this respect is still more pronounced between the discipline of modern life in an industrial community and the discipline of life under the conventions of status and exploit that formerly prevailed.

To return to the benign order of nature, or the meliorative trend,—its passing, as an article of economic faith, was not due to criticism levelled against it by the later classical economists on grounds of its epistemological incongruity. It was tried on its merits, as an alleged account of facts; and the weight of evidence went against it. The belief in a self-realizing trend had no sooner reached a competent and exhaustive statement — *e.g.*, at Bastiat's hands, as a dogma of the harmony of interests specifically applicable to the details of economic life — than it began to lose ground. With his usual concision and incisiveness, Cairnes completed the destruction of Bastiat's special dogma, and put it forever beyond a rehearing. But Cairnes is not a destructive critic of the classical political economy, at least not in intention: he is an interpreter and continuer — perhaps altogether the clearest and truest continuer — of the classical teaching. While he confuted Bastiat and discredited Bastiat's peculiar dogma, he did not thereby put the order of nature bodily out of the science. He qualified and improved it, very much as Mill qualified and improved the tenets of the hedonistic psychology. As Mill and the ethical speculation of his generation threw more of personality into the hedonistic psychology, so Cairnes and the speculators on scientific method (such as Mill and Jevons) attenuated the imputation of personality or teleological content to the process of material cause and effect. The work is of course, by no means, an achievement of Cairnes alone; but he is, perhaps, the best exponent of this advance in economic theory. In Cairnes's redaction this foundation of the science became the concept of a colorless normality.

It was in Cairnes's time the fashion for speculators in other fields than the physical sciences to look to those sciences for guidance in method and for legitimation of the ideals of scientific theory which they were at work to realize. More than that, the large and fruitful achievements of the physical sciences had so far taken men's attention captive as to give an almost instinctive predilection for the methods that had approved themselves in that field. The ways of thinking which had on this ground become familiar to all scholars occupied with any scientific inquiry, had permeated their thinking on any subject whatever. This is eminently true of British thinking.

It had come to be a commonplace of the physical sciences that "natural laws" are of the nature of empirical generalizations simply, or even of the nature of arithmetical averages. Even the underlying preconception of the modern physical sciences — the law of the conservation of energy, or persistence of quantity — was claimed to be an empirical generalization, arrived at inductively and verified by experiment. It is true the alleged proof of the law took the whole conclusion for granted at the start, and used it constantly as a tacit axiom at every step in the argument which was to establish its truth; but that fact serves rather to emphasize than to call in question the abiding faith which these empiricists had in the sole efficacy of empirical generalization. Had they been able overtly to admit any other than an associational origin of knowledge, they would have seen the impossibility of accounting on the mechanical grounds of association for the premise on which all experience of mechanical fact rests. That any other than a mechanical origin should be assigned to experience, or that any other than a so-conceived empirical ground was to be admitted for any general principle, was incompatible with the prejudices of men trained in the school of the associational psychology, however widely they perforce departed from this ideal in practice. Nothing of the nature of a personal element was to be admitted into these fundamental empirical generalizations; and nothing, therefore, of the nature of a discretionary or teleological movement was to be comprised in the generalizations to be accepted as "natural laws." Natural laws must in no degree be imbued with personality, must say nothing of an ulterior end; but for all that they remained "laws" of the sequences subsumed under them. So far is the reduction to colorless terms carried by Mill, for instance, that he formulates the natural laws as empirically ascertained sequences simply, even excluding or avoiding all imputation of causal continuity, as that term is commonly understood by the unsophisticated. In Mill's ideal no more of organic connection or continuity between the members of a sequence is implied in subsuming them under a law of causal relationship than is given by the ampersand. He is busied with dynamic sequences, but he persistently confines himself to static terms.

Under the guidance of the associational psychology, therefore, the extreme of discontinuity in the deliverances of inductive research is aimed at by those economists — Mill and Cairnes being taken as typical — whose names have been associated with deductive methods in modern science. With a fine sense of truth they saw that the notion of causal continuity, as a premise of scientific generalization, is an essentially metaphysical postulate; and they avoided its treacherous ground by denying it, and construing causal sequence to mean a uniformity of coexistences and successions simply. But, since a strict uniformity is nowhere to be observed at first hand in the phenomena with which the investigator is occupied, it has to be found by a laborious interpretation of the phenomena and a diligent abstraction and allowance for disturbing circumstances, whatever may be the meaning of a disturbing circumstance where causal continuity is denied. In this work of interpretation and expurgation the investigator proceeds on a conviction of the orderliness of the natural sequence. "Natura non facit saltum": a maxim which has no meaning within the stricter limits of the associational theory of knowledge.

Before anything can be said as to the orderliness of the sequence, a point of view must be chosen by the speculator, with respect to which the sequence in question does or does not fulfil this condition of orderliness; that is to say, with respect to which it is a sequence. The endeavor to avoid all metaphysical premises fails here as everywhere. The associationists, to whom economics owes its transition from the older classical phase to the modern or quasi-classical, chose as their guiding point of view the metaphysical postulate of congruity,—in substance, the "similarity" of the associationist theory of knowledge. This must be called their *proton pseudos*, if associationism pure and simple is to be accepted. The notion of congruity works out in laws of resemblance and equivalence, in both of which it is plain to the modern psychologist that a metaphysical ground of truth, antecedent to and controlling empirical data, is assumed. But the use of the postulate of congruence as a test of scientific truth has the merit of avoiding all open dealing with an imputed substantiality of the data handled, such as would be involved in the overt use of the concept of causation. The data are congruous among themselves, as items of knowledge; and they may therefore be handled in a logical synthesis and concatenation on the basis of this congruence alone, without committing the scientist to an imputation of a kinetic or motor relation between them. The metaphysics of process is thereby avoided, in appearance. The sequences are uniform or consistent with one another, taken as articles of theoretical synthesis simply; and so they become elements of a system or discipline of knowledge in which the test of theoretical truth is the congruence of the system with its premises.

In all this there is a high-wrought appearance of matter-of-fact, and all metaphysical subreption of a non-empirical or non-mechanical standard of reality or substantiality is avoided in appearance. The generalizations which make up such a system of knowledge are, in this way, stated in terms of the system itself; and when a competent formulation of the alleged uniformities has been so made in terms of their congruity or equivalence with the prime postulates of the system, the work of theoretical inquiry is done.

The concrete premises from which proceeds the systematic knowledge of this generation of economists are certain very concise assumptions concerning human nature, and certain slightly less concise generalizations of physical fact,* presumed to be mechanically empirical generalizations. These postulates afford the standard of normality. Whatever situation or course of events can be shown to express these postulates without mitigation is normal; and wherever a departure from this normal course of things occurs, it is due to disturbing causes,— that is to say, to causes not comprised in the main premises of the science,— and such departures are to be taken account of by way of qualification. Such departures and such qualification are constantly present in the facts to be handled by the science; but, being not congruous with the underlying postulates, they have no place in the body of the science. The laws of the science, that which makes up the economist's theoretical knowledge, are laws of the normal case.

* See, *e.g.*, Cairnes, *Character and Logical Method* (New York), p. 71.

The normal case does not occur in concrete fact. These laws are, therefore, in Cairnes's terminology, "hypothetical" truths; and the science is a "hypothetical" science. They apply to concrete facts only as the facts are interpreted and abstracted from, in the light of the underlying postulates. The science is, therefore, a theory of the normal case, a discussion of the concrete facts of life in respect of their degree of approximation to the normal case. That is to say, it is a taxonomic science.

Of course, in the work actually done by these economists this standpoint of rigorous normality is not consistently maintained; nor is the unsophisticated imputation of causality to the facts under discussion consistently avoided. The associationist postulate, that causal sequence means empirical uniformity simply, is in great measure forgotten when the subject-matter of the science is handled in detail. Especially is it true that in Mill the dry light of normality is greatly relieved by a strong common sense. But the great truths or laws of the science remain hypothetical laws; and the test of scientific reality is congruence with the hypothetical laws, not coincidence with matter-of-fact events.

The earlier, more archaic metaphysics of the science, which saw in the orderly correlation and sequence of events a constraining guidance of an extra-causal, teleological kind, in this way becomes a metaphysics of normality which asserts no extra-causal constraint over events, but contents itself with establishing correlations, equivalencies, homologies, and theories concerning the conditions of an economic equilibrium. The movement, the process of economic life, is not overlooked, and it may even be said that it is not neglected; but the pure theory, in its final deliverances, deals not with the dynamics, but with the statics of the case. The concrete subject-matter of the science is, of course, the process of economic life,—that is unavoidably the case,— and in so far the discussion must be accepted as work bearing on the dynamics of the phenomena discussed; but even then it remains true that the aim of this work in dynamics is a determination and taxis of the outcome of the process under discussion rather than a theory of the process as such. The process is rated in terms of the equilibrium to which it tends or should tend, not conversely. The outcome of the process, taken in its relation of equivalence within the system, is the point at which the inquiry comes to rest. It is not primarily the point of departure for an inquiry into what may follow. The science treats of a balanced system rather than of a proliferation. In this lies its characteristic difference from the later evolutionary sciences. It is this characteristic bent of the science that leads its spokesman, Cairnes, to turn so kindly to chemistry rather than to the organic sciences, when he seeks an analogy to economics among the physical sciences.* What Cairnes has in mind in his appeal to chemistry is, of course, the received, extremely taxonomic (systematic) chemistry of his own time, not the tentatively genetic theories of a slightly later day.

It may seem that in the characterization just offered of the standpoint of normality in economics there is too strong an implication of colorlessness and impartiality. The objection holds as regards much of the work of the modern economists of the classical line. It will hold true even as to much of Cairnes's work; but it cannot be admitted as regards Cairnes's ideal of scientific aim and methods. The economists whose theories Cairnes received and developed, assuredly did not pursue the discussion of the normal case with an utterly dispassionate animus. They had still enough of the older teleological metaphysics left to give color to the accusation brought against them that they were advocates of *laissez-faire*. The preconception of the utilitarians,— in substance the natural-rights pre-

* *Character and Logical Method*, p. 62.

conception,— that unrestrained human conduct will result in the greatest human happiness, retains so much of its force in Cairnes's time as is implied in the then current assumption that what is normal is also right. The economists, and Cairnes among them, not only are concerned to find out what is normal and to determine what consummation answers to the normal, but they also are at pains to approve that consummation. It is this somewhat uncritical and often unavowed identification of the normal with the right that gives colorable ground for the widespread vulgar prejudice, to which Cairnes draws attention,* that political economy "sanctions" one social arrangement and "condemns" another. And it is against this uncritical identification of two essentially unrelated principles or categories that Cairnes's essay on "Political Economy and Laissez-faire," and in good part also that on Bastiat, are directed. But, while this is one of the many points at which Cairnes has substantially advanced the ideals of the science, his own concluding argument shows him to have been but half-way emancipated from the prejudice, even while most effectively combating it.† It is needless to point out that the like prejudice is still present in good vigor in many later economists who have had the full benefit of Cairnes's teachings on this head.‡ Considerable as Cairnes's achievement in this matter undoubtedly was, it effected a mitigation rather than an elimination of the untenable metaphysics against which he contended.

The advance in the general point of view from animistic teleology to taxonomy is shown in a curiously succinct manner in a parenthetical clause of Cairnes's in the chap-

* *Essays in Political Economy*, pp. 260–264.

† See especially *Essays*, pp. 263, 264.

‡ It may be interesting to point out that the like identification of the categories of normality and right gives the dominant note of Mr. Spencer's ethical and social philosophy, and that later economists of the classical line are prone to be Spencerians.

ter on Normal Value.* With his acceptance of the later point of view involved in the use of the new term, Cairnes becomes the interpreter of the received theoretical results. The received positions are not subjected to a destructive criticism. The aim is to complete them where they fall short and to cut off what may be needless or what may run beyond the safe ground of scientific generalization. In his work of redaction, Cairnes does not avow, probably he is not sensible of — any substantial shifting of the point of view or any change in the accepted ground of theoretic reality. But his advance to an unteleological taxonomy none the less changes the scope and aim of his theoretical discussion. The discussion of Normal Value may be taken in illustration.

Cairnes is not content to find (with Adam Smith) that value will "naturally" coincide with or be measured by cost of production, or even (with Mill) that cost of production must, in the long run, "necessarily" determine value. "This . . . is to take a much too limited view of the range of this phenomenon." † He is concerned to determine not only this general tendency of values to a normal, but all those characteristic circumstances as well which condition this tendency and which determine the normal to which values tend. His inquiry pursues the phenomena of value in a normal economic system rather than the manner and rate of approach of value relations to a teleologically or hedonistically defensible consummation. It therefore becomes an exhaustive but very discriminating analysis of the circumstances that bear upon market values, with a view to determine what circumstances are normally present; that is to say, what circumstances conditioning value are commonly effective and at the same time in consonance with the premises of eco-

* "Normal value (called by Adam Smith and Ricardo 'natural value,' and by Mill 'necessary value,' but best expressed, it seems to me, by the term which I have used)." *Leading Principles* (New York), p. 45.

† *Leading Principles*, p. 45.

nomic theory. These effective conditions, in so far as they are not accounted anomalous and, therefore, to be set aside in the theoretical discussion, are the circumstances under which a hedonistic valuation process in any modern industrial community is held perforce to take place,— the circumstances which are held to enforce a recognition and rating of the pleasure-bearing capacity of facts. They are not, as under the earlier cost-of-production doctrines, the circumstances which determine the magnitude of the forces spent in the production of the valuable article. Therefore, the normal (natural) value is no longer (as with Adam Smith, and even to some extent with his classical successors) the primary or initial fact in value theory, the substantial fact of which the market value is an approximate expression and by which the latter is controlled. The argument does not, as formerly, set out from that expenditure of personal force which was once conceived to constitute the substantial value of goods, and then construe market value to be an approximate and uncertain expression of this substantial fact. The direction in which the argument runs is rather the reverse of this. The point of departure is taken from the range of market values and the process of bargaining by which these values are determined. This latter is taken to be a process of discrimination between various kinds and degrees of discomfort, and the average or consistent outcome of such a process of bargaining constitutes normal value. It is only by virtue of a presumed equivalence between the discomfort undergone and the concomitant expenditure, whether of labor or of wealth, that the normal value so determined is conceived to be an expression of the productive force that goes into the creation of the valuable goods. Cost being only in uncertain equivalence with sacrifice or discomfort, as between different persons, the factor of cost falls into the background; and the process of bargaining, which is in the foreground, being a process of valuation, a balancing of individual demand and supply, it follows that a law of reciprocal demand comes in to supplant the law of cost. In all this the proximate causes at work in the determination of values are plainly taken account of more adequately than in earlier cost-of-production doctrines; but they are taken account of with a view to explaining the mutual adjustment and interrelation of elements in a system rather than to explain either a developmental sequence or the working out of a foreordained end.

This revision of the cost-of-production doctrine whereby it takes the form of a law of reciprocal demand is in good part effected by a consistent reduction of cost to terms of sacrifice,—a reduction more consistently carried through by Cairnes than it had been by earlier hedonists, and extended by Cairnes's successors with even more far-reaching results. By this step the doctrine of cost is not only brought into closer accord with the neo-hedonistic premises, in that it in a greater degree throws the stress upon the factor of personal discrimination, but it also gives the doctrine a more general bearing upon economic conduct and increases its serviceability as a comprehensive principle for the classification of economic phenomena. In the further elaboration of the hedonistic theory of value at the hands of Jevons and the Austrians the same principle of sacrifice comes to serve as the chief ground of procedure.

Of the foundations of later theory, in so far as the postulates of later economists differ characteristically from those of Mill and Cairnes, little can be said in this place. Nothing but the very general features of the later development can be taken up; and even these general features of the existing theoretic situation can not be handled with the same confidence as the corresponding features of a past phase of speculation. With respect to writers of the present or the more recent past the work of natural selection, as between variants of scientific aim and animus and between more or less divergent points of view, has not yet taken place; and it would be over-hazardous to attempt an anticipation of the results of the selection that lies in great part yet in the future. As regards the directions of theoretical work suggested by the names of Professor Marshall, Mr. Cannan, Professor Clark, Mr. Pierson, Professor Loria, Professor Schmoller, the Austrian group,— no off-hand decision is admissible as between these candidates for the honor, or, better, for the work, of continuing the main current of economic speculation and inquiry. No attempt will here be made even to pass a verdict on the relative claims of the recognized two or three main "schools" of theory, beyond the somewhat obvious finding that, for the purpose in hand, the so-called Austrian school is scarcely distinguishable from the neo-classical, unless it be in the different distribution of emphasis. The divergence between the modernized classical views, on the one hand, and the historical and Marxist schools, on the other hand, is wider,— so much so, indeed, as to bar out a consideration of the postulates of the latter under the same head of inquiry with the former. The inquiry, therefore, confines itself to the one line standing most obviously in unbroken continuity with that body of classical economics whose life history has been traced in outline above. And, even for this phase of modernized classical economics, it seems necessary to limit discussion, for the present, to a single strain, selected as standing peculiarly close to the classical source, at the same time that it shows unmistakable adaptation to the later habits of thought and methods of knowledge.

For this later development in the classical line of political economy, Mr. Keynes's book may fairly be taken as the maturest exposition of the aims and ideals of the science; while Professor Marshall excellently exemplifies the best work that is being done under the guidance of the classical antecedents. As, after a lapse of a dozen or fifteen years from Cairnes's days of full conviction, Mr. Keynes interprets the aims of modern economic science, it has less of the "hypothetical" character assigned it by Cairnes; that is to say, it confines its inquiry less closely to the ascertainment of the normal case and the interpretative subsumption of facts under the normal. It takes fuller account of the genesis and developmental continuity of all features of modern economic life, gives more and closer attention to institutions and their history. This is, no doubt, due, in part at least, to impulse received from German economists; and in so far it also reflects the peculiarly vague and bewildered attitude of protest that characterizes the earlier expositions of the historical school. To the same essentially extraneous source is traceable the theoretic blur embodied in Mr. Keynes's attitude of tolerance towards the conception of economics as a "normative" science having to do with "economic ideals," or an "applied economics" having to do with "economic precepts."* An inchoate departure from the consistent taxonomic ideal shows itself in the tentative resort to historical and genetic formulations, as well as in Mr. Keynes's pervading inclination to define the scope of the science, not by exclusion of what are conceived to be non-economic phenomena, but by disclosing a point of view from which all phenomena are seen to be economic facts. The science comes to be characterized not by the delimitation of a range of facts, as in Cairnes,† but as an inquiry into the bearing which all facts have upon men's economic activity. It is no longer that certain phenomena belong within the science, but rather that the science is concerned with any and all phenomena as seen from the point of

* *Scope and Method of Political Economy* (London, 1891), chaps. i. and ii.

† *Character and Logical Method; e.g.*, Lecture II., especially pp. 53, 54, and 71.

view of the economic interest. Mr. Keynes does not go fully to the length which this last proposition indicates. He finds * that political economy "treats of the phenomena arising out of the economic activities of mankind in society"; but, while the discussion by which he leads up to this definition might be construed to say that all the activities of mankind in society have an economic bearing, and should therefore come within the view of the science, Mr. Keynes does not carry out his elucidation of the matter to that broad conclusion. Neither can it be said that modern political economy has, in practice, taken on the scope and character which this extreme position would assign it.

The passage from which the above citation is taken is highly significant also in another and related bearing, and it is at the same time highly characteristic of the most effective modernized classical economics. The subject-matter of the science has come to be the "economic activities" of mankind, and the phenomena in which these activities manifest themselves. So Professor Marshall's work, for instance, is, in aim, even if not always in achievement, a theoretical handling of human activity in its economic bearing,— an inquiry into the multiform phases and ramifications of that process of valuation of the material means of life by virtue of which man is an economic agent. And still it remains an inquiry directed to the determination of the conditions of an equilibrium of activities and a quiescent normal situation. It is not in any eminent degree an inquiry into cultural or institutional development as affected by economic exigencies or by the economic interest of the men whose activities are analyzed and portrayed. Any sympathetic reader of Professor Marshall's great work — and that must mean every reader — comes away with a sense of swift and smooth movement and interaction of parts; but it is the movement of a

* *Scope and Method of Political Economy*, chap. iii., particularly p. 97.

consummately conceived and self-balanced mechanism, not that of a cumulatively unfolding process or an institutional adaptation to cumulatively unfolding exigencies. The taxonomic bearing is, after all, the dominant feature. It is significant of the same point that even in his discussion of such vitally dynamic features of the economic process as the differential effectiveness of different laborers or of different industrial plants, as well as of the differential advantages of consumers, Professor Marshall resorts to an adaptation of so essentially taxonomic a category as the received concept of rent. Rent is a pecuniary category, a category of income, which is essentially a final term, not a category of the motor term work or interest.* It is not a factor or a feature of the process of industrial life, but a phenomenon of the pecuniary situation which emerges from this process under given conventional circumstances. However far-reaching and various the employment of the rent concept in economic theory has been, it has through all permutations remained, what it was to begin with, a rubric in the classification of incomes. It is a pecuniary, not an industrial category. In so far as resort is had to the rent concept in the formulation of a theory of the industrial process,—as in Professor Marshall's work,—it comes to a statement of the process in terms of its residue. Let it not seem presumptuous to say that, great and permanent as is the value of Professor Marshall's exposition of quasi-rents and the like, the endeavor which it involves to present in terms of a concluded system what is of the nature of a fluent process has made the exposition unduly bulky, unwieldy, and inconsequent.

There is a curious reminiscence of the perfect taxonomic day in Mr. Keynes's characterization of political economy as a "positive science," "the sole province of which is to establish economic uniformities"; † and, in this resort to

* "Interest" is, of course, here used in the sense which it has in modern psychological discussion.

† *Scope and Method of Political Economy*, p. 46.

the associationist expedient of defining a natural law as a "uniformity," Mr. Keynes is also borne out by Professor Marshall.* But this and other survivals of the taxonomic terminology, or even of the taxonomic canons of procedure, do not hinder the economists of the modern school from doing effective work of a character that must be rated as genetic rather than taxonomic. Professor Marshall's work in economics is not unlike that of Asa Gray in botany, who, while working in great part within the lines of "systematic botany" and adhering to its terminology, and on the whole also to its point of view, very materially furthered the advance of the science outside the scope of taxonomy.

Professor Marshall shows an aspiration to treat economic life as a development; and, at least superficially, much of his work bears the appearance of being a discussion of this kind. In this endeavor his work is typical of what is aimed at by many of the later economists. The aim shows itself with a persistent recurrence in his *Principles*. His chosen maxim is, "Natura non facit saltum," — a maxim that might well serve to designate the prevailing attitude of modern economists towards questions of economic development as well as towards questions of classification or of economic policy. His insistence on the continuity of development and of the economic structure of communities is a characteristic of the best work along the later line of classical political economy. All this gives an air of evolutionism to the work. Indeed, the work of the neo-classical economics might be compared, probably without offending any of its adepts, with that of the early generation of Darwinians, though such a comparison might somewhat shrewdly have to avoid any but superficial features. Economists of the present day are commonly evolutionists, in a general way. They commonly

* *Principles of Economics*, vol. i., Book I., chap. vi., sect. 6, especially p. 105 (3d edition).

accept, as other men do, the general results of the evolutionary speculation in those directions in which the evolutionary method has made its way. But the habit of handling by evolutionist methods the facts with which their own science is concerned has made its way among the economists to but a very uncertain degree.

The prime postulate of evolutionary science, the preconception constantly underlying the inquiry, is the notion of a cumulative causal sequence; and writers on economics are in the habit of recognizing that the phenomena with which they are occupied are subject to such a law of development. Expressions of assent to this proposition abound. But the economists have not worked out or hit upon a method by which the inquiry in economics may consistently be conducted under the guidance of this postulate. Taking Professor Marshall as exponent, it appears that, while the formulations of economic theory are not conceived to be arrived at by way of an inquiry into the developmental variation of economic institutions and the like, the theorems arrived at are held, and no doubt legitimately, to apply to the past,* and with due reserve also to the future, phases of the development. But these theorems apply to the various phases of the development not as accounting for the developmental sequence, but as limiting the range of variation. They say little, if anything, as to the order of succession, as to the derivation and the outcome of any given phase, or as to the causal relation of one phase of any given economic convention or scheme of relations to any other. They indicate the conditions of survival to which any innovation is subject, supposing the innovation to have taken place, not the conditions of variational growth. The economic laws, the "statements of uniformity," are therefore, when construed in an evolutionary bearing, theorems

* See, *e.g.*, Professor Marshall's "Reply" to Professor Cunningham in the *Economic Journal* for 1892, pp. 508–113.

concerning the superior or the inferior limit of persistent innovations, as the case may be.* It is only in this negative, selective bearing that the current economic laws are held to be laws of developmental continuity ; and it should be added that they have hitherto found but relatively scant application at the hands of the economists, even for this purpose.

Again, as applied to economic activities under a given situation, as laws governing activities in equilibrium, the economic laws are, in the main, laws of the limits within which economic action of a given purpose runs. They are theorems as to the limits which the economic (commonly the pecuniary) interest imposes upon the range of activities to which the other life interests of men incite, rather than theorems as to the manner and degree in which the economic interest creatively shapes the general scheme of life. In great part they formulate the normal inhibitory effect of economic exigencies rather than the cumulative modification and diversification of human activities through the economic interest, by initiating and guiding habits of life and of thought. This, of course, does not go to say that economists are at all slow to credit the economic exigencies with a large share in the growth of culture; but, while claims of this kind are large and recurrent, it remains true that the laws which make up the framework of economic doctrine are, when construed as generalizations of causal relation, laws of conservation and selection, not of genesis and proliferation. The truth of this, which is but a commonplace generalization, might be shown in detail with respect to such fundamental theorems as the laws of rent, of profits, of wages, of the increasing or diminishing returns of industry, of population, of competitive prices, of cost of production.

In consonance with this quasi-evolutionary tone of the

* This is well illustrated by what Professor Marshall says of the Ricardian law of rent in his "Reply," cited above.

neo-classical political economy, or as an expression of it, comes the further clarified sense that nowadays attaches to the terms "normal" and economic "laws." The laws have gained in colorlessness, until it can no longer be said that the concept of normality implies approval of the phenomena to which it is applied.* They are in an increasing degree laws of conduct, though they still continue to formulate conduct in hedonistic terms; that is to say, conduct is construed in terms of its sensuous effect, not in terms of its teleological content. The light of the science is a drier light than it was, but it continues to be shed upon the accessories of human action rather than upon the process itself. The categories employed for the purpose of knowing this economic conduct with which the scientists occupy themselves are not the categories under which the men at whose hands the action takes place themselves apprehend their own action at the instant of acting. Therefore, economic conduct still continues to be somewhat mysterious to the economists; and they are forced to content themselves with adumbrations whenever the discussion touches this central, substantial fact.

All this, of course, is intended to convey no dispraise of the work done, nor in any way to disparage the theories which the passing generation of economists have elaborated or the really great and admirable body of knowledge which they have brought under the hand of the science; but only to indicate the direction in which the inquiry in its later phases — not always with full consciousness — is shifting as regards its categories and its point of view. The discipline of life in a modern community, particularly the industrial life, strongly re-enforced by the modern sciences, has divested our knowledge of non-human phenomena of that fulness of self-directing life that was once imputed to them, and has reduced this knowledge to terms

* See, *e.g.*, Marshall, *Principles*, Book I., chap. vi., sect. 6, pp. 105-108. The like dispassionateness is visible in most other modern writers on theory; as, *e.g.*, Clark, Cannan, and the Austrians.

of opaque causal sequence. It has thereby narrowed the range of discretionary, teleological action to the human agent alone; and so it is compelling our knowledge of human conduct, in so far as it is distinguished from the non-human, to fall into teleological terms. Foot-pounds, calories, geometrically progressive procreation, and doses of capital have not been supplanted by the equally uncouth denominations of habits, propensities, aptitudes, and conventions, nor does there seem to be any probability that they will be; but the discussion which continues to run in terms of the former class of concepts is in an increasing degree seeking support in concepts of the latter class.

[4]

Industrial and Pecuniary Employments

Thorstein Bunde Veblen, 'Industrial and Pecuniary Employments', *Publications of the American Economic Association*, Third Series, vol. 2 (1901), pp. 190–235; reprinted in *The Place of Science in Modern Civilization* (New York: Viking Press, 1919) ; reprinted, New Brunswick: Transactions, 1990, pp. 279–323.

One of Veblen's major contributions was to have provided a striking dualism or dichotomy for the interpretation and evaluation of economic affairs. Veblen distinguished between industrial employments and pecuniary employments. The former are activities involved in the actual production of goods and services. The latter are activities involved in the generation of profits through purchase and sale or financial and other maneuvers. In pecuniary activities the production of goods is secondary, and may be incidental or not take place at all. Whereas mainstream economic thought generally projects pecuniary activity as instrumental to the production of a socially optimal allocation of resources, Veblen believed the two to be typically in conflict.

INDUSTRIAL AND PECUNIARY EMPLOYMENTS.

BY THORSTEIN VEBLEN.

For purposes of economic theory, the various activities of men and things about which economists busy themselves were classified by the early writers according to a scheme which has remained substantially unchanged, if not unquestioned, since their time. This scheme is the classical three-fold division of the factors of production under Land, Labor, and Capital. The theoretical aim of the economists in discussing these factors and the activities for which they stand has not remained the same throughout the course of economic discussion, and the three-fold division has not always lent itself with facility to new points of view and new purposes of theory, but the writers who have shaped later theory have, on the whole, not laid violent hands on the sacred formula. These facts must inspire the utmost reserve and circumspection in any one who is moved to propose even a subsidiary distinction of another kind between economic activities or agents. The terminology and the conceptual furniture of economics are complex and parti-colored enough without gratuitous innovation.

It is accordingly not the aim of this paper to set aside the time-honored classification of factors, or even to formulate an iconoclastic amendment, but rather to indicate how and why this classification has proved inadequate for certain purposes of theory which were not contemplated by the men who elaborated it. To this end a bit of preface may be in place as regards the aims which led to its formulation and the uses which the three-fold classification originally served.

The economists of the late eighteenth and early nineteenth centuries were believers in a Providential order, or an order of Nature. How they came by this belief need not occupy us here; neither need we raise a question as to whether their conviction of its truth was well or ill grounded. The Providential order or order of Nature is conceived to work in an effective and just way toward the end to which it tends; and in the economic field this objective end is the material welfare of mankind. The science of that time set itself the task of interpreting the facts with which it dealt, in terms of this natural order. The material circumstances which condition men's life fall within the scope of this natural order of the universe, and as members of the universal scheme of things men fall under the constraining guidance of the laws of Nature, who does all things well. As regards their purely theoretical work, the early economists are occupied with bringing the facts of economic life under natural laws conceived somewhat after the manner indicated; and when the facts handled have been fully interpreted in the light of this fundamental postulate the theoretical work of the scientist is felt to have been successfully done.

The economic laws aimed at and formulated under the guidance of this preconception are laws of what takes place "naturally" or "normally", and it is of the essence of things so conceived that in the natural or normal course there is no wasted or misdirected effort. The standpoint is given by the material interest of mankind, or, more concretely, of the community or "society" in which the economist is placed; the resulting economic theory is formulated as an analysis of the "natural" course of the life of the community, the ultimate theoretical postulate of which might, not unfairly, be stated as in some sort a law of the conservation of economic energy. When the course of things runs off naturally or normally, in accord with the exigencies of human welfare and the constraining laws of nature, economic income and outgo balance one another. The natural forces at play in the economic field may increase indefinitely through accretions brought in under man's dominion and through the natural increase of mankind, and, indeed, it is of the nature of things that an orderly progress of this kind should take place; but within the economic organism, as within the larger organism of the universe, there prevails an equivalence of expenditure and returns, an equilibrium of flux and reflux, which is not broken over in the normal course of things. So it is, by implication, assumed that the product which results from any given industrial process or operation is, in some sense or in some unspecified respect, the equivalent of the expenditure of forces, or of the effort, or what not, that has gone into the process out of which the product emerges.

This theorem of equivalence is the postulate which lies at the root of the classical theory of distribution, but it manifestly does not admit of proof—or of disproof either, for that matter; since neither the economic forces which go into the process nor the product which emerges are, in the economic respect, of such a tangible character as to admit of quantitative determination. They are in fact incommensurable magnitudes. To this last remark the answer may conceivably present itself that the equivalence in question is an equivalence in utility or in exchange value, and that the quantitative determination of the various items in terms of exchange value or of utility is, theoretically, not impossible; but when it is called to mind that the forces or factors which go to the production of a given product take their utility or exchange value from that of the product, it will easily be seen that the expedient will not serve. The equivalence between the aggregate factors of production in any given case and their product remains a dogmatic postulate whose validity cannot be demonstrated in any terms that will not reduce the whole proposition to an aimless fatuity, or to metaphysical grounds which have now been given up.

The point of view from which the early, and even the later classical, economists discussed economic life was that of "the society" taken as a collective whole and conceived as an organic unit. Economic theory sought out and formulated the laws of the normal life of the social organism, as it is conceived to work out in that natural course whereby the material welfare of society is attained. The details of economic life are construed, for purposes of general theory, in terms of their subservience to the aims imputed to the collective life process. Those features of detail which will bear construction as links in the process whereby the collective welfare is furthered, are magnified and brought into the foreground, while such features as will not bear this construction are treated as minor disturbances. Such a procedure is manifestly legitimate and expedient in a theoretical inquiry whose aim is to determine the laws of health of the social organism and the normal functions of this organism in a state of health. The social organism is, in this theory, handled as an individual endowed with a consistent life purpose and something of an intelligent apprehension of what means will serve the ends which it seeks. With these collective ends the interests of the individual members are conceived to be fundamentally at one ; and, while men may not see that their own individual interests coincide with those of the social organism, yet, since men are members of the comprehensive organism of nature and consequently subject to beneficent natural law, the ulterior trend of unrestrained individual action is, on the whole, in the right direction.

The details of individual economic conduct and its consequences are of interest to such a general theory chiefly as they further or disturb the beneficent "natural" course. But if the aims and methods of individual conduct were of minor importance in such an economic theory, that is not the case as regards individual rights. The early political economy was not simply a formulation of the natural course of economic phenomena, but it embodied an insistence on what is called "natural liberty". Whether this insistence on natural liberty is to be traced to utilitarianism or to a less specific faith in natural rights, the outcome for the purpose in hand is substantially the same. To avoid going too far afield, it may serve the turn to say that the law of economic equivalence, or conservation of economic energy, was, in early economics, backed by this second corollary of the order of nature, the closely related postulate of natural rights. The classical doctrine of distribution rests on both of these, and it is consequently not only a doctrine of what must normally take place as regards the course of life of society at large, but it also formulates what ought of right to take place as regards the remuneration for work and the distribution of wealth among men.

Under the resulting natural-economic law of equivalence and equity, it is held that the several participants or factors in the economic process severally get the equivalent of the productive force which they expend. They severally get as much as they produce; and conversely, in the normal case they severally produce as much as they get. In the earlier formulations, as, for example, in the authoritative formulation of Adam Smith, there is no clear or persistent pronouncement as regards the terms in which this equivalence between production and remuneration runs. With the later, classical economists, who had the benefit of a developed utilitarian philosophy, it seems to be somewhat consistently conceived in terms of an ill-defined serviceability. With some later writers it is an equivalence of exchange values; but as this latter reduces itself to tautology, it need scarcely be taken seriously. When we are told in the later political economy that the several agents or factors in production normally earn what they get, it is perhaps fairly to be construed as a claim that the economic service rendered the community by any one of the agents in production equals the service received by the agent in return. In terms of serviceability, then, if not in terms of productive force,[1] the individual agent, or at least the class or group of agents to which the individual belongs, normally gets as much as he contributes and contributes as much as he gets. This applies to all those employments or occupations which are ordinarily carried on in any community, throughout the aggregate of men's dealings with the material means of life. All activity which touches industry comes in under this law of equivalence and equity.

Now, to a theorist whose aim is to find the laws gov-

[1] Some late writers, as, *e. g.*, J. B. Clark, apparently must be held to conceive the equivalence in terms of productive force rather than of serviceability; or, perhaps, in terms of serviceability on one side of the equation and productive force on the other.

erning the economic life of a social organism, and who for this purpose conceives the economic community as a unit, the features of economic life which are of particular consequence are those which show the correlation of efforts and the solidarity of interests. For this purpose, such activities and such interests as do not fit into the scheme of solidarity contemplated are of minor importance, and are rather to be explained away or construed into subservience to the scheme of solidarity than to be incorporated at their face value into the theoretical structure. Of this nature, are what are here to be spoken of under the term "pecuniary employments," and the fortune which these pecuniary employments have met at the hands of classical economic theory is such as is outlined in the last sentence.

In a theory proceeding on the premise of economic solidarity, the important bearing of any activity that is taken up and accounted for, is its bearing upon the furtherance of the collective life process. Viewed from the standpoint of the collective interest, the economic process is rated primarily as a process for the provision of the aggregate material means of life. As a late representative of the classical school expresses it: "Production, in fact, embraces every economic operation except consumption."[1] It is this aggregate productivity, and the bearing of all details upon the aggregate productivity, that constantly occupies the attention of the classical economists. What partially diverts their attention from this central and ubiquitous interest, is their persistent lapse into natural-rights morality.

The result is that acquisition is treated as a sub-head under production, and effort directed to acquisition is

[1] J. B. Clark, The Distribution of Wealth, p. 20.

construed in terms of production. The pecuniary activities of men, efforts directed to acquisition and operations incident to the acquisition or tenure of wealth, are treated as incidental to the distribution to each of his particular proportion in the production of goods. Pecuniary activities, in short, are handled as incidental features of the process of social production and consumption, as details incident to the method whereby the social interests are served, instead of being dealt with as the controlling factor about which the modern economic process turns.

Apart from the metaphysical tenets indicated above as influencing them, there are, of course, reasons of economic history for the procedure of the early economists in so relegating the pecuniary activities to the background of economic theory. In the days of Adam Smith, for instance, economic life still bore much of the character of what Professor Schmoller calls *Stadtwirtschaft*. This was the case to some extent in practice, but still more decidedly in tradition. To a greater extent than has since been the case, households produced goods for their own consumption, without the intervention of sale; and handicraftsmen still produced for consumption by their customers, without the intervention of a market. In a considerable measure, the conditions which the Austrian marginal-utility theory supposes, of a producing seller and a consuming buyer, actually prevailed. It may not be true that in Adam Smith's time the business operations, the bargain and sale of goods, were, in general, obviously subservient to their production and consumption, but it comes nearer being true at that time than at any time since then. And the tradition having once been put into form and authenticated by Adam Smith, that such was the place of pecuniary transactions in economic theory, this tradition has lasted on in the face of later and further changes. Under the shadow of this tradition the pecuniary employments are still dealt with as auxilliary to the process of production, and the gains from such employments are still explained as being due to a productive effect imputed to them.

According to ancient prescription, then, all normal, legitimate economic activities carried on in a well regulated community serve a materially useful end, and so far as they are lucrative they are so by virtue of and in proportion to a productive effect imputed to them. But in the situation as it exists at any time there are activities and classes of persons which are indispensable to the community, or which are at least unavoidably present in modern economic life, and which draw some income from the aggregate product, at the same time that these activities are not patently productive of goods and can not well be classed as industrial, in any but a highly sophisticated sense. Some of these activities, which are concerned with economic matters but are not patently of an industrial character, are integral features of modern economic life, and must therefore be classed as normal; for the existing situation, apart from a few minor discrepancies, is particularly normal in the apprehension of present-day economists. Now, the law of economic equivalence and equity says that those who normally receive an income must perforce serve some productive end; and, since the existing organization of society is conceived to be eminently normal, it becomes imperative to find some ground on which to impute industrial productivity to those classes and employments which do not at the first view appear to be industrial at all.

Hence there is commonly visible in the classical political economy, ancient and modern, a strong inclination to make the schedule of industrially productive employments very comprehensive; so that a good deal of ingenuity has been spent in economically justifying their presence by specifying the productive effect of such non-industrial factors as the courts, the army, the police, the clergy, the schoolmaster, the physician, the opera singer.

But these non-economic employments are not so much to the point in the present inquiry; the point being employments which are unmistakably economic, but not industrial in the naïve sense of the word industry, and which yield an income.

Adam Smith analyzed the process of industry in which he found the community of his time engaged, and found the three classes of agents or factors: Land, Labor, and Capital (stock). The productive factors engaged being thus determined, the norm of natural-economic equivalence and equity already referred to above, indicated what would be the natural sharers in the product. Later economists have shown great reserve about departing from this three-fold division of factors, with its correlated three-fold division of sharers of remuneration; apparently because they have retained an instinctive, indefeasible trust in the law of economic equivalence which underlies it. But circumstances have compelled the tentative intrusion of a fourth class of agent and income. The undertaker and his income presently came to be so large and ubiquitous figures in economic life that their presence could not be overlooked by the most normalizing economist. The undertaker's activity has been interpolated in the scheme of productive factors, as a peculiar and fundamentally distinctive kind of labor, with the function of coördinating and directing industrial processes. Similarly, his income has been interpolated in the scheme of distribution, as a peculiar kind of wages, proportioned to the heightened productivity given the industrial process by his work.[1] His work is discussed in expositions of the theory of production. In discussions of his functions and his income the point of the argument is, how and in what degree does his activity increase the output of goods, or how and in what degree does it save wealth to the community. Beyond his effect in enhancing the effective volume of the aggregate wealth the undertaker receives but scant attention, apparently for the reason that so soon as that point has been disposed of the presence of the undertaker and his income has been reconciled with the tacitly accepted natural law of equivalence between productive service and remuneration. The normal balance has been established, and the undertaker's function has been justified and subsumed under the ancient law that Nature does all things well and equitably.

This holds true of the political economy of our grandfathers. But this aim and method of handling the phenomena of life for theoretical ends, of course, did not go out of vogue abruptly in the days of our grandfathers.[2] There is a large sufficiency of the like aim and animus

[1] The undertaker gets an income; therefore he must produce goods. But human activity directed to the production of goods is labor; therefore the undertaker is a particular kind of laborer. There is, of course, some dissent from this position.

[2] The change which has supervened as regards the habitual resort to a natural law of equivalence is in large part a change with respect to the degree of immediacy and "reality" imputed to this law, and to a still greater extent a change in the degree of overtness with which it is avowed.

in the theoretical discussions of a later time; but specifically to cite and analyse the evidence of its presence would be laborious, nor would it conduce to the general peace of mind.

Some motion towards a further revision of the scheme is to be seen in the attention which has latterly been given to the function and the profits of that peculiar class of undertakers whom we call speculators. But even on this head the argument is apt to turn on the question of how the services which the speculator is conceived to render the community are to be construed into an equivalent of his gains.[1] The difficulty of interpretation encountered at this point is considerable, partly because it is not quite plain whether the speculators as a class come out of their transactions with a net gain or with a net loss. A systematic net loss, or a no-profits balance, would, on the theory of equivalence, mean that the class which gets this loss or doubtful gain is of no service to the community; yet we are, out of the past, committed to the view that the speculator is useful—indeed economically indispenable—and shall therefore have his reward. In the discussions given to the speculator and his function some thought is commonly given to the question of the "legitimacy" of the speculator's traffic. The legitimate speculator is held to earn his gain by services of an economic kind rendered the community. The recourse to this epithet, "legitimate", is chiefly of interest as showing that the tacit postulate of a natural order is still in force. Legitimate are such speculative dealings as are, by the theorist,

[1] See, *e. g.*, a paper by H. C. Emery in the Papers and Proceedings of the Twelfth Annual Meeting of the American Economic Association, on "The Place of the Speculator in the Theory of Distribution," and more particularly the discussion following the paper.

conceived to serve the ends of the community, while illegitimate speculation is that which is conceived to be disserviceable to the community.

The theoretical difficulty about the speculator and his gains (or losses) is that the speculator *ex professo* is quite without interest in or connection with any given industrial enterprise or any industrial plant. He is, industrially speaking, without visible means of support. He may stake his risks on the gain or on the loss of the community with equal chances of success, and he may shift from one side to the other without winking.

The speculator may be treated as an extreme case of undertaker, who deals exclusively with the business side of economic life rather than with the industrial side. But he differs in this respect from the common run of business men in degree rather than in kind. His traffic is a pecuniary traffic, and it touches industry only remotely and uncertainly; while the business man as commonly conceived is more or less immediately interested in the successful operation of some concrete industrial plant. But since the undertaker first broke into economic theory, some change has also taken place as regards the immediacy of the relations of the common run of undertakers to the mechanical facts of the industries in which they are interested. Half a century ago it was still possible to construe the average business manager in industry, as an agent occupied with the superintendence of the mechanical processes involved in the production of goods or services. But in the later development the connection between the business manager and the mechanical processes has, on an average, grown more remote; so much so, that his superintendence of the plant or of the processes is frequently visible only to the scientific imagination. That activity by virtue of which the undertaker is classed as such makes him a business-man, not a mechanic or foreman of the shop. His superintendence is a superintendence of the pecuniary affairs of the concern, rather than of the industrial plant; especially is this true in the higher development of the modern captain of industry. As regards the nature of the employment which characterizes the undertaker, it is possible to distinguish him from the men who are mechanically engaged in the production of goods, and to say that his employment is of a business or pecuniary kind, while theirs is of an industrial or mechanical kind. It is not possible to draw a similar distinction between the undertaker who is in charge of a given industrial concern, and the business man who is in business but is not interested in the production of goods or services. As regards the character of employment, then, the line falls not between legitimate and illegitimate pecuniary transactions, but between business and industry.

The distinction between business and industry has, of course, been possible from the beginning of economic theory, and, indeed, the distinction has from time to time temporarily been made in the contrast frequently pointed out between the proximate interest of the business man and the ulterior interest of society at large. What appears to have hindered the reception of the distinction into economic doctrine, is the constraining presence of a belief in an order of Nature and the habit of conceiving the economic community as an organism. The point of view given by these postulates has made such a distinction between employments not only useless, but even disservicable for the ends to which theory has been directed. But the fact has come to be gradually more and more patent that there are constantly, normally present in modern economic life an important range of activities and classes of persons who work for an income but of whom it cannot be said that they, either proximately or remotely, apply themselves to the production of goods. Their services, proximate or remote, to society are often of quite a problematical character. They are ubiquitous, and it will scarcely do to say that they are anomalous, for they are of ancient prescription, they are within the law and within the pale of popular morals.

Of these strictly economic activities that are lucrative without necessarily being serviceable to the community, the greater part are to be classed as "business". Perhaps the largest and most obvious illustration of these legitimate business employments is afforded by the speculators in securities. By way of further illustration may be mentioned the extensive and varied business of real-estate men (land-agents) engaged in the purchase and sale of property for speculative gain or for a commission; so, also, the closely related business of promoters and boomers of other than real-estate ventures; as also attorneys, brokers, bankers, and the like, although the work performed by these latter will more obviously bear interpretation in terms of social serviceability. The traffic of these business men shades off insensibly from that of the *bona fide* speculator who has no ulterior end of industrial efficiency to serve, to that of the captain of industry or entrepreneur as conventionally set forth in the economic manuals.

The characteristic in which these business employments resemble one another, and in which they differ from the mechanical occupations as well as from other non-economic employments, is that they are concerned primarily with the phenomena of value—with exchange or market values and with purchase and sale—and only indirectly and secondarily, if at all, with mechanical processes. What holds the interest and guides and shifts the attention of men within these employments is the main chance. These activities begin and end within what may broadly be called "the higgling of the market". Of the industrial employments, in the stricter sense, it may be said, on the other hand, that they begin and end outside the higgling of the market. Their proximate aim and effect is the shaping and guiding of material things and processes. Broadly, they may be said to be primarily occupied with the phenomena of material serviceability, rather than with those of exchange value. They are taken up with the phenomena which make the subject matter of Physics and the other material sciences.

The business man enters the economic life process from the pecuniary side, and so far as he works an effect in industry he works it through the pecuniary dispositions which he makes. He takes thought most immediately of men's convictions regarding market values; and his efforts as a business man are directed to the apprehension, and commonly also to the influencing of men's beliefs regarding market values. The objective point of business is the diversion of purchase and sale into some particular channel, commonly involving a diversion from other channels. The laborer and the man engaged in directing industrial processes, on the other hand, enter the economic process from the material side; in their characteristic work they take thought most immediately of mechanical effects, and their attention is directed to turning men and things to account for the compassing of some material end. The ulterior aim, and the ulterior effect, of these industrial employments may be some pecuniary result; work of this class commonly results in an enhancement, or at least an alteration, of market values. Conversely, business activity may, and in a majority of cases it probably does, effect an enhancement of the aggregate material wealth of the community, or the aggregate serviceability of the means at hand; but such an industrial outcome is by no means bound to follow from the nature of the business man's work.

From what has just been said it appears that, if we retain the classical division of economic theory into Production, Distribution, and Consumption, the pecuniary employments do not properly fall under the first of these divisions, Production, if that term is to retain the meaning commonly assigned to it. In an earlier and less specialized organization of economic life, particularly, the undertaker frequently performs the work of a foreman or a technological expert, as well as the work of business management. Hence in most discussions of his work and his theoretical relations his occupation is treated as a composite one. The technological side of his composite occupation has even given a name to his gains (wages of superintendence), as if the undertaker were primarily a master-workman. The distinction at this point has been drawn between classes of persons instead of between classes of employments; with the result that the evident necessity of discussing his technological employment under production has given countenance to the endeavor to dispose of the undertaker's business activity under the same head. This endeavor has, of course, not wholly succeeded.

In the later development, the specialization of work in the economic field has at this point progressed so far, and the undertaker now in many cases comes so near being occupied with business affairs alone, to the exclusion of technological direction and supervision, that, with this object lesson before us, we no longer have the same difficulty in drawing a distinction between business and industrial employments. And even in the earlier days of the doctrines, when the aim was to dispose of the undertaker's work under the theoretical head of Production, the business side of his work persistently obtruded itself for discussion in the books and chapters given to Distribution and Exchange. The course taken by the later theoretical discussion of the entrepreneur, leaves no question but that the characteristic fact about his work is that he is a business man, occupied with pecuniary affairs.

Such pecuniary employments, of which the purely fiscal or financiering forms of business are typical, are nearly all and nearly throughout, conditioned by the institution of property or ownership—an institution which, as John Stuart Mill remarks, belongs entirely within the theoretical realm of Distribution. Ownership, no doubt, has its effect upon productive industry, and, indeed, its effect upon industry is very large, both in scope and range, even if we should not be prepared to go the length of saying that it fundamentally conditions all industry; but ownership is not itself primarily or immediately a contrivance for production. Ownership directly touches the results of industry, and only indirectly the methods and processes of industry. If the institution of property be compared with such a feature of our culture, for instance, as the domestication of plants or the smelting of iron, the meaning of what has just been said may seem clearer.

So much then of the business man's activity as is conditioned by the institution of property, is not to be classed, in economic theory, as productive or industrial activity at all. Its objective point is an alteration of the distribution of wealth. His business is, essentially, to sell and buy—sell in order to buy cheaper, buy in order to sell dearer.[1] It may or may not, indirectly, and in a sense incidentally, result in enhanced production. The business man may be equally successful in his enterprise, and he may be equally well remunerated, whether his activity does or does not enrich the community. Immediately and directly, so long as it is confined to the pecuniary or business sphere, his activity is incapable of enriching or impoverishing the community as a whole except, after the fashion conceived by the mercantilists, through his dealings with men of other communities. The circulation and distribution of goods incidental to the business man's traffic is commonly, though not always or in the nature of the case, serviceable to the community; but the distribution of goods is a mechanical, not a pecuniary transaction, and it is not the objective point of business nor its invariable outcome. From the point of view of business, the distribution or circulation of goods is a means of gain, not an end sought.

It is true, industry is closely conditioned by business. In a modern community, the business man finally decides what may be done in industry, or at least in the greater number and the more conspicuous branches of industry. This is particularly true of those branches that are currently thought of as peculiarly modern. Under existing circumstances of ownership, the discretion in economic matters, industrial or otherwise, ultimately rests in the hands of the business men. It is their business to have to do with property, and property means

[1] Cf., *e.g.*, Marx's Capital, especially bk. I, ch. IV.

the discretionary control of wealth. In point of character, scope and growth, industrial processes and plants adapt themselves to the exigencies of the market, wherever there is a developed market, and the exigencies of the market are pecuniary exigencies. The business man, through his pecuniary dispositions, enforces his choice of what industrial processes shall be in use. He can, of course, not create or initiate methods or aims for industry; if he does so he steps out of the business sphere into the material domain of industry. But he can decide whether and which of the known processes and industrial arts shall be practised, and to what extent. Industry must be conducted to suit the business man in his quest for gain; which is not the same as saying that it must be conducted to suit the needs or the convenience of the community at large. Ever since the institution of property was definitely installed, and in proportion as purchase and sale has been practiced, some approach has been made to a comprehensive system of control of industry by pecuniary transactions and for pecuniary ends, and the industrial organization is nearer such a consummation now than it ever has been. For the great body of modern industry the final term of the sequence is not the production of the goods but their sale; the endeavor is not so much to fit the goods for use as for sale. It is well known that there are many lines of industry in which the cost of marketing the goods equals the cost of making and transporting them.

Any industrial venture which falls short in meeting the pecuniary exigencies of the market declines and yields ground to others that meet them with better effect. Hence shrewd business management is a requisite to success in any industry that is carried on within the scope of the market. Pecuniary failure carries with it industrial failure, whatever may be the cause to which the pecuniary failure is due—whether it be inferiority of the goods produced, lack of salesmanlike tact, popular prejudice, scanty or ill-devised advertising, excessive truthfulness, or what not. In this way industrial results are closely dependent upon the presence of business ability; but the cause of this dependence of industry upon business in a given case is to be sought in the fact that other rival ventures have the backing of shrewd business management, rather than in any help which business management in the aggregate affords to the aggregate industry of the community. Shrewd and farsighted business management is a requisite of survival in the competitive pecuniary struggle in which the several industrial concerns are engaged, because shrewd and farsighted business management abounds and is employed by all the competitors. The ground of survival in the selective process is fitness for pecuniary gain, not fitness for serviceability at large. Pecuniary management is of an emulative character and gives, primarily, relative success only. If the change were equitably distributed, an increase or decrease of the aggregate or average business ability in the community need not immediately affect the industrial efficiency or the material welfare of the community. The like can not be said with respect to the aggregate or average industrial capacity of the men at work. The latter are, on the whole, occupied with production of goods; the business men, on the other hand, are occupied with the acquisition of them.

Theoreticians who are given to looking beneath the facts and to contemplating the profounder philosophical meaning of life speak of the function of the undertaker as being the guidance and coördination of industrial processes with a view to economies of production. No doubt, the remoter effect of business transactions often is such coördination and economy, and, no doubt, also, the undertaker has such economy in view and is stimulated to his manoeuvers of combination by the knowledge that certain economies of this kind are feasible and will inure to his gain if the proper business arrangements can be effected. But it is practicable to class even this indirect furthering of industry by the undertaker as a permissive guidance only. The men in industry must first create the mechanical possibility of such new and more economical methods and arrangements, before the undertaker sees the chance, makes the necessary business arrangements, and gives directions that the more effective working arrangements be adopted.

It is notorious, and it is a matter upon which men dilate, that the wide and comprehensive consolidations and coördinations of industry, which often add so greatly to its effectiveness, take place at the initiative of the business men who are in control. It should be added that the fact of their being in control precludes such coördination from being effected except by their advice and consent. And it should also be added, in order to a passably complete account of the undertaker's function, that he not only can and does effect economizing coördinations of a large scope, but he also can and does at times inhibit the process of consolidation and coördination. It happens so frequently that it might fairly be said to be the common run that business interests and undertaker's manoeuvers delay consolidation, combination, coördination, for some appreciable time after they have become patently advisable on industrial grounds. The industrial advisability or practicability is not the decisive point. Industrial advisability must wait on the eventual convergence of jarring pecuniary interests and on the strategical moves of business men playing for position.

Which of these two offices of the business man in modern industry, the furthering or the inhibitory, has the more serious or more far-reaching consequences is, on the whole, somewhat problematical. The furtherance of coördination by the modern captain of industry bulks large in our vision, in great part because the process of widening coördination is of a cumulative character. After a given step in coördination and combination has been taken, the next step takes place on the basis of the resulting situation. Industry, that is to say the working force engaged in industry, has a chance to develope new and larger possibilities to be taken further advantage of. In this way each successive move in the enhancement of the efficiency of industrial processes, or in the widening of coördination in industrial processes, pushes the captain of industry to a further concession, making possible a still farther industrial growth. But as regards the undertaker's inhibitory dealings with industrial coordination the visible outcome is not so striking. The visible outcome is simply that nothing of the kind then takes place in the premises. The potential cumulative sequence is cut off at the start, and so it does not figure in our appraisement of the disadvantage incurred. The loss does not commonly take the more obtrusive form of an absolute retreat, but only that of a failure to advance where the industrial situation admits of an advance.

It is, of course, impracticable to foot up and compare gain and loss in such a case, where the losses, being of the nature of inhibited growth, cannot be ascertained.

But since the industrial serviceability of the captain of industry is, on the whole, of a problematical complexion, it should be advisable for a cautious economic theory not to rest its discussion of him on his serviceability.[1]

It is not hereby intended to depreciate the services rendered the community by the captain of industry in his management of business. Such services are no doubt rendered and are also no doubt of substantial value. Still less is it the intention to decry the pecuniary incentive as a motive to thrift and diligence. It may well be that the pecuniary traffic which we call business is the most effective method of conducting the industrial policy of the community; not only the most effective that has been contrived, but perhaps the best that can be contrived. But that is a matter of surmise and opinion. In a matter of opinion on a point that cannot be verified, a reasonable course is to say that the majority are presumably in the right. But all that is beside the point. However probable or reasonable such a view may be, it can find no lodgment in modern scientific theory, except as a corollary of secondary importance. Nor can scientific theory build upon the ground it may be conceived to afford. Policy may so build, but science can not. Scientific theory is a formulation of the laws of phenomena in terms of the efficient forces at work in the sequence of phenomena. So long as (under the old dispensation of the order of nature) the animistically conceived natural laws, with their God-given objective end, were considered to exercise a constraining guidance over the course of events whereof they were claimed to be laws, so long it was legitimate scientific procedure for economists to formulate their theory in terms of these laws of the natural course; because so long they were speaking in terms of what was, to them, the efficient forces at work. But so soon as these natural laws were reduced to the plane of colorless empirical generalization as to what commonly happens, while the efficient forces at work are conceived to be of quite another cast, so soon must theory abandon the ground of the natural course, sterile for modern scientific purposes, and shift to the ground of the causal sequence, where alone it will have to do with the forces at work as they are conceived in our time. The generalizations regarding the normal course, as "normal" has been defined in economics since J. S. Mill, are not of the nature of theory, but only rule-of-thumb. And the talk about the "function" of this and that factor of production, etc., in terms of the collective life purpose, goes to the same limbo; since the collective life purpose is no longer avowedly conceived to cut any figure in the every-day guidance of economic activities or the shaping of economic results.

The doctrine of the social-economic function of the undertaker may for the present purpose be illustrated by a suppositious parallel from

It appears, then, as all economists are no doubt aware, that there is in modern society a considerable range of activities, which are not only normally present, but which constitute the vital core of our economic system; which are not directly concerned with production, but which are nevertheless lucrative. Indeed, the group comprises most of the highly remunerative employments in modern economic life. The gains from these employments must plainly be accounted for on other grounds than their productivity, since they need have no productivity.

But it is not only as regards the pecuniary employments that productivity and remuneration are constitutionally out of touch. It seems plain, from what has already been said, that the like is true for the remuneration gained in the industrial employments. Most wages, particularly those paid in the industrial employments proper, as contrasted with those paid for domestic or personal service, are paid on account of pecuniary serviceability to the employer, not on grounds of material

Physics. It is an easy generalization, which will scarcely be questioned, that, in practice, pendulums commonly vibrate in a plane approximately parallel with the nearest wall of the clock-case in which they are placed. The normality of this parallelism is fortified by the further observation that the vibrations are also commonly in a plane parallel with the nearest wall of the room; and when it is further called to mind that the balance which serves the purpose of a pendulum in watches similarly vibrates in a plane parallel with the walls of its case, the absolute normality of the whole arrangement is placed beyond question. It is true, the parallelism is not claimed to be related to the working of the pendulum, except as a matter of fortuitous convenience; but it should be manifest from the generality of the occurrence that in the normal case, in the absence of disturbing causes, and in the long run, all pendulums will "naturally" tend to swing in a plane faultlessly parallel with the nearest wall. The use which has been made of the "organic concept", in economics and in social science at large, is fairly comparable with this suppositious argument concerning the pendulum.

serviceability to mankind at large. The product is valued, sought and paid for on account of and in some proportion to its vendibility, not for more recondite reasons of ulterior human welfare at large. It results that there is no warrant, in general theory, for claiming that the work of highly paid persons (more particularly that of highly paid business men) is of greater substantial use to the community than that of the less highly paid. At the same time, the reverse could, of course, also not be claimed. Wages, resting on a pecuniary basis, afford no consistent indication of the relative productivity of the recipients, except in comparisons between persons or classes whose products are identical except in amount, —that is to say, where a resort to wages as an index of productivity would be of no use anyway.

A result of the acceptance of the theoretical distinction here attempted between industrial and pecuniary employments and an effective recognition of the pecuniary basis of the modern economic organization would be to dissociate the two ideas of productivity and remuneration. In mathematical language, remuneration could no longer be conceived and handled as a "function" of productivity,—unless productivity be taken to mean pecuniary serviceability to the person who pays the remuneration. In modern life remuneration is, in the last analysis, uniformly obtained by virtue of an agreement between individuals who commonly proceed

[1] Since the ground of payment of wages is the vendibility of the product, and since the ground of a difference in wages is the different vendibility of the product acquired through the purchase of the labor for which the wages are paid, it follows that wherever the difference in vendibility rests on a difference in the magnitude of the product alone, there wages should be somewhat in proportion to the magnitude of the product.

on their own interest in point of pecuniary gain. The remuneration may, therefore, be said to be a "function" of the pecuniary service rendered the person who grants the remuneration; but what is pecuniarily serviceable to the individual who exercises the discretion in the matter need not be productive of material gain to the community as a whole. Nor does the algebraic sum of individual pecuniary gains measure the aggregate serviceability of the activities for which the gains are got.

In a community organized, as modern communities are, on a pecuniary basis, the discretion in economic matters rests with the individuals, in severalty; and the aggregate of discrete individual interests nowise expresses the collective interest. Expressions constantly recur in economic discussions which imply that the transactions discussed are carried out for the sake of the collective good or at the initiative of the social organism, or that "society" rewards so and so for their services. Such expressions are commonly of the nature of figures of speech and are serviceable for homiletical rather than for scientific use. They serve to express their user's faith in a beneficent order of nature, rather than to convey or to formulate information in regard to facts.

Of course, it is still possible consistently to hold that there is a natural equivalence between work and its reward, that remuneration is naturally, or normally, or in the long run, proportioned to the material service rendered the community by the recipient; but that proposition will hold true only if "natural" or "normal" be taken in such a sense as to admit of our saying that the natural does not coincide with the actual; and it must be recognized that such a doctrine of the "natural" apportionment of wealth or of income disregards the efficient facts of the case. Apart from effects of this kind in the way of equitable arrangements traceable to grounds of sentiment, the only recourse which modern science would afford the champion of a doctrine of natural distribution, in the sense indicated, would be a doctrine of natural selection; according to which all disserviceable or unproductive, wasteful, employments would, perforce, be weeded out as being incompatible with the continued life of any community that tolerated them. But such a selective elimination of unserviceable or wasteful employments would presume the following two conditions, neither of which need prevail: (1) It must be assumed that the disposable margin between the aggregate productivity of industry and the aggregate necessary consumption is so narrow as to admit of no appreciable waste of energy or of goods; (2) it must be assumed that no deterioration of the condition of society in the economic respect does or can "naturally" take place. As to the former of these two assumptions, it is to be said that in a very poor community, and under exceptionally hard economic circumstances, the margin of production may be as narrow as the theory would require. Something approaching this state of things may be found, for instance, among some Eskimo tribes. But in a modern industrial community—where the margin of admissible waste probably always exceeds fifty per cent. of the output of goods—the facts make no approach to the hypothesis. The second assumed condition is, of course, the old-fashioned assumption of a beneficent, providential order or meliorative trend in human affairs. As such, it needs no argument at this day. Instances are not far to seek of communities in which economic deterioration has taken place while the system of distribution, both of income and of accumulated wealth, has remained on a pecuniary basis.

I am sensible of having dwelt at an unseemly length on this question of an organic or natural equivalence between social service and remuneration, on the one hand, and on the bearing of the attempted distinction between industrial and pecuniary employments upon this theory of a natural equivalence, on the other hand. My excuse for so doing is that this doctrine of a natural equivalence has had a far-reaching and enduring effect upon the received theories of distribution and production, and that, with a change of phrase rather than of substance, it still continues to afford ground for further elaboration of like theories; while at the same time it seems plain that a scrutiny of the metaphysics of the doctrine of equivalence must immediately put it out of court as being groundless as well as useless for the purposes of modern science. I am also sensible of having said very little in the course of this long argument that is not already contained, explicitly or by broad implication, in the accepted body of doctrines. What has been attempted is to follow out the direction of latter-day economic discussion one step beyond the point at which those who have been making economic science have been content to rest their analysis of phenomena. This one step crosses the frontier between the normal and the actual, at a point where the line has not usually been crossed.

To return to the main drift of the argument. The pecuniary employments have to do with wealth in point of ownership, with market values, with transactions of exchange, purchase and sale, bargaining for the purpose of pecuniary gain. These employments make up the characteristic occupations of business men, and the gains of business are derived from successful endeavors of the pecuniary kind. These business employments are the characteristic activity (constitute the "function") of what are in theory called undertakers. The dispositions which undertakers, *qua* business men, make are pecuniary dispositions—whatever industrial sequel they may or may not have—and are carried out with a view to pecuniary gain. The wealth of which they have the discretionary disposal may or may not be in the form of "production goods"; but in whatever form the wealth in question is conceived to exist, it is handled by the undertakers in terms of values and is disposed of by them in the pecuniary respect. When, as may happen, the undertaker steps down from the pecuniary plane and directs the mechanical handling and functioning of "production goods", he becomes for the time a foreman. The undertaker, if his business venture is of the industrial kind, of course takes cognizance of the aptness of a given industrial method or process for his purpose, and he has to choose between different industrial processes in which to invest his values; but his work as undertaker, simply, is the investment and shifting of the values under his hand from the less to the more gainful point of investment. When the investment takes the form of material means of industry, or industrial plant, the sequel of a given business transaction is commonly some particular use of such means; and when such industrial use follows, it commonly takes place at the hands of other men than the undertaker, although it takes place within limits imposed by the pecuniary exigencies of which the undertaker takes cognizance. Wealth turned to account in the way of investment or business management may or may not, in consequence, be turned to account, materially, for industrial effect. Wealth, values, so employed for pecuniary ends is capital in the business sense of the word. Wealth, material means of industry, physically employed for industrial ends is capital in the industrial sense. Theory, therefore, would require that care be taken to distinguish between capital as a pecuniary category, and capital as an industrial category, if the term capital is retained to cover the two concepts.[2] The distinction here made substantially coincides with a distinction which many late writers have arrived at from a different point of approach and have, with varying success, made use of under different terms.[3]

A further corollary touching capital may be pointed out. The gains derived from the handling of capital in the pecuniary respect have no immediate relation, stand in no necessary relation of proportion, to the productive effect compassed by the industrial use of the material means over which the undertaker may dispose; although the gains have a relation of dependence to the effects achieved in point of vendibility. But vendibility need not, even approximately, coincide with serviceability,

[1] All wealth so used is capital, but it does not follow that all pecuniary capital is social wealth.

[2] In current theory the term capital is used in these two senses: while in business usage it is employed pretty consistently in the former sense alone. The current ambiguity in the term capital has often been adverted to by economists, and there may be need of a revision of the terminology at this point; but this paper is not concerned with that question.

[3] Professor Fetter, in a recent paper (*Quarterly Journal of Economics*, November, 1900) is, perhaps, the writer who has gone the farthest in this direction in the definition of the capital concept. Professor Fetter wishes to confine the term capital to pecuniary capital, or rather to such pecuniary capital as is based on the ownership of material goods. The wisdom of such a terminological expedient is, of course, not in question here.

except serviceability be construed in terms of marginal utility or some related conception, in which case the outcome is a tautology. Where, as in the case commonly assumed by economists as typical, the investing undertaker seeks his gain through the production and sale of some useful article, it is commonly also assumed that his effort is directed to the most economical production of as large and serviceable a product as may be, or at least it is assumed that such production is the outcome of his endeavors in the natural course of things. This account of the aim and outcome of business enterprise may be natural, but it does not describe the facts. The facts being, of course, that the undertaker in such a case seeks to produce economically as vendible a product as may be. In the common run vendibility depends in great part on the serviceability of the goods, but it depends also on several other circumstances; and to that highly variable, but nearly always considerable extent to which vendibility depends on other circumstances than the material serviceability of the goods, the pecuniary management of capital must be held not to serve the ends of production. Neither immediately, in his purely pecuniary traffic, nor indirectly, in the business guidance of industry through his pecuniary traffic, therefore, can the undertaker's dealings with his pecuniary capital be accounted a productive occupation, nor can the gains of capital be taken to mark or to measure the productivity due to the investment. The "cost of production" of goods in the case contemplated is to an appreciable, but indeterminable, extent a cost of production of vendibility—an outcome which is often of doubtful service to the body of consumers, and which often counts in the aggregate as waste. The material serviceability of the means employed in industry, that is to say the functioning of industrial capital in the service of the community at large, stands in no necessary or consistent relation to the gainfulness of capital in the pecuniary respect. Productivity can accordingly not be predicted of pecuniary capital. It follows that productivity theories of interest should be as difficult to maintain as productivity theories of the gains of the pecuniary employments, the two resting on the same grounds.

It is, further, to be remarked that pecuniary capital and industrial capital do not coincide in respect of the concrete things comprised under each. From this and from the considerations already indicated above, it follows that the magnitude of pecuniary capital may vary independently of variations in the magnitude of industrial capital—not indefinitely, perhaps, but within a range which, in its nature, is indeterminate. Pecuniary capital is a matter of market values, while industrial capital is, in the last analysis, a matter of mechanical efficiency, or rather of mechanical effects not reducible to a common measure or a collective magnitude. So far as the latter may be spoken of as a homogenous aggregate—itself a doubtful point at best—the two categories of capital are disparate magnitudes, which can be mediated only through a proces of valuation conditioned by other circumstances besides the mechanical efficiency of the material means valued. Market values being a psychological outcome, it follows that pecuniary capital, an aggregate of market values, may vary in magnitude with a freedom which gives the whole an air of caprice,—such as psychological phenomena, particularly the psychological phenomena of crowds, frequently present, and such as becomes strikingly noticeable in times of panic or of speculative inflation. On the other hand, industrial capital, being a matter of mechanical contrivances and adaptation, cannot similarly vary through a revision of valuations. If it is taken as an aggregate, it is a physical magnitude, and as such it does not alter its complexion or its mechanical efficiency in response to the greater or less degree of appreciation with which it is viewed. Capital pecuniarily considered rests on a basis of subjective value; capital industrially considered rests on material circumstances reducible to objective terms of mechanical, chemical and physiological effect.

The point has frequently been noted that it is impossible to get at the aggregate social (industrial) capital by adding up the several items of individual (pecuniary) capital. A reason for this, apart from variations in the market values of given material means of production, is that pecuniary capital comprises not only material things but also conventional facts, psychological phenomena not related in any rigid way to material means of production,—as, *e. g.*, good will, fashions, customs, prestige, effrontery, personal credit. Whatever ownership touches, and whatever affords ground for pecuniary discretion, may be turned to account for pecuniary gain and may therefore be comprised in the aggregate of pecuniary capital. Ownership, the basis of pecuniary capital, being itself a conventional fact, that is to say a matter of habits of thought, it is intelligible that phenomena of convention and opinion should figure in an inventory of pecuniary capital; whereas, industrial capital being of a mechanical character, conventional circumstances do not affect it—except as the future production of material means to replace the existing outfit may be guided by convention—and items having but a conventional existence are, therefore, not comprised in its aggregate. The disparity between pecuniary and industrial capital, therefore, is something more than a matter of an arbitrarily chosen point of view, as some recent discussions of the capital concept would have us believe; just as the difference between the pecuniary and the industrial employments, which are occupied with the one or the other category of capital, means something more than the same thing under different aspects.

But the distinction here attempted has a farther bearing, beyond the possible correction of a given point in the theory of distribution. Modern economic science is to an increasing extent concerning itself with the question of what men do and how and why they do it, as contrasted with the older question of how Nature, working through human nature, maintains a favorable balance in the output of goods. Neither the practical questions of our generation, nor the pressing theoretical questions of the science, run on the adequacy or equity of the share that goes to any class in the normal case. The questions are rather such realistic ones as these: Why do we, now and again, have hard times and unemployment in the midst of excellent resources, high efficiency and plenty of unmet wants? Why is one-half our consumable product contrived for consumption that yields no material benefit? Why are large coordinations of industry, which greatly reduce cost of production, a cause of perplexity and alarm? Why is the family disintegrating among the industrial classes, at the same time that the wherewithal to maintain it is easier to compass? Why are large and increasing portions of the community penniless in spite of a scale of remuneration which is very appreciably above the subsistence minimum? Why is there a widespread disaffection among the intelligent workmen who ought to know better? These and the like questions, being questions of fact, are not to be answered on the grounds of normal equivalence. Perhaps it might better be said that they have so often been answered on those grounds, without any approach to disposing of them, that the outlook for help in that direction has ceased to have a serious meaning. These are, to borrow Professor Clark's phrase, questions to be answered on dynamic, not on static grounds. They are questions of conduct and sentiment, and so far as their solution is looked for at the hands of economists it must be looked for along the line of the bearing which economic life has upon the growth of sentiment and canons of conduct. That is to say, they are questions of the bearing of economic life upon the cultural changes that are going forward.

For the present it is the vogue to hold that economic life, broadly, conditions the rest of social organization or the constitution of society. This vogue of the proposition will serve an excuse from going into an examination of the grounds on which it may be justified, as it is scarcely necessary to persuade any economist that it has substantial merits even if he may not accept it in an unqualified form. What the Marxists have named the "Materialistic Conception of History" is assented to with less and less qualification by those who make the growth of culture their subject of inquiry. This materialistic conception says that institutions are shaped by economic conditions; but, as it left the hands of the Marxists, and as it still functions in the hands of many who knew not Marx, it has very little to say regarding the efficient force, the channels, or the methods by which the economic situation is conceived to have its effect upon institutions. What answer the early Marxists gave to this question, of how the economic situation shapes institutions, was to the effect that the causal connection lies through a selfish, calculating class interest. But, while class interest may count for much in the outcome, this answer is plainly not a competent one, since, for one thing, institutions by no means change with the alacrity which the sole efficiency of a reasoned class interest would require.

Without discrediting the claim that class interest counts for something in the shaping of institutions, and to avoid getting entangled in preliminaries, it may be said that institutions are of the nature of prevalent habits of thought, and that therefore the force which shapes institutions is the force or forces which shape the habits of thought prevalent in the community. But habits of thought are the outcome of habits of life. Whether it is intentionally directed to the education of the individual or not, the discipline of daily life acts to alter or reenforce the received habits of thought, and so acts to fortify the received institutions under which men live. And the direction in which, on the whole, the alteration proceeds is conditioned by the trend of the discipline of daily life. The point here immediately at issue is the divergent trend of this discipline in those occupations which are prevailingly of an industrial character, as contrasted with those which are prevailingly of a pecuniary character. So far as regards the different cultural outcome to be looked for on the basis of the present economic situation as contrasted with the past, therefore, the question immediately in hand is as to the greater or less degree in which occupations are differentiated into industrial and pecuniary in the present as compared with the past.

The characteristic feature which is currently held to differentiate the existing economic situation from that out of which the present has developed, or out of which it is emerging, is the prevalence of the machine industry with the consequent larger and more highly specialized organization of the market and of the industrial force and plant. As has been pointed out above, and as is well enough known from the current discussions of the economists, industrial life is organized on a pecuniary basis and managed from the pecuniary side. This, of course, is true in a degree both of the present and of the nearer past, back at least as far as the middle ages. But the larger scope of organizations in modern industry means that the pecuniary management has been gradually passing into the hands of a relatively decreasing class, whose contact with the industrial classes proper grows continually less immediate. The distinction between employments above spoken of is in an increasing degree coming to coincide with a differentiation of occupations and of economic classes. Some degree of such specialization and differentiation there has, of course, been, one might almost say, always. But in our time, in many branches of industry, the specialization has been carried so far that large bodies of the working population have but an incidental contact with the business side of the enterprise, while a minority have little if any other concern with the enterprise than its pecuniary management. This was not true, *e. g.*, at the time when the undertaker was still salesman, purchasing agent, business manager, foreman of the shop, and master workman. Still less was it true in the days of the self-sufficing manor or household, or in the days of the closed town industry. Neither is it true in our time of what we call the backward or old-fashioned industries. These latter have not been and are not organized on a large scale, with a consistent division of labor between the owners and business managers on the one side and the operative employees on the other. Our standing illustration of this less highly organized class of industries are the surviving handicrafts and the common run of farming as carried on by relatively small proprietors. In that earlier phase of economic life, out of which the modern situation has gradually grown, all the men engaged had to be constantly on their guard, in a pecuniary sense, and were constantly disciplined in the husbanding of their means and in the driving of bargains,—as is still true, *e. g.*, of the American farmer. The like was formerly true also of the consumer, in his purchases, to a greater extent than at present. A good share of the daily attention of those who were engaged in the handicrafts was still perforce given to the pecuniary or business side of their trade. But for that great body of industry which is conventionally recognized as eminently modern, specialization of function has gone so far as, in great measure, to exempt the operative employees from taking thought of pecuniary matters.

Now, as to the bearing of all this upon cultural changes that are in progress or in the outlook. Leaving the "backward," relatively unspecialized, industries on one side, as being of an equivocal character for the point in hand and as not differing characteristically from the corresponding industries in the past so far as regards their disciplinary value; modern occupations may, for the sake of the argument, be broadly distinguished, as economic employments have been distinguished above, into business and industrial. The modern industrial and the modern business occupations are fairly comparable as regards the degree of intelligence required in both, if it be borne in mind that the former occupations comprise the highly trained technological experts and engineers as well as the highly skilled mechanics. The two classes of occupations differ in that the men in the pecuniary occupations work within the lines and under the guidance of the great institution of ownership, with its ramifications of custom, prerogative, and legal right; whereas those in the industrial occupations are, in their work, relatively free from the constraint of this conventional norm of truth and validity. It is, of course, not true that the work of the latter class lies outside the reach of the institution of ownership; but it is true that, in the heat and strain of the work, when the agent's powers and attention are fully taken up with the work which he has in hand, that of which he has perforce to take cognizance is not conventional law, but the conditions impersonally imposed by the nature of material things. This is the meaning of the current commonplace that the required close and continuous application of the operative in mechanical industry bars him out of all chance for an all-around development of the cultural graces and amenities. It is the periods of close attention and hard work that seem to count for most in the formation of habits of thought.

An *a priori* argument as to what cultural effects should naturally follow from such a difference in discipline between occupations, past and present, would probably not be convincing, as *a priori* arguments from half-authenticated premises commonly are not. And the experiments along this line which later economic developments have so far exhibited have been neither neat enough, comprehensive enough, nor long contiued enough to give definitive results. Still, there is something to be said under this latter head, even if this something may turn out to be somewhat familiar.

It is, *e. g.*, a commonplace of current vulgar discussions of existing economic questions, that the classes engaged in the modern mechanical or factory industries are improvident and apparently incompetent to take care of the pecuniary details of their own life. In this indictment may well be included not only factory hands, but the general class of highly skilled mechanics, inventors, technological experts. The rule does not hold in any hard and fast way, but there seems to be a substantial ground of truth in the indictment in this general form. This will be evident on comparison of the present factory population with the class of handicraftsmen of the older culture whom they have displaced, as also on comparison with the farming population of the present time, especially the small proprietors of this and other countries. The inferiority which is currently conceded to the modern industrial classes in this respect is not due to scantier opportunities for saving, whether they are compared with the earlier handicraftsmen or with the modern farmer or peasant. This phenomena is commonly discussed in terms which impute to the improvident industrial classes something in the way of total depravity, and there is much preaching of thrift and steady habits. But the preaching of thrift and self-help, unremitting as it is, is not producing an appreciable effect. The trouble seems to run deeper than exhortation can reach. It seems to be of the nature of habit rather than of reasoned conviction. Other causes may be present and may be competent partially to explain the improvidence of these classes, but the inquiry is at least a pertinent one how far the absence of property and thrift among them may be traceable to the relative absence of pecuniary training in the discipline of their daily life. If, as the general lay of the subject would indicate, this peculiar pecuniary situation of the industrial classes is in any degree due to comprehensive disciplinary causes, there is material in it for an interesting economic inquiry.

The surmise that the trouble with the industrial class is something of this character is strengthened by another feature of modern vulgar life, to which attention is directed as a further, and, for the present, a concluding illustration of the character of the questions that are touched by the distinction here spoken for. The most insidious and most alarming malady, as well as the most perplexing and unprecedented, that threatens the modern social and political structure is what is vaguely called socialism. The point of danger to the social structure, and at the same time the substantial core of the socialistic disaffection, is a growing disloyalty to the institution of property, aided and abetted as it is by a similarly growing lack of deference and affection for other conventional features of social structure. The classes affected by socialistic vagaries are not consistently averse to a competent organization and control of society, particularly not in the economic respect, but they are averse to organization and control on conventional lines. The sense of solidarity does not seem to be either defective or in abeyance, but the ground of solidarity is new and unexpected. What their constructive ideals may be need not concern nor detain us; they are vague and inconsistent and for the most part negative. Their disaffection has been set down to discontent with their lot by comparison with others, and to a mistaken view of their own interests; and much and futile effort has been spent in showing them the error of their ways of thinking. But what the experience of the past suggests that we should expect under the guidance of such motives and reasoning as these would be a demand for a redistribution of property, a reconstitution of the convention of ownership on such new lines as the apprehended interests of these classes would seem to dictate. But such is not the trend of socialistic thinking, which contemplates rather the elimination of the institution of property. To the socialists property or ownership does not seem inevitable or inherent in the nature of things; to those who criticise and admonish them it commonly does.

Compare them in this respect with other classes who have been moved by hardship or discontent, whether well or ill advised, to put forth denunciations and demands for radical economic changes; as *e.g.*, the American farmers in their several movements, of grangerism, populism, and the like. These have been loud enough in their denunciations and complaints, and they have been accused of being socialistic in their demand for a virtual redistribution of property. They have not felt the justice of the accusation, however, and it is to be noted that their demands have consistently run on a rehabilitation of property on some new basis of distribution, and have been uniformly put forth with the avowed purpose of bettering the claimants in point of ownership. Ownership, property "honestly" acquired, has been sacred to the rural malcontents, here and elsewhere; what they have aspired to do has been to remedy what they have conceived to be certain abuses under the institution, without questioning the institution itself.

Not so with the socialists, either in this country or elsewhere. Now, the spread of socialistic sentiment shows a curious tendency to affect those classes particularly who are habitually employed in the specialized industrial occupations, and are thereby in great part exempt from the intellectual discipline of pecuniary management. Among these men, who by the circumstances of their daily life are brought to do their serious and habitual thinking in other than pecuniary terms, it looks as if the ownership preconception were becoming obsolescent through disuse. It is the industrial population, in the modern sense, and particularly the more intelligent and skilled men employed in the mechanical industries, that are most seriously and widely affected. With exceptions both ways, but with a generality that is not to be denied, the socialistic disaffection spreads through the industrial towns, chiefly and most potently among the better classes of operatives in the mechanical employments; whereas the relatively indigent and unintelligent regions and classes, which the differentiation between pecuniary and industrial occupations has not reached, are relatively free from it. In like manner the upper and middle classes, whose employments are of a pecuniary character, if any, are also not seriously affected; and when avowed socialistic sentiment is met with among these upper and middle classes it commonly turns out to be merely a humanitarian aspiration for a more "equitable" redistribution of wealth—a readjustment of ownership under some new and improved method of control—not a contemplation of the traceless disappearance of ownership.

Socialism, in the sense in which the word connotes a

subversion of the economic foundations of modern culture, appears to be found only sporadically and uncertainly outside the limits, in time and space, of the discipline exercised by the modern mechanical, non-pecuniary occupations. This state of the case need of course not be due solely to the disciplinary effects of the industrial employments, nor even solely to effects traceable to those employments whether in the way of disciplinary results, selective development, or what not. Other factors, particularly factors of an ethnic character, seem to cooperate to the result indicated; but, so far as evidence bearing on the point is yet in hand and has been analyzed, it indicates that this differentiation of occupations is a necessary requisite to the growth of a consistent body of socialistic sentiment; and the indication is also that wherever this differentiation prevails in such a degree of accentuation and affects such considerable and compact bodies of people as to afford ground for a consistent growth of common sentiment, a result is some form of iconoclastic socialism. The differentiation may of course have a selective as well as a disciplinary effect upon the population affected, and an off-hand separation of these two modes of influence can of course not be made. In any case, the two modes of influence seem to converge to the outcome indicated; and, for the present purpose of illustration simply, the tracing out of the two strands of sequence in the case neither can nor need be undertaken. By force of this differentiation, in one way and another, the industrial classes are learning to think in terms of material cause and effect, to the neglect of prescription and conventional grounds of validity; just as, in a faintly incipient way, the economists are also learning to do in their discussion of the life of these classes. The resulting decay of the popular sense of conventional validity of course extends to other matters than the pecuniary conventions alone, with the outcome that the socialistically affected industrial classes are pretty uniformly affected with an effortless iconoclasm in other directions as well. For the discipline to which their work and habits of life subject them gives not so much a training away from the pecuniary conventions, specifically, as a positive and somewhat unmitigated training in methods of observation and inference proceeding on grounds alien to all conventional validity. But the practical experiment going on in the specialization of discipline, in the respect contemplated, appears still to be near its beginning, and the growth of aberrant views and habits of thought due to the peculiar disciplinary trend of this late and unprecedented specialization of occupations has not yet had time to work itself clear.

The effects of the like one-sided discipline are similarly visible in the highly irregular, conventionally indefensible attitude of the industrial classes in the current labor and wage disputes, not of an avowedly socialistic aim. So also as regards the departure from the ancient norm in such non-economic, or secondarily economic matters as the family relation and responsibility, where the disintegration of conventionalities in the industrial towns is said to threaten the foundations of domestic life and morality; and again as regards the growing inability of men trained to materialistic, industrial habits of thought to appreciate, or even to apprehend, the meaning of religious appeals and consolations that proceed on the old fashioned conventional or metaphysical grounds of validity. But these and other like directions in which the cultural effects of the modern specialization of occupations, whether in industry or in business, may be traceable can not be followed up here.

[5]

Excerpts from *The Theory of Business Enterprise*

Thorstein Bunde Veblen, 'Business Enterprise', pp. 20–65; 'Modern Business Capital', pp. 133–76; 'The Theory of Modern Welfare', pp. 177–267; 'The Cultural Incidence of the Machine Process', pp. 302–73, *The Theory of Business Enterprise* (New York: Scribner's, 1904).

Veblen juxtaposed the conventional orientations and activities of the modern business enterprise, particularly the modern corporation, to the unappreciated force of modern technology. Business enterprise and capital seen through the eyes of business people (then predominantly men) were different once one appreciated that the progress so readily otherwise attributable to business and capital was really due to the development of new technology. Even the growth of appreciation of this fact, to Veblen, was promoted by an advancing matter-of-fact orientation itself nourished by the machine process and its focus on strict means-ends analysis. The following excerpts are from what many consider to be Veblen's most important analytical work, *The Theory of Business Enterprise*. Here, too, Veblen employs the skills of anthropological deconstruction.

BUSINESS ENTERPRISE

THE motive of business is pecuniary gain, the method is essentially purchase and sale. The aim and usual outcome is an accumulation of wealth.[1] Men whose aim is not increase of possessions do not go into business, particularly not on an independent footing.

How these motives and methods of business work out in the traffic of commercial enterprise proper — in mercantile and banking business — does not concern the present inquiry, except so far as these branches of business affect the course of industrial business in the stricter sense of the term. Nor is it necessary here to describe the details of business routine, whether in the mer-

1 The ulterior ground of efforts directed to the accumulation of wealth is discussed at some length in the *Theory of the Leisure Class*, ch. II. and V., and the economic bearing of the business man's work is treated in a paper on "Industrial and Pecuniary Employments," in the *Proceedings* of the thirteenth annual meeting of the American Economic Association. Cf. also Marshall, *Principles of Economics* (3d ed.), bk. I. ch. III., bk. IV. ch. XII., bk. V. ch. IV., bk. VII. ch. VII. and VIII.; Bagehot, *Economic Studies*, especially pp. 53 *et seq.*; Walker, *Wages Question*, ch. XIV.; and more especially Sombart, *Moderne Kapitalismus*, vol. I. ch. I., VIII., XIV., XV.; Marx, *Kapital*, bk. I. ch. IV.; Schmoller, *Grundriss*, bk. II. ch. VII.

cantile pursuits or in the conduct of an industrial concern. The point of the inquiry is that characteristically modern business that is coextensive with the machine process described above and is occupied with the large mechanical industry. The aim is a theory of such business enterprise in outline sufficiently full to show in what manner business methods and business principles, in conjunction with the mechanical industry, influence the modern cultural situation. To save space and tedium, therefore, features of business traffic that are not of a broad character and not peculiar to this modern situation are left on one side, as being already sufficiently familiar for the purpose in hand.

In early modern times, before the régime of the machine industry set in, business enterprise on any appreciable scale commonly took the form of commercial business — some form of merchandising or banking. Shipping was the only considerable line of business which involved an investment in or management of extensive mechanical appliances and processes, comparable with the facts of the modern mechanical industry.[1] And shipping was

[1] It is significant that joint-stock methods of organization and management — that is to say, impersonally capitalistic methods — are traceable, for their origin and early formulation, to the shipping companies of early modern times. Cf. K. Lehmann, *Die geschichtliche Entwickelung des Aktienrechts bis zum Code de Commerce.* The like view is spoken for by Ehrenberg, *Zeitalter der Fugger;* see vol. II. pp. 325 *et seq.*

commonly combined with merchandising. But even the shipping trade of earlier times had much of a fortuitous character, in this respect resembling agriculture or any other industry in which wind and weather greatly affect the outcome. The fortunes of men in shipping were on a more precarious footing than to-day, and the successful outcome of their ventures was less a matter of shrewd foresight and daily pecuniary strategy than are the affairs of the modern large business concerns in transportation or the foreign trade. Under these circumstances the work of the business man was rather to take advantage of the conjunctures offered by the course of the seasons and the fluctuations of demand and supply than to adapt the course of affairs to his own ends. The large business man was more of a speculative buyer and seller and less of a financiering strategist than he has since become.

Since the advent of the machine age the situation has changed. The methods of business have, of course, not changed fundamentally, whatever may be true of the methods of industry; for they are, as they had been, conditioned by the facts of ownership. But instead of investing in the goods as they pass between producer and consumer, as the merchant does, the business man now invests in the processes of industry; and instead of staking his values on the dimly foreseen conjunctures of the seasons and the act of God, he turns to the conjunctures arising from the interplay of the industrial processes, which are in great measure under the control of business men.

So long as the machine processes were but slightly developed, scattered, relatively isolated, and independent of one another industrially, and so long as they were carried on on a small scale for a relatively narrow market, so long the management of them was conditioned by circumstances in many respects similar to those which conditioned the English domestic industry of the eighteenth century. It was under the conditions of this inchoate phase of the machine age that the earlier generation of economists worked out their theory of the business man's part in industry. It was then still true, in great measure, that the undertaker was the owner of the industrial equipment, and that he kept an immediate oversight of the mechanical processes as well as of the pecuniary transactions in which his enterprise was engaged; and it was also true, with relatively infrequent exceptions, that an unsophisticated productive efficiency was the prime element of business success.[1] A further feature of that precapitalistic business situation is that business, whether handicraft or

[1] Cf. Cantillon, *Essai sur le Commerce*, 1e partie, ch. III., VI., IX., XIV., XV.; *Wealth of Nations*, bk. I.; Bücher, *Enstehung der Volkswirtschaft* (3d ed.), ch. IV. and V.; Sombart, *Kapitalismus*, Vol. I. bk. I.

trade, was customarily managed with a view to earning a livelihood rather than with a view to profits on investment.[1]

In proportion as the machine industry gained ground, and as the modern concatenation of industrial processes and of markets developed, the conjunctures of business grew more varied and of larger scope at the same time that they became more amenable to shrewd manipulation. The pecuniary side of the enterprise came to require more unremitting attention, as the chances for gain or loss through business relations simply, aside from mere industrial efficiency, grew greater in number and magnitude. The same circumstances also provoked a spirit of business enterprise, and brought on a systematic investment for gain. With a fuller development of the modern close-knit and comprehensive industrial system, the point of chief attention for the business man has shifted from the old-fashioned surveillance and regulation of a given industrial process, with which his livelihood was once bound up, to an alert redistribution of investments from less to more gainful ventures,[2] and to a strategic control of the conjunc-

[1] Sombart, vol. I. ch. IV.–VIII. ; Ashley, *Economic History and Theory*, bk. II. ch. VI., especially pp. 389–397.

[2] Cf. Marshall, *Principles of Economics*, on the "Law of Substitution," *e.g.* bk. VI. ch. I. The law of substitution implies freedom of investment and applies fully only in so far as the investor in question is not permanently identified with a given industrial plant or even with a given line of industry. It requires great facility in shifting from one

tures of business through shrewd investments and coalitions with other business men.

As shown above, the modern industrial system is a concatenation of processes which has much of the character of a single, comprehensive, balanced mechanical process. A disturbance of the balance at any point means a differential advantage (or disadvantage) to one or more of the owners of the sub-processes between which the disturbance falls; and it may also frequently mean gain or loss to many remoter members in the concatenation of processes, for the balance throughout the sequence is a delicate one, and the transmission of a disturbance often goes far. It may even take on a cumulative character, and may thereby seriously cripple or accelerate branches of industry that are out of direct touch with those members of the concatenation upon which the initial disturbance falls. Such is the case, for instance, in an industrial crisis, when an apparently slight initial disturbance may become the occasion of a widespread derangement. And such, on the other hand, is also the case when some favorable condition abruptly supervenes in a given

to another point of investment. It is therefore only as the business situation has approached the modern form that the law of substitution has come to be of considerable importance to economic theory; for a theory of business, such as business was in mediæval and early modern times, this law need scarcely have been formulated.

industry; as, *e.g.*, when a sudden demand for war stores starts a wave of prosperity by force of a large and lucrative demand for the products of certain industries, and these in turn draw on their neighbors in the sequence, and so transmit a wave of business activity.

The keeping of the industrial balance, therefore, and adjusting the several industrial processes to one another's work and needs, is a matter of grave and far-reaching consequence in any modern community, as has already been shown. Now, the means by which this balance is kept is business transactions, and the men in whose keeping it lies are the business men. The channel by which disturbances are transmitted from member to member of the comprehensive industrial system is the business relations between the several members of the system; and, under the modern conditions of ownership, disturbances, favorable or unfavorable, in the field of industry are transmitted by nothing but these business relations. Hard times or prosperity spread through the system by means of business relations, and are in their primary expression phenomena of the business situation simply. It is only secondarily that the disturbances in question show themselves as alterations in the character or magnitude of the mechanical processes involved. Industry is carried on for the sake of business, and not conversely; and the progress and activity of industry are conditioned by the outlook of the market, which means the presumptive chance of business profits.

All this is a matter of course which it may seem simply tedious to recite.[1] But its consequences for the theory of business make it necessary to keep the nature of this connection between business and industry in mind. The adjustments of industry take place through the mediation of pecuniary transactions, and these transactions take place at the hands of the business men and are carried on by them for business ends, not for industrial ends in the narrower meaning of the phrase.

The economic welfare of the community at large is best served by a facile and uninterrupted interplay of the various processes which make up the industrial system at large; but the pecuniary interests of the business men in whose hands lies the discretion in the matter are not necessarily best served by an unbroken maintenance of the industrial balance. Especially is this true as regards those greater business men whose interests are very extensive. The pecuniary operations of these latter are of large scope, and their fortunes commonly are not permanently bound up with the smooth working of a given sub-process in the industrial system. Their fortunes are rather related to the larger conjunctures of the industrial

[1] See Sombart, *Kapitalismus*, vol. I. ch. VIII.

system as a whole, the interstitial adjustments, or to conjunctures affecting large ramifications of the system. Nor is it at all uniformly to their interest to enhance the smooth working of the industrial system at large in so far as they are related to it. Gain may come to them from a given disturbance of the system whether the disturbance makes for heightened facility or for widespread hardship, very much as a speculator in grain futures may be either a bull or a bear. To the business man who aims at a differential gain arising out of interstitial adjustments or disturbances of the industrial system, it is not a material question whether his operations have an immediate furthering or hindering effect upon the system at large. The end is pecuniary gain, the means is disturbance of the industrial system, — except so far as the gain is sought by the old-fashioned method of permanent investment in some one industrial or commercial plant, a case which is for the present left on one side as not bearing on the point immediately in hand.[1] The point immediately in question is the part which the business man plays in what are here called the interstitial adjustments of the industrial system; and so far as touches his transactions in this field it is, by

[1] It is chiefly the passive owner of stock and the like that holds permanently to a given enterprise, under the fully developed modern business conditions. The active business man of the larger sort is not in this way bound to the glebe of the given business concern.

and large, a matter of indifference to him whether his traffic affects the system advantageously or disastrously. His gains (or losses) are related to the magnitude of the disturbances that take place, rather than to their bearing upon the welfare of the community.

The outcome of this management of industrial affairs through pecuniary transactions, therefore, has been to dissociate the interests of those men who exercise the discretion from the interests of the community. This is true in a peculiar degree and increasingly since the fuller development of the machine industry has brought about a close-knit and wide-reaching articulation of industrial processes, and has at the same time given rise to a class of pecuniary experts whose business is the strategic management of the interstitial relations of the system. Broadly, this class of business men, in so far as they have no ulterior strategic ends to serve, have an interest in making the disturbances of the system large and frequent, since it is in the conjunctures of change that their gain emerges. Qualifications of this proposition may be needed, and it will be necessary to return to this point presently.

It is, as a business proposition, a matter of indifference to the man of large affairs whether the disturbances which his transactions set up in the industrial system help or hinder the system at large, except in so far as he has ulterior strategic ends to serve. But most of the modern captains of industry have such ulterior ends, and of the greater ones among them this is peculiarly true. Indeed, it is this work of far-reaching business strategy that gives them full title to the designation, "Captains of Industry." This large business strategy is the most admirable trait of the great business men who with force and insight swing the fortunes of civilized mankind. And due qualification is accordingly to be entered in the broad statement made above. The captain's strategy is commonly directed to gaining control of some large portion of the industrial system. When such control has been achieved, it may be to his interest to make and maintain business conditions which shall facilitate the smooth and efficient working of what has come under his control, in case he continues to hold a large interest in it as an investor; for, other things equal, the gains from what has come under his hands permanently in the way of industrial plant are greater the higher and more uninterrupted its industrial efficiency.

An appreciable portion of the larger transactions in railway and "industrial" properties, *e.g.*, are carried out with a view to the permanent ownership of the properties by the business men into whose hands they pass. But also in a large proportion of these transactions the business men's endeavors are directed to a temporary control of the properties in order to close out at an advance or to gain some indirect advantage; that is to say, the transactions have a strategic purpose. The business man aims to gain control of a given block of industrial equipment — as, *e.g.*, given railway lines or iron mills that are strategically important — as a basis for further transactions out of which gain is expected. In such a case his efforts are directed, not to maintaining the permanent efficiency of the industrial equipment, but to influencing the tone of the market for the time being, the apprehensions of other large operators, or the transient faith of investors.[1] His interest in the particular block of industrial equipment is, then, altogether transient, and while it lasts it is of a factitious character.

The exigencies of this business of interstitial disturbance decide that in the common run of cases the proximate aim of the business man is to upset or block the industrial process at some one or more points. His strategy is commonly directed against other business interests and his ends are

[1] Cf. testimony of J. B. Dill, *Report of the Industrial Commission*, vol. I. pp. 1078, 1080–1085; "Digest of Evidence," p. 77; also testimony of various witnesses on stock speculation and corporate management, and particularly the special report to the Commission, on "Securities of Industrial Combinations and Railroads," vol. XIII., especially pp. 920–933.

commonly accomplished by the help of some form of pecuniary coercion. This is not uniformly true, but it seems to be true in appreciably more than half of the transactions in question. In general, transactions which aim to bring a coalition of industrial plants or processes under the control of a given business man are directed to making it difficult for the plants or processes in question to be carried on in severalty by their previous owners or managers.[1] It is commonly a struggle between rival business men, and more often than not the outcome of the struggle depends on which side can inflict or endure the greater pecuniary damage. And pecuniary damage in such a case not uncommonly involves a set-back to the industrial plants concerned and a derangement, more or less extensive, of the industrial system at large.

The work of the greater modern business men, in so far as they have to do with the ordering of the scheme of industrial life, is of this strategic character. The dispositions which they make are

[1] The history of the formation of any one of the great industrial coalitions of modern times will show how great and indispensable a factor in the large business is the invention and organization of difficulties designed to force rival enterprises to come to terms. *E.g.* the manœuvres preliminary to the formation of the United States Steel Corporation, particularly the movements of the Carnegie Company, show how this works on a large scale. Cf. E. S. Meade, *Trust Finance*, pp. 204–217 ; *Report of the Industrial Commission*, vol. XIII., "Review of Evidence," pp. v–vii, with the testimony relating to this topic. The pressure which brings about a new adjustment (coalition) is commonly spoken of as "excessive competition."

business transactions, "deals," as they are called in the business jargon borrowed from gaming slang. These do not always involve coercion of the opposing interests; it is not always necessary to "put a man in a hole" before he is willing to "come in on" a "deal." It may often be that the several parties whose business interests touch one another will each see his interest in reaching an amicable and speedy arrangement; but the interval that elapses between the time when a given "deal" is seen to be advantageous to one of the parties concerned and the time when the terms are finally arranged is commonly occupied with business manœuvres on both or all sides, intended to "bring the others to terms." In so playing for position and endeavoring to secure the largest advantage possible, the manager of such a campaign of reorganization not infrequently aims to "freeze out" a rival or to put a rival's industrial enterprise under suspicion of insolvency and "unsound methods," at the same time that he "puts up a bluff" and manages his own concern with a view to a transient effect on the opinions of the business community. Where these endeavors occur, directed to a transient derangement of a rival's business or to a transient, perhaps specious, exhibition of industrial capacity and earning power on the part of one's own concern, they are commonly detrimental to the industrial system at large; they act temporarily to lower the aggregate serviceability of the comprehensive industrial process within which their effects run, and to make the livelihood and the peace of mind of those involved in these industries more precarious than they would be in the absence of such disturbances. If one is to believe any appreciable proportion of what passes current as information on this head, in print and by word of mouth, business men whose work is not simply routine constantly give some attention to manœuvring of this kind and to the discovery of new opportunities for putting their competitors at a disadvantage. This seems to apply in a peculiar degree, if not chiefly, to those classes of business men whose operations have to do with railways and the class of securities called "industrials." Taking the industrial process as a whole, it is safe to say that at no time is it free from derangements of this character in any of the main branches of modern industry. This chronic state of perturbation is incident to the management of industry by business methods and is unavoidable under existing conditions. So soon as the machine industry had developed to large proportions, it became unavoidable, in the nature of the case, that the business men in whose hands lies the conduct of affairs should play at cross-purposes and endeavor to derange industry. But chronic perturbation is so much a matter of course and prevails with so rare interruptions, that, being the normal state of affairs, it does not attract particular notice.

In current discussion of business, indeed ever since the relation of business men to the industrial system has seriously engaged the attention of economists, the point to which attention has chiefly been directed is the business man's work as an organizer of comprehensive industrial processes. During the later decades of the nineteenth century, particularly, has much interest centred, as there has been much provocation for its doing, on the formation of large industrial consolidations; and the evident good effects of this work in the way of heightened serviceability and economies of production are pointed to as the chief and characteristic end of this work of reorganization. So obvious are these good results and so well and widely has the matter been expounded, theoretically, that it is not only permissible, but it is a point of conscience, to shorten this tale by passing over these good effects as a matter of common notoriety. But there are other features of the case, less obtrusive and less attractive to the theoreticians, which need more detailed attention than they have commonly received.

The circumstances which condition the work of consolidation in industry and which decide whether a given move in the direction of a closer and wider organization of industrial processes will be practicable and will result in economies of production, —these circumstances are of a mechanical nature. They are facts of the comprehensive machine process. The conditions favorable to industrial consolidation on these grounds are not created by the business men. They are matters of "the state of industrial arts," and are the outcome of the work of those men who are engaged in the industrial employments rather than of those who are occupied with business affairs. The inventors, engineers, experts, or whatever name be applied to the comprehensive class that does the intellectual work involved in the modern machine industry, must prepare the way for the man of pecuniary affairs by making possible and putting in evidence the economies and other advantages that will follow from a prospective consolidation.

But it is not enough that the business man should see a chance to effect economies of production and to heighten the efficiency of industry by a new combination. Conditions favorable to consolidation on these grounds must be visible to him before he can make the decisive business arrangements; but these conditions, taken by themselves, do not move him. The motives of the business man are pecuniary motives, inducements in the way of pecuniary gain to him or to the business enterprise with which he is identified. The end of his endeavors is, not simply to effect an industrially advantageous consolidation, but to effect it under such circumstances of ownership as will give him control of large business forces or bring him the largest possible gain. The ulterior end sought is an increase of ownership, not industrial serviceability. His aim is to contrive a consolidation in which he will be at an advantage, and to effect it on the terms most favorable to his own interest.

But it is not commonly evident at the outset what are the most favorable terms that he can get in his dealings with other business men whose interests are touched by the proposed consolidation, or who are ambitious to effect some similar consolidation of the same or of competing industrial elements for their own profit. It rarely happens that the interests of the business men whom the prospective consolidation touches all converge to a coalition on the same basis and under the same management. The consequence is negotiation and delay. It commonly also happens that some of the business men affected see their advantage in staving off the coalition until a time more propitious to their own interest, or until those who have the work of consolidation in hand can be brought to compound with them for the withdrawal of whatever obstruction they are able to offer.[1] Such a coalition involves a loss of independent standing,

[1] Cf., *e.g.*, the accounts of the formation of the United States Steel Corporation or of the Shipbuilding Company.

or even a loss of occupation, to many of the business men interested in the deal. If a prospective industrial consolidation is of such scope as to require the concurrence or consent of many business interests, among which no one is very decidedly preponderant in pecuniary strength or in strategic position, a long time will be consumed in the negotiations and strategy necessary to define the terms on which the several business interests will consent to come in and the degree of solidarity and central control to which they will submit.

It is notorious, beyond the need of specific citation, that the great business coalitions and industrial combinations which have characterized the situation of the last few years have commonly been the outcome of a long-drawn struggle, in which the industrial ends, as contrasted with business ends, have not been seriously considered, and in which great shrewdness and tenacity have commonly been shown in the staving off of a settlement for years in the hope of more advantageous terms. The like is true as regards further coalitions, further consolidations of industrial processes which have not been effected, but which are known to be feasible and desirable so far as regards the mechanical circumstances of the case. The difficulties in the way are difficulties of ownership, of business interest, not of mechanical feasibility.

These negotiations and much of the strategy

that leads up to a business consolidation are of the nature of derangements of industry, after the manner spoken of above. So that business interests and manœuvres commonly delay consolidations, combinations, correlations of the several plants and processes, for some appreciable time after such measures have become patently advisable on industrial grounds. In the meantime the negotiators are working at cross-purposes and endeavoring to put their rivals in as disadvantageous a light as may be, with the result that there is chronic derangement, duplication, and misdirected growth of the industrial equipment while the strategy is going forward, and expensive maladjustment to be overcome when the negotiations are brought to a close.[1]

Serviceability, industrial advisability, is not the decisive point. The decisive point is business expediency and business pressure. In the normal course of business touching this matter of industrial consolidation, therefore, the captain of industry works against, as well as for, a new and more efficient organization. He inhibits as well as furthers the higher organization of industry.[2] Broadly,

[1] Witness the rate wars and the duplications of inefficient track and terminal equipment among the railways, and the similar duplications in the iron and steel industry. The system of railway terminals in Chicago, *e.g.*, is an illuminated object-lesson of systematic ineptitude.

[2] The splendid reach of this inhibitory work of the captain of industry, as well as of his aggressive work of consolidation, is well shown, for instance, in the history and present position of the railway

it may be said that industrial consolidations and the working arrangements made for the more

industry in America. It is and has for a long term of years been obvious that a very comprehensive unification or consolidation, in respect of the mechanical work to be done by the railway system, is eminently desirable and feasible, — consolidation of a scope not only equalling, but far outreaching, the coalitions which have lately been effected or attempted. There is no hazard in venturing the assertion that several hundreds of men who are engaged in the mechanical work of railroading, in one capacity and another, are conversant with feasible plans for economizing work and improving the service by more comprehensive and closer correlation of the work; and it is equally obvious that nothing but the diverging interests of the business men concerned hinders these closer and larger feasible correlations from being put into effect. It is easily within the mark to say that the delay which railway consolidation has suffered up to the present, from business exigencies as distinct from the mechanical circumstances of the case, amounts to an average of at least twenty years. Ever since railroading began in this country there has been going on a process of reluctant consolidation, in which the movements of the business men in control have tardily followed up the opportunities for economy and efficient service which the railroad industry has offered. And their latest and boldest achievements along this line, as seen from the standpoint of mechanical advisability, have been foregone conclusions since a date so far in the past as to be forgotten, and taken at their best they fall short to-day by not less than some fifty per cent. of their opportunities. Cf. *Report of the Industrial Commission*, vol. XIX., "Transportation," especially pp. 304–348.

Like other competitive business, but more particularly such business as has to do with the interstitial adjustments of the industrial system, the business of railway consolidation is of the nature of a game, in which the end sought by the players is their own pecuniary gain and to which the industrial serviceability of the outcome is incidental only. This is recognized by popular opinion and is made much of by popular agitators, who take the view that when once the game between the competing business interests has been played to a finish, in the definitive coalition of the competitors under one management, then the game will go on as a somewhat one-sided conflict between the resulting monopoly and the community at large.

So again, as a further illustration, it is and from the outset has been evident that the iron-ore beds of northern Wisconsin, Michigan, and Minnesota ought, industrially speaking, to have been worked as one collective enterprise. There are also none but business reasons economical utilization of resources and mechanical contrivances are allowed to go into effect only after they are long overdue.

In current economic theory the business man is spoken of under the name of "entrepreneur" or "undertaker," and his function is held to be the coördinating of industrial processes with a view to economics of production and heightened serviceability. The soundness of this view need not be questioned. It has a great sentimental value and is useful in many ways. There is also a modicum of truth in it as an account of facts. In common with other men, the business man is moved by ideals of serviceability and an aspiration to make the way of life easier for his fellows. Like other men, he has something of the instinct of workmanship. No doubt such aspirations move the great business man less urgently than many others, who are, on that account, less successful in business affairs. Motives of this kind detract from business efficiency, and an undue yielding to them on the part of business men is to be deprecated as an infirmity. Still, throughout men's

why practically all the ore beds and iron and steel works in the country are not worked as one collective enterprise. It is equally evident that such correlations of work as are permitted by the business coalitions already effected in this field have resulted in a great economy of production, and that the failure to carry these coalitions farther means an annual waste running up into the millions. Both the economies so effected and the waste so incurred are to be set down to the account of the business managers who have gone so far and have failed to go farther. The like is obvious as regards many other branches of industry and groups of industries.

dealings with one another and with the interests of the community there runs a sense of equity, fair dealing, and workmanlike integrity; and in an uncertain degree this bent discountenances gain that is got at an undue cost to others, or without rendering some colorable equivalent. Business men are also, in a measure, guided by the ambition to effect a creditable improvement in the industrial processes which their business traffic touches. These sentimental factors in business exercise something of a constraint, varying greatly from one person to another, but not measurable in its aggregate results. The careers of most of the illustrious business men show the presence of some salutary constraint of this kind. Not infrequently an excessive sensitiveness of this kind leads to a withdrawal from business, or from certain forms of business which may appeal to a vivid fancy as peculiarly dishonest or peculiarly detrimental to the community.[1] Such

[1] Illustrative instances will readily suggest themselves. Many a business man turns by preference to something less dubious than the distilling of whiskey or the sale of deleterious household remedies. They prefer not to use deleterious adulterants, even within the limits of the law. They will rather use wool than shoddy at the same price. The officials of a railway commonly prefer to avoid wrecks and manslaughter, even if there is no pecuniary advantage in choosing the more humane course. More than that, it will be found true that the more prosperous of the craft, especially, take pride and pains to make the service of their roads or the output of their mills as efficient, not simply as the pecuniary advantage of the concern demands, but as the best pecuniary results will admit. Instances are perhaps not frequent, but they are also not altogether exceptional, where a prosperous captain of industry will go out of his way to heighten the

grounds of action, and perhaps others equally genial and equally unbusinesslike, would probably be discovered by a detailed scrutiny of any large business deal. Probably in many cases the business strategist, infected with this human infirmity, reaches an agreement with his rivals and his neighbors in the industrial system without exacting the last concession that a ruthless business strategy might entitle him to. The result is, probably, a speedier conclusion and a smoother working of the large coalitions than would follow from the unmitigated sway of business principles.[1]

But the sentiment which in this way acts in constraint of business traffic proceeds on such grounds of equity and fair dealing as are afforded by current business ethics; it acts within the range of business principles, not in contravention of them; it acts as a conventional restraint upon pecuniary advantage, not in abrogation of it. This code of business ethics consists, after all, of mitigations of the maxim, *Caveat emptor*. It touches primarily the dealings of man with man,

serviceability of his industry even to a degree that is of doubtful pecuniary expediency for himself. Such aberrations are, of course, not large; and if they are persisted in to any very appreciable extent the result is, of course, disastrous to the enterprise. The enterprise in such a case falls out of the category of business management and falls under the imputation of philanthropy.

[1] The captains of the first class necessarily are relatively exempt from these unbusinesslike scruples.

and only less directly and less searchingly inculcates temperance and circumspection as regards the ulterior interests of the community at large. Where this moral need of a balance between the services rendered the community and the gain derived from a given business transaction asserts itself at all, the balance is commonly sought to be maintained in some sort of pecuniary terms; but pecuniary terms afford only a very inadequate measure of serviceability to the community.

Great and many are the items of service to be set down to the business man's account in connection with the organization of the industrial system, but when all is said, it is still to be kept in mind that his work in the correlation of industrial processes is chiefly of a permissive kind. His furtherance of industry is at the second remove, and is chiefly of a negative character. In his capacity as business man he does not go creatively into the work of perfecting mechanical processes and turning the means at hand to new or larger uses. That is the work of the men who have in hand the devising and oversight of mechanical processes. The men in industry must first create the mechanical possibility of such new and more efficient methods and correlations, before the business man sees the chance, makes the necessary business arrangements, and gives general directions that the contemplated industrial advance shall go into effect. The period between the time of earliest practicability and the effectual completion of a given consolidation in industry marks the interval by which the business man retards the advance of industry. Against this are to be offset the cases, comparatively slight and infrequent, where the business men in control push the advance of industry into new fields and prompt the men concerned with the mechanics of the case to experiment and exploration in new fields of mechanical process.

When the recital is made, therefore, of how the large consolidations take place at the initiative of the business men who are in control, it should be added that the fact of their being in control precludes industrial correlations from taking place except by their advice and consent. The industrial system is organized on business principles and for pecuniary ends. The business man is at the centre; he holds the discretion and he exercises it freely, and his choice falls out now on one side, now on the other. The retardation as well as the advance is to be set down to his account.

As regards the economies in cost of production effected by these consolidations, there is a further characteristic feature to be noted, a feature of some significance for any theory of modern business. In great measure the saving effected is a saving of the costs of business management and of the competitive costs of marketing products and services, rather than a saving in the prime costs of production. The heightened facility and efficiency of the new and larger business combinations primarily affect the expenses of office work and sales, and it is in great part only indirectly that this curtailment and consolidation of business management has an effect upon the methods and aims of industry proper. It touches the pecuniary processes immediately, and the mechanical processes indirectly and in an uncertain degree. It is of the nature of a partial neutralization of the wastes due to the presence of pecuniary motives and business management,—for the business management involves waste wherever a greater number of men or transactions are involved than are necessary to the effective direction of the mechanical processes employed. The amount of "business" that has to be transacted per unit of product is much greater where the various related industrial processes are managed in severalty than where several of them are brought under one business management. A pecuniary discretion has to be exercised at every point of contact or transition, where the process or its product touches or passes the boundary between different spheres of ownership. Business transactions have to do with ownership and changes of ownership. The greater the parcelment in point of ownership, the greater the amount of business work that has to be done in connection with a given output of goods or services, and the slower, less facile, and less accurate, on the whole, is the work. This applies both to the work of bargain and contract, wherein pecuniary initiative and discretion are chiefly exercised, and to the routine work of accounting, and of gathering and applying information and misinformation.

The standardization of industrial processes, products, services, and consumers, spoken of in an earlier chapter, very materially facilitates the business man's work in reorganizing business enterprises on a larger scale; particularly does this standardization serve his ends by permitting a uniform routine in accounting, invoices, contracts, etc., and so admitting a large central accounting system, with homogeneous ramifications, such as will give a competent conspectus of the pecuniary situation of the enterprise at any given time.

The great, at the present stage of development perhaps the greatest, opportunity for saving by consolidation, in the common run of cases, is afforded by the ubiquitous and in a sense excessive presence of business enterprise in the economic system. It is in doing away with unnecessary business transactions and industrially futile manœuvring on the part of independent firms that the promoter of combinations finds his most telling opportunity. So that it is scarcely an overstatement to say that probably the largest, assuredly the securest and most unquestionable, service rendered by the great modern captains of industry is this curtailment of the business to be done,— this sweeping retirement of business men as a class from the service and the definitive cancelment of opportunities for private enterprise.

So long as related industrial units are under different business managements, they are, by the nature of the case, at cross-purposes, and business consolidation remedies this untoward feature of the industrial system by eliminating the pecuniary element from the interstices of the system as far as may be. The interstitial adjustments of the industrial system at large are in this way withdrawn from the discretion of rival business men, and the work of pecuniary management previously involved is in large part dispensed with, with the result that there is a saving of work and an avoidance of that systematic mutual hindrance that characterizes the competitive management of industry. To the community at large the work of pecuniary management, it appears, is less serviceable the more there is of it. The heroic rôle of the captain of industry is that of a deliverer from an excess of business management. It is a casting out of business men by the chief of business men.[1]

The theory of business enterprise sketched above applies to such business as is occupied with the interstitial adjustments of the system of industries. This work of keeping and of disturbing the interstitial adjustments does not look immediately to the output of goods as its source of gain, but to the alterations of values involved in disturbances of the balance, and to the achievement of a more favorable business situation for some of the enterprises engaged. This work lies in the middle, between commercial enterprise proper, on the one hand, and industrial enterprise in the stricter sense, on the other hand. It is directed to the acquisition of gain through taking advantage of those conjunctures of business that arise out of the concatenation of processes in the industrial system.

In a similar manner commercial business may be said to be occupied with conjunctures that arise out of the circumstances of the industrial system at large, but not originating in the mechanical exigencies of the industrial processes. The conjunctures of commercial business proper are in the main fortuitous, in so far that they are

[1] See *Report of the Industrial Commission*, vol. I., Testimony of J. W. Gates, pp. 1029–1039 ; S. Dodd, pp. 1049–1050 ; N. B. Rogers, p. 1068 ; vol. XIII., C. M. Schwab, pp. 451, 459 ; H. B. Butler, p. 490 ; L. R. Hopkins, pp. 346, 347 ; A. S. White, pp. 254, 256.

commonly not initiated by the business men engaged in these commercial pursuits. Commercial business, simply as such, does not aim to guide the course of industry.

On the other hand, the large business enterprise spoken of above initiates changes in industrial organization and seeks its gain in large part through such alterations of value levels as take place on its own initiative. These alterations of the value levels, of course, have their effect upon the output of goods and upon the material welfare of the community; but the effect which they have in this way is only incidental to the quest of profits.

But apart from this remoter and larger guidance of the course of industry, the business men also, and more persistently and pervasively, exercise a guidance over the course of industry in detail. The production of goods and services is carried on for gain, and the output of goods is controlled by business men with a view to gain. Commonly, in ordinary routine business, the gains come from this output of goods and services. By the sale of the output the business man in industry "realizes" his gains. To "realize" means to convert salable goods into money values. The sale is the last step in the process and the end of the business man's endeavor.[1] When he has

[1] Cf. Marx, *Kapital*, bk. I. pt. II.

disposed of the output, and so has converted his holdings of consumable articles into money values, his gains are as nearly secure and definitive as the circumstances of modern life admit. It is in terms of price that he keeps his accounts, and in the same terms he computes his output of products. The vital point of production with him is the vendibility of the output, its convertibility into money values, not its serviceability for the needs of mankind. A modicum of serviceability, for some purpose or other, the output must have if it is to be salable. But it does not follow that the highest serviceability gives the largest gains to the business man in terms of money, nor does it follow that the output need in all cases have other than a factitious serviceability. There is, on the one hand, such a possibility as overstocking the market with any given line of goods, to the detriment of the business man concerned, but not necessarily to the immediate disadvantage of the body of consumers. And there are, on the other hand, certain lines of industry, such as many advertising enterprises, the output of which may be highly effective for its purpose but of quite equivocal use to the community. Many well-known and prosperous enterprises which advertise and sell patent medicines and other proprietary articles might be cited in proof.

In the older days, when handicraft was the rule

of the industrial system, the personal contact between the producer and his customer was somewhat close and lasting. Under these circumstances the factor of personal esteem and disesteem had a considerable play in controlling the purveyors of goods and services. This factor of personal contact counted in two divergent ways: (1) producers were careful of their reputation for workmanship, even apart from the gains which such a reputation might bring; and (2) a degree of irritation and ill-will would arise in many cases, leading to petty trade quarrels and discriminations on other grounds than the gains to be got, at the same time that the detail character of dealings between producer and consumer admitted a degree of petty knavery and huckstering that is no longer practicable in the current large-scale business dealings. Of these two divergent effects resulting from close personal relations between producer and consumer the former seems on the whole to have been of preponderant consequence. Under the system of handicraft and neighborhood industry, the adage that "Honesty is the best policy" seems on the whole to have been accepted and to have been true. This adage has come down from the days before the machine's régime and before modern business enterprise.

Under modern circumstances, where industry is carried on on a large scale, the discretionary head of an industrial enterprise is commonly removed from all personal contact with the body of customers for whom the industrial process under his control purveys goods or services. The mitigating effect which personal contact may have in dealings between man and man is therefore in great measure eliminated. The whole takes on something of an impersonal character. One can with an easier conscience and with less of a sense of meanness take advantage of the necessities of people whom one knows of only as an indiscriminate aggregate of consumers. Particularly is this true when, as frequently happens in the modern situation, this body of consumers belongs in the main to another, inferior class, so that personal contact and cognizance of them is not only not contemplated, but is in a sense impossible. Equity, in excess of the formal modicum specified by law, does not so readily assert its claims where the relations between the parties are remote and impersonal as where one is dealing with one's necessitous neighbors who live on the same social plane. Under these circumstances the adage cited above loses much of its axiomatic force. Business management has a chance to proceed on a temperate and sagacious calculation of profit and loss, untroubled by sentimental considerations of human kindness or irritation or of honesty.

The broad principle which guides producers and merchants, large and small, in fixing the prices at which they offer their wares and services is what is known in the language of the railroads as "charging what the traffic will bear."[1] Where a given enterprise has a strict monopoly of the supply of a given article or of a given class of services this principle applies in the unqualified form in which it has been understood among those who discuss railway charges. But where the monopoly is less strict, where there are competitors, there the competition that has to be met is one of the factors to be taken account of in determining what the traffic will bear; competition may even become the most serious factor in the case if the enterprise in question has little or none of the character of a monopoly. But it is very doubtful if there are any successful business ventures within the range of the modern industries from which the monopoly element is wholly absent.[2] They are, at any rate, few and not of great magnitude. And the endeavor of all such enterprises that look to a permanent continuance of their business is to establish as much of a monopoly as may be.

[1] The economic principle of "charging what the traffic will bear" is discussed with great care and elaboration by R. T. Ely, *Monopolies and Trusts*, ch. III., "The Law of Monopoly Price." Cf., for illustration of the practical working of this principle, testimony of C. M. Schwab, *Report of the Industrial Commission*, vol. XIII. pp. 453–455.

[2] "Monopoly" is here used in that looser sense which it has colloquially, not in the strict sense of an exclusive control of the supply, as employed, *e.g.*, by Mr. Ely in the volume cited above. This usage is the more excusable since Mr. Ely finds that a "monopoly" in the strict sense of the definition practically does not occur in fact. Cf. Jenks, *The Trust Problem*, ch. IV.

Such a monopoly position may be a legally established one, or one due to location or the control of natural resources, or it may be a monopoly of a less definite character resting on custom and prestige (good-will). This latter class of monopolies are not commonly classed as such; although in character and degree the advantage which they give is very much the same as that due to a differential advantage in location or in the command of resources. The end sought by the systematic advertising of the larger business concerns is such a monopoly of custom and prestige. This form of monopoly is sometimes of great value, and is frequently sold under the name of good-will, trademarks, brands, etc. Instances are known where such monopolies of custom, prestige, prejudice, have been sold at prices running up into the millions.[1]

The great end of consistent advertising is to establish such differential monopolies resting on popular conviction. And the advertiser is successful in this endeavor to establish a profitable popular conviction, somewhat in proportion as he correctly apprehends the manner in which a popular conviction on any given topic is built up.[2] The

[1] *E.g.* the prestige value of Ivory Soap.

[2] Cf. W. D. Scott, *The Theory of Advertising;* J. L. Mahin, *The Commercial Value of Advertising*, pp. 4–6, 12–13, 15; E. Fogg-Meade, "The Place of Advertising in Modern Business," *Journal of Political Economy*, March 1901; Sombart, vol. II. ch. XX.–XXI.; G. Tarde, *Psychologie Economique*, vol. I. pp. 187–190. The writing and designing of advertisements (letterpress, display, and illustrations) has

cost, as well as the pecuniary value and the magnitude, of this organized fabrication of popular

grown into a distinct calling; so that the work of a skilled writer of advertisements compares not unfavorably, in point of lucrativeness, with that of the avowed writers of popular fiction.

The psychological principles of advertising may be formulated somewhat as follows: A declaration of fact, made in the form and with the incidents of taste and expression to which a person is accustomed, will be accepted as authentic and will be acted upon if occasion arises, in so far as it does not conflict with opinions already accepted. The acceptance of an opinion seems to be almost entirely a passive matter. The presumption remains in favor of an opinion that has once been accepted, and an appreciable burden of proof falls on the negative. A competent formulation of opinion on a given point is the chief factor in gaining adherents to that opinion, and a reiteration of the statement is the chief factor in carrying conviction. The truth of such a formulation is a matter of secondary consequence, but a wide and patent departure from known fact generally weakens its persuasive effect. The aim of the advertiser is to arrest attention and then present his statement in such a manner that it is easily assimilated into the habits of thought of the person whose conviction is to be influenced. When this is effectually done a reversal of the conviction so established is a matter of considerable difficulty. The tenacity of a view once accepted in this way is evidenced, for instance, by the endless number and variety of testimonials to the merits of well-advertised but notoriously worthless household remedies and the like.

So acute an observer as Mr. Sombart is still able to hold the opinion that "auf Schwindel ist dauernd noch nie ein Unternehmen begründet worden" (*Kapitalismus*, vol. II. p. 376). Mr. Sombart has not made acquaintance with the adventures of Elijah the Restorer, nor is he conversant with American patent-medicine enterprise. With Mr. Sombart's view may be contrasted that of Mr. L. F. Ward, an observer of equally large outlook and acumen: —

"The law of mind as it operates in society as an aid to competition and in the interest of the individual is essentially immoral. It rests primarily on the principle of deception. It is an extension to other human beings of the method applied to the animal world by which the latter was subjected to man. This method was that of the ambush and the snare. Its ruling principle was cunning. Its object was to deceive, circumvent, ensnare, and capture. Low animal cunning was succeeded by more refined kinds of cunning. The more important of these go by the names of business shrewdness, strategy, convictions is indicated by such statements as that the proprietors of a certain well-known household remedy, reputed among medical authorities to be of entirely dubious value, have for a series of years found their profits in spending several million dollars annually in advertisements. This case is by no means unique.

It has been said,[1] no doubt in good faith and certainly with some reason, that advertising as currently carried on gives the body of consumers valuable information and guidance as to the ways and means whereby their wants can be satisfied and their purchasing power can be best utilized. To the extent to which this holds true, advertising is a service to the community. But there is a large reservation to be made on this head. Advertising is competitive; the greater part of it aims to divert purchases, etc., from one channel to another channel of the same general class.[2] And to the extent to which the efforts of advertising in all its branches are spent on this competitive disturbance of trade, they are, on the whole, of

and diplomacy, none of which differ from ordinary cunning in anything but the degree of adroitness by which the victim is outwitted. In this way social life is completely honeycombed with deception." — "The Psychologic Basis of Social Economics," *Ann. of Am. Acad.*, vol. III. pp. 83–84 [475–476].

[1] Fogg-Meade, "Place of Advertising in Modern Business," pp. 218, 224–236.

[2] Advertising and other like expedients for the sale of goods aim at changes in the "substitution values" of the goods in question, not at an enhancement of the aggregate utilities of the available output of goods.

slight if any immediate service to the community. Such advertising, however, is indispensable to most branches of modern industry; but the necessity of most of the advertising is not due to its serving the needs of the community nor to any aggregate advantage accruing to the concerns which advertise, but to the fact that a business concern which falls short in advertising fails to get its share of trade. Each concern must advertise, chiefly because the others do. The aggregate expenditure that could advantageously be put into advertising in the absence of competition would undoubtedly be but an inconsiderable fraction of what is actually incurred, and necessarily incurred under existing circumstances.[1]

Not all advertising is wholly competitive, or at least it is not always obviously so. In proportion as an enterprise has secured a monopoly position, its advertising loses the air of competitive selling and takes on the character of information designed to increase the use of its output independently. But such an increase implies a redistribution of consumption on the part of the customers.[2] So that the element of competitive selling is after all not absent in these cases, but takes the form of competition between different classes of wares

[1] Cf. Jenks, *The Trust Problem*, pp. 21–28; *Report of the Industrial Commission*, vol. XIX. pp. 611–612.

[2] Cf. Böhn-Bawerk, *Positive Theory of Capital*, bk. III., ch. V., VII.–IX., on the value of alternative and complementary goods.

instead of competitive selling of different brands of the same class of wares.

Attention is here called to this matter of advertising and the necessity of it in modern competitive business for the light which it throws on "cost of production" in the modern system, where the process of production is under the control of business men and is carried on for business ends. Competitive advertising is an unavoidable item in the aggregate costs of industry. It does not add to the serviceability of the output, except it be incidentally and unintentionally. What it aims at is the sale of the output, and it is for this purpose that it is useful. It gives vendibility, which is useful to the seller, but has no utility to the last buyer. Its ubiquitous presence in the costs of any business enterprise that has to do with the production of goods for the market enforces the statement that the "cost of production" of commodities under the modern business system is cost incurred with a view to vendibility, not with a view to serviceability of the goods for human use.

There is, of course, much else that goes into the cost of competitive selling, besides the expenses of advertising, although advertising may be the largest and most unequivocal item to be set down to that account. A great part of the work done by merchants and their staff of employees, both wholesale and retail, as well as by sales-agents not exclusively connected with any one mercantile house, belongs under the same head. Just how large a share of the costs of the distribution of goods fairly belongs under the rubric of competitive selling can of course not be made out. It is largest, on the whole, in the case of consumable goods marketed in finished form for the consumer, but there is more or less of it throughout. The goods turned out on a large scale by the modern industrial processes, on the whole, carry a larger portion of such competitive costs than the goods still produced by the old-fashioned detail methods of handicraft and household industry; although this distinction does not hold hard and fast. In some extreme cases the cost of competitive selling may amount to more than ninety per cent. of the total cost of the goods when they reach the consumer. In other lines of business, commonly occupied with the production of staple goods, this constituent of cost may perhaps fall below ten per cent. of the total. Where the average, for the price of finished goods delivered to the consumers, may lie would be a hazardous guess.[1]

It is evident that the gains which accrue from this business of competitive selling and buying bear

[1] Where competitive selling makes up a large proportion of the aggregate final cost of the marketed product, this fact is likely to show itself in an exceptionally large proportion of good-will in the capitalization of the concerns engaged in the given line of business; as, *e.g.*, the American Chicle Company.

no determinable relation to the services which the work in question may render the community. If a comparison may be hazarded between two unknown and indeterminate quantities, it may perhaps be said that the gains from competitive selling bear something more of a stable relation to the service rendered than do the gains derived from speculative transactions or from the financiering operations of the great captains of industry. It seems at least safe to say that the converse will not hold true. Gains and services seem more widely out of touch in the case of the large-scale financiering work. Not that the work of the large business men in reorganizing and consolidating the industrial process is of slight consequence; but as a general proposition, the amount of the business man's gains from any given transaction of this latter class bear no traceable relation to any benefit which the community may derive from the transaction.[1]

As to the wages paid to the men engaged in the routine of competitive selling, as salesmen, buyers, accountants, and the like, — much the same holds true of them as of the income of the business men who carry on the business on their own initiative.

[1] Cf. Ed. Hahn, *Die Wirtschaft der Welt am Ausgang des XIX. Jahrhunderts.* — "In unserem heutigen Wirtschaftsleben ist der Gewinn durch den Zuwachs der Produktion, mit dem frühere Jahrhunderte rechneten, ganz und gar zurückgedrängt, er ist unwesentlich geworden."

Their employers pay the wages of these persons, not because their work is productive of benefit to the community, but because it brings a gain to the employers. The point to which the work is directed is profitable sales, and the wages are in some proportion to the efficiency of this work as counted in terms of heightened vendibility.

The like holds true for the work and pay of the force of workmen engaged in the industrial processes under business management. It holds, in a measure, of all modern industry that produces for the market, but it holds true, in an eminent degree, of those lines of industry that are more fully under the guidance of modern business methods. These are most closely in touch with the market and are most consistently guided by considerations of vendibility. They are also, on the whole, more commonly carried on by hired labor, and the wages paid are competitively adjusted on grounds of the vendibility of the product. The brute serviceability of the output of these industries may be a large factor in its vendibility, perhaps the largest factor; but the fact remains that the end sought by the business men in control is a profitable sale, and the wages are paid as a means to that end, not to the end that the way of life may be smoother for the ultimate consumer of the goods produced.[1]

[1] It might, therefore, be feasible to set up a theory to the effect that wages are competitively proportioned to the vendibility of the

The outcome of this recital, then, is that wherever and in so far as business ends and methods dominate modern industry the relation between the usefulness of the work (for other purposes than pecuniary gain) and the remuneration of it is remote and uncertain to such a degree that no attempt at formulating such a relation is worth while. This is eminently and obviously true of the work and gains of business men, in whatever lines of business they are engaged. This follows as a necessary consequence of the nature of business management.

Work that is, on the whole, useless or detrimental to the community at large may be as gainful to the business man and to the workmen whom he employs as work that contributes substantially to the aggregate livelihood. This seems to be peculiarly true of the bolder flights of business enterprise. In so far as its results are not detrimental to human life at large, such unproductive work directed to securing an income may seem to be

product; but there is no cogent ground for saying that the wages in any department of industry, under a business régime, are proportioned to the utility which the output has to any one else than the employer who sells it. When it is further taken into account that the vendibility of the product in very many lines of production depends chiefly on the wastefulness of the goods (cf. *Theory of the Leisure Class*, ch. V.), the divergence between the usefulness of the work and the wages paid for it seems wide enough to throw the whole question of an equivalence between work and pay out of theoretical consideration. Cf., however, Clark, *The Distribution of Wealth*, especially ch. VII. and XXII.

an idle matter in which the rest of the community has no substantial interests. Such is not the case. In so far as the gains of these unproductive occupations are of a substantial character, they come out of the aggregate product of the other occupations in which the various classes of the community engage. The aggregate profits of the business, whatever its character, are drawn from the aggregate output of goods and services; and whatever goes to the maintenance of the profits of those who contribute nothing substantial to the output is, of course, deducted from the income of the others, whose work tells substantially.

There are, therefore, limits to the growth of the industrially parasitic lines of business just spoken of. A disproportionate growth of parasitic industries, such as most advertising and much of the other efforts that go into competitive selling, as well as warlike expenditure and other industries directed to turning out goods for conspicuously wasteful consumption, would lower the effective vitality of the community to such a degree as to jeopardize its chances of advance or even its life. The limits which the circumstances of life impose in this respect are of a selective character, in the last resort. A persistent excess of parasitic and wasteful efforts over productive industry must bring on a decline. But owing to the very high productive efficiency of the modern mechanical industry, the margin available for wasteful occupations and wasteful expenditures is very great. The requirements of the aggregate livelihood are so far short of the possible output of goods by modern methods as to leave a very wide margin for waste and parasitic income. So that instances of such a decline, due to industrial exhaustion, drawn from the history of any earlier phase of economic life, carry no well-defined lesson as to what a modern industrial community may allow itself in this respect.

While it is in the nature of things unavoidable that the management of industry by modern business methods should involve a large misdirection of effort and a very large waste of goods and services, it is also true that the aims and ideals to which this manner of economic life gives effect act forcibly to offset all this incidental futility. These pecuniary aims and ideals have a very great effect, for instance, in making men work hard and unremittingly, so that on this ground alone the business system probably compensates for any wastes involved in its working. There seems, therefore, to be no tenable ground for thinking that the working of the modern business system involves a curtailment of the community's livelihood. It makes up for its wastefulness by the added strain which it throws upon those engaged in the productive work.

MODERN BUSINESS CAPITAL

WHAT has been said on the use of loan credit has anticipated much of what is peculiar in modern business capital. Such is necessarily the case, since it is in the extensive use of credit that the later phases of the management of capital contrast most strikingly with the corresponding features of earlier business traffic. To follow the terminological precedents set by German writers, the late-modern scheme of economic life is a "credit economy," as contrasted with the "money economy" that characterizes early-modern times. The nature of business capital and its relations to the industrial process under the later, more fully developed, credit economy is in some degree different from what it was before the full and free use of credit came to occupy its present central position in business traffic; and more particularly is it at variance with the theoretical expositions of the economists of the past generation.

It has been the habit of economists and others to speak of "capital" as a stock of the material means by which industry is carried on, — industrial equipment, raw materials, and means of subsistence. This view is carried over from the situation in which business and industry stood at the time of Adam Smith and of the generation before Adam Smith, from whose scheme of life and of thought he drew the commonplace materials and conceptions with which his speculations were occupied. It further carries over the point of view occupied by Adam Smith and the generation to whom he addressed his speculations. That is to say, the received theoretical formulations regarding business capital and its relations to industry proceed on the circumstances that prevailed in the days of the "money economy," before credit and the modern corporation methods became of first-class consequence in economic affairs. They canvass these matters from the point of view of the material welfare of the community at large, as seen from the standpoint of the utilitarian philosophy. In this system of social philosophy the welfare of the community at large is accepted as the central and tone-giving interest, about which a comprehensive, harmonious order of nature circles and gravitates. These early speculations on business traffic turn about the bearing of this traffic upon the wealth of nations, particularly as the wealth of nations would stand in a "natural" scheme of things, in which all things should work together for the welfare of mankind.

The theory, or what there is in the way of a theory, of business capital in the received body of doctrines is worked out from the point of view and for the theoretical purposes of the eighteenth-century scheme of natural liberty, natural rights, and natural law; and the received theorems concerning the part played by capital and by the capitalist are substantially of the character of laws of nature, as that term was understood during the period to which these theorems owe their genesis. What these received theorems declare concerning the nature and normal function of capital and of the capitalist need not be recited here; their content is familiar enough to all readers, lay and learned. Also the merits of such a point of view for purposes of economic theory, and the adequacy of the received concept of capital for the purposes to which it was originally applied, need not detain the inquiry. Modern business management does not take that point of view, nor does "capital" carry such a meaning to the modern business man; because the guiding circumstances under which modern business is carried on are not those supposed to be given by a beneficent order of nature, nor do the controlling purposes of business traffic include that general well-being which constituted the final term of Adam Smith's social philosophy.

As a business proposition, "capital" means a fund of money values; and since the credit economy and corporation finance have come to be the ruling factors in industrial business, this fund of money values (taken as an aggregate) bears but a remote and fluctuating relation to the industrial equipment and the other items which may (perhaps properly) be included under the old-fashioned concept of industrial capital.[1]

Capital has been spoken of as the capitalized (aggregated) cost of industrial equipment, etc.,[2]— a view which had its significance for economic theory a hundred years ago; but since corporation finance has come to pervade the management of

[1] The distinction between business capital and "industrial capital" or "capital goods" has been shown by Knies, *Geld und Credit*, vol. I. ch. II. pp. 40–60. Distinctions having a very similar effect in some bearings are to be found in Rodbertus ("private capital" and "national capital"), in Böhm-Bawerk ("acquisitive capital" and "productive capital," or "private capital" and "social capital"), in Clark ("capital" and "capital goods"). Similar distinctions are made by various writers to help out the incompetency of the received definition of the term. The merit of these distinctions does not concern the present inquiry, since they are made for other purposes than that here aimed at. The distinction made above is not an attempt to recast the terminology of economic theory, but is simply an expedient for present use. It amounts to an unqualified acceptance of the concept (more or less well defined) which business men habitually attach to the term "capital." Mr. F. A. Fetter has latterly spoken for the restriction of "capital," as a technical term, practically to what is here called "business capital." Mr. Fetter's "capital concept," however, should probably not be taken to cover intangible assets. The practical distinction is visible in the testimony of various witnesses before the Industrial Commission, as also in the special report on "Securities," *Report*, vol. XIII.

[2] Even so late and competent a student of corporate capital as J. von Körösi is bound by this antique preconception, and his work has suffered in consequence. See *Finanzielle Ergebnisse der Actiengesellschaften*, p. 3.

business this view is no longer of particular use for a theoretical handling of the facts. To avoid the tedium of argument it may be conceded that under the old dispensation, of partnerships and individual management in business, the basis of capitalization was the cost of the material equipment owned by any given concern; and so far as the methods of partnership and private firms still prevails such may still be the current method of capitalization, especially *de jure*. But in so far as business procedure and business conceptions have been shaped in the image of the modern corporation (or limited liability company), the basis of capitalization has gradually shifted, until the basis is now no longer given by the cost of material equipment owned, but by the earning-capacity of the corporation as a going concern.[1]

A given corporation's capital is, of course, *de jure* a magnitude fixed in the past by an act of legislature chartering the company, or by an issuance of stock by the company under the terms of its charter or of the acts which enable it. But this *de jure* capitalization is nominal only, and there are few, if any, cases in which the effective capital of a company coincides with its *de jure*

[1] This state of the case is brought out, in a veiled manner, by the well-known proposition, expounded in varying form by various writers, that the cost of equipment on which capitalization must, in theory, take place is the cost of reproduction of all valuable items included, tangible and intangible.

capital. Such could be the case only so long as all the securities which go to make up the company's capital were quoted at par on the market. The effective capitalization of any modern company, that is to say, the capitalization which is effective for current business purposes as distinct from the formal requirements of the charter, is given by the quotations of the company's securities, or by some similar but less overt market valuation in case the company's capital is not quotable on the market. The effective (business) capitalization, as distinct from the *de jure* capitalization, is not fixed permanently and inflexibly by a past act of incorporation or stock issue. It is fixed for the time being only, by an ever recurring valuation of the company's properties, tangible and intangible, on the basis of their earning-capacity.[1]

In this capitalization of earning-capacity the nucleus of the capitalization is not the cost of the plant, but the concern's good-will, so called, as has appeared in the last preceding chapter.[2]

[1] "Nothing is more illusive and delusive than the idea that if a corporation's stock be only paid in in money at the outset it is therefore better off than one that has issued its stock for property that could not be converted for one cent on the dollar. The question is what assets the corporation has got at the time of the particular transaction, and that can be ascertained only by present inquiry." —Testimony of F. L. Stetson, *Report of the Industrial Commission*, vol. I. p. 976. Cf. Meade, *Trust Finance*, ch. XVI. and XVIII.

[2] Earning-capacity is practically accepted as the effective basis of capitalization for corporate business concerns, particularly for those

"Good-will" is a somewhat extensible term, and latterly it has a more comprehensive meaning than it once had. Its meaning has, in fact, been gradually extended to meet the requirements of modern business methods. Various items, of very diverse character, are to be included under the head of "good-will"; but the items included have this much in common that they are "immaterial wealth," "intangible assets"; which, it may parenthetically be remarked, signifies among other things that these assets are not serviceable to the community, but only to their owners. Good-will taken in its wider meaning comprises such things as established customary business relations, reputation for upright dealing, franchises and privileges, trade-marks, brands, patent rights, copyrights, exclusive use of special processes guarded by law or by secrecy, exclusive control of particular sources of materials. All these items give a differential advantage to their owners, but they

whose securities are quoted on the market. It is in the stock market that this effective capitalization takes place. But the law does not recognize such a basis of capitalization; nor are business men generally ready to adopt it in set form, although they constantly have recourse to it, in effect, in operations of investment and of credit extension. Cf. *Report of the Industrial Commission*, vol. I. pp. 6, 17, 21 (Test. F. B. Thurber); p. 967 (Test. F. L. Stetson); pp. 585–587 (Test. H. H. Rogers); pp. 110–111, 124 (Test. H. O. Havemeyer); pp. 1021, 1032 (Test. J. W. Gates); pp. 1054–1055 (Test. S. Dodd); vol. XIII. pp. 287–288 (Test. H. Burn); p. 388 (Test. J. Morris); pp. 107–108 (Test. E. R. Chapman). See *Quarterly Journal of Economics*, February 1903, pp. 344–345, "The Holyoke Water Case," for an illustrative decision.

are of no aggregate advantage to the community.[1] They are wealth to the individuals concerned — differential wealth; but they make no part of the wealth of nations.[2]

It is in the industrial corporations that this capitalization of good-will is seen to the best advantage — including, under the term "industrial corporations," railway companies, iron and steel concerns, mines, etc., as well as what are known in the stock market specifically as "industrials." The corporation is, of course, not the only form of business concern in the industrial field, but it is the typical, characteristic form of business organization for the management of industry in modern times, and the peculiarities of modern capital are therefore best seen in these modern corporations. Many of these corporations have grown out of partnerships and firms previously existing, and such is still the genesis of many of the corporations that come forward from time to time. In such a case of conversion from partnership or firm to corporation the rule is that the new cor-

[1] The advantages afforded their owners by these intangible assets have latterly been discussed by economists under such headings as "Rent" or "Quasi-Rent." These discussions, it is believed, are of great theoretical weight. In business practice, however, the items in question are treated as capital, which must avail as an excuse for including them here in business capital.

[2] Compare Böhm-Bawerk's and Clark's distinctions between "private" and "social" capital, and between "capital" and "capital goods."

poration takes over a body of good-will, under one form and name or another, previously pertaining to the partnership which it displaces. Conversely, when a flourishing partnership or similar private firm has gained an assured footing of good-will, in the way of any or all of the items enumerated under that term above, its lot, as prescribed by modern business exigencies, is to go up into a corporation, either by simple conversion into the corporate form or through coalition with other firms into a larger corporate whole. There is in this matter no hard and fast rule, of course. On the one hand, the approved methods of corporation finance may in some measure be resorted to by a private firm, without formal conversion of the concern into the corporate form; and on the other hand, an incorporated company may continue to carry on its business after the manner usual with privately owned concerns. But taken by and large, it will be found that with the assumption of the corporate form is associated a more modern method of capitalization and a freer use of credit. The advantages which the corporate form offers in these respects are commonly not neglected. The more archaic forms of organization and business management, in which recourse is commonly not had to the characteristic methods of corporation finance, prevail chiefly in those "backward" lines of industry in which monopoly or other differential advantages of an intangible nature are not readily attainable; such, *e.g.*, as farming, fishing, local merchandising, and the minor mechanical trades and occupations. In this range of industries large (corporate) organization has hitherto been virtually impracticable, and here at the same time differential advantages, of the nature of good-will (as indicated above), are relatively scant and precarious. Where extensive differential advantages of this kind come in, the corporate form of organization is also likely to come in.

The cases are also frequent where a corporation starts out full-fledged from the beginning, without derivation from a previously existing private firm. Where this happens, the start is commonly made with some substantial body of immaterial goods on which to build up the capitalization; it may be a franchise, as in the case of a railway, telegraph, telephone, street-car, gas, or water company; or it may be the control of peculiar sources of material, as in the case of an oil or natural gas company, or a salt, coal, iron, or lumber company; or it may be a special industrial process, patented or secret; or it may be several of these. When a corporation begins its life history without such a body of immaterial differential advantages, the endeavors of its management are early directed to working up a basis of good-will in the way of trade-marks, clientèle, and trade connections which will place it in something of a monopoly position, locally or generally.[1] Should the management not succeed in these endeavors to gain an assured footing on some such "immaterial" ground, its chances of success among rival corporations are precarious, its standing is insecure, and its managers have not accomplished what is looked for at their hands. The substantial foundation of the industrial corporation is its immaterial assets.

The typical modern industrial corporation is a concern of sufficient magnitude to be of something more than barely local consequence, and extends its trade relations beyond the range of the personal contact of its directive officials. Its properties and its debts are also commonly owned, in part at least, by persons who stand in no direct personal relation to the board of managers. In an up-to-date corporation of this character the typical make-up of the corporate capital, or capitalization, is somewhat as follows: The common stock approximately covers the immaterial properties of the concern, unless these immaterial properties are disproportionately large and valuable; in case of a relatively small and local corporation the common stock will ordinarily somewhat more than cover the value of the immaterial property and comprise something of the plant; in case of the larger concerns the converse is likely to be true, so that here

[1] See Chapter III. above.

the immaterial property, intangible assets, is made to serve in some measure as a basis for other securities as well as for the common stock. The common stock, typically, represents intangible assets and is accounted for by valuable trade-marks, patents, processes, franchises, etc. Whatever material properties, tangible assets, are in hand or to be acquired are covered by preferred stock or other debentures. The various forms of debentures account for the material equipment and the working capital (the latter item corresponding roughly to the economists' categories of raw materials, wages fund, and the like). Of these debentures the preferred stock is the most characteristic modern development. It is, *de jure*, counted as a constituent of the concern's capital and the principal is not repayable; in this (legal) respect it is not an evidence of debt or a credit instrument.[1] But it has little voice in the direction of the concern's business policy.[2] In practice the management rests chiefly on the holdings of common stock. This is due in part to the fact that the preferred bears a stated rate of dividends and is therefore taken up by scattered purchasers as an investment security to a greater extent than the common. In

[1] On the books of the corporation it is, of course, carried as an item of liability; as is the common stock; but that is a technical expedient of accountancy, and does not touch the substantial question.

[2] See testimony of various witnesses on "Capitalization" before the Industrial Commission, vols. I., IX., XIII.

this (practical) respect it amounts to a debenture. Its practical character as a debenture is shown by the stated rate of dividends, and where it is "cumulative" that feature adds a further step of assimilation to the ordinary class of debentures. Indeed, in point of practical effect preferred stock is in some respects commonly a more pronounced credit instrument than the ordinary mortgage; it alienates the control of the property which it represents more effectually than the ordinary bond or mortgage loan, in that it may practically be a debt which, by its own terms, cannot be collected, so that by its own terms it may convey a credit extension from the holder to the issuing corporation in perpetuity. Its effect is to convey the discretionary control of the material properties which it is held to represent into the hands of the holders of the common stock of the concern. The discretionary management of the corporate capital is, by this device, quite as effectually as by the use of ordinary credit instruments, vested in the common stock, which is held to represent the corporation's good-will. The discretionary disposal of the entire capital vests in securities representing the intangible assets. In this sense, then, the nucleus of the modern corporate capitalization is the immaterial goods covered by the common stock.[1]

[1] As one of many illustrative cases, the Rubber Goods Manufacturing Company may be taken as a typical instance of a corporation

This method of capitalization, therefore, effects a somewhat thoroughgoing separation between the management and the ownership of the industrial equipment. Roughly speaking, under corporate organization the owners of the industrial material have no voice in its management, and where preferred stock is a large constituent of the capital this alienation of control on the parts of the owners may be, by so much, irrevocable. Preferred stock is, practically, a device for placing the property it represents in perpetual trust with the holders of the common stock, and, with certain qualifications, these trustees are not answerable for the administration of the property to their trustors. The property relation of the owners to their property is at this point attenuated to an extreme degree. For most business purposes, it should be added, the capital covered by other forms of debentures is in

organized in a conservative but up-to-date manner for permanent success and stable value. Its authorized issue of stock is $25,000,000 7 per cent. cumulative preferred, and $25,000,000 common. The actual issue in 1901 was about $8,000,000 preferred and $17,000,000 common, of which the preferred was presumed to cover the value of the tangible assets. Another coalition organized by the same promoter (Mr. C. R. Flint), the American Chicle Company, illustrates the same general feature. The preferred stock of this company ($3,000,000) "in round numbers was three times the amount of tangible assets," while the common stock ($6,000,000) represents no tangible assets. The aggregate capitalization is about nine times the tangible assets. The witness says that this corporation has been proved by events to be "on a conservative basis from the fact that the company has paid 8 per cent. on its common stock," which has been selling at 80. — *Report of the Industrial Commission*, vol. XIII. pp. 47, 50.

much the same position as that covered by the preferred stock.[1]

[1] It may be argued that this identification of the common stock with the intangible assets holds true in theory only, in the sense that this is the view held by the business men who occupy themselves with such matters; while in point of fact no distinction of this nature between common and preferred stock is or can practically be maintained after the stock has once found its way into the market. It might seem, in other words, that when the stock has once passed the stage of organization and gone into the hands of the purchasers, each share represents nothing but an undivided interest in the aggregate capitalization of the concern, so that the particular item of wealth represented by a given share or given form of security can no longer be identified.

On the face of the situation such appears to be the case, but there are facts which argue for the view set out above. It is, *e.g.*, well known that whenever circumstances arise which immediately affect the value of the good-will of a corporation, it is the quotations of the common stock that first and most decidedly are affected. If the good-will of the concern makes a great and rapid gain, *e.g.* through manœuvres which put it in a position of monopoly or through changes in the goods market which greatly increase the demand for the concern's product, and the like, it is the quotation of the common stock that measures and registers the advantage which thereby accrues to the concern, and the market fluctuation of the common stock is likewise the instrument by means of which manipulations are carried through that affect these intangible assets. At the same time this rule does not hold hard and fast, as is seen in case of a liquidation when the capital of the concern may have shrunk to such dimensions that the entire capital, including the intangible assets, will no more than satisfy the claims represented by the debentures. Still, in point of practical fact, the (theoretical) preconception of business men that the common stock in some intelligible sense covers the intangible assets is fairly borne out by everyday experience, taken by and large.

A curious parallel might be traced between the current endeavors of the business community to organize and manage the industrial equipment on the basis of immaterial assets and the mediæval business perplexities and fictions relative to loans on interest. In both cases the business community has had to face untried exigencies together with a popular, traditional prejudice that discountenances the expedients by which these exigencies are to be met. The mediæval presumption was that the management of productive goods and the

The various descriptions of securities which in this way represent corporate capital are quotable on the market and are subject to market fluctuations; whereby it comes about that the aggregate effective magnitude of the corporate capital varies with the tone of the market, with the manœuvres of the business men to whom is delegated the management of the companies, and with the accidents of the seasons and the chances of peace and war. Accordingly, the amount of the business capital of a given concern, or of the business community as a whole, varies in magnitude in great measure independently of the mechanical facts of industry, as was noted above in speaking of loan credit.[1] The market fluctuations in the amount

profits accruing from their use must go to their users. (Cf. Ashley, *Economic History*, vol. I. ch. III., vol. II. ch. VI.; Endemann, *Die nationalökonomische Grundsätze der kanonistischen Lehre.*) The modern presumption is that the management of the equipment and the gains from such management must vest in the owners. The modern exigencies decide that the equipment must be managed by others than the owners and that profits must largely accrue to those who financially manage the concern. The expedient by which this result is sought to be reached is the fiction of intangible assets and the impersonal, irrevocable credit extension covered by the preferred stock. The effect is to dissociate ownership from management. This is the necessary outcome of a "credit economy" consistently and fully carried through. The management of the material equipment of industry is thrown into the hands of those who own the immaterial wealth; that is to say, those who own the claim to manage the equipment. The current prejudice which insists on management by the owners is set aside by feigning that this claim has an industrial value, and so capitalizing it on the basis of the differential advantage which accrues to its holders.

[1] See also a discussion by E. S. Meade, *Quarterly Journal of Economics*. February 1902, pp. 217 *et seq.*, of how "good-will" may

of capital proceed on variations of confidence on the part of the investors, on current belief as to the probable policy or tactics of the business men in control, on forecasts as to the seasons and the tactics of the guild of politicians, and on the indeterminable, largely instinctive, shifting movements of public sentiment and apprehension. So that under modern conditions the magnitude of the business capital and its mutations from day to day are in great measure a question of folk psychology rather than of material fact.

But in this uncertain and shifting relation of the business capital to the material equipment there are one or two points which may be set down as fairly secure. Since the credit instruments involved in modern capitalization may be used as collateral for a further credit extension, as noted in the chapter on loan credit,[1] the aggregate nominal capital in hand at a given time is, normally, larger by an appreciable amount than the aggregate value of the material properties involved;[2] and at the same time the current value of these material properties is also greater than it would be in the absence of that credit

vary in magnitude, or even disappear, when a concern enters a larger coalition; also, on the same general head, W. F. Willoughby, "Integration of Industry in the United States," *ibid.*, November 1902.

[1] p. 113 above.

[2] $\text{cap}' = \text{cap} + \frac{\text{cap}}{n} > \text{cap}$, in which cap′ is the nominal capital, as increased by the credit element $\frac{\text{cap}}{n}$.

financiering for which corporate capitalization affords a basis.[1]

German writers have familiarized economic readers with the terms "credit economy," "money economy" (Geldwirtschaft), and "natural economy" (Naturalwirtschaft), the later-modern scheme of economic life being characterized as a "credit economy." What characterizes the early-modern scheme, the "money economy," and sets it off in contrast with the natural economy (distribution in kind) that went before it in West-European culture, is the ubiquitous resort to the market as a vent for products and a source of supply of goods. The characteristic feature of this money economy is the goods mar-

[1] $\text{mat}' = \text{mat} + \frac{1}{n}\left(\frac{\text{cap}}{n}\right) > \text{mat}$, in which mat′ is the current value of the material equipment, as increased (over mat) by the competitive demand for equipment due to the credit element $\frac{\text{cap}}{n}$. One of the substantial secondary benefits to be noted as flowing from these modern business expedients is the effect of corporation finance upon the aggregate nominal wealth of the community. A given community, possessed of a given complement of material wealth, is richer in capital if a large proportion of its industrial equipment is capitalized and managed by corporation methods, quite apart from any increase in the material items of which the community is possessed. (Cf. *Twelfth Census of the United States*, "Manufactures," pt. I. p. xcvi.) Wealth may in this way be increased (about twofold on an average), inexpensively, by the simple expedient of incorporating the community's business concerns in the form of joint-stock companies. The more highly involved and the more widely extended the corporation financiering is, the richer, in statistical terms of capital, is the community, other things equal. Among these other things are the material facts of the case.

ket. About the goods market business and industrial interests turn in early modern times; and to this early-modern system of industrial life the current doctrines of political economy are adapted, as indicated above.

The credit economy — the scheme of economic life of the immediate past and the present — has made an advance over the money economy in the respect which chiefly distinguishes the latter. The goods market, of course, in absolute terms is still as powerful an economic factor as ever, but it is no longer the dominant factor in business and industrial traffic, as it once was. The capital market has taken the first place in this respect. The capital market is the modern economic feature which makes and identifies the higher "credit economy" as such. In this credit economy resort is habitually had to the market as a vent for accumulated money values and a source of supply of capital.[1]

Trading under the old régime was a traffic in goods; under the new régime there is added, as the dominant and characteristic trait, trading in capital. Both in the capital and in the goods market there are professional traders, as well as

[1] The commodities bought and sold in the goods market are the outcome of a process of production and are useful for a material purpose; those bought and sold in the capital market are the outcome of a process of valuation and are useful for purposes of pecuniary gain.

buyers and sellers who resort to the market to dispose of their holdings and to supply their needs of what the market affords. In either class of trading the ends sought by those engaged in the business are generically the same. The endeavors of those who are in the business of trading, who buy in order to sell and sell in order to buy, are directed to the pecuniary gain that is to be got through an advantageous discrepancy between the price paid and the price obtained; but on the part of those who resort to the market to supply their needs the end sought is not the same in the two cases. The last buyer of goods buys for consumption, but the last negotiator of capital buys for the sake of the ulterior profit; in substance he buys in order to sell again at an advance. The advance which he has in view is to come out of the prospective earnings of the capital for which he negotiates. What he has in view as his ulterior end in the transaction is the conversion of the values for which he negotiates into a larger outcome of money values, — whatever process of production and the like may intervene between the inception and the goal of his traffic.[1]

The value of any given block of capital, therefore, turns on its earning-capacity; or, as the mathematical expression has it, the value of capital is a func-

[1] Cf. Marx, *Kapital* (4th ed.), bk. I. ch. IV.

tion of its earning-capacity,[1] not of its prime cost or of its mechanical efficiency. It is only more remotely, and through the mediation of the earning-capacity, that these last-named factors sensibly affect the value of the capital. This earning-capacity of capital depends in its turn, not so much on the mechanical efficiency of the valuable items bought and sold in the capital market, as on the tension of the market for goods. To recur to an expression already employed in a similar connection, the question of earning-capacity of capital relates primarily to its effectiveness for purposes of vendibility, and only at the second remove to its effectiveness in the way of material serviceability. But the earning-capacity which in this way affords ground for the valuation of marketable capital (or for the market capitalization of the securities bought and sold) is not its past or actual earning-capacity, but its presumptive future earning-capacity; so that the

[1] Effective capital = current market value of nominal capital = presumptive earning capacity × purchase period, neglecting fortuitous and incalculable items which may affect any given case.

If nominal capital = cap, effective capital = cap′, presumed annual earnings = ea′, and the purchase period of capitalized property (years' purchase) = yp = $\frac{1}{\text{interest rate per annum}}$, we have cap $\lesseqgtr$ cap′ $= \text{ea}' \times \text{yp} = \frac{\text{ea}'}{\text{int}}$.

This equation between cap′ and ea′ is disturbed by the presence in any given case of variable factors which cannot be included in the equation, but it remains true after all qualification has been made that $\text{cap}' = f\left(\frac{\text{ea}'}{\text{int}}\right)$.

fluctuations in the capital market — the varying market capitalization of securities — turn about imagined future events. The forecast in the case may be more or less sagacious, but, however sagacious, it retains the character of a forecast based on other grounds besides the computation of past results.

All capital which is put on the market is in this way subjected to an interminable process of valuation and revaluation — *i.e.* a capitalization and recapitalization — on the basis of its presumptive earning-capacity, whereby it all assumes more or less of a character of intangibility. But the most elusive and intangible items of this marketable capital are, of course, those items which consist of capitalized good-will, since these are intangible goods from start to finish. It is upon this factor of good-will in capital that a change in presumptive earning-capacity falls most immediately, and this factor shows the widest and freest market fluctuations. The variations in the capitalized value of merchantable good-will are relatively wide and unstable, as is shown by the quotations of common stock.

In the capital market the commodity in which trading is done, then, is the capitalized putative earning-capacity of the property covered by the securities bought and sold. This property is in part tangible, in part intangible, the two categories being seldom clearly distinguishable. The items bought and sold are put into merchantable form by being standardized in terms of money and subdivided into convenient imaginary shares, which greatly facilitates the traffic. The earning-capacity on which the market capitalization runs and about which the traffic in merchantable capital turns is a putative earning-capacity. It follows that this putative earning-capacity of a given block of capital, as it takes shape in the surmises of outside investors, may differ appreciably from the actual earning-capacity of the capital as known to its managers; and it may readily be to the latter's interest that such a discrepancy between actual and imputed earning-capacity should arise.[1] When, *e.g.*, the putative earning-capacity of the capital covered by a given line of securities, as shown by the market quotations, rises appreciably above what is known to its managers to be its actual earning-capacity, the latter may find their advantage in selling out, or even in selling short; while in the converse case they will be inclined to buy. Moreover, putative earning-capacity is the outcome of many surmises with respect to prospective earnings and the like; and these surmises

[1] Something of this kind is the usual ground of the obstinate resistance which most business men oppose to publicity of accounts. In lines of business, as, *e.g.*, railroading, in which accounts are readily and effectually sophisticated ("doctored"), the objections to publicity are commonly less strenuous.

will vary from one man to the next, since they proceed on an imperfect, largely conjectural, knowledge of present earning-capacity and on the still more imperfectly known future course of the goods market and of corporate policy. Hence sales of securities are frequent, both because outsiders vary in their estimates and forecasts, and because the information of the outsiders does not coincide with that of the insiders. The consequence is that a given block of capital, representing, *e.g.*, a controlling interest in a given industrial enterprise, may, and in practice it commonly will, change owners much more frequently than a given industrial plant was wont to change owners under the old régime, before the fully developed corporation finance came to occupy the field of industrial business.[1]

It follows, further, that under these circumstances the men who have the management of such an industrial enterprise, capitalized and quotable on the market, will be able to induce a discrepancy between the putative and the actual earning-capacity, by expedients well known and approved for the purpose. Partial information, as well as misinformation, sagaciously given out at a critical juncture, will go far toward producing a favorable temporary discrepancy of this kind, and so enabling the managers to buy or sell the securities of the

[1] Cf., *e.g.*, Eberstadt, *Deutsche Kapitalsmarkt.*

concern with advantage to themselves. If they are shrewd business men, as they commonly are, they will aim to manage the affairs of the concern with a view to an advantageous purchase and sale of its capital rather than with a view to the future prosperity of the concern, or to the continued advantageous sale of the output of goods or services produced by the industrial use of this capital.

That is to say, the interest of the managers of a modern corporation need not coincide with the permanent interest of the corporation as a going concern; neither does it coincide with the interest which the community at large has in the efficient management of the concern as an industrial enterprise. It is to the interest of the community at large that the enterprise should be so managed as to give the best and largest possible output of goods or services; whereas the interest of the corporation as a going concern is that it be managed with a view to maintaining its efficiency and selling as large an output as may be at the best prices obtainable in the long run; but the interest of the managers, and of the owners for the time being, is to so manage the enterprise as to enable them to buy it up or to sell out as expeditiously and as advantageously as may be. The interest of the community at large demands industrial efficiency and serviceability of the product; while the business interest of the concern as such demands vendibility of the product; and the interest of those men who have the final discretion in the management of these corporate enterprises demands vendibility of the corporate capital. The community's interest demands that there should be a favorable difference between the material cost and the material serviceability of the output; the corporation's interest demands a favorable pecuniary difference between expenses and receipts, cost and sale price of the output; the corporation directorate's interest is that there should be a discrepancy, favorable for purchase or for sale as the case may be, between the actual and the putative earning-capacity of the corporation's capital.

It has been noted in an earlier chapter that there unavoidably results a discrepancy, not uncommonly a divergence, between the industrial needs of the community and the business needs of the corporations. Under the régime of the old-fashioned "money economy," with partnership methods and private ownership of industrial enterprises, the discretionary control of the industrial processes is in the hands of men whose interest in the industry is removed by one degree from the interests of the community at large. But under the régime of the more adequately developed "credit economy," with vendible corporate capital,[1] the interest of the men

[1] The capital of any industrial concern under the "money economy" is, of course, also vendible, but with relative difficulty; while

who hold the discretion in industrial affairs is removed by one degree from that of the concerns under their management, and by two degrees from the interests of the community at large.

The business interest of the managers demands, not serviceability of the output, nor even vendibility of the output, but an advantageous discrepancy in the price of the capital which they manage. The ready vendibility of corporate capital has in great measure dissociated the business interest of the directorate from that of the corporation whose affairs they direct and whose business policy they dictate, and has led them to centre their endeavors upon the discrepancy between the actual and the putative earning-capacity rather than upon the permanent efficiency of the concern. Their connection with the concern is essentially transient; it can be terminated speedily and silently whenever their private fortune demands its severance. Instances are abundant, more particularly in railway management, where this discrepancy between the business interest of the concern and the private business interest of the managers for the time being has led to very picturesque developments, such as could not occur if the interests of the man-

the readier vendibility of modern corporate capital is so characteristic and consequential a factor in business and contrasts so broadly with the old-fashioned business methods that it may fairly be spoken of as vendibility *par excellence*. The "holding company" is the mature development of this traffic in vendible capital in industrial business.

agement were bound up with those of the corporation in the manner and degree that once prevailed. The fact is significant that the more frequent and striking instances of such management of corporate affairs for private ends have hitherto occurred in railroading, at the same time that the methods and expedients of modern corporation finance have also first and most widely reached a fair degree of maturity in railroading. It holds out a suggestion as to what may fairly be looked for when corporation finance shall have made itself more thoroughly at home in the "industrials" proper. Indeed, the field of the "industrials" is by no means barren of instances comparable with the maturer and more sagacious railroad financiering.[1]

The stock market interest of those men who have the management of industrial corporations is a wide and multifarious one. It is not confined

[1] It may be noted, by the way, that the question of the turnover (spoken of on p. 95 above) becomes, under the circumstances of the modern corporation finance, in great part a question of the interval between the purchase and sale of the capital engaged in industry on the one hand, and of the magnitude of the discrepancy between actual and putative earning-capacity on the other hand, rather than a question of the period of the industrial process and the magnitude of the output and its price. The formula there shown becomes:—

$$\text{turnover} = \frac{\text{capital}}{\text{time}}\left(\frac{\text{actual earning-capacity}}{n} = \text{putative earning-capacity} - \text{actual earning-capacity}\right),$$

in which capital is the amount of the operator's investment in the concern's securities, the time is the interval between purchase and sale of the securities, and the putative earning-capacity is taken to exceed the actual earning-capacity by an indeterminate fraction of the latter.

to the profitable purchase and sale of properties whose management they may have in hand. They are also interested in making or marring various movements of coalition or reorganization, and to this ulterior end it is incumbent on them to "manipulate" securities with a view to buying and selling in such a manner as to gain control of certain lines of securities.[1] Hence it is a rule of this class of business traffic to cultivate appearance, — to avoid, or sometimes to court, the appearance of sin. So that under this leadership the course of industrial affairs is, in great measure, if not altogether, guided with a view to a plausible appearance of prosperity or of adversity, as the case may be. Under given circumstances it may as well become the aim of men in control to make an adverse showing as a favorable one. The higher exigencies of the captain of industry's personal fortunes, as distinct from those of the corporation controlled by him, may from time to time be best served by an apparent, if not an actual, mismanagement of industrial affairs. A convincing appearance of decline or disaster will lower the putative earning-capacity of the concern below its real earning-capacity and so will afford an advantageous opportunity for buying with a view to future advance or with a view to strategic control. Various other expedients looking to the like outcome are well known to

[1] *Cf.* Chapter III. above.

the craft, besides *bona fide* mismanagement. A given line of securities may be temporarily depressed by less heroic tactics; but the point in question here is the fact that under this system of corporation finance the affairs of the corporation are in good part managed for tactical ends which are of interest to the manager rather than to the corporation as a going concern.

What was said in speaking of credit extension without a determinate time interval[1] applies to this class of business, with a slight change of phrase. In this higher development of corporation finance, in the manipulations of vendible capital, the interval of the turnover spoken of above becomes an indeterminate factor. The gains of the business come to have but an uncertain and shifty relation to the lapse of time and cannot well be calculated per cent. per time-unit. There is, therefore, on these higher levels of business management, properly speaking no ascertainable ordinary rate of earnings. The capital which may be distinctively regarded as operative in the business of manipulation, the valuable items specifically employed in the traffic in vendible corporate capital, is made up of the operator's good-will and his financial solvency. Solvency on a large scale is requisite to carrying on traffic of this class, but the collateral on which this extensive solvency constructively rests is to

[1] Cf. Chapter V. above.

but a partial extent drawn into the business as a basis for an actual credit extension. What counts in the case is the solvency of the operator rather than an outright resort to the credit extension which this solvency might afford. The working capital involved in these transactions is accordingly of a peculiarly elusive character, and the time element in the use of this capital is hard to determine, if such a time element can properly be said to enter into the case at all.

More in detail, the business man in pursuit of gain along this line must, in the ordinary case, be possessed of large holdings of property, this being the basis of the solvency necessary to the business. These holdings are commonly in the form of securities in the concern whose vendible capital is the subject of his traffic, as well as in other corporations. These securities represent capital, tangible and intangible, which is already employed in the ordinary business of the concern by which they have been issued ; the capital, therefore, is already in use to the full extent and is presumably yielding the ordinary rate of earnings. But the solvency for which the ownership of this capital affords a basis may further be useful in enabling the owner to carry on a traffic in vendible corporate capital without withdrawing any appreciable portion of his holdings from the lucrative investments in which they have been placed. In other words, he is able, under modern circumstances, to make a secondary use of his investments for the purpose of trading in vendible corporate capital; but this secondary use of investments bears no hard and fast quantitative relation to the investments in question, nor does it in any determinate way interfere with the ordinary employment of this invested capital in the commonplace conduct of the corporations' business traffic. The capital employed, as well as the potential credit extension which it affords for the purposes of this higher business traffic, is therefore in a peculiar degree intangible, and, in respect of its amount, highly elusive.

Much the same is true of the good-will employed in this traffic. It is also in good part good-will which already serves the purposes of the commonplace business traffic of the corporations on whose securities the business man in question rests his solvency. So that in this higher business traffic the good-will engaged is also here turned to a secondary use. The business economies which are in this way made practicable by a reduplication of uses and made to inure to the greater business men's profit are of great magnitude; but the magnificent additions which are in this way made to the business community's capitalizable forces need scarcely be dwelt on here.

The elusive and flexuous character of the elements of wealth engaged, as well as the absence of an ascertainable ordinary rate of earnings in this line of business, has led economists to speak of this traffic in vendible capital as a "speculative" business.[1] The mere buying and selling of stocks by outsiders for a rise or a decline is of course a speculative business; it is a typical form of speculative business. But in so far as such buying and selling is carried on by the managers of the corporations whose securities are the subject of the traffic, and especially where the securities are bought and sold with a view to the control of the corporations in question and their management for private, tactical ends, a characterization of the business as "speculative" is inadequate and beside the point. This higher reach of corporation financiering has little if any more of a speculative character than what belongs to the commonplace business management of any industrial enterprise. In all business enterprise that stands in relations with the market and depends on vendibility of its output there is more or less uncertainty as to the outcome.[2] In this sense all industrial business, as well as commercial business, has something of a speculative character. But it is little to the purpose on that account to lump industrial enterprises and

[1] Cf. Emery, "Place of the Speculator in the Theory of Distribution," *Proceedings* of the twelfth annual meeting of the American Economic Association; also "Discussion," following Mr. Emery's paper.

[2] Well shown in Mr. Emery's paper cited above.

corporation financiering together as "speculative business" and deal with them as if this were their most salient and consequential bearing. What speculative risk there is in these lines of business is incidental, and it neither affords the incentive to engaging in these pursuits nor does it bound the scope of their bearing upon economic affairs. The speculative risk involved is no greater, relatively to the magnitude of the interests involved, in this larger traffic that deals in vendible capital than it is in the ordinary lines of business traffic that deal in vendible products. In both cases there may be speculation, but in both cases it is a side issue. Indeed, as near as one may confidently hold an opinion on so dark a question, the certainty of gain, though perhaps not the relative amount of it, seems rather more assured in the large-scale manipulation of vendible capital than in business management with a view to a vendible product.

What may obscure the question is the fact that the manipulations involved in this traffic in vendible capital commonly impose increased risks upon the business concerns engaged in industry — the corporations whose capital is involved, as well as other firms. The everyday business of the corporations whose securities are involved, as well as of other business concerns engaged in rival or related lines of industry, is rendered more hazardous than it might be in the absence of this financiering traffic in vendible capital. The manipulations carry risk, not so much to the manipulators as such, as to the corporations whose properties are the subject of manipulation; but since the manipulators commonly own but a relatively small proportion of the properties involved or touched by their manipulations, the risks which arise do not fall chiefly on them. To this is to be added, as of prime importance for the whole question, that the manipulators have the advantage of being able, in great part, to foresee the nature, magnitude, and incidence of the risks which they create. Rightly seen, this, of course, goes to say that the increased speculative risk due to the traffic in vendible capital does not fall on that traffic, but on the business enterprise engaged about the output of vendible goods. The traffic in vendible capital is not without its speculative risks, but the risks which it creates fall with relatively greater weight upon the business men who are not immediately concerned in this traffic. Indeed, so secure and lucrative is this class of business, that it is chiefly out of gains accruing, directly and indirectly, from such traffic in vendible capital that the great modern fortunes are being accumulated; and both the rate and the magnitude of these accumulations, whether taken absolutely or relatively to the total increase of wealth, surpass all recorded phenomena of their kind. Nothing so effective for the accumulation of private wealth is known to the history of human culture.

The aim and substantial significance of the "manipulations" of vendible capital here spoken of is an ever recurring recapitalization of the properties involved, whereby the effective capitalization of the corporations whose securities are the subject of the traffic is increased and decreased from time to time. The fluctuations, or pulsations, of this effective capitalization are shown by the market quotations of the securities, as noted above.[1] It is out of these variations in capitalization that the gains of the traffic arise, and it is also through the means of these variations of capitalization that the business men engaged in this higher finance are enabled to control the fortunes of the corporations and to effect their strategic work of coalition and reorganization of business enterprises. Hence this traffic in vendible capital is the pivotal and dominant factor in the modern situation of business and industry.[2]

[1] p. 154.

[2] As is true of good-will and credit extensions generally, so with respect to the good-will and credit strength of these greater business men; it affords a differential advantage and gives a differential gain. In the traffic of corporation finance this differential gain is thrown immediately into the form of capital and so is added to the nominal capitalized wealth of the community. What it gives to its holders in this capitalized form is a claim to a proportionate share in the existing wealth. If other things are supposed to remain the same (which may not be the case), the claim so enforced by the great financiers on the basis of good-will and credit extension deducts that much from the wealth held by the rest, the previous holders, as counted in

It has been noted above that what may be called the working capital on which this higher corpora-

terms of material wealth; as counted in terms of money value, of course, the holdings of previous holders do (or need) not suffer, since the new claims take the form of an addition to the number of capitalized value units, although the increased aggregate number of value units constitutes a claim on the same aggregate mass of wealth as before. The *pro rata* reduction of the material magnitude of the several shares of wealth is not felt as an impoverishment, because it does not take the form of a reduction of the nominal value of the shares.

This capitalization of the gains arising from a differential advantage results in a large "saving" and increase of capital. The wealth so drawn in by the financiers (entrepreneurs) is nearly all held as capital, very little of it being consumed in current expenses of living. It has been cogently argued that the profits of the undertakers is the chief and normal source of capitalized savings in the modern situation, and the method here indicated seems to be the method by which such saving is chiefly effected. An extremely suggestive discussion of the undertaker's gains in this connection occurs in a paper by L. V. Birck ("Driftsherrens Gevinst"), read before the Danish Economic Association, December 1901. More immediately to the point still is V. Schou's discussion of Mr. Birck's paper. (See *Nationalökonomisk Tidsskrift*, January–February 1902, pp. 76, 78–80.) J. B. Clark, in lectures hitherto unprinted, follows a line of analysis somewhat closely parallel with Schou, though not carried to quite the same length.

This process of combined recapitalization and saving may be stated formally as follows: The initial value of the properties submitted for coalition and recapitalization, cap, is in the normal case augmented by the increment Δ, making the effective value of the properties $=$ cap $+ \Delta$, in effective units, U_e. This augmented effective value of the properties $= U_e(\text{cap} + \Delta)$ is capitalized at a nominal value of $\text{cap}' = U_n(\text{cap} + \Delta)$, in nominal units, U_n, nominally equivalent to U_e. In the recapitalization the number of units of capitalization is increased by an element of intangible assets assigned the owners on account of a presumed increase of earning-capacity due to the coalition. This element of good-will due to coalition may be called co. Further there is added the bonus of the promoter, taken as a block of stock in the new capitalization, pro. Hence $U_n(\text{cap}') \approx U_n(\text{cap} + \Delta) \approx U_n(\text{cap} + \text{co} + \text{pro})$. $U_n(\text{pro}) \approx U_n(\text{cap}' - \text{cap} - \text{co}) \approx U_n(\Delta - \text{co})$ is evidently a secure gain to the promoter of $U_e(\Delta - \text{co})$, which is a fraction of the effective value $U_e(\text{cap} + \Delta)$. This is saved by him in the capitalized form. The account of the former owners of the properties will then stand as follows:

tion finance proceeds is made up, chiefly, of two elements: the solvency (and consequent potential credit) of the men engaged, and the "good-will" of these men. Both of these elements are of a somewhat intangible and elusive character, resting, as they do, somewhat indirectly and shiftily on elements already elsewhere engaged in business enterprise. The solvency in question rests in large part on the capital of the corporations whose capitalization is subject to the fluctuations induced by the traffic in vendible capital. It is therefore necessarily a somewhat indeterminate and unstable magnitude. To this is to be added the "floating

$U_e(\text{cap} + \Delta - \text{pro}) \lesseqgtr U_e(\text{cap})$ according as $U_e \Delta \lesseqgtr U^e(\text{pro})$. The nominal gain of the owners, co, may or may not be a real gain according as the event may prove that the promoter's bonus has not or has absorbed the entire effective augmentation of value, Δ, due to the coalition; it is therefore a problematical gain, which may or may not, in the event, prove to be an effective element of capitalized savings.

The constitution of Δ will decide what is the ultimate source of the savings effected by this transaction. If Δ consists entirely of economies of production, the capitalized savings held by the promoter and former owners as a result of the transaction represent new values added to, or saved to, the aggregate wealth of the community. If Δ consists entirely of good-will in the shape of monopoly advantage, the saving is effected at the cost of the community and for the benefit of the promoter and owners; it is then an involuntary or subconscious saving on the part of the community, whereby a part of the community's wealth at large passes into the hands of the recapitalized corporation. Where Δ is made up of these two constituents together, the result, as regards the present point, should be plain without discussion. If, on the other hand, $\Delta = 0$, so that $\text{cap}' = \text{cap}$, then the promoter's savings, pro, are secured at the cost of the former owners; $U_e(\text{cap}' - \text{pro}) = U_e(\text{cap} + (\Delta = 0) - \text{pro}) \backsimeq U_e(\text{cap} - \text{pro})$. Whereas if $U_e(\text{pro}) = U_e(\Delta)$, $U_e(\text{co}) = 0$, leaving the owners without effective profit or loss in spite of any nominal increase of the capitalization.

capital" and banking capital at the disposal of these men. If a common-sense view be taken of the business, the good-will engaged must also be added to the assets. There is involved a very considerable and very valuable body of good-will, appertaining to the financiers engaged and to the financing firms associated with them.[1] This good-will and this solvency is capital, for the purpose in hand, as effectually as the good-will and securities incorporated in the capitalization of any corporation engaged in industrial business.

But hitherto this particular category of good-will has not been formally capitalized. There may be peculiar difficulties in the way of reducing this good-will to the form of a fund, expressing it in terms of a standard unit, and so converting it into quotable common stock, as has been done with the corresponding good-will of incorporated industrial enterprises. So also as regards the body of solvency engaged, — the potential credit, or credit capacity, of the promoters and financiers. Perhaps this latter had best also be treated as an element

[1] "Good-will" in this field of enterprise most frequently takes the form of a large ability to help or hinder other financiers and financing houses in any similar manœuvres in which they may be engaged, or an ability to put them in the way of lucrative financing transactions. The guild of financiers is commonly split up into more or less well-defined factions, each comprising an extensive ramification of financing houses and financiers furthering one another's endeavors under more or less settled working arrangements. These working arrangements are a large part of the financiers' "good-will."

of good-will; it is difficult to handle under any other, more tangible, conception. It may be difficult to standardize, fund, and capitalize these unstable but highly efficient factors of business enterprise; but the successful capitalization of good-will and credit extensions in the case of the modern industrial corporations argues that this difficulty should not be insurmountable in case an urgent need,—that is to say, the prospect of a profitably vendible result,—should press for a formal capitalization of these peculiar elements of business wealth. There can be no question, *e.g.*, but that the good-will and large solvency belonging to such a firm as J. P. Morgan and Company for the purposes of this class of business enterprise are an extremely valuable and substantial asset, as is also, and more unequivocally, the good-will of the head of that firm. These intangible assets, immaterial goods, should, in all consistency, be reduced to standard units, funded, issued as common stock, and so added to the statistical aggregate of the country's capitalized wealth.

It is safe to affirm that this good-will of the great reorganizer has in some measure entered in capitalized form into the common stock of the United States Steel Corporation, as also into that of some of the other great combinations that have latterly been effected. The "good-will" of Mr. Carnegie and his lieutenants, as well as of many other large business men connected with the steel industry, has also no doubt gone to swell the capitalization of the great corporation. But good-will on this higher level of business enterprise has a certain character of inexhaustibility, so that its use and capitalization in one corporation need not, and indeed does not, hinder or diminish the extent to which it may be used and capitalized in any other corporation.[1] The case is analogous, though scarcely similar, to that of the workmanlike or artistic skill of a handicraftsman, or an artist, which may be embodied in a given product without abating the degree of skill possessed by the workman. Like other good-will, though perhaps in a higher degree of sublimation, it is of a spiritual nature, such that, by virtue of the ubiquity proper to spiritual bodies, the whole of it may undividedly be present in every part of the various structures which it has created. Indeed, the fact of such good-will having been incorporated in capitalized form in the stock of any given corporation seems rather to augment than to diminish the amount at which it may advantageously be capitalized in the stock of the next corporation into which it enters. It has also the correlative spiritual attribute that it may imperceptibly and inscru-

[1] This category of good-will stands in a relation to the creation of vendible capital similar to that which the corporate good-will of an industrial business concern bears to the creation of vendible products.

tably withdraw its animating force from any one of its creatures without thereby altering the material circumstances of the corporation which suffers such an intangible shrinkage of its forces.

There can be no question but that the good-will of the various great organizers and their financiering houses has repeatedly been capitalized, probably to its full amount, in the common stock of the various corporations which they have created; but taken in the sense of an asset belonging to the financing house as a corporation, it is not known that this item of immaterial wealth has yet been formally capitalized and offered in quotable shares on the market or included in the schedules of personal property.[1]

The sublimation of business capital that has been going forward in recent times has grave consequences for the owners of property as well as for the conduct of industry. In so far as invested property is managed by the methods of modern corporation finance, it is evident that the management is separated from the ownership of

[1] Parenthetically it may be remarked that the failure to capitalize such items of good-will is likely to involve a virtual evasion of the tax on personal property, and may, therefore, be questionable on moral grounds.

The case of J. P. Morgan and Company is, of course, not here cited as being a unique or peculiar instance, but simply as a typical and striking illustration of what happens and of what might be accomplished in a number of large and very consequential cases of the same class.

the property, more and more widely as the scope of corporation finance widens. The discretion, the management, lies in the hands of the holders of the intangible forms of property; and with the extension of corporation methods it is increasingly true that this management, again, centres in the hands of those greater business men who hold large blocks of these intangible assets. The reach of a business man's discretionary control, under corporation methods, is not proportioned simply to the amount of his holdings. If his holdings are relatively small, they give him virtually no discretion. Whereas if they are relatively large, they may give him a business discretion of much more than a proportionate reach. The effective reach of a business man's discretion might be said to increase as the square of his holdings; although this is to be taken as a suggestive characterization rather than as an exact formula.

Among the holdings of industrial property that count in this way toward control of the business situation, the intangible assets (represented by common stock, good-will, and the like) are chiefly of consequence. Hence follow these two results: the fortunes of property owners are in large measure dependent on the discretion of others — the owners of intangible property; and the management of the industrial equipment tends strongly to centre in the hands of men who do not own the industrial equipment, and who have only a remote interest in the efficient working of this equipment. The property of those who own less, or who own only material goods, is administered by those who own more, especially of immaterial goods; and the material processes of industry are under the control of men whose interest centres on an increased value of the immaterial assets.[1]

[1] This dissociation of the business control from workmanlike efficiency and from immediate contact with or ownership of the industrial plant gives the existing situation a superficial resemblance to the feudal system, in so far as touches the immateriality of the captain's connections with the everyday life and interests of the community of whose affairs he is master. It gives a certain plausibility to the attempted interpretation of latter-day economic developments in feudalistic terms. —See Ghent, *Our Benevolent Feudalism*.

THE THEORY OF MODERN WELFARE

BEFORE business principles came to dominate everyday life the common welfare, when it was not a question of peace and war, turned on the ease and certainty with which enough of the means of life could be supplied. Since business has become the central and controlling interest, the question of welfare has become a question of price. Under the old régime of handicraft and petty trade, dearth (high prices) meant privation and might mean famine and pestilence; under the new régime low prices commonly mean privation and may on occasion mean famine. Under the old régime the question was whether the community's work was adequate to supply the community's needs; under the new régime that question is not seriously entertained.

But the common welfare is in no less precarious a case. The productive efficiency of modern industry has not done away with the recurrence of hard times, or of privation for those classes whose assured pecuniary position does not place them above the chances of hard times. Distress may not be so extreme in modern industrial communities, it does not readily reach the famine mark; but such a degree of privation as is implied in the term "hard times" recurs quite as freely in modern civilized countries as among the industrially less efficient peoples on a lower level of culture. The oscillation between good times and bad is as wide and as frequent as ever, although the average level of material well-being runs at a higher mark than was the case before the machine industry came in.

This visible difference between the old order and the new is closely dependent on the difference between the purposes that guide the older scheme of economic life and those of the new. Under the old order, industry, and even such trade as there was, was a quest of livelihood; under the new order industry is directed by the quest of profits. Formerly, therefore, times were good or bad according as the industrial processes yielded a sufficient or an insufficient output of the means of life. Latterly times are good or bad according as the process of business yields an adequate or inadequate rate of profits. The controlling end is different in the present, and the question of welfare turns on the degree of success with which this different ulterior end is achieved. Prosperity now means, primarily, business prosperity; whereas it used to mean industrial sufficiency.

A theory of welfare which shall account for the phenomena of prosperity and adversity under the modern economic order must, accordingly, proceed on the circumstances which condition the modern situation, and need not greatly concern itself with the range of circumstances that made or marred the common welfare under the older régime, before the age of machine industry and business enterprise.[1] Under the old order, when those in whose hands lay the discretion in economic affairs looked to a livelihood as the end of their endeavors, the welfare of the community was regulated "by the skill, dexterity, and judgment with which its labor was generally applied."[2] What would mar this common welfare was the occasionally disastrous act of God in the way of unpropitious seasons and the like, or the act of man in the way of war and untoward governmental exactions. Price variations, except as conditioned by these untoward intrusive agencies, had commonly neither a wide nor a profound effect upon the even course of the community's welfare. This holds true, in a general way, even after resort to the market had come to be a fact of great importance in the life of large classes, both as an outlet for their products and as

[1] Such a discussion as Patten's *Theory of Prosperity* applies to the régime of "natural economy," and passably also to that of handicraft and petty trade, but does not seriously touch the modern situation. The like is true generally for current discussions of this topic.

[2] *Wealth of Nations*, Introduction.

a base of supplies of consumable goods or of raw materials, — as in the better days of the handicraft system.

Until the machine industry came forward, commerce (with its handmaiden, banking) was the only branch of economic activity that was in any sensible degree organized in a close and comprehensive system of business relations. "Business" would then mean "commerce," and little else. This was the only field in which men habitually took account of their own economic circumstances in terms of price rather than in terms of livelihood. Price disturbances, even when they were of considerable magnitude, seem to have had grave consequences only in commerce, and to have passed over without being transmitted much beyond the commercial houses and the fringe of occupations immediately subsidiary to commercial business.

Crises, depressions, hard times, dull times, brisk times, periods of speculative advance, "eras of prosperity," are primarily phenomena of business; they are, in their origin and primary incidence, phenomena of price disturbance, either of decline or advance. It is only secondarily, through the mediation of business traffic, that these matters involve the industrial process or the livelihood of the community. They affect industry because industry is managed on a business footing, in terms of price and for the sake of profits. So long as business enterprise habitually ran its course within commercial traffic proper, apart from the industrial process as such, so long these recurring periods of depression and exaltation began and ended within the domain of commerce.[1] The greatest field for

[1] This means, in concrete terms, prior to the régime of the machine industry. Since the coming in of the machine, modern business enterprise has taken over the management of industry; that is to say, industry has come to be managed by the method of investment for a profit — by what is in aim and animus essentially the commercial method. As has been remarked above, capital has become vendible in a decisive degree. The material factors engaged in industry, particularly in the machine industry proper, are vendible in about the same (perhaps on an average in a higher) degree as the material items handled by commercial traffic are vendible. This is true of raw materials, labor power, and industrial equipment, but it is peculiarly true of the industrial equipment — the mechanical factors in the stricter sense. It is in these mechanical appliances primarily, but in the other factors of the machine industry in only a slightly lower degree, that the traffic of investment, and of purchase and sale connected with investment, is particularly active. Within these wider limits a further limitation may be made. "Vendibility" of all items involved is, as a broadly general rule, carried to the highest pitch in those branches of industry that have to do with the production of "producer's goods." These branches are at the same time, and partly in consequence of this fact, more widely and intimately related to other branches of industry than are any other group of industrial processes that might be named. It seems to be this extreme prevalence of vendibility, together with this more far-reaching and more exacting articulation with the industrial process at large, that chiefly gives substantial significance to a classification of these lines of industry as "Produktivmittel-Industrien" by late German writers. There is, for business purposes, a difference of degree, in both of the respects named, between this (ill-defined) group of industrial processes on the one hand, and the contrasted group occupied with the production of consumption goods on the other hand. The "productive-goods industries" show the modern industrial and business traits in an accentuated form and force, and they are, by consequence, in a strategetically primary position in the business situation.

Cf., *e. g.*, A. Spiethoff, *Jahrbuch f. Gesetzgebung Verwaltung u. Volkswirtschaft*, vol. XXVI. Heft 2. "Vorbemerkungen zu einer Theorie

business profits is now afforded, not by commercial traffic in the stricter sense, but by the industries engaged in producing goods and services for the market. And the close-knit, far-reaching articulation of the industrial processes in a balanced system, in which the interstitial adjustments are made and kept in terms of price, enables price disturbances to be transmitted throughout the industrial community with such celerity and effect that a wave of depression or exaltation passes over the whole community and touches every class employed in industry within a few weeks. And somewhat in the same measure as the several modern industrial peoples are bound together by the business ties of the world market, do these peoples also share in common any wave of prosperity or depression which may initially fall upon any one member of this business community of nations. Exceptions from this rule, of course, are such periods of prosperity or depression as result from local (material) accidents of the seasons and the like,—accidents that may inflict upon one community hardships which through the mediation of prices are transmuted into gain for the other communities that are not touched by the calamitous act of God to which the disturbance is due.

der Überproducktion," and vol. XXVII. pp. 343–353; Tugan-Baranowsky, *Theorie und Geschichte der Handelskrisen in England*, pp. 18–28; L. Pohle, *Periodische Wirtschaftskrisen*, especially sec. II. with subjoined notes.

The true, or what may be called the normal, crises, depressions, and exaltations in the business world are not the result of accidents, such as the failure of a crop. They come in the regular course of business. The depression and the exaltation are in a measure bound together. In the recent past, since depression and exaltation have been normal features of the situation, every strongly marked period of exaltation (prosperity) has had its attendant period of depression; although it does not seem to follow in the nature of things that a wave of depression necessarily has its attendant reaction in the way of a period of business exaltation. In the recent past — the last twenty years or so — it has been by no means anomalous to have a period of hard times, or even a fairly pronounced crisis, without a wave of marked exaltation either preceding or following it in such close sequence as conveniently to connect the two as action and reaction. But it would be a matter of some perplexity to a student of this class of phenomena to come upon a wave of marked business exaltation (prosperity) that was not promptly followed by a crisis or by a period of depression more or less pronounced and prolonged. Indeed, as the organization of business has approached more and more nearly to the relatively consummate situation of to-day, — say during the last twenty years of the nineteenth century, — periods of exaltation have, on the whole, grown less pronounced and less frequent, whereas periods of depression or "hard times" have grown more frequent and prolonged, if not more pronounced. It might even be a tenable generalization, though perhaps unnecessarily broad, to say that for a couple of decades past the normal condition of industrial business has been a mild but chronic state of depression, and that any marked departure from commonplace dull times has attracted attention as a particular case calling for a particular explanation. The causes which have given rise to any one of the more pronounced intervals of prosperity during the past two decades are commonly not very difficult to trace; but it would be a bootless quest to go out in search of special causes to which to trace back each of the several periods of dull times that account for the greater portion of the past quarter of a century. Under the more fully developed business system as it has stood during the close of the century dull times are, in a way, the course of nature; whereas brisk times are an exceptional invention of man or a rare bounty of Providence.

What current economic theory has to say on the common welfare is more frequently found under the caption of crisis and depression than in any other one connection. And the theory of crisis and depression has, as is well known, been one of the less happy passages in the economists' repertory of doctrines. It has been customary to approach the problem from the side of the industrial phenomena involved — the mechanical facts of production and consumption; rather than from the side of business enterprise — the phenomena of price, earnings, and capitalization. This untoward accident of a false start is probably accountable for the fact that no tenable theory of these phenomena has yet been offered. The solutions attempted have commonly proceeded by an analysis of industrial life apart from business enterprise; that is to say, they have sought to explain the occurrence of crises under that old-fashioned "natural economy" or "money economy" under which crises did not normally occur.[1]

Taking as a point of departure the patent fact that crises, depressions, and brisk times are in their first incidence phenomena of business, of prices and capitalization, an explanation of their appearance and disappearance, and of their bearing upon the common welfare, may be sought by harking back to those business principles that underlie

[1] This is well exemplified in Tugan-Baranowsky (*Handelskrisen*), who declares at the outset (p. 17) that money and price are negligible factors for the purpose in hand. He thereby commits himself to the position that these crises are phenomena of the material processes of economic life (production and consumption), not of business traffic. Hence the ultimate failure of this acute observer and theoretician to reach a tenable solution of the question. Substantially the same is true of Marx, whom Tugan follows, though with large reservations. (Cf. Marx, *Kapital*, vol. III. ch. XV.)

modern capitalistic enterprise. An analysis of the current, common-sense business views of price and investment should indicate the genesis and manner of growth of these mass movements of the business community, as well as the character of those circumstances which may further or inhibit such movements. Business depression and exaltation are, at least in their first incidence, of the nature of psychological fact, just as price movements are a psychological phenomenon.

The everyday circumstances which condition the modern business management of industry are sufficiently well known, and they have already been reviewed in some detail in earlier chapters; but they may perhaps advantageously be outlined again in so far as they bear immediately on the question in hand.

(1) Industry is carried on by means of investment, which is made with a view to pecuniary gain (the earnings). The business man's endeavors in managing the affairs of the concern in which investment has been made look to the same end. The gains are kept account of as a percentage on the investment, and both they and the industrial plant or process through the management of which they are procured are counted in terms of money, and, indeed, in no other terms. The plant or process (or the investment, whatever form it takes) is capitalized on the basis of the gains which accrue

from it, and this capitalization proceeds on the ground afforded by the current rate of interest, weighted by consideration of any prospective change in the earning-capacity of the concern. The management of the concern is effected by a more or less intricate and multifarious sequence of bargains. The decisive consideration at every point in this traffic of investment and administration is the consideration of price in one relation or another.

(2) The industry to which the business men in this way resort as the ways and means of gain is of the nature of a mechanical process, or it is some employment (as commerce or banking) that is closely bound up with the mechanical industries. Broadly, it is such industry as lies under the dominion of the machine, in that it is involved in that comprehensive quasi-mechanical process of modern industrial life that has been discussed in an earlier chapter. This implication of each industry in a comprehensive system, or this articulation with other branches of industry, is of such a nature as to place each industrial concern in dependence on one or more other branches of industry, from which it draws its materials, appliances, etc., and to which it disposes of its output; and these relations of dependence and articulation form an endless sequence. That is to say, the interindustrial relations into which any branch of industry necessarily enters do not run to a final term in any

direction; within the process of industry at large there is no member that stands in the relation of an initial term to any sequence of processes. The ramification of industrial dependence is without limits. The method of these relations of one concern to another, or of one branch of industry to another, is that of bargaining, contracts of purchase and sale. It is a pecuniary relation, in the last resort a price relation, and the balance of this system of interstitial relations is a price balance.

(3) These interstitial pecuniary relations, between the several concerns or branches of industry that make up the comprehensive industrial system at large, involve credit relations of greater or less duration. The bargaining, by means of which industry is managed and the interstitial relations adjusted, takes the form of contracts for future performance. All industrial concerns of appreciable size are constantly involved in such contracts, which are, on an average, of considerable magnitude and duration, and commonly extend in several directions. These contracts may be of the nature of loans, advances, outstanding accounts, engagements for future delivery or future acceptance, but in the nature of the case they involve credit obligations. Credit, whether under that name or under the name of orders, contracts, accounts, and the like, is inseparable from the management of modern industry in all that con-

cerns the working relations between businesses that are not under one ownership, or between which the relations resting on separate ownership have not been placed in abeyance by some such expedient as lease, pool, syndicate, trust agreement, and the like. Credit relations of one kind and another are also found expedient and profitable at many points where their employment is not precisely unavoidable. These extended credit relations are requisite to the most expeditious and profitable conduct of business, and so to the highest degree of success of the business. Under the régime of the machine industry and modern business methods it is probably fair to say that the use of credit, apart from loan capital and leases, unavoidably goes to the extent required to cover all goods in process of elaboration, from the raw material to the finished goods, in so far as the goods change hands (in point of ownership) during the process.

(4) The conduct of industry by competing business concerns involves an extensive use of loan credit, as spoken of in Chapter V. above.

The four conditions recited are characteristic features of that recent past during which brisk times, crises, and depressions followed one another with some regularity as incidents of the normal course of business.[1] Certain qualifications of this

[1] The "cycle" of exaltation, crisis, and depression has frequently been described. Perhaps as effective a description and analysis as any is that of Tugan-Baranowsky, *Handelskrisen*, chap. VIII.

characterization are necessary to fit the immediate present. These will be indicated presently.

In brisk times the use of credit is large; it may be as a cause or an effect of the acceleration of business; most commonly it seems to be both a cause and an effect. No appreciable business acceleration takes place without an extension of credit, at least in the form of contracts of purchase and sale for future performance, if not also in the form of loans. In times of protracted depression the use of credit seems on the whole to be somewhat restricted, at least such is the current apprehension of the case among business men. Still, it cannot confidently be said that seasons of protracted depression are due solely to an absence of credit relations or to an unwillingness to enter into credit relations. A comparison of the course of interest rates, *e.g.*, does not warrant the generalization that the readiness with which loans can be negotiated need be appreciably different in brisk and in dull times.[1] The readiness with which contracts of purchase and sale are negotiated is appreciably greater in brisk times than in times of depression; that, indeed, is the obvious difference between the two.

Of the three phases of business activity, depression, exaltation, and crisis, the last named has

Cf., however, Cassel, "Om Kriser och Dåliga Tider," *Ekonomisk Tidskrift*, vol. VI. No. 2, pp. 59–78.

claimed the larger and livelier attention from students, as it is also the more picturesque phenomenon. An industrial crisis is a period of liquidation, cancelment of credits, high discount rates, falling prices and "forced sales," and shrinkage of values. It has as a sequel, both severe and lasting, a shrinkage of capitalization throughout the field affected by it. It leaves the business men collectively poorer, in terms of money value; but the property which they hold between them may not be appreciably smaller in point of physical magnitude or of mechanical efficiency than it was before the liquidation set in. It commonly also involves an appreciable curtailment of industry, more severe than lasting; but the effects which a crisis has in industry proper are commonly not commensurate with its consequences in business or with the importance attached to a crisis by the business community. It does not commonly involve an appreciable destruction of property or a large waste of the material articles of wealth. It leaves the community at large poorer in point of market values, but not necessarily in terms of the material means of life. The shrinkage incident to a crisis is chiefly a pecuniary, not a material, shrinkage; it takes place primarily in the intangible items of wealth, secondarily in the price rating of the tangible items. Apart from such rerating of wealth, the most substantial immediate effect of a crisis is an extensive redistribution of the ownership of the industrial equipment, as noted in speaking of the use of credit.

The play of business exigencies which lead to such a period of liquidation seems to run somewhat as follows: Many firms have large bills payable falling due at near dates, at the same time that they hold bills receivable also in large amounts. To meet the demand of their creditors they call upon their debtors, who may in their turn have bills receivable or may hold loans on collateral. The initial move in the sequence of liquidation may be the calling in of a call loan, or a call for additional collateral on a call loan. At some point, earlier or later, in the sequence of liabilities the demand falls upon the holder of a loan on collateral which is, in the apprehension of his creditor, insufficient to secure ready liquidation, either by a shifting of the loan or by a sale of the collateral. The collateral is commonly a block of securities representing capitalized wealth, and the apprehension of the creditor may be formulated as a doubt of the conservative character of the effective capitalization on which it rests. In other words, there is an apprehension that the property represented by the collateral is overcapitalized, as tested by the current quotations, or by the apprehended future quotations, of the securities in question. The market capitalization of the collateral has taken place on the basis of high prices and brisk trade which prevail in such a period of business exaltation as always precedes an acute crisis. When such a call comes upon a given debtor, the call is passed along to the debtors farther along in the sequence of liabilities, and the sequence of liquidations thereby gets under way, with the effect, notorious through unbroken experience, that the collateral all along the line declines in the market. The crisis is thereby in action, and the further consequences follow as a well-known matter of course. All this is familiar matter, known to business men and students by common notoriety.

The immediate occasion of such a crisis, then, is that there arises a practical discrepancy between the earlier effective capitalization on which the collateral has been accepted by the creditors, and the subsequent effective capitalization of the same collateral shown by quotations and sales of the securities on the market. But since the earlier capitalization commonly, in the normal case, comes out of a period of business prosperity, the point of inquiry is as to the ground and method of this effective capitalization of collateral during the period of prosperity that goes before a crisis, and this, in turn, involves the question of the nature and causes of a period of prosperity.

The manner in which the capitalization of collateral, and thereby the discrepancy between the putative and actual earning-capacity of capital, is increased by loan credit during an era of prosperity has been indicated in some detail in Chapter V. above. But it may serve to enforce the view there taken, if it can be shown on similar lines that a period of prosperity will bring on a like discrepancy between putative and actual earning-capacity, and therefore between putative and eventual capitalization of collateral, even independently of the expansion effected by loan credit.

A period of prosperity is no more a matter of course than a crisis. It has its beginning in some specific combination of circumstances. It takes its rise from some traceable favorable disturbance of the course of business. In such a period the potent fact which serves as incentive to the acceleration of business is a rise of prices. This rise of prices presently becomes general as prosperity progresses and becomes an habitual fact, but it takes its start from some specific initial disturbance of prices. That is to say, prices rise first in some one industry or line of industries.[1]

[1] As, *e.g.*, the era of prosperity 1897–1902 took its start from the demand for supplies caused by the Spanish-American War, though other favorable circumstances acted to give it volume. Mr. Carver, possibly following suggestions given by Spiethoff's discussion, has suggested that the lines of business in which the favorable initial disturbance arises are necessarily those engaged in the production of "producer's goods"; the reason for this being that, in the nature of the case, "the value of producer's goods tends to fluctuate more vio-

By new investments, as well as by extending the operations of the plants already employed, business men forthwith endeavor to take advantage of such a rise. The endeavor to market an increased supply of the things for which there is an enlarged demand, brings on an increased demand and an advance of prices in those lines of industry from which the concerns that had the initial advantage draw their supplies. In part by actual increase of demand and in part through a lively anticipation of an advanced demand, aggressive business enterprise extends its ventures and pushes up prices in remoter lines of industry. This transmission of the favorable disturbance of business (substantially a psychological phenomenon) follows very promptly under modern conditions, so that any differential advantage that accrues at the outset to the particular line of industry upon which the initial disturbance falls is presently lost or greatly lessened. In the meantime extensive contracts for future performance are entered into in all directions, and this extensive implication of

lently than the value of consumer's goods," inasmuch as the value of producer's goods varies somewhat as the magnitude of the margin of profits, while that of the consumer's goods varies somewhat as the magnitude of the entire demand on which this margin of profits rests as an increment. (The value of producer's goods $= f(\Delta)$, that of consumer's goods $= f(\text{demand} + \Delta)$.) From the like line of argument it should follow that the initial break in time of crisis must come in some line of business occupied with producer's goods. Cf. *Quarterly Journal of Economics*, May 1903, pp. 497–500. See also foot-note on p. 181 above.

the various lines of industry serves, of itself, to maintain the prosperity for the time being. If the original favorable disturbance of demand and prices, to which the prosperity owes its rise, falls off to the earlier level of demand, the era of prosperity has thereby a term set to its run; although the date of its termination is always at some distance in the future, beyond the time when the original demand has ceased to act. The reason for this retardation, whereby the close of an era of prosperity is always delayed, other things equal, beyond the lapse of the cause from which it has arisen, is (1) the habit of buoyancy, or speculative recklessness, which grows up in any business community under such circumstances, (2) the continued life of a considerable body of contracts for future performance, which acts to keep up the demand for such things as are required in order to fill these contracts and thereby keeps up prices in so far. In general it may be said that after the failure of the favorable price disturbance to which it is due, an era of prosperity will continue for that (indefinite) further period during which the fringe of outstanding contracts continues to dominate the business situation. Some further, new contracts will always continue to be made during this period, and some unfilled contracts will always be left standing over when the liquidation sets in; but, broadly speaking, the wind-up comes, not when this body of outstanding contracts have run out or been filled, but when the business of filling them and of filling the orders to which they give rise no longer occupies the attention of the business community in greater measure than the rest of current business.

The run of business exigencies on which an era of prosperity goes forward may be sketched in its general features somewhat as follows: Increased demand and enhanced prices, with the large contracts which follow from such a state of the market, increase the prospective earnings of the several concerns engaged. These prospective earnings may eventually be realized in full measure, or they may turn out to have been putative earnings only; that is largely a question of how far in the future the liquidation lies. The business effect of increased prospective earnings, however, is much the same whether the event proves the expectation of increased earnings to have been well grounded or not. The expectation in either case leads the business men to bid high for equipment and supplies. Thereby the effective (market) capitalization is increased to answer to the increased prospective earnings. This recapitalization of industrial property, on the basis of heightened expectation, increases the value of this property as collateral. The inflated property becomes, in effect, collateral even without a formal extension of credit in the way of loans; because, in effect, the contracts entered into are a credit extension, and because the property of the contracting parties is liable to be drawn into liquidation in case of non-fulfilment of the contracts. But during the free swing of that buoyant enterprise that characterizes an era of prosperity contracts are entered into with a somewhat easy scrutiny of the property values available to secure a contract. So that as regards this point not only is the capitalization of the industrial property inflated on the basis of expectation, but in the making of contracts the margin of security is less closely looked after than it is in the making of loans on collateral. There results a discrepancy between the effective capitalization during prosperity and the capitalization as it stood before the prosperity set in, and the heightened capitalization becomes the basis of an extensive ramification of credit in the way of contracts (orders); at the same time the volume of loan credit, in set form, is also greatly increased during an era of prosperity.[1]

An era of prosperity is an era of rising prices. When prices cease to rise prosperity is on the wane, although it may not promptly terminate at that juncture. This follows from the fact that the

[1] Cf. Sombart, *Kapitalismus*, vol. II. ch. I., on the motive forces at work in advancing business enterprise.

putative increase of earnings on which prosperity rests is in substance an apprehended differential gain in increased selling price of the output over the expenses of production of the output. Only so long as the selling price of the output realizes such a differential gain over the expenses of production, is the putative increased rate of earnings realized; and so soon as such a differential advantage ceases, the era of prosperity enters on its closing phase.

Such a differential advantage arises mainly from two causes: (1) The lines of industry which are remote, industrially speaking, from the point of initial disturbance, — from which, that is to say, the lines of industry first and chiefly affected by the rise draw supplies of one kind or another, — these remote lines of industry are less promptly and less acutely affected by the favorable disturbance of the price level; this retardation of the disturbance affords the industries nearer the seat of disturbance a differential advantage, which grows less the farther removed the given enterprise is from the point of initial disturbance.[1] (2) The chief and most secure differential advantage in the case is that due to

[1] The "initial disturbance" here spoken of may of course be of a progressive or recurring character, and so may keep the differential advantage going in a progressive manner; as, *e.g.*, in the case of a progressive demand for supplies due to a protracted war or to a period of continued preparation for war, such as has occurred in America during the last few years.

the relatively slow advance in the cost of labor during an era of prosperity. Wages ordinarily are not advanced at all for a considerable period after such an era of prosperity has set in; and so long as the eventual advance of wages does not overtake the advance in prices (which in the common run of cases it never does in full measure), so long, of course, a differential gain in the selling price accrues, other things equal, to virtually all business enterprises engaged in the industries affected by the prosperity.

There are, further, certain (outlying) lines of industry, as, *e.g.*, farming, which may not be drawn into the movement in any appreciable degree, and the price of supplies drawn from these outlying industries need not rise; particularly they need not advance in a degree proportionate to the advance in the prices of the goods into which they enter as an element of their expenses of production. To an uncertain but commonly appreciable extent there is also a progressive cheapening of the processes of production during such an era, and this cheapening, particularly in so far as it affects the production of the goods contracted for, as contrasted with the appliances of production, serves also to maintain the differential advantage between the contracted sale price and the expenses of production of the goods contracted for.

In the ordinary course, however, the necessary

expenses of production presently overtake or nearly overtake the prospective selling price of the output. The differential advantage, on which business prosperity rests, then fails; the rate of earnings falls off; the enhanced capitalization based on enhanced putative earnings proves greater than the earnings realized or in prospect on the basis of an enhanced scale of expenses of production; the collateral consequently shrinks to a point where it will not support the credit extension resting on it in the way of outstanding contracts and loans; and liquidation ensues, after the manner frequently set forth by those who have written on these subjects.[1]

At some point in the system of investment and business extension will be found some branches of industry which have gradually lost what differen-

[1] There is a point or two of further detail in what may be called the method of prosperity and crisis, which are best discussed in connection with the phenomena of depression. These will, therefore, be taken up presently. The above characterization of an era of prosperity and the manner of its exhausting itself will serve as a description of the course which such an era takes under the régime of the more highly developed business methods of the high tide of the nineteenth century. For the earlier, less fully developed, business situation of the early nineteenth century the corresponding course of events runs somewhat different, owing, chiefly at least, (1) to a slower rate of transmission of any price disturbance, and (2) to the greater range and value of "outlying" industries which are very tardily if at all drawn into the exuberant movement of prosperity. In this connection it is worth noting that during this earlier period of the ninteenth century the production of specifically productive goods had not been carried to the point afterward attained, either in the differentiation and specialization of industries occupied with this class of goods or in the relative volume of this class of industries.

tial advantage they started out with when they entered on the era of prosperity; and if these are involved in large contracts and undertakings which are carried over into the phase of the movement at which this particular branch of industry has ceased to have a differential advantage in the price of its output over the cost of its supplies of material or labor, then what may have been a conservative capitalization of their holdings at an early phase, while their earning-capacity rested on a large differential advantage, will become an excessive capitalization after their earning-capacity has declined through loss of their differential advantage. Some branch or branches and some firms or class of firms necessarily fall into this position in the course of a period of phenomenally brisk times. A business concern so placed necessarily becomes a debtor, and its liabilities necessarily become, in some degree, bad debts. It is forced by circumstances to deliver its output at prices which preclude its obtaining such a margin as its extension of business presupposed. That is to say, its capitalization becomes excessive through shrinkage of its earning-capacity (as counted in terms of price). A concern of this class which is a debtor is precluded from meeting its obligations out of its current earnings; and if, as commonly happens in an appreciable proportion of cases, its obligations have already been augmented to the extent which its recent earning-capacity would warrant, then the concern is insolvent for the time being. If the claims against it are pressed, it has no recourse but liquidation through forced sales or bankruptcy. Either expedient, if the case is one of considerable magnitude, is disastrous to the balanced sequence of credit relations in which the business community is involved. The system of credit relations prevailing at such a time has grown up on the basis of an earning-capacity transiently enhanced by a wave of differential price advantage; and when this wave has passed, even if it leaves prices higher all around, the differential advantage of at least most concerns is past. The differential price advantage has come to the several branches or firms in succession, and has, in the typical case, successively left each with an excessive capitalization, and has left many with a body of liabilities out of proportion to their subsequent earning-capacity. This situation may, evidently, come about in this manner, even without lowering the aggregate (pecuniary) earning-capacity of the business community to the level at which it stood before the wave of prosperity set in.[1]

[1] The several phases of this sequence of exaltation and depression, for any given business concern, may be stated as follows:—

Let ea = earnings; pr = sale price of output; exp = expenses of production of output; mar = margin of gain on output = pr − exp; cap = initial effective capitalization; yp = year's purchase at (current

But when such a situation has come, all that is required to bring on the general catastrophe is that some considerable creditor find out that the present earning-capacity of his debtor will probably not warrant the capitalization on which his collateral is appraised. In self-defence he must decline the extension of a loan, and forced liquidation must follow. Such a liquidation involves

rates = int) $= \frac{1}{\text{int}}$, disregarding risk; cr = normal credit extension on given cap $= \frac{\text{cap}}{n} = f\left(\frac{\text{cap}}{\text{int}}\right)$.

Then at the initial phase,

$$\text{ea} = (\text{mar} = \text{pr} - \text{exp})\text{outp},$$
$$\text{cap} = \text{ea} \times \text{yp} = \frac{\text{ea}}{\text{int}},$$
$$\text{cr} = \frac{\text{cap}}{n}.$$

At the subsequent phase, of exaltation,

$$\begin{aligned}\text{ea}' &= \text{ea} + \Delta\text{ea} = \text{mar}' \times \text{outp}\\ &= [(\text{pr}' = \text{pr} + \Delta\text{pr}) - \text{exp}]\,\text{outp}\\ &= (\text{mar} + \Delta\text{mar})\,\text{outp} > \text{ea},\end{aligned}$$
$$\text{cap}' = \frac{\text{ea}'}{\text{int}} = \frac{\text{ea} + \Delta\text{ea}}{\text{int}} > \text{cap},$$
$$\text{cr}' = \frac{\text{cap}'}{n} = \frac{\text{cap} + \Delta\text{cap}}{n} > \text{cr}.$$

At the concluding phase, of depression,

$$\begin{aligned}\text{ea}'' &= \text{ea}' - \Delta\text{ea}' = \text{mar}'' \times \text{outp}\\ &= [\text{pr}' - (\text{exp}' = \text{exp} + \Delta\text{exp})]\,\text{outp} < \text{ea}'\end{aligned}$$
$$\text{cap}'' = \frac{\text{ea}''}{\text{int}} = \frac{\text{ea}' - \Delta\text{ea}'}{\text{int}} < \text{cap}',$$
$$\text{cr}'' = \frac{\text{cap}''}{n} = \frac{\text{cap}' - \Delta\text{cap}'}{n} < \text{cr}'.$$

For simplicity of statement, in all this no account is taken of the element of risk, nor of the fluctuations of discount rates or the variations of volume of output. If these be included in the calculation as variables, the result is much the same. They are functions of the variables already included, and their inclusion would, on the whole, accentuate the oscillations shown by the computation as it stands.

cutting under the ruling prices of products, which lessens the profits of competing firms and throws them into the class of insolvents, and so extends the readjustment of capitalization.

The point of departure for the ensuing sequence of liquidation is not infrequently the failure of some banking house, but when this is the case it is pretty sure to be a bank whose funds have been "tied up" in "unwise" loans to industrial enterprises of the class spoken of above.[1]

The abruptness of the recapitalization and of the redistribution of ownership involved in a period of liquidation may be greatly mitigated, and the incidence of the shrinkage of values may be more equably distributed, by a judicious leniency on the part of the creditors or by a well-advised and discreetly weighted extension of credit by the government to certain sections of the business community. Such measures of alleviation were had, with happy effect, in the case of a recent stringency which is sometimes spoken of as an averted crisis. But where the situation answers the specifications

[1] A crisis may take its rise from credit extension in other than properly industrial business. Such, *e.g.*, was in great measure the American crisis in 1837, when the most obvious and disastrous inflation was in speculative land values and the credits based on them. But it is no stretch of the concept to say that in that case the situation out of which the crisis arose was an overcapitalization of the land values in question. Capitalized land is, of course, "capital" for business purposes as truly as any other body of values that are capitalized and drawn into the money market.

recited above, in respect of a large and widely prevalent discrepancy between earning-capacity and capitalization, a drastic readjustment of values is apparently unavoidable.

The point has already been adverted to once or twice that the most substantial immediate outcome of such a liquidation as is involved in a crisis is a redistribution of the ownership of the property concerned in the liquidation, whereby creditors and similar claimants gain at the expense of the solvent debtors. Such being the case, it would logically follow that the large creditors should see and follow up their advantage by concertedly pushing the body of debtors to an abrupt liquidation, and so realizing as large a gain as possible with the least practicable delay, whenever the situation offers.

Such may be the logic of the circumstances, but such is not the course practically taken by the large creditors under the circumstances. For this there is more than one reason. It is not, apparently, that human kindness overrules the creditors' impulse to gain at the expense of the debtors. The ever recurring object-lessons afforded by operations in the stock and money market enforce the belief that when one business man gets the advantage of another he will commonly use the advantage without humanitarian reserve, if only the advantage is offered him in terms which he can comprehend. But short-sightedness and lack of insight beyond the conventional routine seem to be fairly universal traits of the class of men who engage in the larger business activities. So that, while it would be to the unequivocal advantage of the large creditor, in point of material gain, to draw in his debtor's property at such a reduced valuation as comes in a period of abrupt liquidation, yet he does not ordinarily see the matter in that light; because the liquidation involves a shrinkage of the money value of the property concerned, and the business man, creditor or debtor, is not in the habit of looking beyond the money rating of the property in question or beyond the most immediate future. The conventional base line of business traffic, of course, is the money value, and a recognition of the patent fact that this base line wavers incontinently, and that it may on occasion shift very abruptly, apparently exceeds the business man's practical powers of comprehension. Money value is his habitual bench-mark, and he holds to the conviction that this bench-mark is stable, in spite of the facts.[1]

[1] It is, in great part, through or by force of fluctuations of this base line of money values that large accumulations of wealth are made. One might almost say that this is the "normal" method by which savings are made and capitalized in later modern times. Fluctuations in the stock market, of course, are of this character, as are commonly also large variations of the course of prices outside the stock market, as well as fluctuations of the money market. The great gains of successful promoters of corporations and the like come in this manner usually. They are due to enlargement of the money value of a given block of industrial equipment independently of any change in the physical

It is true, cases occur, from time to time, of transactions of some appreciable magnitude in which some degree of recognition of this fact is met with. Some large business man may yet rise to the requisite level of intelligence, and may comprehend and unreservedly act upon the fact that the money base line of business traffic at large is thoroughly unstable and may readily be manipulated, and it will be worth going out of one's way to see the phenomenal gains and the picturesque accompaniments of such a man's work. Parenthetically it may be remarked that if such a degree of insight should become the common property of the business community, business traffic as now carried on might conceivably collapse through loss of its base line. What is yet lacking in order to such a consummation is perhaps nothing more serious than that business capital be reduced to a somewhat more thorough state of intangibility than it has yet attained, and that does not seem a remote contingency.[1]

character of the equipment. Which comes near saying that the large fortunes originate in such changes of the base line, — from which it follows that the larger accretions to the volume of capital are of this origin. The large profits are made in the form of capital, which is acquired by virtue of a price variation. See foot-note, pp. 168–170.

[1] A substantial move in this direction would be that advocated by Mr. F. S. Stetson before the New York Bar Association, and reiterated before the United States Industrial Commission: "To permit the formation of a distinct class of business stock corporations whose capital stock may be issued as representing proportional parts of the whole capital without any nominal or money value." The market value of

There is, however, another and more constraining circumstance which hinders the large creditors from wilfully pushing the debtors to a reckoning when things are ripe for liquidation. As was indicated above, the sequence of credit relations in an era of prosperity is endlessly ramified through the business community; whereby it happens that very few creditors are not also debtors, or stand in such relation to debtors as would involve them in some loss, even if this loss should not be commensurate with their eventual gain at the cost of other debtors. This circumstance by itself has a strong deterrent effect, and when taken in connection with what was said above of the habitual inability of the men in business to appreciate the instability of money values, it is probably sufficient to explain the apparently short-sighted conduct of those large creditors to seek to mitigate the severity of liquidation when the liquidation has come due.

The account here offered of the "method" of crises and eras of prosperity does not differ greatly from accounts usually met with, except in explaining these phenomena as primarily phenomena of business rather than of industry. The disturbances of the mechanical processes of industry, which are

such shares would be the only value assigned them, and little of a base line in the way of a legally imputed value would remain. The *de jure* value would no longer hinder a free recognition of the facts. — *Report of the Industrial Commission*, vol. I. p. 976.

a conspicuous feature of any period of crisis, follow from the disturbance set up in the pecuniary traffic instead of leading up to the latter. While industry and business stand in a relation of mutual cause and effect, in this as in other cases, the initiative in such a movement belongs with the business traffic rather than with the industrial processes.

Industry is controlled by business exigencies and is carried on for business ends. The effects of a wide disturbance in business, therefore, reach the industrial processes pretty directly, and the consequences, in the way of an expansion or curtailment of industrial activity and an enlarged or shortened output of product, are, of course, both immediate and important. As a primary effect, on the industrial side, of an era of prosperity, the community gains greatly in aggregate material wealth. The gain in material wealth, of course, is not equably distributed; most of it goes to the larger business men, eventually in great part to those who come out of the subsequent liquidation on the credit side. To some extent this aggregate material gain is offset by the unavoidable waste incident to the stagnation that attends upon an era of prosperity. It is further offset by the fact that good times carry with them an exceptionally wasteful expenditure in current consumption. Also, the usual and more effectual impetus to an era of prosperity, when it is not an inflation of the currency, is some form of wasteful expenditure, as, *e.g.*, a sustained war demand or the demand due to the increase of armaments, naval and military, or again, such an interference with the course of business as is wrought by a differentially protective tariff. The later history of America and Germany illustrates both these methods of procuring an era of prosperity. These methods, it will be noticed, are, in their primary incidence, of the nature of a waste of industrial output or energy; but the prosperity achieved is, none the less, to be recognized as a beneficial outcome in point of heightened industrial activity as well as in point of increased comfort for the industrial classes.

To the workmen engaged in industry, particularly, substantial benefits accrue from an era of prosperity. These benefits come, not in the way of larger returns for a given amount of work, but more work, fuller employment, at about the earlier rate of pay. To the workmen it often means a very substantial gain if they can get a fuller livelihood by working harder or longer, and an era of prosperity gives them a chance of this kind. Gradually, however, as prosperity—that is to say, the advancing price level—rises and spreads, the increased cost of living neutralizes the gain due to fuller employment, and after the era of prosperity has been under way for some time the gain in the amount of work obtainable is likely to be fairly offset by the increased cost of living. As noted above, much of the business advantage gained in an era of prosperity is due to the fact that wages advance more tardily than the prices of goods. An era of prosperity does not commonly bring an increase of wages until the era is about to close. The advance of wages in such a case is not only a symptom indicating that the season of prosperity is passing, but it is a business factor which must by its own proper effect close the season of prosperity as soon as the advance in wages becomes somewhat general. Increasing wages cut away the securest ground of that differential price advantage on which an era of prosperity runs.

Periods of crisis or of prosperity are, after all, relatively simple phenomena with strongly marked features, and a passable explanation of them is correspondingly easy. They have also the advantage of having received much attention at the hands of the students of economic history. On the other hand, protracted depression, not traceable to widespread hardship or calamity arising from circumstances outside the range of business transactions, is a relatively new and untried subject for economic theory. Newer, more obscure, with less pronounced features and less definite limits than movements of speculative advance or speculative crises, this phenomenon has to a less extent engaged the steady attention of students. An inquiry into the life history and the causes and effects of depression, from the point of view of a theory of business, may therefore scarcely be expected to yield concise or secure conclusions.

Since industry waits upon business, it is a matter of course that industrial depression is primarily a depression in business. It is in business that depression is felt, since it is on the business side of economic activity that the seat of economic sensibility may be said to lie; it is also in business (pecuniary) terms that the depression is measured whenever a measure or estimate of the matter is attempted. In so far as there is an attendant derangement of the mechanical processes and of the mechanical articulation of processes in industry, the derangement follows from the pecuniary exigencies of business. Depression and industrial stagnation follow only in case the pecuniary exigencies of the situation are of such a character as to affect the traffic of the business community in an inhibitory way. But business is the quest of profits, and an inhibition of this quest must touch the seat of its vital motives. Industrial depression means that the business men engaged do not see their way to derive a satisfactory gain from letting the industrial process go forward on the lines and in the volume for which the material equipment of industry is designed. It is not worth their while, and it might even work them pecuniary harm. Commonly their apprehension of the discrepancy which forbids an aggressive pursuit of industrial business is expressed by the phrase "overproduction." An alternative phrase, intended to cover the same concept, but less frequently employed, is "underconsumption." [1]

The controversial question as to the tenability of any given "overproduction" doctrine may, for the present purpose, be left on one side; it lies outside the theory of business and it has no merits or demerits for the purposes of a theory of business. The point of interest here is rather the ground of its acceptation among business men and the meaning which this notion has for them; that is to say, it is chiefly of interest here to inquire into the habits of thought which give cogency and effect to the dogma of "overproduction" as practically held by the body of business men,—what it practically means, why the dogma is held, and what is its effect on the course of business enterprise.

"Overproduction," or "underconsumption," as it is met with in the views of business men, is neither a vacant dogma nor a shifty apology wherewith to cover their own delinquencies, but a very concretely real state of affairs. It is a state of affairs that prevails when business is persistently

[1] Cf. Hobson, *Problem of the Unemployed*, ch. V.; Vialles, *La consommation et les crises economiques*, especially "Introduction" and ch. III.

dull; and the concept covered by the term comprises the sufficient cause of the dulness, in the apprehension of the business community, even though they may not always speak of the difficulty by that name. It may be worth while, even at the risk of tedium, to point out that this concept of "overproduction" applies, not to the material, mechanical bearing of the situation, but to its pecuniary bearing. The notion is never seriously entertained that there is or may be an embarrassing excess of goods, or of the appliances for their production, above what would be of some human use if the business situation permitted them to be turned to use.

(1) The supply of consumable goods is, practically, never greater than the community's capacity for consuming them. An embarrassing excess in any line is practically a remote contingency at the most.[1] There are many eloquent passages in the economic manuals which may be called in witness of this truism, where much pains is taken to show that human wants are, in the nature of the case, indefinitely extensible. Nothing stands in the way, we are told, but "difficulty of attainment" of the goods with which to satisfy these wants. (2) In times of depression, or "hard times," there

[1] Something that might bear such a construction occurs, *e.g.*, locally, when a run of fish exceeds the ability of the workmen to take care of them. The fatuity of appealing to such an example is plain.

is, under the modern industrial system at least, no overproduction in the sense of a production so large as to overtax the working capacity of the industrial appliances and processes employed, nor so large, even, as to overtax the normal powers of the force of workmen or require them to work overtime and holidays. Quite the contrary. That sort of thing happens only in brisk times, when there is no overproduction. Seriously to recite such platitudes as these may seem like a trifling with the patience of the printer, or it may be taken for a light-headed excess of "wissenschaftlicher Methode"; but these two formulations appear to cover all the conceivable ways in which overproduction may occur, so long as the term is construed from the point of view of the mechanical facts of the case. Seen from this side a period of depression is a period of underproduction; mills run on half time or none, and the supply of goods that finds its way into the hands of consumers is sensibly scant for the demands of comfort.

The difficulty is, of course, a pecuniary one, and the phrase is used by business men in that pecuniary sense in which it has an immediate bearing on business. "Excessive competition" is an alternative phrase. There is an excess of goods, or of the means of producing them, above what is expedient on pecuniary grounds, — above what there is an effective demand for at prices that will repay the cost of production of the goods and leave something appreciable over as a profit. It is a question of prices and earnings. The difficulty is that not enough of a product can be disposed of at fair prices to warrant the running of the mills at their full capacity, or running them at a rate near enough to their capacity to yield a fair profit. Or, to turn the proposition about, as business men are in the habit of doing, there is more of an output offered than will be carried off at a fair price,— such a price as will afford fair or ordinary profits on the investment and the running expenses. There is too large a productive capacity; there are too many competitive producers and too much industrial apparatus to supply the market at reasonable prices. The matter reduces itself to a question of fair prices and ordinary profits.[1]

If there is a large volume of outstanding credit obligations, that will complicate the situation. There is always a considerable amount of interest-bearing securities outstanding, and the claims of these securities have to be satisfied before dividends can be paid on stock, or before profits accrue to industrial ventures which have issued the securities. These fixed charges, together with others of a like kind, narrow the margin from which profits are derived and increase the handicap which a season of dull times brings to the business

[1] Cf. Smart, *Studies in Economics*, ch. VII.

men in charge of industry. At the same time fixed charges preclude shutting down, except at a sure and considerable loss. The business men involved are constrained to go on, and in the absence of wide combinations in industry they are constrained to go on at such competitive prices as to preclude reasonable profits.

The question of fair prices and reasonable profits has some reference to current rates of interest. A "fair" rate of profits is such a rate as bears a reasonable relation to the current rate of interest, although this relation of profits to interest rates does not appear to be a strict one. Still, there undoubtedly is some reference to the current rate of interest as a sort of zero line to which profits should not decline. New investments are made on the basis of current rates of interest and with a view to securing the differential gain promised by the excess of prospective profits over interest rates.

In a period of depression the aggregate industrial equipment is, notoriously, not running at its full capacity; there are many idle and half-idle plants and many idle workmen. The concerns in question find themselves unable to do a full run of business at reasonable profits. Still, unless the depression is of exceptionally short duration, there is always some new investment going on. More or less of new capital continues to find its way into industrial business in competition with the concerns that are already in the field.[1] In case of a protracted depression the aggregate of new investments so made may, in the course of years, amount to a very considerable addition to the industrial outfit, and the production of the new establishments may very appreciably increase the aggregate output. Indeed, the output of the new establishments is a notable factor in swelling the supply and keeping down prices. But the new investments made during the depression are profitable, at least at the start. Or even if this should be questioned when stated in this broad way, it will at least hold true that they are commonly entered upon with a well-advised expectation of their being profitable if the situation does not materially change between the time when the new venture was entered upon and the time when the new equipment has got under way. If the interval between the inception of the new enterprise and its completion is a long one, the situation may so change in the meantime as to leave it unprofitable even if it has been conservatively planned. There are also, of course, fraudulent enterprises which are not expected by their promoters to pay a profit on the investment; and there are probably, also,

[1] For the present purpose a concern which passes through a liquidation and reappears with a rerated and reorganized capitalization and body of liabilities also has much of the character of a new investment.

always some ventures entered upon during dull times with a view to being beforehand in preparation for better times. But after all has been said in qualification of the main proposition, it remains true that some new investment is going on with a well-advised expectation of reasonable profits on the basis of current costs, prices, and rates of interest.[1]

The rate of interest in times of depression may be unsatisfactory to lenders; it may be discouraging by comparison with the customary range of interest rates during better times. Still, the obstacle to business is not to be sought in an effectual discouragement of lenders, for in point of fact money

[1] Cf. L. Pohle, *Bevölkerungsbewegung, Kapitalbildung und periodische Wirtschaftskrisen*, who concludes that depression is due to a scarcity of capital as compared with population; the rate of increase of capital is conceived to fall short of the rate of increase of population, hence periodical depression.

Cf., on the other hand, Macrosty, *Trusts and the State*, p. 133, who finds, by recourse to the testimony before the Royal Commission on the Depression of Trade and Industry, that there is at such times capital constantly seeking investment and entering into competition with what is already invested. Cf. *Final Report of the Royal Commission on Depression of Trade and Industry* (1886). "The replies received from Chambers of Commerce to the inquiries we addressed to them confirm the statements made by the witnesses who appeared before us. Those replies testify to the general maintenance or increase of the volume of trade, accompanied in many cases by a shrinkage in its value, and in all cases by a serious diminution of profit. They also show how general is the belief in commercial circles that overproduction, the fall of prices, and more effective foreign competition assisted by high tariffs, go far to account for the existing position of trade and industry in this country" (pp. ix–x). Cf. also pp. xi–xv of the *Report*.

is readily to be had on good security during any protracted depression.[1] There is also the fact that investment is continually going on, which argues that the difficulty is neither that capital cannot be found for investment, nor that investment has no prospect of reasonable profits. Practically, no exceptional amount of fluent funds is withheld from the market, — except in time of panic, which is another matter. It may be added that the rate of interest need not be notably low in time of depression, just as, on the other hand, a period of business exaltation is not uniformly accompanied by a notably high rate of interest.

But a low or declining rate of interest is effective in the way of depressing the business situation, even though a depression may go on without it. The line of its bearing upon business depression, or at least one line, is as follows: Established business concerns (particularly corporations) engaged in industry have some appreciable fixed (interest) charges to meet — on leases, mortgages, and interest-bearing securities (preferred stock and bonds). These outstanding obligations and securities may have been negotiated, "floated," at an earlier period of higher interest rates and higher profits, or they may have been carried over through a period of higher interest rates. In the former

[1] Cf., *e.g.*, Burton, *Crises and Depressions*, ch. IV., especially pp 113–115.

case these interest charges are excessively high as compared with the present capitalized value of the property on which they rest, computing the capitalization on the basis of the present cost of replacing this property and the present interest charge which this cost of replacement would bear. In the latter case the original capitalization of the corresponding items of property will have undergone a practical (effective) recapitalization at a lower figure to correspond with the higher rate of interest prevalent during the interval in question; and in the subsequent period of low interest, the fixed charge on this recapitalization is excessively high as compared with the current effective capitalization of the property. The liabilities are excessive, in respect of their interest charges, as compared with the present earning-capacity of the property represented by them.[1]

[1] More in detail, what happens in connection with interest-bearing securities carried over an interval of high interest rates and business activity may be formulated as follows: When current interest rates advance, securities bearing a fixed rate (of dividends or interest) decline on the market. That is to say, the effective capitalized value of the claim to these fixed rates of income, as shown by the market quotations, shrinks. At the same time, since the period during which this readjustment occurs is a period of acceleration in business, the earning-capacity (actual or putative) of the property on which these securities rest has increased over what it was at the time the securities were floated. Hence this property (industrial equipment) is also recapitalized, in the market quotations, at a higher value than it had when the securities were floated. The effective recapitalization carried out by the market quotations acts, for the present purpose, to the same effect upon the value of both of the items considered, this effect being to leave a margin of the property previously covered by the securities

What gives effect to this drawback for the business enterprises which have such fixed interest

uncovered and available as collateral on which to float a new extension of credit, in the form of mortgage loan or interest-bearing security. In the common run of business procedure this available margin, between the current (higher) capitalized value of the property (collateral) and the current (lower) capitalized value of the securities resting upon it is promptly covered by a fresh credit extension ; whether this extension takes the set form of loan, bonds, preferred stock, and the like, or the less patent form of a larger volume of obligations in the way of contracts and the like, — the result, as touches the securities and their basis, being that the same nominal volume of securities with the same aggregate interest charge rests on a (materially) smaller block of the industrial equipment after this readjustment of capitalization is had than it did when the securities were placed. When depression ensues, and the rate of earnings and interest declines, the effective capitalization of the securities with a fixed rate of income is increased (if the securities are felt to be secure) to correspond with the lower rate of interest; whereas the capitalized value of the block of industrial equipment on which these securities (plus whatever may have been added in the interval) rest shrinks to correspond with the same facts. A discrepancy, such as was adjusted by a recapitalization during the interval of high rates, reappears, but in the inverse sense. And this discrepancy cannot be corrected, since the margin on which the previous adjustment was made has disappeared, and no corresponding margin on the other side emerges. Business accounts do not deal in negative quantities, except under stress of a necessity that violates the premises on which business accountancy proceeds.

Recurring to the notation employed on page 153, and letting l = par value of securities with fixed charges, r = rate per annum of fixed charges, l′ = market value (effective capitalization) of these securities,

$$\text{cap}' = \text{ea}\left(\text{yp} = \frac{1}{\text{int}}\right), \quad \text{l}' = \frac{\text{lr}}{\text{int}};$$

but if int becomes int′ (= int + Δ int), l′ becomes

$$\text{l}'' = \frac{\text{lr}}{(\text{int} + \Delta\,\text{int} = \text{int}')} < \text{l}'.$$

cap′ at the same time becomes $\text{cap}'' = \dfrac{\text{ea} + \Delta\,\text{ea}}{\text{int} + \Delta\,\text{int}} = \dfrac{\text{ea}'}{\text{int}'}$;

whereas in a period of falling interest,

$$\text{int}' = \text{int} - \Delta\,\text{int}, \text{ and } \text{l}'' = \frac{\text{lr}}{\text{int}' = (\text{int} - \Delta\,\text{int})} > \text{l}'.$$

charges to meet is the fact that the new investments, and those concerns that have gone into bankruptcy or receivers' hands, come into competition with the old. These new or rejuvenated concerns are not committed to a scale of fixed charges carried over from a higher interest level; and these are therefore carrying only such interest charges as the current effective capitalization of their property will warrant, whether effective capitalization be taken to mean cost of production of the equipment, earning-capacity of the concern, or market quotation of its securities. These unincumbered competitors are presumed to be making reasonable profits at current prices, and their presence in the competitive market therefore precludes an advance of prices to such a scale as would afford a reasonable profit to the other establishments after paying their interest charges on what is, in effect, overcapitalized property.

This tentative explanation of depression applies only so far as the period of depression is a time of relatively low rates of interest. But depression does not uniformly coincide with low interest rates; besides which, there are other facts in the case which limit the applicability of the explanation formulated above. To explain protracted depression, *e.g.*, this line of argument would be convincing only on the supposition of a progressively falling rate of interest, — a condition not commonly met with in a protracted period of depression.

But this explanation, applicable within a limited range of the phenomena that make up a period of depression, points the way to another class of considerations that go far toward explaining the rest. It appears that the phase of the difficulty covered by this explanation is traceable to a discrepancy between the accepted capitalization, the interest charges, and the earning-capacity. And it appears equally plain that the only remedy applicable to the case (barring a speculative exaltation of business) is a recapitalization of the concerns affected on a lower basis, to fit the lowered cost of production of the equipment and its lowered earning-capacity. But under existing conditions of law such a remedy cannot be applied to the interest-bearing securities,—except by process of insolvency,—and it is very reluctantly applied to other capitalized wealth; besides which it is, practically, very difficult to effect such an avowed recapitalization as applied to the stock of incorporated companies, particularly in the case of those whose stock is ostensibly the capitalized value of their plant.

Such a readjustment of nominal value to actual value as shown by the facts of earning-capacity is continually going on, in some measure; but it does not cover the entire range of facts involved, and it is nearly always of the nature of a reluctant concession, following only after the need of it has become somewhat pressing. It can, therefore, in the common run of cases, not catch up with the progressive difficulty which it is designed to meet, in so far as the difficulty is of a progressive character.

A discrepancy between accepted capitalization and current earning-capacity, similar to the discrepancy discussed above but of a progressive character, arises under modern conditions apart from a fall in the rate of interest. The discrepancy pointed out and provisionally disposed of above, due to a fall in interest rates, is a discrepancy between the nominal value (accepted capitalization) of the older establishments, computed on their earlier earning-capacity or on the original cost of their equipment, on the one hand, and their present actual value on the other hand, computed on their current earning-capacity in competition with rivals that have the advantage of a lower cost of equipment, or, in other words, a lower interest charge per unit of earning-capacity. Under the régime of the later, more fully developed machine production, a discrepancy having a similar effect arises out of a persistent divergence between the past cost of production of a given equipment and the current cost of a like or equivalent equipment at any subsequent date, — supposing that there intervenes no inflation of prices and no extraneous cause making for a speculative advance.[1]

Suppose prices of finished goods to be stable or to vary by inconsequential fluctuations, negligible for purposes of the argument, and suppose the rate of interest to be in a similarly negligible position. In other words, suppose such a condition as the business community would recognize as ordinary, normal, sound, without ground for pronounced hopes or fears. Under modern circumstances, dominated as the modern situation is by the machine industry, such a state of affairs is unstable, even apart from any disturbance of an extraneous kind. It is unstable by virtue of the forces at work in its own process, and these forces, on the whole, make for a progressive change in the direction of depression.

It has appeared above that the depressing effect which a relatively low (declining) rate of interest has upon industrial business is due to its setting up a discrepancy between the accepted capitalization of older establishments and the cost of new establishments of an equivalent earning-capacity.

[1] Compare Hobson, *Problem of the Unemployed*, ch. V., and Tugan-Baranowsky, *Handelskrisen*, ch. I. and VI. In his criticism (pp. 191–193) Tugan has quite missed the point of Hobson's theory as well as of his illustration, having apparently not understood Hobson's exposition, which is, in effect, very similar to his own. See also Hobson, *Modern Capitalism*, ch. VII., especially secs. 8 and 16.

Now, under the circumstances of the more fully developed machine industry, such as it has stood for a couple of decades past, a similar discrepancy results from the gradual but uninterrupted progressive improvements of industrial processes. "The state of the industrial arts," as the older economists are in the habit of calling it, is no longer to be conceived as stationary, even for the time being. No "statical" theory of the industrial arts or of business prosperity is tenable, even for the purposes of a "statical" theory of the industrial situation. Progressively increasing efficiency of the processes in use is a pervading trait of the industrial situation. No two successive years are now on the same, or virtually the same, plane in respect of the efficiency of the industrial arts; indeed, the "period of production" can no longer safely be construed to begin and end on the same level in this respect. At the same time the progressively wider and more close-knit articulation of the several industries in a comprehensive process is also going forward, and this also affects all branches of industrial business in some degree and in the same direction, as will appear presently.

The items of the equipment (plant, materials, and in a measure even good-will) in which any industrial enterprise invests, and by the use of which the business men in industry turn out their output of vendible goods, are themselves products of the machine industry. Machine processes, ever increasing in efficiency, turn out the mechanical appliances and materials with which the processes are carried on, at an ever decreasing cost; so that at each successive step the result is a process having a higher efficiency at a lower cost.[1] This is now no longer a sporadic effect of ingenious contrivances having a local and limited application, to be handled as trade secrets and exploited as an enduring differential advantage.

The cost of production of "capital goods" is steadily and progressively lowered, as counted in terms of the processes involved in their production. In a competitive market this is reflected, with greater or less promptitude, in the prices of such capital goods to all buyers. But the buyers whose purposes this lower scale of prices particularly subserves are chiefly the new investors who go into business in the way of new industrial establishments or extensions of the old. Each new venture or extension goes into the competitive traffic of producing and selling any line of staple goods with a differential advantage, as against those that have gone before it, in the way of a lower scale of costs. A successively smaller aggregate value of new equipment will turn out a given volume of

[1] The typical form taken by this acceleration is the machine production of machinery, but in fact it involves the production of other material factors as well as the mechanical apparatus, notably the materials used in industry.

vendible product. In so far as there is no collusive control of the output or the prices, this means that the newcomers will cut under the scale of prices at which their predecessors have been content to supply the goods. The run of competitive prices is lowered; which means that at the new competitive prices, and with their output remaining on its old footing as regards expenses of production, the older establishments and processes will no longer yield returns commensurate with the old accepted capitalization.[1] From the inherent character of the machine industry itself, therefore, it follows that the earning-capacity of any industrial enterprise enters on a decline from the outset, and that its capitalization, based on its initial putative earning-capacity, grows progressively antiquated from the start. The efficiency of the machine process in the "instrumental industries" sets up a discrepancy between cost and capitalization. So that a progressive readjustment of capitalization to correspond with the lowered earning-capacity is required by the nature of the case It is also, in the nature of the case, impracticable.

[1] The established concerns having been capitalized on the basis of past cost, we can say that in the older establishments, cap $= f$ (cost), but in the new establishments with an equal earning-capacity, $\text{cap}_1 = f\ (\text{cost}_1 = \text{cost} - \Delta\ \text{cost})$; hence the rate of earnings $\left[= f\left(\frac{\text{ea}}{\text{cost}}\right)\right]$ will be progressively higher as cost decreases: —

$$f\left(\frac{\text{ea}}{\text{cost}}\right) < f\left(\frac{\text{ea}}{\text{cost} - \Delta\ \text{cost}}\right) < f\left(\frac{\text{ea}}{\text{cost} - 2\ \Delta\ \text{cost}}\right), \text{ etc.}$$

In so far as the process of investment and business management involves the use of credit, in the way of interest-bearing securities or loans equivalent to such securities, this element of credit retards the readjustment by force of the fixed charges which it involves. This retardation (aided as it is by the reluctance of business men to lower their capitalization) is of sufficient effect to hinder recapitalization, on the whole, from overtaking the progressive need of it, with the result that a fair or "ordinary" rate of profits on industrial investments is not permanently attainable in the field of open competition. In order that the rate of interest should effectually further business depression in this way, therefore, it is not necessary that the rate should rise or fall, or that it should be relatively high or low, or that it should be uniform over the field, but only that there should be a rate of interest in each case, and that there should be some appreciable volume of credit involved in industrial investments. Credit is, in fact, a ubiquitous factor in modern industrial business, and its effects in the way indicated are therefore to be counted in as a constant force in the situation.

However, even apart from the presence of this ubiquitous credit element, a similar effect would probably result from the progressive enhancement of industrial efficiency when this enhancement proceeds at such a rate as has been the case for some time past. As has been shown in an earlier chapter, business men keep account of their wealth, their outgo and their income, in terms of money value, not in terms of mechanical serviceability or of consumptive effect. Business traffic and business outcome are standardized in terms of the money unit, while the industrial process and its output are standardized in terms of physical measurements (mechanical efficiency). In the current habits and conventions of the business community, the unit of money is accepted and dealt with as a standard measure. The stability of the standard unit cannot be effectually questioned within the scope of business traffic. According to the practical metaphysics of the business community, the money unit is an invariable magnitude, whatever may be true of it in fact. A man imbued with these business metaphysics and not given to fine-spun reflection, as business men commonly are not, is richer or poorer in his own apprehension, according as his balance sheet shows a greater or less number of these standard units of value. Investment, expenses, vendible output, earnings, fixed charges, and capitalization run in terms of this value unit. A reduction of earnings or of capitalization, as rated in terms of the value unit, is felt as an impoverishment. The reduction of capitalization in these terms is, therefore, a hardship, which is only reluctantly and tardily submitted to, even if it carries no hardship in the way of a reduced command over the material means of production, of life, or of comfort. A business man's rating in the business community likewise rests on the pecuniary magnitude of his holdings and his transactions, not on the mechanical serviceability of his establishment or his output; and this business rating is a large part of the business man's everyday ambition. An enhancement of it is a source of secure gratification and self-respect, and a reduction of it has a very substantial contrary effect.[1] A reduction of the pecuniary showing is submitted to only reluctantly and tardily, after it has become unavoid-

[1] Recurring to the notation employed in note 2, page 168, and letting U_m = unit of material efficiency, then a given established concern, A, with a given equipment $U_m(\text{cap})_a \Leftrightarrow U_e(\text{cap}) \Leftrightarrow U_n(\text{cap}) \Leftrightarrow U_e\left(\frac{\text{ea}}{\text{int}}\right)$, presently finds itself in competition with a younger concern, B, having an equivalent material equipment $= U_m(\text{cap})_b$ procured at a lower cost and requiring lower earnings ($=\text{ea}'$) and lower fixed charges.

$$U_m(\text{cap})_b \Leftrightarrow U_e\left(\frac{\text{ea}'}{\text{int}} = \frac{\text{ea} - \Delta\,\text{ea}}{\text{int}}\right) = U_e(\text{cap}' = \text{cap} - \Delta\,\text{cap}).$$

But $U_m(\text{cap})_a = U_m(\text{cap})_b$ as competitors in the market. Hence, with the competitive lowering of earnings, and therefore of effective capitalization, A's account comes to stand: —

$$U_m(\text{cap})_a \Leftrightarrow U_e(\text{cap}') = U_e(\text{cap} - \Delta\,\text{cap}) < U_n(\text{cap}).$$

In effect A is overcapitalized by $U_e(\text{cap} - \text{cap}')$. A's nominal capital, $U_n(\text{cap})_a \Leftrightarrow U_e(\text{cap}' + \Delta\,\text{cap})$, while A's effective capitalization

$$U_e(\text{cap}')_a = U_e(\text{cap} - \Delta\,\text{cap}).$$

The business man's sensibilities in the case, therefore, suffer a lesion

$$= f\left[U_n\left(\frac{\text{ea}}{\text{int}}\right) - U_e\left(\frac{\text{ea} - \Delta\,\text{ea}}{\text{int}}\right)\right],$$

which is a monotonic function. The discrepancy between $U_n(\text{cap})_a$ and $U_e(\text{cap}')$ is, in large part, embodied in securities with fixed charges; which makes a readjustment very difficult even apart from A's reluctance.

able, and only to the least feasible extent. But under conditions, such as now prevail, which involve the requirement of a progressive rerating of this kind, this reluctant concession never overtakes the need of readjustment, — and the discrepancy between capitalization and earning-capacity is therefore chronic so long as no extraneous circumstances come in temporarily to set aside the trend of business affairs in this respect. It may, therefore, be said, on the basis of this view, that chronic depression, more or less pronounced, is normal to business under the fully developed régime of the machine industry.[1]

This deplorable trend given to business by the excessive prevalence and efficiency of the machine industry can, however, be set aside by several factors more or less extraneous to the industrial system proper. Even within the mechanical system of industry there is at least one factor of some consequence that consistently acts to mitigate the trend indicated, and that may even put it in abeyance from time to time. As has been pointed out above, questions of business are fundamentally questions of price. A decline of prices which

[1] With the above analysis may be contrasted Marx's discussion of the declining rate of profits and the manner in which he conceives overproduction, speculation, and crises to arise out of the tendency of profits to a minimum. (*Kapital*, vol. III. ch. XV.) In the same connection, see Tugan-Baranowsky's criticism of Marx, *Handelskrisen*, ch. VII.

widely touches business interests brings depression. Conversely, an appreciable advance in prices, from whatever cause, means improvement in business. Such an advance in prices may come of a speculative movement; which in turn may arise from a variety of circumstances, for the most part circumstances extraneous to the industrial process. For the present, however, the question of a speculative movement is best left on one side. Another factor touches the case more intimately. As has more than once been the case, prices may be advanced through a freer supply of the precious metals, or by an inflation of the currency, or a more facile use of credit instruments as a subsidiary currency mechanism. Now, the growing efficiency of industry has an effect in lowering the (material) cost of production of the precious metals and so increasing the ease with which they are supplied, after the same manner as it affects the supply of goods for industrial or consumptive use. But the increased supply of the precious metals has, of course, an effect upon prices contrary to that exerted by the increasing supply of goods. In so far as this effect is had, it acts to correct or mitigate the trend of business toward chronic depression.[1]

[1] In point of direct material serviceability, no doubt, a fresh supply of the precious metals is one of the least useful forms of wealth to the production of which industrial effort can be directed, but for the purposes of business prosperity at large it is probably the most serviceable addition that can be made to the aggregate wealth. Rapidly

But certain circumstances come in to qualify the salutary effect of a lowered cost of the precious metals. Improvements in the industrial processes affect the (industrial) cost of production of the precious metals in a less degree than the cost of other goods; at least, such seems to have been the case recently. But beyond this, and of graver consequence, is a peculiarity affecting the value of the money metals. The annual product of the money metals is not annually consumed, nor nearly. The use of them as money does not consume them except incidentally and very slowly. The mass of these metals in hand at any given time is very considerable and is relatively imperishable, so that the annual accretion is but a small fraction of the aggregate supply. The lowered cost of the annual supply has therefore but a relatively slight effect upon the aggregate value of the available supply.

The case is different as regards the annual output of vendible products, whether for industrial or consumptive use. In this case, and particularly as regards this matter of new investments and extensions of industrial equipment, the annual output counts for by far the greater factor in making the current value of the available supply, if indeed it

increasing efficiency in the production of other forms of wealth is detrimental to the business interests, in that it brings depression; but a rapid increase of the precious metals is the most fortunate material circumstance for the business interests that industrial activity can bring, because it puts off depression by keeping up prices.

is not to be regarded as substantially the only factor that comes in question here. Accordingly, it is only under very exceptional circumstances, at times when the precious metals are supplied with extraordinary freedom, that the increased output of these metals can offset the trend of business toward depression. Ordinarily this factor can count for no more than a mitigation of the "tendency of profits to a minimum." And even this mitigating effect, it may be remarked, appears to be of less radical consequence for the general situation of business now than it was during the earlier phases of the machine industry's régime. The most telling effect of an increased supply of the precious metals seems to be the incitement which it gives to speculative inflation.[1]

It will be noted that the explanation here offered of depression makes it a malady of the affections. The discrepancy which discourages business men is a discrepancy between that nominal capitalization which they have set their hearts upon through habituation in the immediate past and that actual capitalizable value of their property which its current earning-capacity will warrant. But where the preconceptions of the business men engaged have, as commonly happens, in great part been

[1] Cf. Smart, *Studies in Economics*, Essay VI., "Must Prices Fall?" *Distribution of Income*, bk. II, ch. III.

fixed and legalized in the form of interest-bearing securities, this malady of the affections becomes extremely difficult to remedy, even though it be true that these legalized affections, preconceptions, or what not, centre upon the metaphysical stability of the money unit.

But while it is true that depression is primarily a business difficulty and rests on emotional grounds, that does not hinder its having grave consequences for industry and for the material welfare of the community outside the range of business interests. Business enterprise, it is true, proceeds on metaphysical grounds and is swayed by considerations of nominal wealth rather than by considerations of material serviceability; but, none the less, business enterprise and business metaphysics control the course of industry.

Dull times in business means dull times in industry, of course. But a caution is necessary on this head. The yearly output does not usually vary extremely between brisk and dull times, except as measured in price. As measured in material terms the discrepancy in the volume of output between brisk and dull times is much less. The gross output as measured by weight and tale is less in dull than in brisk times, other things equal; but the deficiency as measured in these terms is much less than the price returns would indicate. Indeed, the output as measured by weight and tale need not average very appreciably less during a protracted depression than during a preceding period of good times.[1] The volume of business as well as the volume of output (by weight and tale) of industry may increase during a few years of depression at nearly if not quite as high a rate as during a corresponding period of good times. A transition from dull to brisk times, however, commonly if not invariably involves a rapid increase in values, while a converse transition involves a corresponding shrinkage of values, though commonly a slower shrinkage, — except where a crisis intervenes.

The primary hardship of a period of depression is a persistent lesion of the affections of the business men; the greatest secondary hardship is what falls upon the workmen, in the way of partial unemployment and a decline in wages, with consequent precariousness and reduction of their liveli-

[1] Work goes on during dull times, though at a slackened pace, and extensions and improvements are continually being made. The volume of output consequently increases, so that, even if there has been a setback to production at the beginning of the depression, the aggregate output presently again reaches the volume which it had when the dull times set in. It may be added that the rate of consumption is also appreciably lower during dull times, particularly in the more wasteful forms of consumption. This lowered aggregate consumption offsets the lowered intensity of production during dull times to such an extent that it is probably safe to say that the net surplus product, measured by weight and tale, is at least not appreciably smaller during depression than during prosperity. Cf. Carroll D. Wright, Testimony in *Report of the Industrial Commission*, vol. VII. p. 25.

hood.[1] For those workmen who continue to find fairly steady employment during the depression, however, even at reduced wages, the loss is more apparent than real; since the cheapening of goods offsets the decline in wages. Indeed, the cheapening of the means of living is apt to offset the fall in wages fully, for such workmen as have steady work. So that in the case of the workmen also, as well as in that of the business men, the distress which dull times brings is in some part a spiritual, emotional matter.

To the rest of the community, those classes that are outside of business enterprise and outside of the industrial occupations proper, that is to say, those (non-industrial) classes who live on a fixed salary or similar fixed income, dull times are a thinly disguised blessing. They suffer in their affections from the reflected emotional detriment of the business community, but they gain in their ease of livelihood and in their savings by all the difference between the price scale of brisk and of dull times. To these classes an era of prosperity brings substantially nothing but detriment.[2]

[1] The reduced scale of living of the working population is the chief factor that counts as an offset against the reduction of the gross production during dull times, as indicated above.

[2] Cf. articles by G. Cassel, "Om Kriser och Daliga Tider," now running in *Ekonomisk Tidskrift* (1904, Nos. 1 and 2), for a parallel discussion of the topics here dealt with. Mr. Cassel's exposition connects more closely with the received notions of Capital, Production, etc., and goes more into detail at certain points, particularly on Saving,

Depression is primarily a malady of the affections of the business men. That is the seat of the difficulty. The stagnation of industry and the hardships suffered by the workmen and other classes are of the nature of symptoms and secondary effects. Any proposed remedy, therefore, must be of such a nature as to reach this emotional seat of the trouble and restore the balance between the nominal value of the business capital engaged and the earnings of the business; that is to say, a remedy, to be efficacious, must restore profits to a "reasonable" rate; which means, practically, that prices must be brought to the level on which the accepted capitalization has been made. Such a remedy, to offset the disastrous cheapening of products through mechanical improvements, has been found in business coalitions and working arrangements of one kind and another, looking to the "regulation" of prices and output. Latterly this remedy is becoming familiar to the business community as well as to students of the business situation, and its tangible, direct, and unequivocal efficiency in correcting this main infirmity of modern business is well recognized. So much so, indeed, that its urgent advisability has been formulated in the maxim that "Where

Investment (Kapitalbildning), and Pecuniary Expectancy (Väntandet). His exposition is not yet completed, but so far as may be gathered from what has come to hand, he should reach substantially the same outcome as that given above.

combination is possible competition is impossible." What is required is a business coalition on such a scale as to regulate the output and eliminate competitive sales and competitive investment within a field large enough to make up a self-balanced, passably independent industrial system, — such a coalition of business enterprises as is loosely called a "trust."

Such a business coalition, if it is comprehensive and closely controlled, can adjust the output of goods and services to the market with some nicety, and can maintain the balance of the ruling prices, or the price scale agreed upon, with such effect that the received capitalization need not become obsolete even in the face of very radical improvements in the processes of industry. Its effect, in the case of ideal success, is to neutralize the cheapening of goods and services effected by current industrial progress. It offsets industrial improvements in so far as these improvements affect the cost of goods more than they affect the value of the money metals. It might seem at first sight that by this inhibitory effect of the trust the entire advantage derivable from industrial improvements within the scope of the trust should inure to the gain of the business men in the combination, but such does not appear to be the practical outcome. The practical outcome appears more nearly to be that material advantage inures to no one from industrial improvements under the control of the trust, in so far as the trust successfully carries its point. This feature of trust management will be taken up again in a different connection.

In addition to its prime purpose of checking the decline of earnings on past investments, such a business coalition is also enabled to distribute any unavoidable effect of the progressively reduced cost of production of the productive goods employed, somewhat equably over the entire field of industry comprised in the coalition, and so obviate the pressure of this untoward industrial progress falling with exceptional severity at any given point. Economies effected are at the same time made to accrue to the collective business organization, showing themselves in the way of increased dividends and increased effective (market) capitalization of the coalition's property, instead of being dissipated in competitive selling, and so going to the body of consumers or to the industrial system at large.

To return to a point temporarily set aside above. By supposition, in what has just been said, anything like a speculative inflation has been excluded from the discussion of business depression; and necessarily so, since the two do not come at the same time. But at one point the two show a feature in common. Under both of these two widely different conditions of the business situation there is a discrepancy between the accepted capitalization and the actual earning-capacity.[1] But the two differ even at this point in that, in the case of inflation, the discrepancy is not felt until the climax, when a widespread realization of the discrepancy brings on an abrupt readjustment, in the crisis which follows inflation; whereas in a period of depression the sense of this discrepancy and the protest against it is the most striking circumstance of the case. The discrepancy between capitalization and earning-capacity in a period of speculative movement comes of an inflation of capitalization; whereas in time of depression the discrepancy is due to a shrinkage of earning-capacity, — both capitalization and earning-capacity being, of course, counted in terms of money values. A speculative movement offsets or checks the trend to depression whenever it occurs; and for some appreciable time past, such speculative movements appear to have been the only force which has from time to time broken the otherwise uninterrupted course of business depression. Under the régime of a perfected

[1] In the case of a speculative inflation,

$$\text{cap} = \frac{\text{ea}}{\text{cost}} \times \frac{1}{\text{int}} < \text{cap}' = \frac{\text{ea} + \Delta\,\text{ea}}{\text{cost}} \times \frac{1}{\text{int}};$$

in case of depression,

$$\text{cap}' = \frac{\text{ea}}{\text{cost} \times \text{int}} > \text{cap}'' = \frac{\text{ea} - \Delta\,\text{ea}}{\text{cost} \times \text{int}}.$$

In the former case the current capitalization during inflation, being cap′, exceeds the bona fide capital value as proved by events, cap; while in the case of depression the nominal capital, being cap′, exceeds the capitalization warranted by current earning-capacity, cap″.

machine industry and a perfect business organization, with active competition throughout, it is at least probable that depression would not be seriously interrupted by any other cause.

But it has been a point of economic dogma in modern times — not to call it a point of theory, since it is not held on reasoned grounds — that depression and inflation, followed by crisis, succeed one another with a rough periodicity, interminably and in the nature of the case. The periodicity (with an interval of some ten to twelve years from phase to phase) has not been established with any cogent show of evidence, except for the period from 1816 to 1873; and even within that period the evidence has not been convincing to all students of these phenomena. A tentative explanation of the periodicity, such as there may have been within that period, as well as of its absence before and after the period in question, may be offered on the basis of the views here set forth. Keeping in mind the point that the disturbance, both in the case of inflation and in that of depression, is a discrepancy between capitalization and earning-capacity, and also the manner in which this discrepancy arises, it may be said that prior to the earlier date mentioned the modern industrial system was not such a comprehensive and articulate process that a disturbance in one part or one member of the system need be transmitted forthwith through the channels of business to all the rest. A speculative movement need not spread forthwith throughout the industrial system. The great episodes of speculation and collapse that occurred during earlier modern times were not of the nature of speculative inflation affecting the entire business community occupied with industry. They are rather of the nature of commercial speculation verging on gambling.[1] So also, the crises of that earlier time, when they were not collapses of gambling ventures, were commonly produced by some great disaster which brought an absolute material loss upon the community, such as crop failures, invasions, or heavy war expenditures. On the other hand, as regards periods of depression prior to the early years of the nineteenth century, they were also rare if not unknown, except when due to failure of resources or the burdens of government. The conditions out of which depression could come, as a persistent disturbance of business through a divergence between the capitalization and the earning-capacity of investments, were not had. The developed machine system was absent, and without this the cost of production of productive goods could not

[1] So impressive a fact has the gambling character of early periods of inflation and crises been that it has led economists to look for gambling as a matter of course in later phenomena that have been classed as inflation and crises, even when no gambling element has been obviously present. It has been felt that gambling must presumptively be present whenever there is inflation or crises, because the showing of earlier history runs that way.

be progressively lowered at a rate large enough to set up and maintain a persistent divergence between capitalization and earning-capacity in industrial enterprises.

At some uncertain point in the first half of the nineteenth century the system of machine industry, and the business system based upon it, attained such a breadth and consistency that business disturbances of appreciable magnitude in any part would affect values throughout the system. It had then grown so large and was so closely articulated a structure that the relations of its members to one another and to the system as a whole were of greater moment for the fortunes of these members and for the orderly process of the whole than were the relations of the members to industrial factors lying outside the system of the machine industry and the business community. Hence industrial crises in the proper sense of the word seem well at home in this period. They spread with great force and facility whenever they came; and they had the true character of business crises, in that they ran with great severity without involving an appreciable aggregate loss of material wealth, except in terms of price. They commonly meant a cancelment of values, without appreciable aggregate loss of goods. They seem also to have been true to the staple definition of crises in that they followed upon a period of speculative inflation in industrial investments.

Chronic depression, however, does not seem to belong, as a consistent feature of the course of things, in this nineteenth-century period, prior to the eighties or the middle of the seventies. The usual course, it is commonly held, was rather: inflation, crisis, transient depression, gradual advance to inflation, and so on over again.[1]

On the view of these phenomena here spoken for, an attempt at explaining this circuit may be made as follows: A crisis, under this early nineteenth-century situation, was an abrupt collapse of capitalized values, in which the capitalization was not only brought to the level of the earning-capacity which the investments would have shown in quiet times, but appreciably below that level. The efficiency and the reach of the machine industry in the production of productive goods was not then so great as to lower the cost of their production rapidly enough to overtake the shrinkage in capitalization and so prevent the latter from rising again in response to the stimulus of a relatively high earning-capacity. The shock-effect of the liquidation passed off before the cheapening of the means of production had time to catch up with the shrinkage of capitalization due to the crisis, so that after the shock-effect had passed there still remained an appreciable undercapitalization as a

[1] Cf., *e.g.*, Burton, *Crises and Depressions*, ch. VIII., for a succinct account of depressions and crises in the United States during this period.

sequel of the period of liquidation. Therefore there did not result a persistent unfavorable discrepancy between capitalization and earning-capacity, with a consequent chronic depression. On the other hand, the earning-capacity of investments was high relatively to their reduced capitalization after the crisis. Actual earning-capacity exceeded the nominal earning-capacity of industrial plants by so appreciable a margin as to encourage a bold competitive advance and a sanguine financiering on the part of the various business men, so soon as the shock of the liquidation had passed and business had again fallen into settled channels. But such a bold competitive advance means the beginning of an extension of credit and a speculative movement in industry, such as has been discussed some pages back in connection with crises. This movement has a cumulative character, after the manner there indicated, and its outcome is an inflation of capitalization and a large extension of credit, which normally ends in a period of liquidation.

Within the period spoken of (1816–1873) this liquidation is apparently always brought on by some extraneous disturbance. But it seems that the theory would require us to say that the extraneous disturbance requisite to bring such a speculative movement to a head will be slighter the farther the movement has gone; so that in the earlier stages of a given period of inflation a liquidation could be brought on only by some relatively violent disturbance, whereas at a higher phase of speculative inflation a relatively slight disturbance would suffice.

Now, it takes some time for such a speculative movement to bring on so large a discrepancy between capitalization and earning-capacity as may not be adjusted by other means than a widespread and severe liquidation.[1] Hence a rough periodicity in the recurrence of these seasons of buoyancy and of collapse in capitalized values. Other factors, and varying ones, have, no doubt, been present in each of the historic crises of the nineteenth century, and these other factors would have to be taken due account of in any history of crises, and even in any theory of crises, which aimed at anything like an exhaustive treatment; but the factors here pointed out seem to be the characteristic and constant ones in the sequence of crises within this period, at the same time that they are the factors which are in a peculiar degree connected with that process of business management in modern industry which is the objective point of the present inquiry.

Since the seventies, as an approximate date and

[1] The speculative movement requires time, because the inflation is a cumulative one and is carried out unintentionally and in a sense unconsciously.

as applying particularly to America and in a less degree to Great Britain, the course of affairs in business has apparently taken a permanent change as regards crises and depression. During this recent period, and with increasing persistency, chronic depression has been the rule rather than the exception in business. Seasons of easy times, "ordinary prosperity," during this period are pretty uniformly traceable to specific causes extraneous to the process of industrial business proper. In one case, the early nineties, it seems to have been a peculiar crop situation, and in the most notable case of a speculative inflation, the one now (1904) apparently drawing to a close, it was the Spanish-American War, coupled with the expenditures for stores, munitions, and services incident to placing the country on a war footing, that lifted the depression and brought prosperity to the business community. If the outside stimulus from which the present prosperity takes its impulse be continued at an adequate pitch, the season of prosperity may be prolonged; otherwise there seems little reason to expect any other outcome than a more or less abrupt and searching liquidation.

What would be an adequate pitch of the stimulus making for prosperity is, of course, not easy to say, but it is probably safe to say that in order to keep up the season of prosperity for a considerable number of years the stimulus would have to be gradually increased. That is to say in other words, the absorption of goods and services by extra-industrial expenditures, expenditures which as seen from the standpoint of industry are pure waste, would have to go on in an increasing volume. If the wasteful expenditure slackens, the logical outcome should be a considerable perturbation of business and industry, followed by depression; if the waste on war, colonization, provincial investment, and the like, comes to an abrupt stop, the logical consequence, in the absence of other counteracting factors, should be a crisis of some severity.[1]

[1] These extra-industrial expenditures that have brought prosperity are here spoken of as wasteful, not thereby implying that they may not be beneficial to the community even in respect to their effect upon the aggregate income or the aggregate accumulation of wealth in the community. They are called wasteful simply because these expenditures directly, in their first incidence, merely withdraw and dissipate wealth and work from the industrial process, and unproductively consume the products of industry. Indirectly they have a beneficial aggregate effect upon industry by inducing an employment of the full productive efficiency of the industrial apparatus; so that in a very short time, it is at least conceivable, the aggregate net output of the industrial process may be as large and serviceable as before the wasteful expenditures were entered upon, even with the destruction of that portion of the product which goes to maintain the wasteful expenditures. At the same time, the effect upon business must be held to be patently favorable. The wasteful expenditures enhance demand and so increase the vendibility of the output, — they increase profits and raise capitalization. They therefore act unequivocally to advance the values of the business men's holdings and increase their gains, as counted in business terms. The wasteful expenditure is good for trade. It is only in the eventual liquidation that a disadvantageous business consequence comes in view.

It was said above that since the seventies the ordinary course of affairs in business, when undisturbed by transient circumstances extraneous to the industrial system proper, has been chronic depression. The fact of such prevalent depression will probably not be denied by any student of the situation during this period, so far as regards America and, in a degree, England.[1] For the Continent of Europe this characterization would have to be materially qualified. But the reply is ready to hand that governmental interferences with trade have been so ubiquitous on the Continent, particularly in the German-speaking communities, that their case is fairly to be thrown out of any general theory. It may also be questioned whether the industrial system of Germany, *e.g.*, throughout this period conforms to the requirements of the theory in respect of the degree of development of

It will be seen that on this view of the effect of wasteful expenditure the position occupied by some early economists, as Malthus, Lauderdale, Chalmers, and others, as well as by some later ones, as Robertson, Hobson, is substantially well taken, although the defence of waste which these economists offer may be incomplete. Waste seems necessary to keep trade brisk, and therefore to keep the industrial processes working at their full capacity. The ulterior reason for this state of the case being the fact that the decisive ground which determines the margin of activity in business, and therefore in industry, is the business men's reluctance to accept a reduction of profits as measured in terms of price. The opponents of the Malthusian view failed to appreciate the decisive importance of price, as contrasted with serviceability, among the motives on which business proceeds.

[1] The objection would not come unexpected that this state of the case is not to be taken as normal,—a point of opinion not readily to be decided, since it rests on a difference in the point of view.

the machine industry which such a state of affairs supposes.[1]

The explanation of this persistent business depression, in those countries where it has prevailed, is, on the view here spoken for, quite simple. By an uncertain date toward the close of the seventies the advancing efficiency and articulation of the processes of the machine industry reached such a pitch that the cost of production of productive goods has since then persistently outstripped such readjustment of capitalization as has from time to time been made. The persistent decline of profits, due to this relative overproduction of industrial apparatus, has not permitted a consistent speculative expansion, of the kind which abounds in the earlier half of the nineteenth century, to get under way. When a speculative movement has been set up by extraneous stimuli, during this late period, the inherent and relatively rapid decline of earning-capacity on the part of older investments has brought the speculative inflation to book before it has reached such dimensions as would bring on a violent crisis. And when a crisis of some appreciable severity has come and has lowered the capitalization, the persistent efficiency and facile balance of processes in the modern machine industry has overtaken the decline in capitalization without allowing time for

[1] Cf. Sombart, *Kapitalismus*, vol. I. ch. XVIII.-XX.

recovery and consequent boom. The cheapening of capital goods has overtaken the lowered capitalization of investments before the shock-effect of the liquidation has worn off. Hence depression is normal to the industrial situation under the consummate régime of the machine, so long as competition is unchecked and no *deus ex machina* interposes.[1]

The persistent defection of reasonable profits calls for a remedy. The remedy may be sought in one or the other of two directions: (1) in an increased unproductive consumption of goods; or (2) in an elimination of that "cutthroat" competition that keeps profits below the "reasonable" level. If enough of the work or of the output is turned to wasteful expenditures, so as to admit of but a relatively slight aggregate saving, as counted by weight and tale, profitable prices can be maintained on the old basis of capitalization. If the waste is sufficiently large, the current investment in additional industrial equipment will not be sufficient to lower prices appreciably through competition.[2]

Wasteful expenditure on a scale adequate to offset the surplus productivity of modern industry is nearly out of the question. Private initiative

[1] Cf. Hobson, *Problem of the Unemployed*, Appendix to ch. V.

[2] Cf. Hobson, *Problem of the Unemployed*, ch. VI. Mr. Hobson does not use the term "waste" in this connection. Also Vialles, *Consommation*, final chapter.

cannot carry the waste of goods and services to nearly the point required by the business situation. Private waste is no doubt large, but business principles, leading to saving and shrewd investment, are too ingrained in the habits of modern men to admit an effective retardation of the rate of saving.[1] Something more to the point can be done, and indeed is being done, by the civilized governments in the way of effectual waste. Armaments, public edifices, courtly and diplomatic establishments, and the like, are almost altogether wasteful, so far as bears on the present question. They have the additional advantage that the public securities which represent this waste serve as attractive investment securities for private savings, at the same time that, taken in the aggregate, the savings so invested are purely fictitious savings and therefore do not act to lower profits or prices. Expenditures met by taxation are less expedient for this purpose; although indirect taxes have the peculiar advantage of keeping up the prices of the goods on which they are imposed, and thereby act directly toward the desired end. The waste of time and effort that goes into military service, as well as the employment of the courtly, diplomatic, and ecclesiastical personnel, counts effectually in

1 "Saving" at the same time takes place automatically in the current operations of coalition and incorporation, as indicated above, pp. 166–176.

the same direction. But however extraordinary this public waste of substance latterly has been, it is apparently altogether inadequate to offset the surplus productivity of the machine industry, particularly when this productivity is seconded by the great facility which the modern business organization affords for the accumulation of savings in relatively few hands. There is also the drawback that the waste of time involved in military service reduces the purchasing power of the classes that are drawn into the service, and so reduces the amount of wasteful consumption which these classes might otherwise accomplish.[1]

So long as industry remains at its present level

[1] Hobson (*Problem of the Unemployed*), whose analysis of overproduction and its relation to depression goes farther than any other, reviews and criticises (ch. VIII.) the palliative measures that have been advocated. He finds them, all and several, inadequate and inconsequent, in that they do not touch the root of the evil — oversaving or "underconsumption." They do not touch this because they do not mitigate the automatic saving and investment process that necessarily goes with the possession of large private incomes. But in point of practical efficiency his own proposed remedies must also be scheduled under the head of "palliatives." These proposed remedies are measures looking to a "Reformed Distribution of Consuming Power" (ch. VI.), such as taxation of "unearned" incomes, higher wages, shorter working day. The aim is "to increase the proportion of the total wealth of the community, which falling to them as wages shall be spent in raising the general standard of working-class consumption." The contemplated move is manifestly chimerical in any community, such as the modern industrial communities, where public policy is with growing singleness of purpose guided by business interests with a naïve view to an increase of profits.

Cf. also Smart, *Studies in Economics*, Essay VIII., on "Overproduction"; also Essay IX., "The Socializing of Consumption," particularly sec. 8, on "The Limits of Consumption," pp. 293–298.

of efficiency, and especially so long as incomes continue to be distributed somewhat after the present scheme, waste cannot be expected to overtake production, and can therefore not check the untoward tendency to depression. But if the balance cannot be maintained by accelerating wasteful consumption, it may be maintained by curtailing and regulating the output of goods.

"Cutthroat" competition, that is to say, free competitive selling, can be done away by "pooling the interests" of the competitors, so soon as all or an effective majority of the business concerns which are rivals in the market combine and place their business management under one directive head. When this is done, by whatever method, selling of goods or services at competitively varying prices is replaced by collective selling ("collective bargaining") at prices fixed on the basis of "what the traffic will bear." That is to say, prices are fixed by consideration of what scale of prices will bring the largest aggregate net earnings, due regard being had to the effect of a lower price in increasing sales as well as to the reduction of cost through the increase of output. The outcome, as regards the scale of prices, may easily be a reduction of the price to consumers; but it may also, and equally readily, be an increase of the average price. But the prices of the output which is in this way brought to a monopoly basis are nearly certain to run more even than prices of the like output while sold competitively by rival concerns.

What has been said in the last paragraph supposes that the combination of business enterprises is so comprehensive as to place the resulting coalition in a position of practical monopoly. Such a result is not always attained, however, especially not in the earlier attempts at coalition in any particular branch of industry; although the endeavor is commonly repeated until at last a virtual monopoly is achieved. But even where no effective monopoly is achieved, a coalition of this kind has a salutary effect, at least temporarily. In almost all cases a consolidation of this kind is able to effect considerable economies in the cost of production, as pointed out in an earlier chapter, and such economies bring relief through enabling the combined industrial ventures to earn a reasonable profit at a lower price for their product than before. They are therefore able to go on on a scale of prices which was not remunerative while they stood on their old footing of severalty. But the relief which comes of such measures, so long as competitive selling goes on in rivalry with concerns standing outside the coalition, is only transient. The declining cost of production, and the consequent competitive investment and extension in the industry, presently catches up with the gain in economy; the margin of advantage in the competition is lost, and depression again overtakes the consolidated enterprises on their new footing. The remedy again is a wider coalition, making possible farther economies, and making some approach to a position of secure monopoly.

It is only on a footing of monopoly that this grinding depression can be definitively set aside. But the monopoly need not be absolute in order to afford a somewhat enduring relief. What is necessary is that the monopoly should comprehend all but a negligible fraction of the business concerns and the equipment engaged in the field within which competition has kept profits below a reasonable level. What is a negligible quantity in such a case is not to be determined on general considerations, since it depends in each case on circumstances affecting the particular industry. But, in a general way, the more nearly complete the monopoly, the more effectually is it likely to serve its purpose.[1]

Such business coalitions have the effect of bringing profits to a reasonable level, not only by

[1] The obvious remark may be added, for completeness of statement, that the various branches of industry lend themselves to management by monopoly in extremely varying degrees, some, *e.g.*, farming, as an extreme instance, not being amenable to this method of management under existing circumstances; others, again, as, *e.g.*, retail merchandising, can be managed by this method only to a very restricted extent; while at the other end of the scale, in such industries as railroading, monopoly management, more or less unqualified, is fairly unavoidable.

making it possible to regulate output and prices, but also by the economies which are made practicable on this footing. Coalitions of a less comprehensive character, as spoken of above, also effect economies in the cost of production. But the larger coalitions which bring the business to a monopoly basis have not only the advantage which comes of the large-scale organization of the industrial process, but they also enjoy peculiar advantages in the matter of cost, due to their monopoly position. These added advantages are more particularly advantages in buying or bargaining for all goods, materials, and services required, as well as in selling the output. So long as the coalitions are not comprehensive enough effectually to eliminate competition, they are constrained to both buy and sell in competition with others. But when the coalition comes effectually to cover its special field of operation, it is able, not only to fix the prices which it will accept (on the basis of what the traffic will bear), but also in a considerable measure to fix the prices or rates which it will pay for materials, labor, and other services (such as transportation) on a similar basis, — unless it should necessarily have to do with another coalition that is in a similar position of monopoly.

The rule which governs the fixing of rates on this side of the business dealings of a monopolistic coalition is similar to that which guides its transactions in the matter of sales. Prices and rates, as, *e.g.*, for materials and labor, are not depressed to the lowest possible point, but to the lowest practicable point,—to the point compatible with the largest net profits. This may or may not be a point below the rates necessary under a régime of competitive buying. It may be added that only in rare cases does a coalition attain so strong a position in respect of its purchases (of materials or services) as to lift this side of its business entirely above the reach of competition.[1]

Wherever this expedient of coalition has been found practicable, the chronic depression of recent times and the confusion and uncertainty which goes with a depressed competitive business situation have been obviated. The great coalitions do not suffer acutely from the ills of depression, except in cases where their industrial processes are to a peculiar degree in the position of intermediaries within the range of the competitive industries, as is the case, *e.g.*, with most railroads. But

[1] Hitherto probably none of the American coalitions have succeeded in freeing themselves from the inconveniences of competitive bidding for labor, and very few have achieved a purely monopolistic buying, either of materials or of any of the various kinds of services which they require. With regard to raw materials alone have some, as, *e.g.*, the Standard Oil Company, been able to compass an effectual monopoly. Something approaching this position has been accomplished by a very few other coalitions, as, *e.g.*, the Sugar Refineries, the Cotton Seed Oil Company, the United States Steel Corporation, and in a local way certain coal, railway, lumber, and warehouse companies.

even in such a case the coalition which has a monopoly is more fortunate as regards the stability of its balance sheet than the same traffic would be without the advantage of monopoly.

Barring providential intervention, then, the only refuge from chronic depression, according to the view here set forth, is thoroughgoing coalition in those lines of business in which coalition is practicable. But since this would include the greater part of those lines of industry which are dominated by the machine process, it seems reasonable to expect that the remedy should be efficacious. The higher development of the machine process makes competitive business impracticable, but it carries a remedy for its own evils in that it makes coalition practicable. The ulterior effects of thoroughgoing monopoly, as regards the efficiency of industry, the constancy of employment, the rates of wages, the prices of goods to consumers, and the like, are, of course, largely matter of surmise, and cannot be taken up in this inquiry, the present purpose being merely to give in outline an economic theory of current business enterprise.

A further consideration bearing on the later phases of the business situation may be added. The great coalitions and the business manœuvres connected with them have the effect of adding to the large fortunes of the greater business men; which adds to the large incomes that cannot be spent in consumptive expenditures; which accelerates the increase of investments; which brings competition if there is a chance for it; which tends to bring on depression, in the manner already indicated. The great coalitions, therefore, seem to carry the seed of this malady of competition, and this evil consequence can accordingly be avoided only on the basis of so comprehensive and rigorous a coalition of business concerns as shall wholly exclude competition, even in the face of any conceivable amount of new capital seeking investment.

What has made chronic depression the normal course of things in modern industrial business is the higher development of the machine process,—given, of course, the traits of human nature as it manifests itself in business traffic. The machine process works this effect by virtue, chiefly if not altogether, of these two characteristics: (1) a relatively rapid rate of increasing efficiency; and (2) the close interdependence of the several lines of industrial activity in a comprehensive system, which is growing more comprehensive and close-knit as improvement and specialization of industrial processes go on. The last-named factor counts for more in proportion as the interdependence grows closer and more comprehensive. Disturbances are progressively transmitted with greater facility and effect throughout the system, and each line of industrial business comes to stand in relatively intimate relations to an ever increasing range of other lines with which it carries on a traffic of purchase or sale. A consequence of this state of things is that any business coalition, in order effectually to serve its purpose of maintaining earnings and capitalization, is required to be of larger scope and closer texture. As the exigencies which enforce the resort to coalition uninterruptedly gain in scope and urgency, the "trust" must take the same course of growth to meet these exigencies; until, with some slight further advance along the accustomed lines, the trust which shall serve the modern business situation must comprehend in one close business coalition virtually the whole field of industry within which the machine process is the dominant industrial factor.[1]

To this there is a broad exception, given by the circumstances of the industrial organization. This organization rests on the distinction between business management and ownership. The workmen do not and cannot own or direct the industrial equipment and processes, so long as ownership prevails and industry is to be managed on business principles. The labor supply, or the working population, can therefore not be included in the ideally

[1] It is, *e.g.*, already apparent that the general railway system of America must presently come under one management, and it must fall into a coalition with the group of industries that are occupied with the supply and elaboration of iron, coal, and lumber.

complete business coalition suggested above, however consummate the machine system and the business organization built upon it may become. So that when the last step in business coalition has been taken, there remains the competitive friction between the combined business capital and the combined workmen.

From the considerations recited above it appears that the competitive management of industry becomes incompatible with continued prosperity so soon as the machine process has been developed to its fuller efficiency. Further technological advance must act to heighten the impracticability of competitive business. As it is sometimes expressed, the tendency to consolidation is irresistible. Modern circumstances do not permit the competitive management of property invested in industrial enterprise, much less its management in detail by the individual owners. In short, the exercise of free contract, and the other powers inhering in the natural right of ownership, are incompatible with the modern machine technology. Business discretion necessarily centres in other hands than those of the general body of owners. In the ideal case, so far as the machine technology and its business concomitants are consistently carried through, the general body of owners are necessarily reduced to the practical status of pensioners dependent on the discretion of the great holders of immaterial wealth; the general body of business men are similarly, in the ideal outcome, disfranchised in point of business initiative and reduced to a bureaucratic hierarchy under the same guidance; and the rest, the populace, is very difficult to bring into the schedule except as raw material of industry. What may take place to accentuate or mitigate this tendency is a question of the drift of sentiment on the matter of property rights, business obligations, and economic policy. So far as the economic factors at play in the modern situation shape this drift of sentiment they do so in large part indirectly, through the disciplinary effect of new and untried circumstances of politics and legal relation to which their working gives rise.

THE CULTURAL INCIDENCE OF THE MACHINE PROCESS

So far as regards the non-mechanical factors of culture, such as religion, politics, and even business enterprise, the present is in a very large degree comparable with the scheme of things that prevailed on the Continent of Europe in the seventeenth century. And so far as the working of these cultural factors is undisturbed by forces that were not present in the older days, they should logically again work out in such a situation as came to prevail in Central Europe in the course of the eighteenth century. The modern situation, of course, is drawn on a larger scale; but that is due to the intrusion of a new technology, a different "state of the industrial arts," and not to a substantially altered range of religious, political, or business conceptions. The pitch of squalor that characterized vulgar life in the busier Continental countries at the close of the great era of politics could probably not be reached again, but that again, is due, not to these spiritual factors of cultural growth, but to the altered state of the industrial arts. The factor in the modern situation that is alien to the ancient regime is the machine technology, with its many and wide ramifications.

Business conceptions and business methods were present in vigorous growth in Central Europe in the sixteenth and seventeenth centuries, as they had been in South Europe from a slightly earlier date; although the large sweep of business enterprise is not had until a later date, being conditioned by the machine technology. Business methods and the apparatus of business traffic develop very promptly whenever and wherever the situation calls for them; such is the teaching of economic history.[1] There is nothing recondite about them, little that has to be acquired by a protracted, cumulative experience running over many generations, such as is involved in technological development. This business development in earlier modern times, together with the accumulations of funded wealth that came of this business enterprise, ran their course to a finish in Continental Europe, leaving no basis for a new start. The new start from which the current situation takes its rise, in Europe and elsewhere, was given to the Continental peoples by

[1] The perfected system of business principles rests on the historical basis of free institutions, and so presumes a protracted historical growth of these institutions; but a highly efficient, though less perfect, business system was worked out in a relatively short time by the South and Central European peoples in early modern times on the basis of a less consummate system of rights. — Cf. Ehrenberg, *Zeitalter der Fugger*; Sombart, *Kapitalismus*, vol. II. ch. VIII., XIV., XV.

the English, ready-made, in the so-called Industrial Revolution. The natural-rights metaphysics, to which the eventual breakdown of the old Continental system owed its specific character, came also from the English.[1]

In point of blood and cultural descent the population of Great Britain did not differ materially from their neighbors across the Channel or across the North Sea.[2] But from the beginning of the modern cultural era Great Britain stood outside of the general European situation, by force of its physical isolation. So that during the modern era, down to the close of the eighteenth century, the British community was in the position of an interested third party rather than a participant in the political concert of Europe. The era of "state-making," so called, is an era in which England interferes, but is, on the whole, not greatly interfered with, so far as her own home affairs are concerned. England, and presently Great Britain, being reduced to law and order under one crown and living in a condition of isolation and (relatively) of internal peace, the cultural growth of that country took a relatively peaceable direction. The dominant note of everyday life was industry and trade, not dynastic politics and war. This na-

[1] See Chapter IV. above.

[2] Cf. Keane, *Man, Past and Present*, ch. XIV.; W. Z. Ripley, *Races of Europe*; Lapouge, *L'Aryen*; Montelius, *Les temps préhistoriques en Suède*, etc.; Andreas Hansen, *Menneskeslægtens Ælde*.

tional experience gave as its outcome constitutional government and the modern industrial technology, together with the animus and the point of view of the modern materialistic science. The point of departure for the more recent, current situation, therefore, is a twofold one: (1) the British peaceable variant of the Western culture has contributed constitutional methods and natural rights, together with the machine technology brought in under the head of the "industrial revolution"; and (2) there are the patriotic ideals and animosities left as a residue of the warlike political traffic in Continental Europe.

Since the new departure, made on the basis of natural rights and modern industrial and scientific methods, the complex of nations and of international relations is a single, not a twofold one. The stage over which affairs, political, industrial and cultural, run their course is no longer Continental or British, but cosmopolitan, comprising all civilized communities and all civilized interests. So that there is not now, as there was in the sixteenth and seventeenth centuries, an isolation hospital for technology, science, and civil rights, set apart from the general current of cultural development. Whatever the forces at work in the modern situation may eventually bring to pass, therefore, the outcome must touch all communities in the same way and in approximately the same degree. If the outcome is dynastic politics and armament again played to a finish in popular squalor, aristocratic virtues, and universal bankruptcy, there will be no peaceable community of matter-of-fact mechanics and shopkeepers left in reserve from which to make a new cultural and industrial start. The modern technology has, in a manner, cut away the ground out of which it first grew and from which it gathered force to reshape the course of history. It has made it impossible for any community to stand peaceably outside of the great complex of nations.

But within the comprehensive situation of to-day there is this new factor, the machine process. In an earlier chapter (II.) the technological character of this machine process has been set forth at some length. The machine process pervades the modern life and dominates it in a mechanical sense. Its dominance is seen in the enforcement of precise mechanical measurements and adjustment and the reduction of all manner of things, purposes and acts, necessities, conveniences, and amenities of life, to standard units. The bearing of this sweeping mechanical standardization upon business traffic is a large part of the subject-matter of the foregoing chapters. The point of immediate interest here is the further bearing of the machine process upon the growth of culture,— the disciplinary effect which this movement for standardization and mechanical equivalence has upon the human material.

This discipline falls more immediately on the workmen engaged in the mechanical industries, and only less immediately on the rest of the community which lives in contact with this sweeping machine process. Wherever the machine process extends, it sets the pace for the workmen, great and small. The pace is set, not wholly by the particular processes in the details of which the given workman is immediately engaged, but in some degree by the more comprehensive process at large into which the given detail process fits. It is no longer simply that the individual workman makes use of one or more mechanical contrivances for effecting certain results. Such used to be his office in the earlier phases of the use of machines, and the work which he now has in hand still has much of that character. But such a characterization of the workman's part in industry misses the peculiarly modern feature of the case. He now does this work as a factor involved in a mechanical process whose movement controls his motions. It remains true, of course, as it always has been true, that he is the intelligent agent concerned in the process, while the machine, furnace, roadway, or retort are inanimate structures devised by man and subject to the workman's supervision. But the process comprises him and his intelligent motions, and it is by virtue of his necessarily taking an intelligent part in what is going forward that the mechanical process has its chief effect upon him. The process standardizes his supervision and guidance of the machine. Mechanically speaking, the machine is not his to do with it as his fancy may suggest. His place is to take thought of the machine and its work in terms given him by the process that is going forward. His thinking in the premises is reduced to standard units of gauge and grade. If he fails of the precise measure, by more or less, the exigencies of the process check the aberration and drive home the absolute need of conformity.

There results a standardization of the workman's intellectual life in terms of mechanical process, which is more unmitigated and precise the more comprehensive and consummate the industrial process in which he plays a part. This must not be taken to mean that such work need lower the degree of intelligence of the workman. No doubt the contrary is nearer the truth. He is a more efficient workman the more intelligent he is, and the discipline of the machine process ordinarily increases his efficiency even for work in a different line from that by which the discipline is given. But the intelligence required and inculcated in the machine industry is of a peculiar character. The machine process is a severe and insistent disciplinarian in point of intelligence. It requires close and unremitting thought, but it is thought which runs in standard terms of quantitative precision. Broadly, other intelligence on the part of the workman is useless; or it is even worse than useless, for a habit of thinking in other than quantitative terms blurs the workman's quantitative apprehension of the facts with which he has to do.[1]

In so far as he is a rightly gifted and fully disciplined workman, the final term of his *habitual* thinking is mechanical efficiency, understanding "mechanical" in the sense in which it is used above. But mechanical efficiency is a matter of precisely adjusted cause and effect. What the discipline of the machine industry inculcates, therefore, in the habits of life and of thought of the workman, is regularity of sequence and mechanical precision; and the intellectual outcome is an habitual resort to terms of measurable cause and effect, together with a relative neglect and disparagement of such exercise of the intellectual faculties as does not run on these lines.

Of course, in no case and with no class does the discipline of the machine process mould the habits of life and of thought fully into its own image. There is present in the human nature of all classes too large a residue of the propensities and aptitudes carried over from the past and working to a different result. The machine's regime has been of too

[1] If, *e.g.*, he takes to myth-making and personifies the machine or the process and imputes purpose and benevolence to the mechanical appliances, after the manner of current nursery tales and pulpit oratory, he is sure to go wrong.

short duration, strict as its discipline may be, and the body of inherited traits and traditions is too comprehensive and consistent to admit of anything more than a remote approach to such a consummation.

The machine process compels a more or less unremitting attention to phenomena of an impersonal character and to sequences and correlations not dependent for their force upon human predilection nor created by habit and custom. The machine throws out anthropomorphic habits of thought. It compels the adaptation of the workman to his work, rather than the adaptation of the work to the workman. The machine technology rests on a knowledge of impersonal, material cause and effect, not on the dexterity, diligence, or personal force of the workman, still less on the habits and propensities of the workman's superiors. Within the range of this machine-guided work, and within the range of modern life so far as it is guided by the machine process, the course of things is given mechanically, impersonally, and the resultant discipline is a discipline in the handling of impersonal facts for mechanical effect. It inculcates thinking in terms of opaque, impersonal cause and effect, to the neglect of those norms of validity that rest on usage and on the conventional standards handed down by usage. Usage counts for little in shaping the processes of work of this kind or in shaping the modes of thought induced by work of this kind.

The machine process gives no insight into questions of good and evil, merit and demerit, except in point of material causation, nor into the foundations or the constraining force of law and order, except such mechanically enforced law and order as may be stated in terms of pressure, temperature, velocity, tensile strength, etc.[1] The machine technology takes no cognizance of conventionally established rules of precedence; it knows neither manners nor breeding and can make no use of any of the attributes of worth. Its scheme of knowledge and of inference is based on the laws of material causation, not on those of immemorial custom, authenticity, or authoritative enactment. Its metaphysical basis is the law of cause and effect, which in the thinking of its adepts has displaced even the law of sufficient reason.[2]

The range of conventional truths, or of institutional legacies, which it traverses is very comprehensive, being, indeed, all-inclusive. It is but little more in accord with the newer, eighteenth-century conventional truths of natural rights,

[1] Such expressions as "good and ill," "merit and demerit," "law and order," when applied to technological facts or to the outcome of material science, are evidently only metaphorical expressions, borrowed from older usage and serviceable only as figures of speech.

[2] Tarde, *Psychologic Economique*, vol. I. pp. 122–131, offers a characterization of the psychology of modern work, contrasting, among other things, the work of the machine workman with that of the handicraftsman in respect of its psychological requirements and effects. It may be taken as a temperate formulation of the current commonplaces on this topic, and seems to be fairly wide of the mark.

natural liberty, natural law, or natural religion, than with the older norms of the true, the beautiful, and the good which these displaced. Anthropomorphism, under whatever disguise, is of no use and of no force here.

The discipline exercised by the mechanical occupations, in so far as it is in question here, is a discipline of the habits of thought. It is, therefore, as processes of thought, methods of apperception, and sequences of reasoning, that these occupations are of interest for the present purpose; it is as such that they have whatever cultural value belongs to them. They have such a value, therefore, somewhat in proportion as they tax the mental faculties of those employed; and the largest effects are to be looked for among those industrial classes who are required to comprehend and guide the processes, rather than among those who serve merely as mechanical auxiliaries of the machine process. Not that the latter are exempt from the machine's discipline, but it falls upon them blindly and enforces an uncritical acceptance of opaque results, rather than a theoretical insight into the causal sequences which make up the machine process. The higher degree of training in such matter-of-fact habits of thought is accordingly to be looked for among the higher ranks of skilled mechanics, and perhaps still more decisively among those who stand in an engineering or supervisory relation to the processes. It counts more forcibly and farthest among those who are required to exercise what may be called a mechanical discretion in the guidance of the industrial processes, who, as one might say, are required to administer the laws of causal sequence that run through material phenomena, who therefore must learn to think in the terms in which the machine processes work.[1] The metaphysical ground, the assumptions, on which such thinking proceeds must be such as will hold good for the sequence of material phenomena; that is to say, it

[1] For something more than a hundred years past this change in the habits of thought of the workman has been commonly spoken of as a deterioration or numbing of his intelligence. But that seems too sweeping a characterization of the change brought on by habituation to machine work. It is safe to say that such habituation brings a change in the workman's habits of thought, — in the direction, method, and content of his thinking, — heightening his intelligence for some purposes and lowering it for certain others. No doubt, on the whole, the machine's discipline lowers the intelligence of the workman for such purposes as were rated high as marks of intelligence before the coming of the machine, but it appears likewise to heighten his intelligence for such purposes as have been brought to the front by the machine. If he is by nature scantily endowed with the aptitudes that would make him think effectively in terms of the machine process, if he has intellectual capacity for other things and not for this, then the training of the machine may fairly be said to lower his intelligence, since it hinders the full development of the only capacities of which he is possessed. The resulting difference in intellectual training is a difference in kind and direction, not necessarily in degree. Cf. Schmoller, *Grundriss der Volkswirtschaftslehre*, vol. I. secs. 85–86, 132; Hobson, *Evolution of Modern Capitalism*, ch. IX. secs. 4 and 5; Cooke Taylor, *Modern Factory System*, pp. 434–435; Sidney and Beatrice Webb, *Industrial Democracy*, *e.g.* pp. 327 *et seq.*; K. Th. Reinhold, *Arbeit und Werkzeug*, ch. X. (particularly pp. 190–198) and ch. XI. (particularly pp. 221–240).

is the metaphysical assumptions of modern material science, — the law of cause and effect, cumulative causation, conservation of energy, persistence of quantity, or whatever phrase be chosen to cover the concept. The men occupied with the modern material sciences are, accordingly, for the purpose in hand, in somewhat the same case as the higher ranks of those employed in mechanical industry.[1]

Leaving aside the archaic vocations of war, politics, fashion, and religion, the employments in which men are engaged may be distinguished as pecuniary or business employments on the one hand, and industrial or mechanical employments on the other hand.[2] In earlier times, and indeed until an uncertain point in the nineteenth century, such a distinction between employments would not to any great extent have coincided with a difference between occupations. But gradually, as time has passed and production for a market has come to be the rule in industry, there has supervened a differentiation of occupations, or a division of labor, whereby one class of men have taken over the work of purchase and sale and of husbanding a store of accumulated values. Concomitantly, of course, the rest, who may, for lack of means or of

[1] Cf. J. C. Sutherland, "The Engineering Mind," *Popular Science Monthly*, January 1903, pp. 254–256.

[2] Cf. "Industrial and Pecuniary Employments," especially pp. 198–218.

pecuniary aptitude, have been less well fitted for pecuniary pursuits, have been relieved of the cares of business and have with increasing specialization given their attention to the mechanical processes involved in this production for a market. In this way the distinction between pecuniary and industrial activities or employments has come to coincide more and more nearly with a difference between occupations. Not that the specialization has even yet gone so far as to exempt any class from all pecuniary care;[1] for even those whose daily occupation is mechanical work still habitually bargain with their employers for their wages and with others for their supplies. So that none of the active classes in modern life is fully exempt from pecuniary work.

But the need of attention to pecuniary matters is less and less exacting, even in the matter of wages and supplies. The scale of wages, for instance, is, for the body of workmen, and also for what may be called the engineering force, becoming more and more a matter of routine, thereby lessening at least the constancy with which occasions

[1] As G. F. Steffen has described it: "Those who hire out their labor power or their capital or their land to the entrepreneurs are as a rule not absolutely passive as seen from the point of view of business enterprise. They are not simply inanimate implements in the hands of the entrepreneurs. They are 'enterprising implements' (företagande verktyg) who surrender their undertaking functions only to the extent designated in the contract with the entrepreneur." — *Ekonomisk Tidskrift*, vol. V. p. 256.

for detail bargaining in this respect recur. So also as regards the purchase of consumable goods. In the cities and industrial towns, particularly, the supplying of the means of subsistence has, in great part, become a matter of routine. Retail prices are in an increasing degree fixed by the seller, and in great measure fixed in an impersonal way. This occurs in a particularly evident and instructive way in the practice of the department stores, where the seller fixes the price, and comes in contact with the buyer only through the intervention of a salesman who has no discretion as to the terms of sale. The change that has taken place and that is still going on in this respect is sufficiently striking on comparison with the past in any industrial community, or with the present in any of those communities which we are in the habit of calling "industrially backward."

Conversely, as regards the men in the pecuniary occupations, the business men. Their exemption from taking thought of mechanical facts and processes is likewise only relative. Even those business men whose business is in a peculiar degree remote from the handling of tools or goods, and from the oversight of mechanical processes, as, for example, bankers, lawyers, brokers, and the like, have still, at the best, to take some cognizance of the mechanical apparatus of everyday life; they are at least compelled to take some thought of what may be called the mechanics of consumption. Whereas those business men whose business is more immediately concerned with industry commonly have some knowledge and take some thought of the processes of industry; to some appreciable extent they habitually think in mechanical terms. Their cogitations may habitually run to pecuniary conclusions, and the test to which the force and validity of their reasoning is brought may habitually be the pecuniary outcome; the beginning and end of their more serious thinking is of a pecuniary kind, but it always takes in some general features of the mechanical process along the way. Their exemption from mechanical thinking, from thinking in terms of cause and effect, is, therefore, materially qualified.

But after all qualifications have been made, the fact still is apparent that the everyday life of those classes which are engaged in business differs materially in the respect cited from the life of the classes engaged in industry proper. There is an appreciable and widening difference between the habits of life of the two classes; and this carries with it a widening difference in the discipline to which the two classes are subjected. It induces a difference in the habits of thought and the habitual grounds and methods of reasoning resorted to by each class. There results a difference in the point of view, in the facts dwelt upon, in the methods of argument, in the grounds of validity appealed to; and this difference gains in magnitude and consistency as the differentiation of occupations goes on. So that the two classes come to have an increasing difficulty in understanding one another and appreciating one another's convictions, ideals, capacities, and shortcomings.

The ultimate ground of validity for the thinking of the business classes is the natural-rights ground of property,—a conventional, anthropomorphic fact having an institutional validity, rather than a matter-of-fact validity such as can be formulated in terms of material cause and effect; while the classes engaged in the machine industry are habitually occupied with matters of causal sequence, which do not lend themselves to statement in anthropomorphic terms of natural rights and which afford no guidance in questions of institutional right and wrong, or of conventional reason and consequence. Arguments which proceed on material cause and effect cannot be met with arguments from conventional precedent or dialectically sufficient reason, and conversely.

The thinking required by the pecuniary occupations proceeds on grounds of conventionality, whereas that involved in the industrial occupations runs, in the main, on grounds of mechanical sequence or causation, to the neglect of conventionality. The institution (habit of thought) of ownership or property is a conventional fact; and the logic of pecuniary thinking — that is to say, of thinking on matters of ownership — is a working out of the implications of this postulate, this concept of ownership or property. The characteristic habits of thought given by such work are habits of recourse to conventional grounds of finality or validity, to anthropomorphism, to explanations of phenomena in terms of human relation, discretion, authenticity, and choice. The final ground of certainty in inquiries on this natural-rights plane is always a ground of authenticity, of precedent, or accepted decision. The argument is an argument *de jure*, not *de facto*, and the training given lends facility and certainty in the pursuit of *de jure* distinctions and generalizations, rather than in the pursuit or the assimilation of a *de facto* knowledge of impersonal phenomena. The end of such reasoning is the interpretation of new facts in terms of accredited precedents, rather than a revision of the knowledge drawn from past experience in the matter-of-fact light of new phenomena. The endeavor is to make facts conform to law, not to make the law or general rule conform to facts. The bent so given favors the acceptance of the general, abstract, custom-made rule as something real with a reality superior to the reality of impersonal, non-conventional facts. Such training gives reach and subtlety in metaphysical argument and in what is known as the "practical" management of affairs; it gives executive or administrative efficiency, so-called, as distinguished from mechanical work. "Practical" efficiency means the ability to turn facts to account for the purposes of the accepted conventions, to give a large effect to the situation in terms of the pecuniary conventions in force.[1]

The spiritual attitude given by this training in reasoning *de jure*, from pecuniary premises to pecuniary conclusions, is necessarily conservative. This species of reasoning assumes the validity of the conventionally established postulates, and is consequently unable to take a sceptical attitude toward these postulates or toward the institutions in which these postulates are embodied. It may lead to scepticism touching other, older, institutions that are at variance with its own (natural-rights) postulates, but its scepticism cannot touch the natural-rights ground on which it rests its own case. In the same manner, of course, the thinking which runs in material causal sequence cannot take a sceptical attitude toward its fundamental postulate, the law of cause and effect; but since reasoning on this materialistic basis does not visibly go to uphold the received

[1] Cf., on the other hand, Reinhold, *Arbeit und Werkzeug*, ch. XII. and XIV., where double dealing is confused with workmanship, very much after the manner familiar to readers of expositions of the "wages of superintendence," but more broadly and ingeniously than usual.

institutions, the attitude given by the discipline of the machine technology cannot, for the present, be called a conservative attitude.

The business classes are conservative, on the whole, but such a conservative bent is, of course, not peculiar to them. These occupations are not the only ones whose reasoning prevailingly moves on a conventional plane. Indeed, the intellectual activity of other classes, such as soldiers, politicians, the clergy, and men of fashion, moves on a plane of still older conventions; so that if the training given by business employments is to be characterized as conservative, that given by these other, more archaic employments should be called reactionary.[1] Extreme conventionalization means

[1] Individual exceptions are, of course, to be found in all classes, but there is, after all, a more or less consistent, prevalent class attitude. As is well known, clergymen, lawyers, soldiers, civil servants, and the like, are popularly held to be of a conservative, if not reactionary temper. This vulgar apprehension may be faulty in detail, and especially it may be too sweeping in its generalizations; but there are, after all, few persons not belonging to these classes who will not immediately recognize that this vulgar appraisement of them rests on substantial grounds, even though the appraisement may need qualification. So, also, a conservative animus is seen to pervade all classes more generally in earlier times or on more archaic levels of culture than our own. At the same time, in those early days and in the more archaic cultural regions, the structure of conventionally accepted truths and the body of accredited spiritual or extra-material facts are more comprehensive and rigid, and the thinking on all topics is more consistently held to tests of authenticity as contrasted with tests of sense perception. On the whole, the number and variety of things that are fundamentally and eternally true and good increase as one goes outward from the modern West-European cultural centres into the earlier barbarian past or into the remoter barbarian present.

extreme conservatism. Conservatism means the maintenance of conventions already in force. On this head, therefore, the discipline of modern business life may be said simply to retain something of the complexion which marks the life of the higher barbarian culture, at the same time that it has not retained the disciplinary force of the barbarian culture in so high a state of preservation as some of the other occupations just named.

The discipline of the modern industrial employments is relatively free from the bias of conventionality, but the difference between the mechanical and the business occupations in this respect is a difference of degree. It is not simply that conventional standards of certainty fall into abeyance for lack of exercise, among the industrial classes. The positive discipline exercised by their work in good part runs counter to the habit of thinking in conventional, anthropomorphic terms, whether the conventionality is that of natural rights or any other. And in respect of this positive training away from conventional norms, there is a large divergence between the several lines of industrial employment. In proportion as a given line of employment has more of the character of a machine process and less of the character of handicraft, the matter-of-fact training which it gives is more pronounced. In a sense more intimate than the inventors of the phrase seem to have appreciated, the machine has become the master of the man who works with it and an arbiter in the cultural fortunes of the community into whose life it has entered.

The intellectual and spiritual training of the machine in modern life, therefore, is very far-reaching. It leaves but a small proportion of the community untouched; but while its constraint is ramified throughout the body of the population, and constrains virtually all classes at some points in their daily life, it falls with the most direct, intimate, and unmitigated impact upon the skilled mechanical classes, for these have no respite from its mastery, whether they are at work or at play.

The ubiquitous presence of the machine, with its spiritual concomitant — workday ideals and scepticism of what is only conventionally valid — is the unequivocal mark of the Western culture of to-day as contrasted with the culture of other times and places. It pervades all classes and strata in a varying degree, but on an average in a greater degree than at any time in the past, and most potently in the advanced industrial communities and in the classes immediately in contact with the mechanical occupations.[1] As the comprehensive mechanical organization of the material side of life has gone on, a heightening of this cultural effect throughout the community has also super-

[1] See Chapter II. above.

vened, and with a farther and faster movement in the same direction a farther accentuation of this "modern" complexion of culture is fairly to be looked for, unless some remedy be found. And as the concomitant differentiation and specialization of occupations goes on, a still more unmitigated discipline falls upon ever widening classes of the population, resulting in an ever weakening sense of conviction, allegiance, or piety toward the received institutions.

It is a matter of common notoriety that the modern industrial populations are improvident in a high degree and are apparently incapable of taking care of the pecuniary details of their own life. This applies, not only to factory hands, but also to the general class of highly skilled mechanics, inventors, technological experts. The rule does not hold in any hard and fast way, but it holds with such generality as may fairly be looked for. The present factory population may be compared in this respect with the class of handicraftsmen whom they have displaced, as also with the farming population of the present time, especially the class of small proprietary farmers. The failure of the modern industrial classes on this head is not due to scantier opportunities for saving, whether they are compared with the earlier handicraftsmen or with the modern farmer or peasant; nor is it due to a lack of general intelligence, for a comparison in point of intelligence falls out in favor of the modern industrial workmen. This improvidence is commonly discussed in terms of deprecation, and there is much preaching of thrift and steady habits. But the preaching has no appreciable effect. The trouble seems to be of the nature of habit rather than of reasoned conviction. Other causes may partially explain this improvidence, but the inquiry is at least pertinent how far the absence of property and thrift among them may be traceable to the relative absence of pecuniary training and to the presence of a discipline which is at variance with habits of thrift.

Mere exemption from pecuniary training is not competent alone to explain the patent thriftlessness of modern workmen; the more so since this exemption is but partial and relative. Also, the thriftless classes commonly have an envious appreciation of pecuniary advantages. It is rather the composite effect of exemption from pecuniary training and certain positive requirements of modern life. Among these positive requirements is what has been called the canon of conspicuous waste. Under modern conditions a free expenditure in consumable goods is a condition requisite to good repute.[1] This conduces to immediate consumption rather than to saving. What is perhaps

[1] Cf. *Theory of the Leisure Class*, especially ch. IV. and V.

still more decisive against thrift on the part of workmen is the fact that the modern large organization of industry requires a high degree of mobility on the part of employees. It requires, in fact, that the labor force and the labor units be mobile, interchangeable, distributable, after the same impersonal fashion as the mechanical contrivances engaged are movable and distributable. The working population is required to be standardized, movable, and interchangeable in much the same impersonal manner as the raw or half-wrought materials of industry. From which it follows that the modern workman cannot advantageously own a home. By force of this latter feature of the case he is discouraged from investing his savings in real property, or, indeed, in any of the impedimenta of living. And the savings-bank account, it may be added, offers no adequate substitute, as an incentive to thrift, in the place of such property as a dwelling-place, which is tangibly and usefully under the owner's hand and persistently requires maintenance and improvement.

The conditions of life imposed upon the working population by the machine industry discourage thrift. But after allowance has been made for this almost physical restraint upon the aquisition of property by the working classes, something is apparently left over, to be ascribed to the moral effect of the machine technology. The industrial classes appear to be losing the instinct of individual ownership. The acquisition of property is ceasing to appeal to them as a natural, self-evident source of comfort and strength. The natural right of property no longer means so much to them as it once did.

A like weakening of the natural-rights animus is visible at another point in the current frame of mind of these classes. The growth of trade-unionism and of what is called the trade-union spirit is a concomitant of industry organized after the manner of a machine process. Historically this growth begins, virtually, with the industrial revolution, coming in sporadically, loosely, tentatively, with no precise assignable date, very much as the revolution does. England is the land of its genesis, its "area of characterization," and the place where it has reached its fullest degree of specification and its largest force; just as England is the country in which the modern machine industry took its rise and in which it has had the longest and most consistent life and growth. In this matter other countries are followers of the British lead and apparently borrowers of British precedents and working concepts. Still, the history of the trade-union movement in other countries seems to say that the working classes elsewhere have not advisedly borrowed ideals and methods of organization from their British congeners so much as they have been pushed into the same general attitude and line of conduct by the same general line of exigencies and experiences. Particularly, experience seems to say that it is not feasible to introduce the trade-union spirit or the trade-union rules into any community until the machine industry has had time extensively to standardize the scheme of work and of life for the working classes on mechanical lines. Workmen do not take to full-blown trade-union ideals abruptly on the introduction of those modern business methods which make trade-union action advisable for the working class. A certain interval elapses between the time when business conditions first make trade-union action feasible, as a business proposition, and the time when the body of workmen are ready to act in the spirit of trade-unionism and along the lines which the union animus presently accepts as normal for men in the mechanically organized industries. An interval of discipline in the ways of the mechanically standardized industry, more or less protracted and severe, seems necessary to bring such a proportion of the workmen into line as will give a consensus of sentiment and opinion favorable to trade-union action.

The pervading characteristic of the trade-union animus is the denial of the received natural-rights dogmas wherever the mechanical standardization of modern industry traverses the working of these received natural rights. Recent court decisions in America, as well as decisions in analogous cases in England at that earlier period when the British development was at about the same stage of maturity as the current American situation, testify unequivocally that the common run of trade-union action is at variance with the natural-rights foundation of the common law. Trade-unionism denies individual freedom of contract to the workman, as well as free discretion to the employer to carry on his business as may suit his own ends. Many pious phrases have been invented to disguise this iconoclastic trend of trade-union aims and endeavors; but the courts, standing on a secure and familiar natural-rights footing, have commonly made short work of the shifty sophistications which trade-union advocates have offered for their consideration. They have struck at the root of the matter in declaring trade-union regulations inimical to the natural rights of workman and employer alike, in that they hamper individual liberty and act in restraint of trade. The regulations, therefore, violate that system of law and order which rests on natural rights, although they may be enforced by that *de facto* law and order which is embodied in the mechanical standardization of the industrial processes.

Trade-unionism is an outgrowth of relatively late industrial conditions and has come on gradually as an adaptation of old methods and working arrangements carried over from the days of handicraft and petty trade. It is a movement to adapt, construe, recast, earlier working arrangements with as little lesion to received preconceptions as the new exigencies and the habits of thought bred by them will permit. It is, on its face, an endeavor of compromise between received notions of what "naturally" ought to be in matters of industrial business, on the one hand, and what the new exigencies of industry demand and what the new animus of the workman will tolerate, on the other hand. Trade-unionism is therefore to be taken as a somewhat mitigated expression of what the mechanical standardization of industry inculcates. Hitherto the movement has shown a fairly uninterrupted growth, not only in the numbers of its membership, but in the range and scope of its aims as well; and hitherto it has reached no halting-place in its tentative, shifty, but ever widening crusade of iconoclasm against the received body of natural rights. The latest, maturest expressions of trade-unionism are, on the whole, the most extreme, in so far as they are directed against the natural rights of property and pecuniary contract.

The nature of the compromise offered by trade-unionism is shown by a schedule of its demands: collective bargaining for wages and employment;

arbitration of differences between owners and workmen; standard rates of wages; normal working day, with penalized regulation of hours for men, women, and children; penalized regulation of sanitary and safety appliances; mutual insurance of workmen, to cover accident, disability, and unemployment. In all of this the aim of unionism seldom goes the length of overtly disputing the merits of any given article of natural-rights dogma. It only endeavors to cut into these articles, in point of fact, at points where the dogmas patently traverse the conditions of life imposed on the workmen by the modern industrial system or where they traverse the consensus of sentiment that is coming to prevail among these workmen.

When unionism takes an attitude of overt hostility to the natural-rights institutions of property and free contract, it ceases to be unionism simply and passes over into something else, which may be called socialism for want of a better term. Such an extreme iconoclastic position, which would overtly assert the mechanical standardization of industry as against the common-law standardization of business, seems to be the logical outcome to which the trade-union animus tends, and to which some approach has latterly been made by more than one trade-unionist body, but which is, on the whole, yet in the future, if, indeed, it is to be reached at all. On the whole, the later expressions go farther in this direction than the earlier; and the animus of the leaders, as well as of the more wide-awake body of unionist workmen, appears to go farther than their official utterances.

A detail of trade-union history may be cited in illustration of their attitude toward the natural-rights principles that underlie modern business relations. As is well known, trade-unions have somewhat consistently avoided pecuniary responsibility for the actions of their members or officials. They avoid incorporation. Practically an employer has had no recourse in case he suffers from a failure on the part of his union workmen to live up to the terms of an agreement made with the union. In English practice this exemption from pecuniary responsibility has acquired much of the force of law, and indeed was supposed to have gained the countenance of statutory enactment, until, within the past few months, the so-called Taff Vale decision of the House of Lords reversed the views which had come to prevail on this head. This decision, by the most conservative tribunal of the British nation, is too recent to permit its consequences for trade-unionism to be appreciated. But it seems fair to expect that the question which the decision brings home to the unions will be, How is this court-made pecuniary responsibility to be evaded? not, How is it to be lived up to? Patently,[1] the decision is unexceptionable under common law rules; but, also patently,[2] it broadly traverses trade-union practice and is wholly alien to the attitude of the trade-unionists.[3]

The animus shown by the trade-unionists in this shirking of pecuniary responsibility is characteristic of their attitude toward common law rules. The unions and their methods of work are essentially extra-legal. It is only reluctantly, as defendants if at all, that unions are accustomed to appear in court. When they make a move for statutory enactment, as for the enforcement of a normal day or of sanitary and safeguarding regulations, it is prevailingly to criminal law that they turn.

To all this it might, of course, be said that the

[1] As, *e.g.*, Mr. W. G. S. Adams cogently points out in a recent number of the *Journal of Political Economy* (December 1902).

[2] As Mr. Webb shows (*Industrial Democracy*, 1902, pp. xxiv-xxxvi).

[3] The historical explanation of this House of Lords reversal of trade-union practice is probably to be found in the conservative, or rather reactionary, trend given to British sentiment by the imperialist policy of the last two or three decades, accentuated by the experiences of the Boer War. The Boer War seems to mark a turning-point in the growth of sentiment and institutions. Since the seventies the imperialist interest, that is to say, the dynastic interest, has been coming into the foreground among the interests that engage the attention of the British community. It seems now to have definitively gained the first place, and may be expected in the immediate future to dominate British policy both at home and abroad. Concomitantly, it may be remarked, the British community has been slowing down, if not losing ground, in industrial animus, technological efficiency, and scientific spirit. Cf. Hobson, *Imperialism*, part II. ch. I. and III.

workmen who make up the trade-union element take the course indicated simply because their selfish interest urges them to this course; that their common necessities and common weakness constrains them to stand together and to act collectively in dealing with their employers; while the fact that their demands have no standing in court constrains them to seek their ends by extra-legal means of coercion. But this objection is little else than another way of saying that the exigencies forced upon the workmen by the mechanically standardized industrial system are extra-legal exigencies — exigencies which do not run in business terms and therefore are not amenable to the natural-rights principles of property and contract that underlie business relations; that they can therefore not be met on common law ground; and that they therefore compel the workmen to see them from another point of view and seek to dispose of them by an appeal to other principles than those afforded by the common law standpoint. That is to say, in other words, these exigencies which compel the trade-unionists to take thought of their case in other terms than those afforded by existing legal institutions are the means whereby the discipline of the machine industry is enforced and made effective for recasting the habits of thought of the workmen. The harsh discipline of these exigencies of livelihood drives home the new point of view and holds the workmen consistently to it. But that is not all that the mechanical standardization of industry does in the case; it also furnishes the new terms in which the revised scheme of economic life takes form. The revision of the scheme aimed at by trade-union action runs, not in terms of natural liberty, individual property rights, individual discretion, but in terms of standardized livelihood and mechanical necessity; it is formulated, not in terms of business expediency, but in terms of industrial, technological standard units and standard relations.

The above presentation of the case of trade-unionism is of course somewhat schematic, as such a meagre, incidental discussion necessarily must be. It takes account only of those features of trade-unionism which characteristically mark it off from that business scheme of things with which it comes in conflict. There are, of course, many survivals, pecuniary and others, in the current body of trade-union demands, and much of the trade-union argument is carried on in business terms. The crudities and iniquities of the trade-union campaign are sufficiently many and notorious to require no rehearsal here. These crudities and iniquities commonly bulk large in the eyes of critics who pass an opinion on trade-unionism from the natural-rights point of view; and, indeed, they may deserve all the disparaging attention that is given them. Trade-unionism does not fit into the natural-rights scheme of right and honest living; but therein, in great part, lies its cultural significance. It is of the essence of the case that the new aims, ideals, and expedients do not fit into the received institutional structure; and that the classes who move in trade-unions are, however crudely and blindly, endeavoring, under the compulsion of the machine process, to construct an institutional scheme on the lines imposed by the new exigencies given by the machine process.

The point primarily had in view in entering on this characterization of trade-unionism was that under the discipline of the mechanically standardized industry certain natural rights, particularly, those of property and free contract, are in a degree falling into abeyance among those classes who are most immediately subjected to this discipline. It may be added that other classes also, to an uncertain extent, sympathize with the trade-unionists and are affected with a similar (mild and equivocal) distrust of the principles of natural liberty. When distrust of business principles rises to such a pitch as to become intolerant of all pecuniary institutions, and leads to a demand for the abrogation of property rights rather than a limitation of them, it is spoken of as "socialism" or "anarchism." This socialistic disaffection is widespread among the advanced industrial peoples. No other cultural phenomenon is so threatening to the received economic and political structure; none is so unprecedented or so perplexing for practical men of affairs to deal with. The immediate point of danger in the socialistic disaffection is a growing disloyalty to the natural-rights institution of property, but this is backed by a similar failure of regard for other articles of the institutional furniture handed down from the past. The classes affected with socialistic vagaries protest against the existing economic organization, but they are not necessarily averse to a somewhat rigorous economic organization on new lines of their own choosing. They demand an organization on industrial as contrasted with business lines. Their sense of economic solidarity does not seem to be defective, indeed it seems to many of their critics to be unnecessarily pronounced; but it runs on lines of industrial coherence and mechanical constraint, not on lines given by pecuniary conjunctures and conventional principles of economic right and wrong.

There is little agreement among socialists as to a programme for the future. Their constructive proposals are ill-defined and inconsistent and almost entirely negative. The negative character of the socialistic propaganda has been made a point of disparagement by its critics, perhaps justly. But their predilection for shifty iconoclasm, as well as the vagueness and inconsistency of their constructive proposals, are in the present connection to be taken as evidence that the attitude of the socialists cannot be expressed in positive terms given by the institutions at present in force. It may also be evidence of the untenability of the socialistic ideals; but the merits of the socialist contentions do not concern the present inquiry. The question here is as to the nature and causes of the socialist disaffection; it does not concern the profounder and more delicate point, as to the validity of the socialist contentions. Current socialism is an animus of dissent from received traditions. The degree and the direction of this dissent varies greatly, but it is, within the socialist scheme of thought, agreed that the institutional forms of the past are unfit for the work of the future.[1]

The socialistic disaffection has been set down

[1] All this applies to anarchism as well as to socialism; similarly to several minor categories of dissentients. In their negative proposals the socialists and anarchists are fairly agreed. It is in the metaphysical postulates of their protest and in their constructive aims that they part company. Of the two, the socialists are more widely out of touch with the established order. They are also more hopelessly negative and destructive in their ideals, as seen from the standpoint of the established order. This applies to the later socialists rather than to the earlier, and it applies, of course, only to the lower-class, "democratic" socialists, not to the so-called state and Christian socialists.

Anarchism proceeds on natural-rights ground, and is accordingly in touch with the postulates of the existing property arrangements to that extent. It is a more unmitigated working out of the same postulates. It is a system of "natural liberty" unqualified to the extent even of not admitting prescriptive ownership. Its basis is a (divinely to envy, class hatred, discontent with their own lot by comparison with that of others, and to a mistaken view of their own interests. This criticism may be well enough as far as it goes, but it does not touch socialism in those respects in which it differs from other movements into which this range of motives enters; that is to say, it touches, not the specific traits of socialism, but the common features of popular discontent. History shows many such movements of discontent, pushed on by real or fancied privation and iniquity; and past experience recorded in history should lead us to expect that, under the guidance

instituted) order of nature, the keynote of which is an inalienable freedom and equality of the individual, quite in the eighteenth-century spirit. It is in this sense an offshoot of the Romantic school of thought. Anarchism is a *de jure* scheme, which takes no account of mechanical exigencies but rests its case altogether on anthropomorphic postulates of natural rights. It is, from the natural-rights standpoint, substantially sound, though senselessly extreme.

What may be called the normal socialism, socialism of the later, more dangerous, and more perplexing, kind, does not build on the received metaphysical basis of the "natural order." It demands a reconstruction of the social fabric, but it does not know on what lines the reconstruction is to be carried out. The natural rights of the individual are not accepted as the standard (except by certain large bodies of neophytes, especially rural American, who are carrying under socialist mottoes the burden of animosities and preconceptions that once made populism), but nothing definite is put in the place of this outworn standard. The socialists of the line, in so far as there is any consensus among them, profess that the mechanical exigencies of the industrial system must decide what the social structure is to be, but beyond this vague generality they have little to offer. And this mechanical standardization can manifestly afford no basis for legislation on civil rights. Indeed, it is difficult to see how any scheme of civil rights, much or little, can find a place in a socialistic reorganization.

of such motives and such reasoning as is currently imputed to the socialists by their conservative critics, the malcontents would demand a redistribution of property, a reorganization of ownership on such new lines as would favor the discontented classes. But such is not the trend of socialistic thinking. It looks to the disappearance of property rights rather than their redistribution. The entire range of doctrines covered by the theory of distribution in the received economics is essentially (and characteristically) neglected by the modern socialist speculations.[1]

The perplexity of those who protest against a supposedly imminent socialistic subversion of property rights is of a twofold kind: (1) The absence of proprietary rights is incomprehensible, and a living together in society without defined ownership of the means of living is held to be impracticable; ownership of goods, in the apprehension of

[1] The "scientific socialism" of Marx and Engels as promulgated during the third quarter of the nineteenth century was not of this negative character. It was a product of Hegelianism blended with the conceptions of natural rights, its chief count being the "claim to the full product of labor." This socialism never made serious inroads among the working classes outside of Germany — the home of Hegelianism. Even in that country the most vigorous growth of socialistic sentiment came after Hegelianism had begun to yield to Darwinian methods of thought, and this later growth has been progressively less Marxian and less positive. Marxism is now little more than a *pro forma* confession of faith. Avowed socialism is practically taking on the character described above, except so far as it has grown opportunist and has sought affiliation with the liberal democratic movement and the reformers.

the conservative critics, is involved in the presence of goods. (2) Ownership of the means of living is an inalienable right of man, ethically inevitable; the cancelment of property rights is felt to violate a fundamental principle of morals. All this, of course, proceeds on the assumption that the institution of ownership cannot be abrogated, as being an elemental function of human nature and an integral factor in the order of things in which human life belongs.

To the modern socialist all this is coming to be less and less convincing. In this respect there is a fairly well marked progressive change in the attitude of the professed socialists. Their position is progressively less capable of being formulated as a business proposition; their demands are progressively more difficult to state in the form of a pecuniary claim. The claim to the full product of labor, which once filled a large place in socialistic clamors and had a great carrying force during the earlier three-quarters of the nineteenth century, has gradually fallen into abeyance, both with the agitators and the adherents of the propaganda, during the last generation. To-day this claim is an afterthought in the advocate's presentation of socialism, more frequently than it is a point of departure for the argument, and it is made more of by the proselytes, who have carried the metaphysics of it over from the current common sense of the business community, than by the socialists of confirmed standing. The claim to the full product is an article of natural-rights dogma, and as such it is a reminiscence of the institutional situation from which socialism departs, rather than a feature of the prospective situation to which socialistic sentiment looks.

The like obsolescence of the sense of equity in ownership is visible in the attitude taken by strikers in the large, mechanically organized industries, outside of the ranks of avowed socialism. These strikers are less and less deterred by considerations of vested rights, property rights, owner's interests, and the like. The principle that a man may do what he will with his own is losing its binding force with large classes in the community, apparently because the spiritual ground on which rests the notion of "his own" is being cut away by the latter-day experience of these classes. Abridgment of proprietary discretion, confiscation of proprietary rights, is growing gradually less repugnant to the industrial populace; and the question of indemnity for eventual loss is more and more falling into neglect. With the socialistic element the question is not, what shall be done in the way of readjustment of property claims, but what is to be done to abolish them.[1]

[1] Where members of the well-to-do classes avow socialistic sentiments and ideals it commonly turns out to be a merely humanitarian

The question of equity or inequity in the distribution of wealth presumes the validity of ownership rights on some basis or other, or at least it presumes the validity of some basis on which the claims of ownership may be discussed. Ownership is the major premise of any argument as to the equity of distribution, and it is this major premise that is being forgotten by the classes among whom socialistic sentiment is gaining. Equity in this connection seems not to belong in the repertory of socialist concepts. It is at this point — the point of a common ground of argument — that the discrepancy occurs which stands in the way, not only of an eventual agreement between the socialists and their conservative critics, but even of their meeting one another's reasoning with any substantial effect. In the equipment of common-sense ideas on the basis of which the conservatives reason on this matter, there is included the conventional article of ownership, as a prime fact; in the common-sense basis of socialistic thinking this conventional premise has no secure place. There

aspiration for a more "equitable" redistribution of wealth, a readjustment of the scheme of ownership with some improved safeguarding of the "reasonable" property claims of all members of the community. What "socialist" reform commonly means to this contingent of well-to-do irregulars is some scheme of equal rights of ownership for all. Whereas to socialists of the line equal rights of ownership is as idle a proposition as an equal right of citizens to sell their votes. Instead of a reform of ownership the socialists contemplate the traceless disappearance of ownership.

is, therefore, a discrepancy in respect of the metaphysics underlying the knowledge and reasoning of the two parties to the controversy, and the outlook for a common understanding is accordingly vain. No substantial agreement upon a point of knowledge or conviction is possible between persons who proceed from disparate preconceptions.

Still the conservative reformers and the iconoclasts have a good deal in common. The prevalent habit of mind of both classes is a hybrid product of conventional principles and matter-of-fact insight. But these two contrasted grounds of opinion and aspiration are present in unequal degrees in the two contrasted classes; in the conservatives the conventional grounds of finality dominate and bear down the matter-of-fact knowledge of things, while the converse is true of the iconoclasts. Contrasted with earlier times and other cultural regions the consensus, the general drift, of the modern Western culture as a whole is of an iconoclastic character; while the class contrast here in question lies only within the range of this Western cultural consensus. As one or the other of the two contrasted proclivities — recourse to conventional precedents and recourse to matter-of-fact insight — gains and overbalances the other, the general cultural movement will drift toward a more conservative (archaic), conventional position or toward a more iconoclastic, materialistic position. During modern times the cultural drift has set in the latter direction. With due but not large exceptions, the effective body of the modern population has been growing more matter-of-fact in their thinking, less romantic, less idealistic in their aspirations, less bound by metaphysical considerations in their view of human relations, less mannerly, less devout.

The discrepancy between the conservatives and the iconoclasts need not be taken to mean that the two contrasted classes are moving in opposite directions, nor even in widely divergent directions. Neither class can properly be said to be reactionary.[1] Taken generally, both wings have been moving in the direction of a more impersonal, more matter-of-fact, less conventional point of view. In this composite cultural growth the matter-of-fact habit of mind has on the whole been gaining at the expense of the conventional, and the conventional premises that have been retained have also come to bear more of a matter-of-fact character,—as, *e.g.*, in the supersession of feudalistic or theocratic principles of law by natural rights. So that the position for which the effective body of conservatives now stand is not in substance a very archaic one. It is a more matter-of-fact position, less

[1] Unless it be in the latest extremes of conservatism, such as is shown in the recent success of dynastic politics in Germany, Tory policy in England, and predatory political ideals in America.

closely bound by authentic conventions, than the position effectively occupied by the iconoclastic wing a hundred years ago.

Throughout the modern cultural complex there is a somewhat variable, scattering shifting of ground to a more matter-of-fact basis. The direction of spiritual growth or change is much the same throughout the general body of the population; but the rate of change, the rate at which matter-of-fact ideals are superseding ideals of conventional authenticity, is not the same for all classes. Hence the class discrepancy here spoken of. The coefficient of change is so much larger in the vulgar, industrial classes as progressively to widen the cultural interval between them and the conservatives in the respect which is here in question. And the resulting discrepancy of institutional aims and ideals may have none the less serious consequences for being due to a differential rate of movement rather than to a divergent cultural trend.

In this differential rate of movement the departure from the ancient landmarks has now gone so far (or is reaching such a point) among the socialistic vulgar as to place their thinking substantially on a plane of material matter of fact, particularly as regards economic institutions. Whereas in the conservative classes the change is not yet large enough to take them off the plane of received conventional truth, particularly as regards economic institutions and such social questions as are of an economic complexion. In the case of the former this change in habit of mind has been so considerable as, in effect, to constitute a change in kind; crude matter of fact has come to be the dominant note of their attitude, and conventional authenticity has been relegated to a subsidiary place; that is to say, the change is of a revolutionary character. In the case of the conservative classes, so far as touches the institutional notions here under inquiry, the corresponding change has not yet gone so far as to amount to a change in kind; it is not of a revolutionary nature. The views current among the respectable classes on these matters still, in effect, run on the ancient levels on which were built up the pecuniary institutions about which the controversy circles. For the present there need be no apprehension that the more respectable classes will reach a mature revolutionary frame of mind. The discipline of their daily life does not, on the whole, favor such a result.

This, in substance, is also the view taken by the socialistic revolutionaries, particularly by those that are of Marxian antecedents. It is a point of conviction with them, though not wholly of reasoned conviction, that the socialistic movement is, in the nature of the case, a proletarian movement, in which the respectable, that is to say the pecuniarily competent, classes can have no organic part even if they try. It is held, in effect, that the well-to-do are, by force of their economic circumstances, incapable of assimilating the socialist ideas. The argument here set forth may serve to enforce this view, but with a difference. Instead of contrasting the well-to-do with the indigent, the line of demarcation between those available for the socialist propaganda and those not so available is rather to be drawn between the classes employed in the industrial and those employed in the pecuniary occupations. It is a question not so much of possessions as of employments; not of relative wealth, but of work. It is a question of work because it is a question of habits of thought, and work shapes the habits of thought. The socialists themselves construe the distinction to be a distinction in respect of habits of thought; and habits of thought are made by habits of life rather than by a legal relation to accumulated goods. This legal relation may count materially in shaping the animus of the several economic classes; but it appears not to be competent of itself to explain the limitations observable in the spread of socialistic sentiment.

The socialistic disaffection shows a curious tendency to overrun certain classes and to miss certain others. The men in the skilled mechanical trades are peculiarly liable to it, while at the extreme of immunity is probably the profession of the law. Bankers and other like classes of business men, together with clergymen and politicians, are also to be held free of serious aspersion; similarly, the great body of the rural population are immune, including the population of the country towns, and in an eminent degree the small farmers of the remoter country districts[1]; so also the delinquent classes of the cities and the populace of half-civilized and barbarous countries. The body of unskilled laborers, especially those not associated with the men in the skilled mechanical trades, are not seriously affected. The centres of socialistic disaffection are the more important industrial towns, and the effective nucleus of the socialistic malcontents is made up of the more intelligent body of workmen in the highly organized and specialized industries. Not that socialism does not spread in virulent form outside this narrow range, but at a farther remove from the centre of dispersion it appears rather sporadically and uncertainly, while within this field it is fairly endemic. As regards the educated classes, socialistic views are particularly likely to crop out among the men in the material sciences.

[1] Socialistic notions are apparently making some inroads among the rural population of the American prairie region, where a mechanically organized and standardized method of farming prevails, with a large use of mechanical appliances.

The advocates of the new creed have made little headway among the rural classes of Europe, whether peasant farmers or farm laborers. The rural proletariat has hitherto proved virtually impermeable.[1] The discipline of their daily life leaves their spirit undisturbed on the plane of conventionality and anthropomorphism, and the changes to which they aspire lie within the scope of the conventionalities which have grown out of these circumstances of their life and which express the habit of mind enforced by these circumstances.

Without claiming that this explanation is competent to cover the case of socialism in all its bearings, it may be pointed out that this socialistic bias has effectively spread among the people only within the last quarter of a century, which is also approximately the period since which the machine process and the mechanical standardization of industry has reached its fuller development, both as regards the extent of its field and as regards the extent of its technological requirements; that it is found in vigorous growth only in those communities and partic-

[1] So striking has been the failure of the German socialists, for instance, in their attempts upon the integrity of the farming community, that they have latterly changed their tactics, and instead of attempting to convert the peasants to a full socialistic programme, they have turned to measures of compromise, in which the characteristic and revolutionary features of the socialistic programme are softened beyond recognition, if not suppressed. The habits of life, and therefore the habits of thought, of the peasant farmers move on the ancient levels of handicraft, pecuniary management, personal consequence, and prescriptive custom.

ularly among those classes whose life is closely regulated by the machine technology; and that the discipline of this machine technology is peculiarly designed to inculcate such iconoclastic habits of thought as come to a head in the socialistic bias. Socialism, in so far as the term means the subversion of the economic foundations of modern culture, occurs only sporadically and dubiously outside the limits, in time and space, of the discipline of the machine technology. While among those classes whose everyday life schools them to do their habitual serious thinking in terms of material cause and effect, the preconceptions of ownership are apparently becoming obsolescent through disuse and through supersession by other methods of apprehending things.[1]

[1] If this account of the class limitation of the socialist bias is accepted, it has an immediate bearing upon a question which is latterly engaging the attention of the advocates of socialism. The question is as to the part played by propertyless office employees and by the business men whom the modern consolidations of business reduce to the position of salaried managers and superintendents. With a faith prompted by their own hopes rather than by observed facts or by the logic of events, the spokesmen for socialism are strongly inclined to claim this "business proletariat" as a contingent which the course of economic development is bound to throw into the socialist camp. The facts do not in any appreciable degree countenance such an expectation. The unpropertied classes employed in business do not take to socialistic vagaries with such alacrity as should inspire a confident hope in the advocates of socialism or a serious apprehension in those who stand for law and order. This pecuniarily disfranchised business population, in its revulsion against unassimilated facts, turns rather to some excursion into pragmatic romance, such as Social Settlements, Prohibition, Clean Politics, Single Tax, Arts and Crafts, Neighborhood Guilds, Institutional Church, Christian Science, New

But the machine technology not only trains the workmen into materialistic iconoclasm, it has also a selective effect. Persons endowed with propensities and aptitudes of a materialistic, matter-of-fact kind are drafted into the mechanical employments, and such are also peculiarly available socialistic material. Aptitude for the matter-of-fact work of the machine technology means, in a general way, ineptitude for an uncritical acceptance of institutional truths. It is probable, therefore, that the apparent facility with which the mechanical employments (and the material sciences) induce a socialistic or iconoclastic bent is to be set down in part to the fact that the human material in these employments is picked material, peculiarly amen-

Thought, or some such cultural thimblerig. The work of the captain of industry in curtailing the range of individual discretion in business and in reducing the lesser undertakers to the rank of clerks and subalterns need not be looked upon as unavoidably furthering the spread of the socialistic bias, except in so far as the change results in throwing the men affected by it out of the pecuniary or business occupations and subjecting them to the discipline of the mechanical industry. At the most, apparently, the change from an independent to a dependent business life serves to weaken the men's interest in the question of property; it does not appear that it throws them into an attitude of substantial distrust or iconoclasm. Their interest in this particular institution slackens through the loss of that emulative motive on which pecuniary endeavor proceeds, but their faith in its intrinsic fitness is not thereby shaken, nor are they thrown into the ranks of the chronic dissentients. The training given by their life continues prevailingly to run on conventional grounds; that is to say, on grounds of legal relation, solvency, and the like. Accountants and office employees are nearly as conservative as clergymen and lawyers, and their being so is apparently due to the fact that their experience runs on much the same ground of conventional finality.

able to this discipline. There is a sifting of the working classes, whereby the socialistic and mechanically capable are roughly segregated out from the rest and subjected to the iconoclastic discipline of the mechanical employments and matter-of-fact thinking; while the residue, which is on the whole made up of the persons that are relatively least capable of revolutionary socialism, is at the same time less exposed to the discipline that might fit them for the socialistic movement. This sifting is, of course, a rough one, and leaves many exceptions both ways.

In the light of this consideration, then, it is to be noted: (1) that the dominance of the machine process in modern industry is not so potent a factor for the inculcation of socialistic notions — it does not so irresistibly shape men's habit of mind in the socialistic sense — as the first survey of the facts would suggest; and (2) that the differentiation of occupations involved in modern industrial methods selectively bunches the socialistic elements together, and so heightens their sense of class solidarity and acts to accentuate their bias, gives consistency to their ideals, and induces that boldness of conviction and action which is to be had only in a compact body of men.

But in either case, whether the visible outcome is chiefly due to their selective or to their disciplinary effect, the bearing of the industrial occupations upon the growth of socialism seems equally close and undeniable. The two modes of influence seem to converge to the outcome indicated above, and for the purpose of the present inquiry a detailed tracing out of the two strands of sequence in the case neither can nor need be undertaken.[1]

With such generality as commonly holds in statements of this kind, it may be said that the modern socialistic disaffection is loosely bound up with the machine industry — spreading where this industry spreads and flourishing where this indus-

[1] Connected with this apparent selective action which the modern specialization of occupations exerts, there is a further, and at first sight more singular, point of disparity between the socialists and the conservatives; and this difference has also a curious correlation with the distribution of the machine industry. In a degree, — slight and uncertain, perhaps, but scarcely to be mistaken, — the socialists and the conservatives are apparently of different racial antecedents. It has been seen above that the propaganda is most vital and widespread in the industrial towns, as contrasted with the agricultural country. But if the researches of such students as Ammon, Ripley, Lapouge, Closson, and others that might be named, are taken at their face value, it appears that the towns differ perceptibly from the open country in point of race; and that the migration from the country into the industrial towns has a selective effect of such a kind that a larger proportion of one racial stock than of another resorts to the towns. The towns, in those countries where data are available, show a larger admixture of the dolicho-blond stock than the open country. This seems to argue that the dolicho-blond stock, or the racial mixture of the towns in which there is a relatively large admixture of the dolicho-blond, is perceptibly more efficient in the machine industries, more readily inclined to think in materialistic terms, more given to radical innovation, less bound by convention and prescription. This generalization is strengthened by the fact that the more dolicho-blond regions are also, on the whole, more socialistic than those in which this element is less in evidence. At the same time they are industrially in advance of the latter in the matter of machine industry; and they are also Protestant (irreligious) rather than Catholic.

try gives the dominant note of life. The correlation between the two phenomena is of such a kind as to leave no doubt that they are causally connected; which means either that the machine industry, directly or indirectly, gives rise to socialism, or that the two are expressions of the same complex of causes. The former statement probably expresses the truth of the case in great part, but the latter need not therefore be false. Wherever and in so far as the increase and diffusion of knowledge has made the machine process and the mechanical technology the tone-giving factor in men's scheme of thought, there modern socialistic iconoclasm follows by easy consequence.

The socialistic bias primarily touches economic institutions proper. But that is not the whole of it. When the term is used without modifying phrase it carries a certain implication touching other than primarily economic matters. The political bias of this unmitigated socialism is always radically democratic, to the extent that these socialists are in a high degree intolerant of any monarchical, aristocratic, or other prescriptive government. The state is doomed in the socialistic view.[1] The

[1] This, of course, does not hold for the inoffensive pseudo-socialistic diversions set afoot by various well-meaning politicians and clergymen, known by various qualifying designations, such as "State," "Christian," "Catholic," etc., and designed to act as correctives of the socialistic distemper..

socialist antagonism to the state takes various forms and goes to varying degrees of intemperance, but it is consistently negative. Except in their destructively hostile attitude to existing political organizations, the socialists have nothing consistent to offer on the head of political institutions, less, indeed, latterly than in the earlier days of the propaganda. There seems to be a growing shiftlessness of opinion on this head; one gets the impression that the sense of the socialist malcontents, as near as it may be permissible to use that word in this connection, is that the community can best get along without political institutions.

There is a like departure from the ancient norms touching domestic relations. This is not confined to those portions of the community that avowedly affect socialistic views, although it has, on the whole, gone farthest among the classes among whom the socialistic views prevail. There is a visible weakening of the family ties, a disintegration of the conventions of household life, throughout large classes. The defection is even felt, by sensitive and solicitous persons, to be of such grave proportions as to threaten the foundations of domestic life and morality. This disintegration of the family ties shows itself most alarmingly among the socialistic classes, with whom it all wears such an air of unconcern as argues that in this respect they are incorrigible. To these the conventional form of the household has in good part ceased to appeal as something sacred. It is no longer one of their secure spiritual assets.

What appears to be in jeopardy, should this socialistic defection gain ground, is the headship of the male in the household economy. The family, as it has come down from the mediæval past, under the shelter of the church, is of a patriarchal constitution, at least in theory. The man has been vested with discretionary control in domestic affairs. In the earlier days his discretion was very direct and full, comprising corporal coercion. Latterly, after and so far as mastery and servitude have passed off the field and natural rights have come to rule, this direct coercive control has been superseded by a pecuniary discretion; so that the male head of the household is alone competent to exercise a proprietary control of household affairs. This latter-day conventional headship of the man is now in its turn beginning to lose the respect of a good share of the populace. The disintegration of the patriarchal tradition has gone farthest among those industrial classes who are at the same time inclined to socialistic views.

At this point in the institutional structure, as well as at other points where the industrial classes are giving evidence of a loss of spiritual ground, there is little indication of a constructive movement toward any specific arrangement to take the place of the institution whose existence is threatened. There is a loosening of the bonds, a weakening of conviction as to the full truth and beauty of the received domestic institutions, without much of a consensus as to what is to be done about it, if anything. In this, as at other junctures of a similar kind, the mechanically employed classes, trained to matter-of-fact habits of thought, show a notable lack of spontaneity in the construction of new myths or conventions as well as in the reconstruction of the old.

All this disintegration of the spiritual foundations of our domestic institutions spreads with the most telling effect, because most heedlessly, among the population of the industrial towns. But it spreads also outside the limits of the industrial classes; for the habits of life and of thought inculcated by the machine technology are not limited to them, even if these classes are the ones who suffer most and most severely from the machine discipline. The disintegration shows itself, in varying degree, in all modern industrial communities, and it is visible somewhat in proportion as the community is modern and industrial. The machine is a leveller, a vulgarizer, whose end seems to be the extirpation of all that is respectable, noble, and dignified in human intercourse and ideals.

What happens within the narrow range of the institutions of domestic life repeats itself in substance in the larger field of national life and ideals. Fealty to a superior installed by law or custom suffers under the discipline of a life which, as regards its most formative exigencies, is not guided by conventional grounds of validity. And the transmuted form of fealty called patriotism is in much the same insecure case. The new ground of class solidarity and antagonism, for which these extreme spokesmen of the industrial régime stand, is neither ecclesiastic, dynastic, territorial, nor linguistic; it is industrial and materialistic. But in their attitude of heedlessness toward the dynastic and national conventions the socialists are merely the extreme exponents of the spirit of the age in the modern industrial communities.

So, again, as regards the religious life. Men trained by the mechanical occupations to materialistic, industrial habits of thought are beset with a growing inability to appreciate, or even to apprehend, the meaning of religious appeals that proceed on the old-fashioned grounds of metaphysical validity. The consolations of a personal relation (of subservience) to a supernatural master do not appeal to men whose habit of life is shaped by a familiarity with the relations of impersonal cause and effect, rather than by relations of personal dominance and fealty. It does not come as a matter of course for such men to give the catechism's answer to the question, What is the chief end of man? Nor do they instinctively feel themselves to be sinners by virtue of a congenital, hereditary taint or obliquity. Indeed, they can only with great difficulty be seriously persuaded that they are sinners at all. They are in danger of losing the point of view of sin. The relation of status or fealty involved in the concept of sin is becoming alien to their habit of mind. They are therefore slow to realize that their past life has violated such a relation of fealty, on the one hand, and that it is of vital consequence to reëstablish such a relation of status by a work of salvation or redemption. The kindly ministrations of the church and the clergy grate on the sensibilities of men so trained, as being so much ado about nothing. The machine, their master, is no respecter of persons and knows neither morality nor dignity nor prescriptive right, divine or human; its teaching is training them into insensibility of the whole range of concepts on which these ministrations proceed.[1]

Not alone in the direction of growth given to vulgar sentiment and to the vulgar insight into facts is the matter-of-fact discipline of the machine technology apparent, but also in the scope and

[1] The cultural era of Natural Rights, Natural Liberty, and Natural Religion reduced God to the rank of a "Great Artificer," and the machine technology is, in turn, relegating Him to that fringe of minor employments and those outlying industrial regions to which the handicraftsmen have been retired.

method of that scientific knowledge that has had the vogue since the advent of the machine industry. Scientific inquiry is directed to a different end and carried out under the guidance of a different range of principles or preconceptions in the modern industrial communities than in earlier days or in cultural centres lying outside the machine's dominion. Modern science is single-minded in its pursuit of impersonal relations of causal sequence in the phenomena with which it is occupied.

The line of descent of this matter-of-fact modern science is essentially British, as is that of the machine technology and of the characteristically modern civil and political institutions. It is true, beginnings of the modern scientific movement were made in Italy in the days of the Renaissance, and Central Europe had its share in the enlightenment; but these early modern risings of the scientific spirit presently ran into the sand, when war, politics, and religion reasserted their sway in the south of Europe. Similar tentative stirrings of matter-of-fact thought were had in Spain and France before and during the early phases of the state-making era; but here, again, war and politics rendered these onsets nearly nugatory, so that the intellectual output was more speculation than science. In the Low Countries something similar holds true, with a larger qualification. The British community made a later and slower start, coming out of barbarism at a later date and with a heavier handicap of physical obstructions. But being, relatively, sheltered from war and politics, the British were able to take up the fund of scientific gains made by the South-European men of workday insight, to turn it to account and to carry it over the era of state-making and so prepare the way for the modern scientific, technological era.

Of course, nothing but the most meagre and sketchiest outline of this matter is practicable in this place, and even that only in its relation to the machine industry during the past one hundred years or so. What is said above of the British lead in modern science may perhaps be questioned, and it is not necessary for the present purpose to insist on its truth; but so much seems beyond hazard as that the lead in the material sciences lay with the British through the early machine age, and that the provenance of this modern scientific research to-day does not extend, in any pronounced degree, beyond those communities that lie within the area of the modern machine industry.

In time and space the prevalence of the modern materialistic science is roughly coextensive with that of the machine process. It is, no doubt, related to it both as cause and as effect; but that its relation to modern industry is more that of effect than cause seems at least broadly suggested by the decay which presently overtook scientific research, *e.g.*, in the south of Europe when those peoples turned their attention from material to spiritual and political affairs.[1]

What is of immediate interest is the change that has come over the scope and method of scientific research since the dominance of the machine process, in comparison with what preceded the coming of the machine age. The beginnings of modern science are older than the industrial revolution; the principles of scientific research (causal explanation and exact measurement) antedate the régime of the machine process. But a change has taken place in the postulates and animus of scientific research since modern science first began, and this change in the postulates of scientific knowledge is related to the growth of the machine technology.

It is unnecessary here to hark back to that scholastic science or philosophy that served as an intellectual expression of the ecclesiastical and political culture of the Middle Ages. Its character, as compared with later science, is sufficiently notorious. By the change from scholastic knowledge to modern science, to the extent to which the change was carried through, the principle (habit of

[1] There is a similar suggestion in the relative (slight but perceptible) decline of scientific animus in England since the English community has turned its attention and aspirations to imperialistic feats of prowess more than to industrial matters.

mind) of adequate cause was substituted for that of sufficient reason. The law of causation as it is found at work, in the maturer science of the eighteenth and early nineteenth centuries, comprises two distinguishable postulates: (1) equality (quantitative equivalence) of cause and effect; and (2) similarity (qualitative equivalence) of cause and effect. The former may, without forcing it, be referred to commercial accountancy as its analogue in practical life and as the probable cultural ground out of which the habit of insisting on an inviolable quantitative equivalence gathered consistency. The ascendancy of the latter seems in a similar manner to be referable to the prevalence of handicraft as its cultural ground. Stated negatively, it asserts that nothing appears in the effect but what was contained in the cause, in a manner which suggests the rule that nothing appears in the product of handicraft but what was present in the skill of the artificer. "Natural causes," which are made much of in this middle period of modern science, are conceived to work according to certain "natural laws." These natural laws, laws of the "normal course" of things, are felt to tend to a rational end and to have something of a coercive force. So that Nature makes no mistakes, Nature does nothing in vain, Nature takes the most economical course to its end, Nature makes no jumps, etc. Under this law of natural causation every effect must have a cause which resembles it in the particular respect which claims the inquirer's attention. Among other consequences of this view it follows that, since the details as well as the whole of the material universe are construed to show adaptation to a preconceived end, this "natural order" of things must be the outcome of preëxistent design residing in the "first cause," which is postulated by virtue of this imputed design and is designated the "Great Artificer." There is an element of conation in this original modern postulate of cause and effect. The shadow of the artificer, with his intelligence and manual skill, is forever in the background of the concepts of natural law. The "cause" dealt with in a given case is not thought of as an effect; and the effect is treated as a finality, not as a phase of a complex sequence of causation. When such a sequence is under inquiry, as in the earlier, pre-Darwinian theories of evolution, it is not handled as a cumulative sequence whose character may blindly change from better to worse, or conversely, at any point; but rather as an unfolding of a certain prime cause in which is contained, implicitly, all that presently appears in explicit form.

In the conception of the causal relation as it may be seen at work a hundred years ago, cause and effect are felt to stand over against one another, so that the cause controls, determines the effect by transmitting its own character to it. The cause is the producer, the effect the product. Relatively little emphasis or interest falls upon the process out of which the product emerges; the interest being centred upon the latter and its relation to the efficient cause out of which it has come. The theories constructed under the guidance of this conception are generalizations as to an equivalence between the producing cause and the effect-product. The cause "makes" the effect, in much the same sense as the craftsman is apprehended to make the article on which he is engaged. There is a felt distinction between the cause and the environing circumstances, much as there is between the workman on the one hand and his tools and materials on the other hand. The intervening process is simply the manner of functioning of the efficient cause, much as the workman's work is the functioning of the workman in the interval between the inception and the completion of the product. The effect is subsequent to the cause, as the workman's product is subsequent to and consequent upon his putting forth his productive efficiency. It is a relation of before and after, in which the process comes in for attention as covering and accounting for the time interval which, in analogy with workmanlike endeavor, is required for the functioning of the efficient cause.[1]

[1] Compare, however, Sombart, *Kapitalismus*, especially vol. I. ch. VIII and XV. Sombart finds the modern scientific concept of

But as time passes and habituation to the exigencies of the machine technology gains in range and consistency, the quasi-personal, handicraft conception of causation decays, — first and most notably in those material, inorganic sciences that stand in the closest relation to the mechanical technology, but presently also in the organic sciences, and even in the moral sciences. The machine technology is a mechanical or material process, and requires the attention to be centred upon this process and the exigencies of the process. In such a process no one factor stands out as unequivocally the efficient cause in the case, whose personal char-

cause and effect to be essentially an outcome of the discipline of accountancy enforced by business traffic. So that he makes business enterprise rather than mechanical industry accountable for the rise of modern science and for the matter-of-fact character which distinguishes this science. In this view there is, no doubt, a large and valuable element of truth. To the end of a mathematical formulation of causal phenomena as well as a tenacious grasp of the principle of quantitative equivalence, the accountancy enforced by the petty trade of early modern times, as well as by commercial traffic proper, appears to have given the most effective training. In so far as this element of quantitative equivalence, simply, has dominated the growth of science, it has given, as its most perfect product, Positivism. Positivism flourished at its best and freest in France, where the modern economic culture was commercial rather than mechanical. And when the machine discipline seriously invaded France, Positivism languished and died. But modern science is not a calculus simply. It deals not with calculations of quantitative equivalence only, but with efficient causes, active relations, creative forces. The concept of efficient cause is not a derivative of accountancy, nor is it formed in the image of accountancy. But this generic concept of efficient cause, the kinetic concept, antedates Positivism and has outlived it. In its earlier (eighteenth-century) phase this concept shows close relationship with the notion of workmanship, in its later (nineteenth-century) use it has much in common with the notion of mechanical efficiency.

acter, so to speak, is transfused into the product, and to whose workings the rest of the complex of causes are related only as subsidiary or conditioning circumstances. To the technologist the process comes necessarily to count, not simply as the interval of functioning of an initial efficient cause, but as the substantial fact that engages his attention. He learns to think in terms of the process, rather than in terms of a productive cause and a product between which the process intervenes in such a manner as to afford a transition from one to the other. The process is always complex; always a delicately balanced interplay of forces that work blindly, insensibly, heedlessly; in which any appreciable deviation may forthwith count in a cumulative manner, the further consequences of which stand in no organic relation to the purpose for which the process has been set going. The prime efficient cause falls, relatively, into the background and yields precedence to the process as the point of technological interest.

This machine technology, with its accompanying discipline in mechanical adaptations and object-lessons, came on gradually and rose to a dominating place in the cultural environment during the closing years of the eighteenth and the course of the nineteenth century; and as fast as men learned to think in terms of technological process, they went on at an accelerated pace in the further invention of mechanical processes, so that from that time the progress of inventions has been of a cumulative character and has cumulatively heightened the disciplinary force of the machine process. This early technological advance, of course, took place in the British community, where the machine process first gained headway and where the discipline of a prevalent machine industry inculcated thinking in terms of the machine process. So also it was in the British community that modern science fell into the lines marked out by technological thinking and began to formulate its theories in terms of process rather than in terms of prime causes and the like. While something of this kind is noticeable relatively early in some of the inorganic sciences, as, *e.g.*, Geology, the striking and decisive move in this direction was taken toward the middle of the century by Darwin and his contemporaries.[1] Without much preliminary exposition and without feeling himself to be out of touch with his contemporaries, Darwin set to work to explain species in terms of the process out of which they have arisen, rather than out of the prime cause to which the distinction between them may be due.[2] Denying nothing as to the substantial services of the

[1] Darwin, of course, does not stand alone. He is the great exponent of a mass movement which involves a shifting of the point of veiw and of the point of interest in scientific research and speculation.

[2] This is the substance of Darwin's advance over Lamarck, for instance.

Great Artificer in the development of species, he simply and naïvely left Him out of the scheme, because, as being a personal factor, He could not be stated and handled in terms of process. So Darwin offered a tentative account of the descent of man, without recourse to divine or human directive endeavor and without inquiry as to whence man ultimately came and why, or as to what fortune would ultimately overtake him. His inquiry characteristically confines itself to the process of cumulative change. His results, as well as his specific determination of the factors at work in this process of cumulative change, have been questioned; perhaps they are open to all the criticisms levelled against them as well as to a few more not yet thought of; but the scope and method given to scientific inquiry by Darwin and the generation whose spokesman he is has substantially not been questioned, except by that diminishing contingent of the faithful who by force of special training or by native gift are not amenable to the discipline of the machine process. The characteristically modern science does not inquire about prime causes, design in nature, desirability of effects, ultimate results, or eschatological consequences.

Of the two postulates of earlier modern science, — the quantitative equivalence and the qualitative equivalence of cause and effect, — the former has come practically to signify the balanced articulation of the process of cumulative change; the endeavor of the Positivists to erect this canon of quantitative equivalence into the sole canon of scientific truth, and so to reduce scientific theory to a system of accountancy, having failed. The latter thesis, that like causes produce like effects, or that the effect is, in some sense, of the same character as the cause, has fallen into decay as holding true only in such tenuously general terms as to leave it without particular force. The scientists are learning more and more consistently to think in the opaque, impersonal terms of strains, mechanical structures, displacement, and the like; terms which are convertible into the working drawings and specifications of the mechanical engineer.

The older preconceptions are, of course, not wholly eliminated from the intellectual apparatus of scientific research and generalization. The cultural situation whose discipline gives the outcome is made up of inherited traditional notions at least as much as of the notions brought in by the machine process. Even among the scientific adepts there has been no complete break with the past; necessarily not, since they are, after all, creatures of their own generation. Many of them, but more especially those who are engaged in upholding the authentic results of scientific research, are somewhat prone to make much of the definitive results achieved, rather than of the process of research in which these results are provisional appliances of work. And many of these, together with the great part of those well-meaning persons who exploit the sciences for purposes of edification, such as clergymen and naturalistic myth-makers, still personify the process of cause and effect and find in it a well-advised meliorative trend. But that work of research which effectually extends the borders of scientific knowledge is nearly all done under the guidance of highly impersonal, mechanical, morally and æsthetically colorless conceptions of causal sequence. And this scientific work is carried out only in those communities which are in due contact with the modern mechanically organized industrial system, — only under the shadow of the machine technology.

In the nature of the case the cultural growth dominated by the machine industry is of a sceptical, matter-of-fact complexion, materialistic, unmoral, unpatriotic, undevout. The growth of habits of thought, in the industrial regions and centres particularly, runs in this direction; but hitherto there has enough of the ancient norms of Western Christendom remained intact to make a very respectable protest against that deterioration of the cultural tissues which the ferment of the machine industry unremittingly pushes on. The machine discipline, however, touches wider and wider circles of the population, and touches them in an increasingly intimate and coercive manner. In the nature of the case, therefore, the resistance opposed to this cultural trend given by the machine discipline on grounds of received conventions weakens with the passage of time. The spread of materialistic, matter-of-fact preconceptions takes place at a cumulatively accelerating rate, except in so far as some other cultural factor, alien to the machine discipline, comes in to inhibit its spread and keep its disintegrating influence within bounds.

[6]

The Place of Science in Modern Civilization

Thorstein Bunde Veblen, 'The Place of Science in Modern Civilization', *American Journal of Sociology*, vol. 11 (1906), pp. 585–609; reprinted in *The Place of Science in Modern Civilization* (New York: Viking Press, 1919) ; reprinted, New Brunswick: Transactions, 1990, pp. 1–31.

Veblen's unique approach to institutions and culture is perhaps nowhere deployed more effectively than in his analysis of the culture of science and of the impact of science, and of scientific modes of thought, on culture itself. Here we have the matter-of-fact contrasted to the teleological mode of thought, with telling consequences for conventional habits of thought.

THE PLACE OF SCIENCE IN MODERN CIVILIZATION

THORSTEIN VEBLEN
The University of Chicago

It is commonly held that modern Christendom is superior to any and all other systems of civilized life. Other ages and other cultural regions are by contrast spoken of as lower, or more archaic, or less mature. The claim is that the modern culture is superior on the whole, not that it is the best or highest in all respects and at every point. It has, in fact, not an all-around superiority, but a superiority within a closely limited range of intellectual activities, while outside this range many other civilizations surpass that of the modern occidental peoples. But the peculiar excellence of the modern culture is of such a nature as to give it a decisive practical advantage over all other cultural schemes that have gone before or that have come into competition with it. It has proved itself fit to survive in a struggle for existence as against those civilizations which differ from it in respect of its distinctive traits.

Modern civilization is peculiarly matter-of-fact. It contains many elements that are not of this character, but these other elements do not belong exclusively or characteristically to it. The modern civilized peoples are in a peculiar degree capable of an impersonal, dispassionate insight into the material facts with which mankind has to deal. The apex of cultural growth is at this point. Compared with this trait the rest of what is comprised in the cultural scheme is adventitious, or at the best it is a by-product of this hard-headed apprehension of facts. This quality may be a matter of habit or of racial endowment, or it may be an outcome of both; but whatever be the explanation of its prevalence, the immediate consequence is much the same for the growth of civilization. A civilization which is dominated by this matter-of-fact insight must prevail against any cultural scheme that lacks this element. This characteristic of western civilization comes to a head in modern science, and it finds its highest material expression in the technology of the machine industry. In these things modern culture is creative and self-sufficient; and these being given, the rest of what may seem characteristic in western civilization follows by easy consequence. The cultural structure clusters about this body of matter-of-fact knowledge as its substantial core. Whatever is not consonant with these opaque creations of science is an intrusive feature in the modern scheme, borrowed or standing over from the barbarian past.

Other ages and other peoples excel in other things and are known by other virtues. In creative art, as well as in critical taste, the faltering talent of Christendom can at the best follow the lead of the ancient Greeks and the Japanese. In deft workmanship the handicraftsmen of the middle Orient, as well as of the Far East, stand on a level securely above the highest European achievement, old or new. In myth-making, folklore, and occult symbolism many of the lower barbarians have achieved things beyond what the latter-day priests and poets know how to propose. In metaphysical insight and dialectical versatility many orientals, as well as the Schoolmen of the Middle Ages, easily surpass the highest reaches of the New Thought and the Higher Criticism. In a shrewd sense of the religious verities, as well as in an unsparing faith in devout observances, the people of India or Thibet, or even the mediæval Christians, are past-masters in comparison even with the select of the faith of modern times. In political finesse, as well as in unreasoning, brute loyalty, more than one of the ancient peoples give evidence of a capacity to which no modern civilized nation may aspire. In warlike malevolence and abandon, the hosts of Islam, the Sioux Indian, and the "heathen of the northern sea" have set the mark above the reach of the most strenuous civilized warlord.

To modern civilized men, especially in their intervals of sober reflection, all these things that distinguish the barbarian civilizations seem of dubious value and are required to show cause why they should not be slighted. It is not so with the knowledge of facts. The making of states and dynasties, the founding of families, the prosecution of feuds, the propagation of creeds and the creation of sects, the accumulation of fortunes, the consumption of superfluities—these have all in their time been felt to justify themselves as an end of endeavor; but in the eyes of modern civilized men all these things seem futile in comparison with the achievements of science. They dwindle in men's esteem as time passes, while the achievements of science are held higher as time passes. This is the one secure holding-ground of latter-day conviction, that "the increase and diffusion of knowledge among men" is indefeasibly right and good. When seen in such perspective as will clear it of the trivial perplexities of workday life, this proposition is not questioned within the horizon of the western culture, and no other cultural ideal holds a similar unquestioned place in the convictions of civilized mankind.

On any large question which is to be disposed of for good and all the final appeal is by common consent taken to the scientist. The solution offered in the name of science is decisive so long as it is not set aside by a still more searching scientific inquiry. This state of things may not be altogether fortunate, but such is the fact. There are other, older grounds of finality that may conceivably be better, nobler, worthier, more profound, more beautiful. It might conceivably be preferable, as a matter of cultural ideals, to leave the last word with the lawyer, the duelist, the priest, the moralist, or the college of heraldry. In past times people have been content to leave their weightiest questions to the decision of some one or other of these tribunals, and, it cannot be denied, with very happy results in those respects that were then looked to with the greatest solicitude. But whatever the common-sense of earlier generations may have held in this respect, modern common-sense holds that the scientist's answer is the only ultimately true one. In the last resort enlightened common-sense sticks by the opaque truth and refuses to go behind the returns given by the tangible facts.

Quasi lignum vitae in paradiso Dei, et quasi lucerna fulgoris in domo Domini, such is the place of science in modern civilization. This latter-day faith in matter-of-fact knowledge may be well grounded or it may not. It has come about that men assign it this high place, perhaps idolatrously, perhaps to the detriment of the best and most intimate interests of the race. There is room for much more than a vague doubt that this cult of science is not altogether a wholesome growth—that the unmitigated quest of knowledge, of this matter-of-fact kind, makes for race-deterioration and discomfort on the whole, both in its immediate effects upon the spiritual life of mankind, and in the material consequences that follow from a great advance in matter-of-fact knowledge.

But we are not here concerned with the merits of the case. The question here is: How has this cult of science arisen? What are its cultural antecedents? How far is it in consonance with hereditary human nature? and, What is the nature of its hold on the convictions of civilized men?

In dealing with pedagogical problems and the theory of education, current psychology is nearly at one in saying that all learning is of a "pragmatic" character; that knowledge is inchoate action inchoately directed to an end; that all knowledge is "functional;" that it is of the nature of use. This, of course, is only a corollary under the main postulate of the latter-day psychologists, whose catchword is that The Idea is essentially active. There is no need of quarreling with this "pragmatic" school of psychologists. Their aphorism may not contain the whole truth, perhaps, but at least it goes nearer to the heart of the epistemological problem than any earlier formulation. It may confidently be said to do so because, for one thing, its argument meets the requirements of modern science. It is such a concept as matter-of-fact science can make effective use of; it is drawn in terms which are, in the last analysis, of an impersonal, not to say tropismatic, character; such as is demanded by science, with its insistence on opaque cause and effect. While knowledge is construed in teleological terms, in terms of personal interest and attention, this teleological aptitude is itself reducible to a product of unteleological natural selection. The teleological bent of intelligence is a hereditary trait settled upon the race by the selective action of forces that look to no end. The foundations of pragmatic intelligence are not pragmatic, nor even personal or sensible.

This impersonal character of intelligence is, of course, most evident on the lower levels of life. If we follow Mr. Loeb, e. g., in his inquiries into the psychology of that life that lies below the threshold of intelligence, what we meet with is an aimless but unwavering motor response to stimulus.[1] The response is of the nature of motor impulse, and in so far it is "pragmatic," if that term may fairly be applied to so rudimentary a phase of sensibility. The responding organism may be called an "agent" in so far. It is only by a figure of speech that these terms are made to apply to tropismatic reactions. Higher in the scale of sensibility and nervous complication instincts work to a somewhat similar outcome. On the human plane, intelligence (the selective effect of inhibitive complication) may throw the response into the form of a reasoned line of conduct looking to an outcome that shall be expedient for the agent. This is naïve pragmatism of the developed kind. There is no longer a question but that the responding organism is an "agent," and that his intelligent response to stimulus is of a teleological character. But that is not all. The inhibitive nervous complication may also detach another chain of response to the given stimulus, which does not spend itself in a line of motor conduct and does not fall into a system of uses. Pragmatically speaking, this outlying chain of response is unintended and irrelevant. Except in urgent cases, such an idle response seems commonly to be present as a subsidiary phenomenon. If credence is given to the view

[1] Jacques Loeb, *Heliotropismus der Thiere* and *Comparative Psychology and Physiology of the Brain.*

that intelligence is, in its elements, of the nature of an inhibitive selection, it seems necessary to assume some such chain of idle and irrelevant response to account for the further course of the elements eliminated in giving the motor response the character of a reasoned line of conduct. So that associated with the pragmatic attention there is found more or less of an irrelevant attention, or idle curiosity. This is more particularly the case where a higher range of intelligence is present. This idle curiosity is, perhaps, closely related to the aptitude for play, observed both in man and in the lower animals.[2] The aptitude for play, as well as the functioning of idle curiosity, seems peculiarly lively in the young, whose aptitude for sustained pragmatism is at the same time relatively vague and unreliable.

This idle curiosity formulates its response to stimulus, not in terms of an expedient line of conduct, nor even necessarily in a chain of motor activity, but in terms of the sequence of activities going on in the observed phenomena. The "interpretation" of the facts under the guidance of this idle curiosity may take the form of anthropomorphic or animistic explanations of the "conduct" of the objects observed. The interpretation of the facts takes a dramatic form. The facts are conceived in an animistic way, and a pragmatic animus is imputed to them. Their behavior is construed as a reasoned procedure on their part looking to the advantage of these animistically conceived objects, or looking to the achievement of some end which these objects are conceived to have at heart for reasons of their own.

Among the savage and lower barbarian peoples there is commonly current a large body of knowledge organized in this way into myths and legends, which need have no pragmatic value for the learner of them and no intended bearing on his conduct of practical affairs. They may come to have a practical value imputed to them as a ground of superstitious observances, but they may also not.[3] All students of the lower cultures are aware of

[2] Cf. Gross, *Spiele der Thiere*, chap. 2 (esp. pp. 65–76), and chap. 5; *The Play of Man*, Part III, sec. 3; Spencer, *Principles of Psychology*, secs. 533-35.

[3] The myths and legendary lore of the Eskimo, the Pueblo Indians, and some tribes of the northwest coast afford good instances of such idle creations. Cf. various *Reports* of the Bureau of American Ethnology; also, e. g., Tylor, *Primitive Culture*, esp. the chapters on "Mythology" and "Animism."

the dramatic character of the myths current among these peoples, and they are also aware that, particularly among the peaceable communities, the great body of mythical lore is of an idle kind, as having very little intended bearing on the practical conduct of those who believe in these myth-dramas. The myths on the one hand, and the workday knowledge of uses, materials, appliances, and expedients on the other hand, may be nearly independent of one another. Such is the case in an especial degree among those peoples who are prevailingly of a peaceable habit of life, among whom the myths have not in any great measure been canonized into precedents of divine malevolence.

The lower barbarian's knowledge of the phenomena of nature, in so far as they are made the subject of deliberate speculation and are organized into a consistent body, is of the nature of life-histories. This body of knowledge is in the main organized under the guidance of an idle curiosity. In so far as it is systematized under the canons of curiosity rather than of expediency, the test of truth applied throughout this body of barbarian knowledge is the test of dramatic consistency. In addition to their dramatic cosmology and folk legends, it is needless to say, these peoples have also a considerable body of worldly wisdom in a more or less systematic form. In this the test of validity is usefulness.[4]

The pragmatic knowledge of the early days differs scarcely at all in character from that of the maturest phases of culture. Its highest achievements in the direction of systematic formulation consist of didactic exhortations to thrift, prudence, equanimity, and shrewd management—a body of maxims of expedient con-

[4] "Pragmatic" is here used in a more restricted sense than the distinctively pragmatic school of modern psychologists would commonly assign the term. "Pragmatic," "teleological," and the like terms have been extended to cover imputation of purpose as well as conversion to use. It is not intended to criticise this ambiguous use of terms, nor to correct it; but the terms are here used only in the latter sense, which alone belongs to them by force of early usage and etymology. "Pragmatic" knowledge, therefore, is such as is designed to serve an expedient end for the knower, and is here contrasted with the imputation of expedient conduct to the facts observed. The reason for preserving this distinction is simply the present need of a simple term by which to mark the distinction between worldly wisdom and idle learning.

duct. In this field there is scarcely a degree of advance from Confucius to Samuel Smiles. Under the guidance of the idle curiosity, on the other hand, there has been a continued advance toward a more and more comprehensive system of knowledge. With the advance in intelligence and experience there come closer observation and more detailed analysis of facts.[5] The dramatization of the sequence of phenomena may then fall into somewhat less personal, less anthropomorphic formulations of the processes observed; but at no stage of its growth—at least at no stage hitherto reached—does the output of this work of the idle curiosity lose its dramatic character. Comprehensive generalizations are made and cosmologies are built up, but always in dramatic form. General principles of explanation are settled on, which in the earlier days of theoretical speculation seem invariably to run back to the broad vital principle of generation. Procreation, birth, growth, and decay constitute the cycle of postulates within which the dramatized processes of natural phenomena run their course. Creation is procreation in these archaic theoretical systems, and causation is gestation and birth. The archaic cosmological schemes of Greece, India, Japan, China, Polynesia, and America, all run to the same general effect on this head.[6]

Throughout this biological speculation there is present, obscurely in the background, the tacit recognition of a material causation, such as conditions the vulgar operations of workday life from hour to hour. But this causal relation between vulgar work and product is vaguely taken for granted and not made a principle for comprehensive generalizations. It is overlooked as a trivial matter of course. The higher generalizations take their color from the broader features of the current scheme of life. The habits of thought that rule in the working-out of a system of knowledge are such as are fostered by the more impressive affairs of life, by the institutional structure under which the community lives. So long as the ruling institutions are those of blood-relationship, descent, and clannish discrimination, so long the canons of knowledge are of the same complexion.

[5] Cf. Ward, *Pure Sociology*, esp. pp. 437–48.

[6] Cf., e. g., Tylor, *Primitive Culture*, chap. 8.

When presently a transformation is made in the scheme of culture from peaceable life with sporadic predation to a settled scheme of predaceous life, involving mastery and servitude, gradations of privilege and honor, coercion and personal dependence, then the scheme of knowledge undergoes an analogous change. The predaceous, or higher barbarian, culture is, for the present purpose, peculiar in that it is ruled by an accentuated pragmatism. The institutions of this cultural phase are conventionalized relations of force and fraud. The questions of life are questions of expedient conduct as carried on under the current relations of mastery and subservience. The habitual distinctions are distinctions of personal force, advantage, precedence, and authority. A shrewd adaptation to this system of graded dignity and servitude becomes a matter of life and death, and men learn to think in these terms as ultimate and definitive. The system of knowledge, even in so far as its motives are of a dispassionate or idle kind, falls into the like terms, because such are the habits of thought and the standards of discrimination enforced by daily life.[7]

The theoretical work of such a cultural era, as, for instance, the Middle Ages, still takes the general shape of dramatization, but the postulates of the dramaturgic theories and the tests of theoretic validity are no longer the same as before the scheme of graded servitude came to occupy the field. The canons which guide the work of the idle curiosity are no longer those of generation, blood-relationship, and homely life, but rather those of graded dignity, authenticity, and dependence. The higher generalizations take on a new complexion, it may be without formally discarding the older articles of belief. The cosmologies of these higher barbarians are cast in terms of a feudalistic hierarchy of agents and elements, and the causal nexus between phenomena is conceived animistically after the manner of sympathetic magic. The laws that are sought to be discovered in the natural universe are sought in terms of authoritative enactment. The relation in which the deity, or deities, are conceived to stand to facts is no longer the relation of progenitor, so much as that

[7] Cf. James, *Psychology*, chap. 9, esp. sec. 5.

of suzerainty. Natural laws are corollaries under the arbitrary rules of status imposed on the natural universe by an all-powerful Providence with a view to the maintenance of his own prestige. The science that grows in such a spiritual environment is of the class represented by alchemy and astrology, in which the imputed degree of nobility and prepotency of the objects and the symbolic force of their names are looked to for an explanation of what takes place.

The theoretical output of the Schoolmen has necessarily an accentuated pragmatic complexion, since the whole cultural scheme under which they lived and worked was of a strenuously pragmatic character. The current concepts of things were then drawn in terms of expediency, personal force, exploit, prescriptive authority, and the like, and this range of concepts was by force of habit employed in the correlation of facts for purposes of knowledge even where no immediate practical use of the knowledge so gained was had in view. At the same time a very large proportion of the scholastic researches and speculations aimed directly at rules of expedient conduct, whether it took the form of a philosophy of life under temporal law and custom, or of a scheme of salvation under the decrees of an autocratic Providence. A naïve apprehension of the dictum that all knowledge is pragmatic would find more satisfactory corroboration in the intellectual output of scholasticism than in any system of knowledge of an older or a later date.

With the advent of modern times a change comes over the nature of the inquiries and formulations worked out under the guidance of the idle curiosity—which from this epoch is often spoken of as the scientific spirit. The change in question is closely correlated with an analogous change in institutions and habits of life, particularly with the changes which the modern era brings in industry and in the economic organization of society. It is doubtful whether the characteristic intellectual interests and teachings of the new era can properly be spoken of as less "pragmatic," as that term is sometimes understood, than those of the scholastic times; but they are of another kind, being conditioned by a different cultural and industrial situation.[8] In the life of the new era conceptions of authentic rank and differential dignity have grown weaker in practical affairs, and notions of preferential reality and authentic tradition similarly count for less in the new science. The forces at work in the external world are conceived in a less animistic manner, although anthropomorphism still prevails, at least to the degree required in order to give a dramatic interpretation of the sequence of phenomena.

The changes in the cultural situation which seem to have had the most serious consequences for the methods and animus of scientific inquiry are those changes that took place in the field of industry. Industry in early modern times is a fact of relatively greater preponderance, more of a tone-giving factor, than it was under the régime of feudal status. It is the characteristic trait of the modern culture, very much as exploit and fealty were the characteristic cultural traits of the earlier times. This early-modern industry is, in an obvious and convincing degree, a matter of workmanship. The same has not been true in the same degree either before or since. The workman, more or less skilled and with more or less specialized efficiency, was the central figure in the cultural situation of the time; and so the concepts of the scientists came to be drawn in the image of the workman. The dramatizations of the seqence of external phenomena worked out under the impulse of the idle curiosity were then conceived in terms of workmanship. Workmanship gradually supplanted differential dignity as the authoritative canon of scientific truth, even on the higher levels of speculation and research. This, of course, amounts to saying in other words that the law of cause and effect was given the first place, as contrasted with dialectical consistency and authentic tradition. But this early-modern law of cause and effect—the law of efficient causes—is of an anthropomorphic kind. "Like causes produce like effects," in much the

[8] As currently employed, the term "pragmatic" is made to cover both conduct looking to the agent's preferential advantage, expedient conduct, and workmanship directed to the production of things that may or may not be of advantage to the agent. If the term be taken in the latter meaning, the culture of modern times is no less "pragmatic" than that of the Middle Ages. It is here intended to be used in the former sense.

same sense as the skilled workman's product is like the workman; "nothing is found in the effect that was not contained in the cause," in much the same manner.

These dicta are, of course, older than modern science, but it is only in the early days of modern science that they come to rule the field with an unquestioned sway and to push the higher grounds of dialectical validity to one side. They invade even the highest and most recondite fields of speculation, so that at the approach to the transition from the early-modern to the late-modern period, in the eighteenth century, they determine the outcome even in the counsels of the theologians. The deity, from having been in mediæval times primarily a suzerain concerned with the maintenance of his own prestige, becomes primarily a creator engaged in the workmanlike occupation of making things useful for man. His relation to man and the natural universe is no longer primarily that of a progenitor, as it is in the lower barbarian culture, but rather that of a talented mechanic. The "natural laws" which the scientists of that era make so much of are no longer decrees of a preternatural legislative authority, but rather details of the workshop specifications handed down by the master-craftsman for the guidance of handicraftsmen working out his designs. In the eighteenth-century science these natural laws are laws specifying the sequence of cause and effect, and will bear characterization as a dramatic interpretation of the activity of the causes at work, and these causes are conceived in a quasi-personal manner. In later modern times the formulations of causal sequence grow more impersonal and more objective, more matter-of-fact; but the imputation of activity to the observed objects never ceases, and even in the latest and maturest formulations of scientific research the dramatic tone is not wholly lost. The causes at work are conceived in a highly impersonal way, but hitherto no science (except ostensibly mathematics) has been content to do its theoretical work in terms of inert magnitude alone. Activity continues to be imputed to the phenomena with which science deals; and activity is, of course, not a fact of observation, but is imputed to the phenomena by the observer.[9] This is, also

[9] Epistemologically speaking, activity is imputed to phenomena for the purpose of organizing them into a dramatically consistent system.

of course, denied by those who insist on a purely mathematical formulation of scientific theories, but the denial is maintained only at the cost of consistency. Those eminent authorities who speak for a colorless mathematical formulation invariably and necessarily fall back on the (essentially metaphysical) preconception of causation as soon as they go into the actual work of scientific inquiry.[10]

Since the machine technology has made great advances, during the nineteenth century, and has become a cultural force of wide-reaching consequence, the formulations of science have made another move in the direction of impersonal matter-of-fact. The machine process has displaced the workman as the archetype in whose image causation is conceived by the scientific investigators. The dramatic interpretation of natural phenomena has thereby become less anthropomorphic; it no longer constructs the life-history of a cause working to produce a given effect—after the manner of a skilled workman producing a piece of wrought goods—but it constructs the life-history of a process in which the distinction between cause and effect need scarcely be observed in an itemized and specific way, but in which the run of causation unfolds itself in an unbroken sequence of cumulative change. By contrast with the pragmatic formulations of worldly wisdom these latter-day theories of the scientists appear highly opaque, impersonal, and matter-of-fact; but taken by themselves they must be admitted still to show the constraint of the dramatic prepossessions that once guided the savage myth-makers.

In so far as touches the aims and the animus of scientific inquiry, as seen from the point of view of the scientist, it is a wholly fortuitous and insubstantial coincidence that much of the knowledge gained under machine-made canons of research can be turned to practical account. Much of this knowledge is useful, or may be made so, by applying it to the control of the processes in which natural forces are engaged. This employment of scien-

[10] Cf., e. g., Karl Pearson, *Grammar of Science*, and compare his ideal of inert magnitudes as set forth in his exposition with his actual work as shown in chaps. 9, 10, and 12, and more particularly in his discussions of "Mother Right" and related topics in *The Chances of Death*.

tific knowledge for useful ends in technology, in the broad sense in which the term includes, besides the machine industry proper, such branches of practice as engineering, agriculture, medicine, sanitation, and economic reforms. The reason why scientific theories can be turned to account for these practical ends is not that these ends are included in the scope of scientific inquiry. These useful purposes lie outside the scientist's interest. It is not that he aims, or can aim, at technological improvements. His inquiry is as "idle" as that of the Pueblo myth-maker. But the canons of validity under whose guidance he works are those imposed by the modern technology, through habituation to its requirements; and therefore his results are available for the technological purpose. His canons of validity are made for him by the cultural situation; they are habits of thought imposed on him by the scheme of life current in the community in which he lives; and under modern conditions this scheme of life is largely machine-made. In the modern culture, industry, industrial processes, and industrial products have progressively gained upon humanity, until these creations of man's ingenuity have latterly come to take the dominant place in the cultural scheme; and it is not too much to say that they have become the chief force in shaping men's daily life, and therefore the chief factor in shaping men's habits of thought. Hence men have learned to think in the terms in which the technological processes act. This is particularly true of those men who by virtue of a peculiarly strong susceptibility in this direction become addicted to that habit of matter-of-fact inquiry that constitutes scientific research.

Modern technology makes use of the same range of concepts, thinks in the same terms, and applies the same tests of validity as modern science. In both, the terms of standardization, validity, and finality are always terms of impersonal sequence, not terms of human nature or of preternatural agencies. Hence the easy copartnership between the two. Science and technology play into one another's hands. The processes of nature with which science deals and which technology turns to account, the sequence of changes in the external world, animate and inanimate, run in terms of brute causation, as do the theories of science. These processes take no thought of human expediency or inexpediency. To make use of them they must be taken as they are, opaque and unsympathetic. Technology, therefore, has come to proceed on an interpretation of these phenomena in mechanical terms, not in terms of imputed personality nor even of workmanship. Modern science, deriving its concepts from the same source, carries on its inquiries and states its conclusions in terms of the same objective character as those employed by the mechanical engineer.

So it has come about, through the progressive change of the ruling habits of thought in the community, that the theories of science have progressively diverged from the formulations of pragmatism, ever since the modern era set in. From an organization of knowledge on the basis of imputed personal or animistic propensity the theory has changed its base to an imputation of brute activity only, and this latter is conceived in an increasingly matter-of-fact manner; until, latterly, the pragmatic range of knowledge and the scientific are more widely out of touch than ever, differing not only in aim, but in matter as well. In both domains knowledge runs in terms of activity, but it is on the one hand knowledge of what had best be done, and on the other hand knowledge of what takes place; on the one hand knowledge of ways and means, on the other hand knowledge without any ulterior purpose. The latter range of knowledge may serve the ends of the former, but the converse does not hold true.

These two divergent ranges of inquiry are to be found together in all phases of human culture. What distinguishes the present phase is that the discrepancy between the two is now wider than ever before. The present is nowise distinguished above other cultural eras by any exceptional urgency or acumen in the search for pragmatic expedients. Neither is it safe to assert that the present excels all other civilizations in the volume or the workmanship of that body of knowledge that is to be credited to the idle curiosity. What distinguishes the present in these premises is (1) that the primacy in the cultural scheme has passed from pragmatism to a disinterested inquiry whose motive is idle curiosity, and (2) that in the domain of the latter the making of myths and legends in terms of imputed personality, as well as the construction of dialectical systems in terms of differential reality, has yielded the first place to the making of theories in terms of matter-of-fact sequence.[11]

Pragmatism creates nothing but maxims of expedient conduct. Science creates nothing but theories.[12] It knows nothing of policy or utility, of better or worse. None of all that is comprised in what is today accounted scientific knowledge. Wisdom and proficiency of the pragmatic sort does not contribute to the advance of a knowledge of fact. It has only an incidental bearing on scientific research, and its bearing is chiefly that of inhibition and misdirection. Wherever canons of expediency are intruded into or are attempted to be incorporated in the inquiry, the consequence is an unhappy one for science, however happy it may be for some other purpose extraneous to science. The mental attitude of worldly wisdom is at cross-purposes with the disinterested scientific spirit, and the pursuit of it induces an intellectual bias that is incompatible with scientific insight. Its intellectual output is a body of shrewd rules of conduct, in great part designed to take advantage of human infirmity. Its habitual terms of standardization and validity are terms of human nature, of human preference, prejudice, aspiration, endeavor, and disability, and the habit of mind that goes with it is such as is consonant with these terms. No doubt, the all-pervading pragmatic animus of the older and non-European civilizations has had more than anything else to do with their relatively slight and slow advance in scientific knowledge. In the modern scheme of knowledge it holds true, in a similar manner and with analogous effect, that training in divinity, in law, and in the related branches of diplomacy, business tactics, military affairs, and political theory, is alien to the skeptical scientific spirit and subversive of it.

The modern scheme of culture comprises a large body of worldly wisdom, as well as of science. This pragmatic lore stands over against science with something of a jealous reserve. The pragmatists value themselves somewhat on being useful as

[11] Cf. James, *Psychology*, Vol. II, chap. 28, pp. 633–71, esp. p. 640 note.

[12] Cf. Ward, *Principles of Psychology*, pp. 439-43.

well as being efficient for good and evil. They feel the inherent antagonism between themselves and the scientists, and look with some doubt on the latter as being merely decorative triflers, although they sometimes borrow the prestige of the name of science —as is only good and well, since it is of the essence of worldly wisdom to borrow anything that can be turned to account. The reasoning in these fields turns about questions of personal advantage of one kind or another, and the merits of the claims canvassed in these discussions are decided on grounds of authenticity. Personal claims make up the subject of the inquiry, and these claims are construed and decided in terms of precedent and choice, use and wont, prescriptive authority, and the like. The higher reaches of generalization in these pragmatic inquiries are of the nature of deductions from authentic tradition, and the training in this class of reasoning gives discrimination in respect of authenticity and expediency. The resulting habit of mind is a bias for substituting dialectical distinctions and decisions *de jure* in the place of explanations *de facto*. The so-called "sciences" associated with these pragmatic disciplines, such as jurisprudence, political science, and the like, is a taxonomy of credenda. Of this character was the greater part of the "science" cultivated by the Schoolmen, and large remnants of the same kind of authentic convictions are, of course, still found among the tenets of the scientists, particularly in the social sciences, and no small solicitude is still given to their cultivation. Substantially the same value as that of the temporal pragmatic inquiries belongs also, of course, to the "science" of divinity. Here the questions to which an answer is sought, as well as the aim and method of inquiry, are of the same pragmatic character, although the argument runs on a higher plane of personality, and seeks a solution in terms of a remoter and more metaphysical expediency.

In the light of what has been said above, the questions recur: How far is the scientific quest of matter-of-fact knowledge consonant with the inherited intellectual aptitudes and propensities of the normal man? and, What foothold has science in the modern culture? The former is a question of the temperamental heritage of civilized mankind, and therefore it is in large part a question of the circumstances which have in the past selectively shaped the human nature of civilized mankind. Under the barbarian culture, as well as on the lower levels of what is currently called civilized life, the dominant note has been that of competitive expediency for the individual or the group, great or small, in an avowed struggle for the means of life. Such is still the ideal of the politician and business man, as well as of other classes whose habits of life lead them to cling to the inherited barbarian traditions. The upper-barbarian and lower-civilized culture, as has already been indicated, is pragmatic, with a thoroughness that nearly bars out any non-pragmatic ideal of life or of knowledge. Where this tradition is strong there is but a precarious chance for any consistent effort to formulate knowledge in other terms than those drawn from the prevalent relations of personal mastery and subservience and the ideals of personal gain.

During the Dark and Middle Ages, for instance, it is true in the main that any movement of thought not controlled by considerations of expediency and conventions of status are to be found only in the obscure depths of vulgar life, among those neglected elements of the population that lived below the reach of the active class struggle. What there is surviving of this vulgar, non-pragmatic intellectual output takes the form of legends and folk-tales, often embroidered on the authentic documents of the Faith. These are less alien to the latest and highest culture of Christendom than are the dogmatic, dialectical, and chivalric productions that occupied the attention of the upper classes in mediæval times. It may seem a curious paradox that the latest and most perfect flower of the western civilization is more nearly akin to the spiritual life of the serfs and villeins than it is to that of the grange or the abbey. The courtly life and the chivalric habits of thought of that past phase of culture have left as nearly no trace in the cultural scheme of later modern times as could well be. Even the romancers who ostensibly rehearse the phenomena of chivalry, unavoidably make their knights and ladies speak the language and the sentiments of the slums of that time, tempered with certain schematized modern reflections and speculations.

The gallantries, the genteel inanities and devout imbecilities of mediæval high-life would be insufferable even to the meanest and most romantic modern intelligence. So that in a later, less barbarian age the precarious remnants of folklore that have come down through that vulgar channel—half savage and more than half pagan—are treasured as containing the largest spiritual gains which the barbarian ages of Europe have to offer.

The sway of barbarian pragmatism has, everywhere in the western world, been relatively brief and relatively light; the only exceptions would be found in certain parts of the Mediterranean seaboard. But wherever the barbarian culture has been sufficiently long-lived and unmitigated to work out a thoroughly selective effect in the human material subjected to it, there the pragmatic animus may be expected to have become supreme and to inhibit all movement in the direction of scientific inquiry and eliminate all effective aptitude for other than worldly wisdom. What the selective consequences of such a protracted régime of pragmatism would be for the temper of the race may be seen in the human flotsam left by the great civilizations of antiquity, such as Egypt, India, and Persia. Science is not at home among these leavings of barbarism. In these instances of its long and unmitigated dominion the barbarian culture has selectively worked out a temperamental bias and a scheme of life from which objective, matter-of-fact knowledge is virtually excluded in favor of pragmatism, secular and religious. But for the greater part of the race, at least for the greater part of civilized mankind, the régime of the mature barbarian culture has been of relatively short duration, and has had a correspondingly superficial and transient selective effect. It has not had force and time to eliminate certain elements of human nature handed down from an earlier phase of life, which are not in full consonance with the barbarian animus or with the demands of the pragmatic scheme of thought. The barbarian-pragmatic habit of mind, therefore, is not properly speaking a temperamental trait of the civilized peoples, except possibly within certain class limits (as, e. g., the German nobility). It is rather a tradition, and it does not constitute so tenacious a bias as to make head against the strongly materialistic drift of modern conditions and set aside that increasingly urgent resort to matter-of-fact conceptions that makes for the primacy of science. Civilized mankind does not in any great measure take back atavistically to the upper-barbarian habit of mind. Barbarism covers too small a segment of the life-history of the race to have given an enduring temperamental result. The unmitigated discipline of the higher barbarism in Europe fell on a relatively small proportion of the population, and in the course of time this select element of the population was crossed and blended with the blood of the lower elements whose life always continued to run in the ruts of savagery rather than in those of the high-strung, finished barbarian culture that gave rise to the chivalric scheme of life.

Of the several phases of human culture the most protracted, and the one which has counted for most in shaping the abiding traits of the race, is unquestionably that of savagery. With savagery, for the purpose in hand, is to be classed that lower, relatively peaceable barbarism that is not characterized by wide and sharp class discrepancies or by an unremitting endeavor of one individual or group to get the better of another. Even under the full-grown barbarian culture—as, for instance, during the Middle Ages—the habits of life and the spiritual interests of the great body of the population continue in large measure to bear the character of savagery. The savage phase of culture accounts for by far the greater portion of the life-history of mankind, particularly if the lower barbarism and the vulgar life of later barbarism be counted in with savagery, as in a measure they properly should. This is particularly true of those racial elements that have entered into the composition of the leading peoples of Christendom.

The savage culture is characterized by the relative absence of pragmatism from the higher generalizations of its knowledge and beliefs. As has been noted above, its theoretical creations are chiefly of the nature of mythology shading off into folklore. This genial spinning of apocryphal yarns is, at its best, an amiably inefficient formulation of experiences and observations in terms of something like a life-history of the phenomena observed. It has, on the one hand, little value, and little purpose, in the way of pragmatic expediency, and so it is not closely akin to the pragmatic-barbarian scheme of life; while, on the other hand, it is also ineffectual as a systematic knowledge of matter-of-fact. It is a quest of knowledge, perhaps of systematic knowledge, and it is carried on under the incentive of the idle curiosity. In this respect it falls in the same class with the civilized man's science; but it seeks knowledge not in terms of opaque matter-of-fact, but in terms of some sort of a spiritual life imputed to the facts. It is romantic and Hegelian rather than realistic and Darwinian. The logical necessities of its scheme of thought are necessities of spiritual consistency rather than of quantitative equivalence. It is like science in that it has no ulterior motive beyond the idle craving for a systematic correlation of data; but it is unlike science in that its standardization and correlation of data run in terms of the free play of imputed personal initiative rather than in terms of the constraint of objective cause and effect.

By force of the protracted selective discipline of this past phase of culture, the human nature of civilized mankind is still substantially the human nature of savage man. The ancient equipment of congenital aptitudes and propensities stands over substantially unchanged, though overlaid with barbarian traditions and conventionalities and readjusted by habituation to the exigencies of civilized life. In a measure, therefore, but by no means altogether, scientific inquiry is native to civilized man with his savage heritage, since scientific inquiry proceeds on the same general motive of idle curiosity as guided the savage myth-makers, though it makes use of concepts and standards in great measure alien to the myth-makers' habit of mind. The ancient human predilection for discovering a dramatic play of passion and intrigue in the phenomena of nature still asserts itself. In the most advanced communities, and even among the adepts of modern science, there comes up persistently the revulsion of the native savage against the inhumanly dispassionate sweep of the scientific quest, as well as against the inhumanly ruthless fabric of technological processes that have come out of this search for matter-of-fact knowledge. Very often the savage need of a spiritual interpretation (dramatization) of phenomena breaks through the crust of acquired materialistic habits of thought, to find such refuge as may be had in articles of faith seized on and held by sheer force of instinctive conviction. Science and its creations are more or less uncanny, more or less alien, to that fashion of craving for knowledge that by ancient inheritance animates mankind. Furtively or by an overt breach of consistency, men still seek comfort in marvelous articles of savage-born lore, which contradict the truths of that modern science whose dominion they dare not question, but whose findings at the same time go beyond the breaking point of their jungle-fed spiritual sensibilities.

The ancient ruts of savage thought and conviction are smooth and easy; but however sweet and indispensable the archaic ways of thinking may be to the civilized man's peace of mind, yet such is the binding force of matter-of-fact analysis and inference under modern conditions that the findings of science are not questioned on the whole. The name of science is after all a word to conjure with. So much so that the name and the mannerisms, at least, if nothing more of science, have invaded all fields of learning and have even overrun territory that belongs to the enemy. So there are "sciences" of theology, law, and medicine, as has already been noted above. And there are such things as Christian Science, and "scientific" astrology, palmistry, and the like. But within the field of learning proper there is a similar predilection for an air of scientific acumen and precision where science does not belong. So that even that large range of knowledge that has to do with general information rather than with theory—what is loosely termed scholarship—tends strongly to take on the name and forms of theoretical statement. However decided the contrast between these branches of knowledge on the one hand, and science properly so called on the other hand, yet even the classical learning, and the humanities generally, fall in with this predilection more and more with each succeeding generation of students. The students of literature, for instance, are more and more prone to substitute critical analysis and linguistic speculation, as the end of their endeavors, in the place of that discipline of taste and that cultivated sense of literary form and literary feeling that must always remain the chief end of literary training, as distinct from philology and the social sciences. There is, of course, no intention to question the legitimacy of a science of philology or of the analytical study of literature as a fact in cultural history, but these things do not constitute training in literary taste, nor can they take the place of it. The effect of this straining after scientific formulations in a field alien to the scientific spirit is as curious as it is wasteful. Scientifically speaking, those quasi-scientific inquiries necessarily begin nowhere and end in the same place; while in point of cultural gain they commonly come to nothing better than spiritual abnegation. But these blindfold endeavors to conform to the canons of science serve to show how wide and unmitigated the sway of science is in the modern community.

Scholarship—that is to say an intimate and systematic familiarity with past cultural achievements—still holds its place in the scheme of learning, in spite of the unadvised efforts of the short-sighted to blend it with the work of science, for it affords play for the ancient genial propensities that ruled men's quest of knowledge before the coming of science or of the outspoken pragmatic barbarism. Its place may not be so large in proportion to the entire field of learning as it was before the scientific era got fully under way. But there is no intrinsic antagonism between science and scholarship, as there is between pragmatic training and scientific inquiry. Modern scholarship shares with modern science the quality of not being pragmatic in its aim. Like science it has no ulterior end. It may be difficult here and there to draw the line between science and scholarship, and it may even more be unnecessary to draw such a line; yet while the two ranges of discipline belong together in many ways, and while there are many points of contact and sympathy between the two; while the two together make up the modern scheme of learning; yet there is no need of confounding the one with the other, nor can the one do the work of the other. The scheme of learning has changed in such manner as to give science the more commanding place, but the scholar's domain has not thereby been invaded, nor has it suffered contraction at the hands of science, whatever may be said of the weak-kneed abnegation of some whose place, if they have one, is in the field of scholarship rather than of science.

All that has been said above has of course nothing to say as to the intrinsic merits of this quest of matter-of-fact knowledge. In point of fact, science gives its tone to modern culture. One may approve or one may deprecate the fact that this opaque, materialistic interpretation of things pervades modern thinking. That is a question of taste, about which there is no disputing. The prevalence of this matter-of-fact inquiry is a feature of modern culture, and the attitude which critics take toward this phenomenon is chiefly significant as indicating how far their own habit of mind coincides with the enlightened common-sense of civilized mankind. It shows in what degree they are abreast of the advance of culture. Those in whom the savage predilection or the barbarian tradition is stronger than their habituation to civilized life will find that this dominant factor of modern life is perverse, if not calamitous; those whose habits of thought have been fully shaped by the machine process and scientific inquiry are likely to find it good. The modern western culture, with its core of matter-of-fact knowledge, may be better or worse than some other cultural scheme, such as the classic Greek, the mediæval Christian, the Hindu, or the Pueblo Indian. Seen in certain lights, tested by certain standards, it is doubtless better; by other standards, worse. But the fact remains that the current cultural scheme, in its maturest growth, is of that complexion; its characteristic force lies in this matter-of-fact insight; its highest discipline and its maturest aspirations are these.

In point of fact, the sober common-sense of civilized mankind accepts no other end of endeavor as self-sufficient and ultimate. That such is the case seems to be due chiefly to the ubiquitous presence of the machine technology and its creations in the life of modern communities. And so long as the machine process continues to hold its dominant place as a disciplinary factor in modern culture, so long must the spiritual and intellectual life of this cultural era maintain the character which the machine process gives it.

But while the scientist's spirit and his achievements stir an unqualified admiration in modern men, and while his discoveries carry conviction as nothing else does, it does not follow that the manner of man which this quest of knowledge produces or requires comes near answering to the current ideal of manhood, or that his conclusions are felt to be as good and beautiful as they are true. The ideal man, and the ideal of human life, even in the apprehension of those who most rejoice in the advances of science, is neither the finikin skeptic in the laboratory nor the animated slide-rule. The quest of science is relatively new. It is a cultural factor not comprised, in anything like its modern force, among those circumstances whose selective action in the far past has given to the race the human nature which it now has. The race reached the human plane with little of this searching knowledge of facts; and throughout the greater part of its life-history on the human plane it has been accustomed to make its higher generalizations and to formulate its larger principles of life in other terms than those of passionless matter-of-fact. This manner of knowledge has occupied an increasing share of men's attention in the past, since it bears in a decisive way upon the minor affairs of workday life; but it has never until now been put in the first place, as the dominant note of human culture. The normal man, such as his inheritance has made him, has therefore good cause to be restive under its dominion.